American Literature and the Culture of Reprinting, 1834–1853

American Literature and the Culture of Reprinting, 1834–1853

Meredith L. McGill

PENN

UNIVERSITY OF PENNSYLVANIA PRESS

Philadelphia

10   9   8   7   6   5   4   3   2   1

Published by
University of Pennsylvania Press
Philadelphia, Pennsylvania 19104–4011

Library of Congress Cataloging-in-Publication Data

McGill, Meredith L.
    American literature and the culture of reprinting, 1834–1853/Meredith L. McGill
        p. cm. (Material texts)
    ISBN 0-8122-3698-X (cloth : alk. paper)
    Includes bibliographical references (p.) and index.
        1. Hawthorne, Nathaniel, 1804–1864—Relations with publishers. 2. Poe, Edgar Allan,
1809–1849—Relations with publishers. 3. Dickens, Charles, 1812–1870—Relations with
publishers. 4. American literature—19th century—History and criticism. 5. Literature
publishing—United States—History—19th century. 6. Authors and publishers—
United States—History—19th century. 7. Copyright—United States—History—
19th century. I. Title. II. Series
PS208 .M38 2002
810.9´003—dc 21   2002029146

For my parents, and for Andy

Contents

Introduction: The Matter of the Text

American Literature and the Culture of Reprinting is a case study of the dynamic relationship between conceptions of literary property and American cultural production, focusing on an extraordinarily vibrant period of publishing in the 1830s and '40s, just prior to what literary critics call the "American Renaissance." In this period, legal and political resistance to tight controls over intellectual property produced a literary marketplace suffused with unauthorized publications. Not only was the mass-market for literature in America built and sustained by the publication of cheap reprints of foreign books and periodicals, the primary vehicles for the circulation of literature were uncopyrighted newspapers and magazines. I will argue that antebellum ideas about intellectual property helped to produce a distinctive literary culture that cannot adequately be perceived through the optics of national literary study, a paradigm that we have all but naturalized. Although we have come to think of the classic works of mid-nineteenth-century American authors as national property, these texts emerged from a literary culture that was regional in articulation and transnational in scope.

As William Charvat and others have noted, the hallmark of the antebellum literary marketplace was its decentralization. Not only was the national market for books distributed across multiple, loosely affiliated, regional publishing centers, each of the major cities—Philadelphia, New York, and Boston—claimed to be the center of national culture. Cutting across these internal divisions was a flourishing trade in cheap, reprinted British books, which, because unconstrained by copyright, achieved a remarkable national distribution in the form of competing, regionally produced editions. A handful of literary periodicals, which also commonly circulated without the benefit of copyright protection, were able to achieve something like national distribution through the mails. Yet not only did many of these magazines remain unprofitable (subscription payments were notoriously difficulty to collect, due in part to the lack of a national currency), they were freely excerpted by other periodicals, some of which amounted to little more than compilations of reprinted texts. Unauthorized reprinting was so widely practiced in this period that the designation of a poem, article, or tale as an "original" referred not to the quality of its contents, but to the fact that the book or periodical in which it appeared was the site of its first printing. Within the culture of reprinting, dissemination ran in advance of, and often stood in lieu of, payment. Circulation outstripped authorial and editorial control.

While literary critics have assumed that the trade in books offered a stable counterweight to the volatile world of the magazines, close ties between book publishers and magazine editors, who offered one of the few outlets for book promotion in the form of reviews, involved publishers in intricate dealings with cliques of literati who traded in favorable notices. Not only was the market for books heavily dependent on the climates of opinion and networks of readers constructed by the literary periodicals, books themselves were often difficult to distinguish from newspapers and magazines. For example, the extraordinary demand for cheap literature, brought on in part by the depression of the late 1830s, gave rise to an intermediary form of publishing whereby entire books were printed as magazine "extras" and circulated in looseleaf format through the mail. Held together by a single stitch so that they could qualify as newspapers under the postal code, these supplements were published in a standard quarto size so that the reader could have them bound to create a uniform but personalized library. Typical of the hybrid publishing formats of the 1840s, the magazine extra decentralized book production, blurring the line between publisher and reader as well as that between low and high culture—disposable literature, and books that were worth preserving. The proliferation of cheap, reprinted texts and the reliance of the book trade on periodical publishing realigned relations between author, publisher, editor, and reader, upended the hierarchy of genres, and troubled the boundaries of the text-as-object.

The central aim of my study is to understand the consequences for American literary history of this radically different way of conceiving of the production and circulation of texts. The literature that was published under the system of reprinting has eluded critical scrutiny for reasons that are bound up with its vexed relation to author-centered literary nationalisms, past and present. Texts that circulate without authors' names attached frequently remain unindexed and untraceable, as do authored texts that are published without their authors' knowledge or consent. Unauthorized reprinting escapes the enumerative strategies of bibliographers and collectors who remain tied to authorial intention and the principle of scarcity as grounds of value. The mass-cultural circulation of high-cultural texts confounds our critical taxonomies even as the transnational status of reprinted texts makes it difficult for us to assimilate them into national literary narratives. Americanist critics tend to sift through this literature for signs of an original, national difference rather than to recognize American authors' complex negotiations with European culture or to assess the ways in which foreign literature is repackaged and redeployed. Depicting American authors more as victims than as products of these conditions of publication, critics have rescued anonymous and pseudonymous texts from their disseminated condition and reissued them in standard, multi-volume authors' editions, creating composite figures and bodies of work that did not exist and could not have existed in the era in which these texts were written.

My book attempts to remedy this narrowing of the cultural field by addressing the complexity and instability of the antebellum literary marketplace on its own terms. I am interested not only in recovering the vibrancy and importance of the literature that thrived under conditions of decentralized mass-production, but also in unfolding the legal arguments and political struggles that produced the culture of reprinting and held it in place for approximately twenty years. In turning to nineteenth-century case law and to publishers' agitation against an international copyright law, I seek to restore a political dimension to recent accounts of the economic grounds of antebellum literary culture, arguing that the decentralization of the literary marketplace was upheld by a strong appeal to republican values. Focusing on the ways in which the problematic property status of their texts transforms the careers and writing of Charles Dickens, Edgar Allan Poe, and Nathaniel Hawthorne, I seek both to show how changes in the conditions of publication make themselves felt at the level of literary form, and to take the measure of what was lost as literary markets became centralized and literary culture became stratified in the early 1850s.

Throughout this book I will use the term reprinting and not piracy in order to emphasize the fact that the republication of foreign works and particular kinds of domestic texts was perfectly legal; it was not a violation of law or custom, but a cultural norm. Indeed, the proliferation of general interest periodicals and affordable editions of foreign books was considered by many to be proof of democratic institutions' remarkable powers of enlightenment. Although there was substantial domestic opposition to the culture of reprinting, particularly as the literary nationalist movement

gained strength and prominence in the early 1840s, American defenders of
the reprint trade wielded considerable political power, holding off an international copyright agreement until late in the nineteenth century. By the
time a modest international copyright law was finally passed in 1891, reprinting was only one facet of a highly centralized publishing industry that was
increasingly interested in using copyright to regulate national and international trade. But in the 1830s and '40s, reprinting was implicated in the
larger struggle over the course of national development. Regional print
centers were only provisionally linked to one another, westward expansion
kept redefining the boundaries of the nation, and the very terms of national
union were vigorously under debate. In bringing the system of reprinting
into focus, I take up the question of the cultural coherence of the nation
rather than assuming the existence of a national literature as a threshold
condition for literary study. Taking reprinting as my point of entry into
antebellum culture enables me to reach back through the foundational
anxieties of literary nationalism to uncover a literature defined by its exuberant understanding of culture as iteration and not origination.

In describing this system of production and reproduction as a "culture of reprinting," I seek to go beyond literary histories that invoke antebellum publishing conditions as an index of the hardships American authors
faced in gaining access to print. Critics most often turn to the unstable
and disjointed nature of the literary marketplace to account for an author's
falling short of modern standards of achievement, praising writers for
having produced valuable work despite these conditions of publication.
This approach not only presumes that texts and authors could somehow
inhabit this market without being shaped by it, it naturalizes the workings
of a centralized, stratified, and author-centered market, dismissing the
primary features of antebellum literary culture as aberrations that will be
corrected over time. I will argue to the contrary that antebellum Americans' commitment to the circulation of unauthorized reprints constituted
a "culture," by which I mean (1) that the decentralization of publishing
was systematic, not simply the product of geographic and historical contingencies; (2) that this publishing system was distinctive, explicitly defined
and defended against other systems; and (3) that it was also part of the
horizon of the ordinary, and as such, often unconscious as a principle of
organization to members of this culture. The redundancies and manifold
inefficiencies of the antebellum literary marketplace were not the mis-
firings of a system in a primitive stage development, they were characteristic features of a social structure that many thought could fend off the

stultifying effects of British publishing monopolies. Those who explicitly defended the culture of reprinting maintained that it operated as a hedge against the concentration of economic and political power.

While this book is framed as a study of a historical period that is defined by the dominance of a particular system of publishing, it is also an extended experiment in thinking about the relations of literary texts to their conditions of production. In tracing multiple forms of this relation, I draw on the interpretive strategies of the history of the book, a cross-pollination of the methods of bibliography, social history, and cultural history. This interdisciplinary field takes as its subject the material grounds of discourse, the mediation of culture by historically specific practices of textual production, distribution, and reception. My study is richly indebted to book history's attention to the physical form of printed texts and to its understanding of the complexity of the social processes by which communities of readers are formed.[1]

Indeed, broadly considered, reprinting is a remarkably promising subject for book historians. Reprinting is a form of textual production that is inseparable from distribution and reception. Running counter to the avowed intentions (if not always the interests) of authors and their publishers, unauthorized reprinting makes publication distinctly legible as an independently signifying act. In the multiplicity of their formats and points of origin, and in the staggered temporality of their production, reprinted texts call attention to the repeated acts of articulation by which culture and its audiences are constituted. From the vantage point of the interdisciplinary field of the history of the book, the subject of reprinting is significantly larger than the question of how authors are situated or how literary texts circulate and signify within this system. In focusing on the intersection of antebellum literature and the system of reprinting, then, I offer neither an exhaustive survey of the sites or kinds of reprinting, nor a history of American publishing that illuminates the centrality of reprinting to the growth of the industry itself.[2]

I remark on the importance of reprinting to a general history of antebellum print culture not only to identify my study as a subset of a larger field of inquiry, but also to signal a difference in methodology. Book historians' commitment to documenting the material processes of publication and reception and their interest in the social locations of culture have often rendered the rhetorical analysis of texts of secondary importance. Much of book history turns to texts to illustrate the ways in which they are subject to determining forces imagined as wholly exterior to them. In many studies, the physical form of the book is invoked as a principle of constraint, the details of its embodiment delimiting the range of possible meanings of a particular text.[3] In other studies, the history of a text's publication and reception is used to bring into focus the material (but often invisible) social networks across which books travel as they are solicited, published, bought and sold, borrowed and exchanged.[4] In these modes of analysis, a text's structure, its negotiations with genre, its thematic preoccupations and figures of address are invoked only insofar as they are impinged on from without. Either a text's field of signification is limited and disciplined by history, or the text is used to illuminate a set of social structures that are imagined to surround and contain it.

If book historians have found textual analysis to be of limited usefulness, the dominant modes of literary criticism of the past two decades have found surprisingly little use for the book. Deconstructive criticism has generally associated the book with the grounding interpretive conventions of "author" and "work" against which it defines its object of study. For example, in his classic essay "From Work to Text," Roland Barthes uses the physical form of the book to figure the essential boundedness of the concept of the work, proposing in its place a theory of the text as an impossibly plural, ineradicably present-tense, and inherently slippery field of signification.[5] In practice, however, deconstructive readings of literary texts tend to assume rather than to move beyond the stabilizing categories of the author and the work. In framing their object of study as the entanglement of literary texts with a thematics of writing, deconstructive critics have tended to take the category of literature for granted, relegating publishing history to at best a supporting role. In Americanist criticism, it is most often classic works that are submitted to deconstructive reading and canonical authors who emerge as the motive force behind masterfully self-deconstructing literary artifacts.[6]

Critics writing in the wake of deconstruction have also largely failed to take advantage of the way in which book history can illuminate the contingency of the category of the literary. The centrality of the concept of discourse to the critical practice of New Historicism has placed a premium on charting the intersection of literary and nonliterary discourses. And yet re-imagining literary texts as sites in which a range of discourses contend with one another often renders the material conditions of their production oddly transparent. New Historicist critics are often more interested in the discursive mediation of social relations than they are in the mediation of discourses themselves.[7] The shift of the object of study within literary criticism from texts to discourses has left open the question of what to do about the book: how do changes in the material conditions of textual production, distribution, and reception affect the relationship between literature and other discourses?

Located at the intersection between book history and literary criticism and theory, *American Literature and the Culture of Reprinting* attempts to speak across these disciplinary and methodological divides. I am interested in the way in which debates about books have material consequences for their production and distribution—both how legal and political discourses shape the literary marketplace, and how the market for books carries with it all kinds of fantasies about political power. And while I am concerned to read the materiality of reprinted texts as fully rhetorical, I regard rhetorical structures as no less material than publication processes. This book takes as its subject the problematic property status of printed texts, but it will not center on the book-as-object. That is to say, this is not a study of reprints themselves but of the ways in which the system of reprinting recasts the reading and writing of poetry and fiction.[8] Although, as I hope to demonstrate, the values of the system of reprinting are visible in its characteristic formats, its significance as a system lies in the traffic across them, the relays by which elite culture is redistributed in a variety of mass-cultural formats, by which authors are detached from and reattached to their texts, and by which European works are reshuffled for American purposes. I will treat reprinting not only as a means of distribution but also in terms of its transformation of antebellum assumptions about literariness, assumptions that affect literary works whether they are reprinted or not.

My focus, then, will be on the rhetorical origins and interpretive consequences of the material practices of reprinting. Throughout, I invoke textual materiality not as an answer to but as a means of reframing questions about the nature and limits of antebellum literary culture, hoping thereby to expand what scholars understand to comprise the matter of the text. At its simplest, "the matter of the text" is a synonym for textual embodiment that suggests the many insights that can be gleaned from an analysis of the formats in which antebellum literature appeared. Shifting my gaze from first and authorized editions to unauthorized reprints, from the form of the book to the intersection of book and periodical publishing, and from a national literature to an internally divided and transatlantic literary marketplace, I will trace some of the changing definitions and locations of the literary as authors and editors struggled to bring textual circulation under their control.

I also intend "the matter of the text," however, as a synonym for concern or issue, suggesting in this way the rhetorical nature of the problem of textual materiality. As legal and political struggles over copyright make abundantly clear, the property status of the printed text was by no means a settled question in the antebellum period. Debates over literary property not only gave substance to the laws that governed the circulation of texts, they were bound up with larger struggles over the centralization of power. The capitalization of the publishing industry, the formats publishers favored, and even the structure of the transportation networks across which books and periodicals traveled were materially influenced by these debates.

Referring, then, both to the text-as-object and to the essence of thought, the phrase "the matter of the text" suggests a productive encounter between the materiality of the book and the materiality of writing. My most general aim in this book is to use reprinting to illustrate the complex reciprocity between the discourses and practices of a particular print culture—to show how a political struggle over property rights comes to structure the literary field, and how the question of the cultural status of the literary gets folded into texts themselves.

*   *   *

Books are extraordinary objects. If you're inclined to be skeptical about this claim, look back at this volume's copyright page, which you'll find in its legally prescribed place on the verso of the title page, the page that claims property in the names of both author and publisher. In contrast to the title page's elegant simplicity, its acknowledgment of individual authorial agency and the name and location of the publishing house that brought the book into existence, the copyright page bears the marks of a tangle of national and international regulations and agencies. This book is an object of property that is produced, sold, bought, and consumed under a complex set of constraints that are governed by federal law and international treaty, including domestic and international copyright law, International Standards agreements, which govern the assignment of the International Standard Book Number, and the protocols of the Library of Congress, which supplies both a control number and cataloging data for the use of libraries. While similar bureaucracies affect trade in any commodity that is subject to health and safety laws, state or federal taxes, or international tariff agreements, books are unusual in that they explicitly invoke the power of the state to enforce an abstract and changing set of property rights. The University of Pennsylvania Press could pursue damages against you in a federal court should you exercise any of the rights that it has "reserved," such as copying large portions of this book by machine or by hand, dramatizing or otherwise adapting it, uploading pages onto the web, or transferring them via reprographic technologies that we have yet to imagine. However unlikely these scenarios may be in this particular case, so long as the publication of this book complies with the processes of the official regulatory agencies, the University of Pennsylvania Press and I retain a whole host of property rights in it past the point of sale.

And yet the state's considerable investment in this book also takes it out of the hands of its author, publisher, and buyer. Although it is nowhere mentioned on the copyright page, while this book circulates in the United States it is subject to obscenity laws and protected by the First Amendment. If the acknowledgments page, the notes, and the bibliography are sites where authors formally (if at times reluctantly) recognize the collaborative nature of authorial labor, the copyright page bears witness to the way in which public property in printed texts outruns the control of authors. At least two state-enforced limits to my title are clearly visible here: the subject of the book has been broken down into a set of categories that are created and applied by the Library of Congress; and the copyright notice signals an as yet open-ended period of time at the close of which this text is transformed from an odd kind of private property into part of the public domain. Under the Sonny Bono Copyright Term Extension Act of 1998 (112 Stat. 2827), the timespan during which federal copyright law limits how this book may be used is defined as "the life of the author and 70 years after the author's death" (17 USCS 302a). If the title page of the book provides a set of names that enable reference to the text—names that sustain the image of the author as originator, denominator, and individual proprietor—inscribed on its back is a property-granting formula that is administered by the press, enforced by the state, and calculated in terms of the death of the author. It is no wonder we tend to avoid reading it.

I call your attention to this twenty-first-century copyright page, which differs in crucial ways from its nineteenth-century precursors, to suggest that even in an era of tight control over intellectual property, the public investment in printed texts transforms them into something less and something more than ordinary commodities. Something less, because copyright law acknowledges that objects defined as intellectual property cannot simply be subjected to the laws that govern ordinary things. In order for them to be recognized by the state as private property, printed texts have required the development of a separate and increasingly arcane domain of law.[9] Something more, because state intervention assures that the individual ownership of copyrighted texts carries the weight of collective interests. Copyrighted texts are objects that, as a condition of sale, are jointly and provisionally held by numerous parties.

As defined by the U.S. Constitution, copyright is a property right of limited duration granted by the state on the grounds that it advances the public good, promoting "the Progress of Science and useful Arts."[10] Writing pseudonymously in defense of this provision in *Federalist* 43 (1788), James Madison argued that copyright and patent laws were clearly in the public interest: "the public good fully coincides in both cases with the claims of individuals."[11] However, in a letter to Thomas Jefferson, Madison took a decidedly less sanguine view of the matter, speculating on the available forms of redress should private property and public good fail to coincide: "With regard to Monopolies, they are justly classed among the greatest nuisances in Government. But is it clear that as encouragements to literary works and ingenious discoveries, they are not too valuable to be wholly renounced? Would it not suffice to reserve in all cases a right to the public to abolish the privilege at a price to be specified in the grant of it?"[12] Madison's wariness about copyright's constraint of the very public that grants this privilege is reflected in the first legislative act describing the parameters of copyright. As it was initially defined in 1790,[13] copyright was hedged about by qualifications: it was restricted to citizens and residents, limited to a period of fourteen years, and renewable for a second term of fourteen years only if the author were living at the time that his copyright expired. Although in 1831 copyright was redefined as heritable property and the initial term was doubled to twenty-eight years, it was still possible to calculate the moment at which a text was transformed from private into public property by looking at the date of registry on the copyright page. In recent years, the radical extension of the term of copyright, combined with the indexing of this right to the life of the author, has made the reversion of copyrighted works into the public domain both rarely experienced and difficult to forecast. The postponement of this reversion into an indefinite future has made intellectual property seem more like real estate than the limited monopoly right imagined by Madison. Indeed, terms of copyright that ordinarily extend beyond one hundred years have enabled intellectual property to become the bedrock of substantial businesses and a form of inheritance on which multiple generations depend. While today's copyrights, then, are far less provisionally held than they were in the nineteenth century, they continue to represent corporate interests that necessarily exceed the grasp of the individual in whose name they are held.

The radical extension of the rights conferred by copyright under the sign of authorial ownership suggests a final reason for the volatile relation between title-page and copyright-page understandings of authorship. If books are extraordinary objects, they are also exemplary objects; in announcing their reliance on state protection they threaten to lay bare the condition of ordinary possessions. At least since Jeremy Bentham, legal scholars have insisted on the conventional nature of all property: we don't own things, but rather rights to things that are secured by laws that make possession possible.[14] Clearly grounded in statutory law and not common law or natural right, copyright threatens to expose by analogy the artificial and state-mediated nature of all property. This paradox can help to explain why some of the most brazen attempts to extend the purview of copyright are also accompanied by appeals to the sanctity of individual rights and by strenuous denials or evasions of the corporate interests that are vested in intellectual property. Frequently using an overstrained analogy with ordinary things to confer extraordinary rights under copyright and patent law, contemporary courts are caught between an understanding of intellectual property as a matter of individual rights, and an awareness of the many interests that converge on an object of intellectual property.[15]

I dwell on the paradoxical status of intellectual property under contemporary law in order to suggest some of the challenges that attend my own attempt to understand how property rights in printed texts shaped the market for books in the antebellum United States. In considering the relation of the book market to the development of market culture in general, I will argue that the market for books is exceptional, that a long-standing tradition of considering print as public property arrayed book and periodical publishers against the consolidating forces of the general economy. But I am also interested in the ways in which books and authors take on an exemplary status within market culture. Printed texts and authorial labor were idealized both by those who called on the government to regulate and nationalize the trade in books, and by those who argued forcefully for the book market's decentralization.

These arguments put me at odds with the consensus position, forged by Michael T. Gilmore, that in the antebellum period "writing and publishing developed along roughly the same lines as the economy at large."[16] Following in the footsteps of William Charvat's groundbreaking studies of literary publishing and the profession of authorship, Gilmore argues that antebellum American writers struggled to adapt themselves and their writing to the "commercialization" of literature as a rapidly advancing market economy brought all aspects of social life "under the dominion of exchange" (4). Gilmore is interested in how authors such as Emerson, Thoreau, Hawthorne, and Melville became attuned to the impact of the market on society through their more immediate experience of alienation from the reading public. Outlining broad patterns of socioeconomic change, Gilmore holds the category of the market stable in order to chronicle a range of authors' responses to the market-mediation of their writing. Although he acknowledges that the structural conditions for the national distribution of American literature were not in place until the early 1850s, Gilmore argues that subjection to the market is a national phenomenon, a common denominator that cuts through differences in the pace and scope of change: "that the Age of Jackson was a time of transition should not obscure the fact that the extension of the commodity form over man and nature proceeded inexorably throughout the period" (17). For Gilmore, the most significant consequence of the emergence of a market for literary works is the dependence of authors on a readership that they grow to resent. According to Gilmore, the mass-market provokes a split between high and low culture, leaving little space for serious art. The story of American romantics' relation to the marketplace becomes one of failed communication: authorial subjection to market forces produces a literature of dissent fueled by radical ambivalence towards the market. Paradoxically, this ambivalence is shared by the very reading public that canonical American authors largely fail to reach.

My closer focus on the development of the literary marketplace challenges this narrative in a number of respects. I will argue that it is not the fact of the market but its structure that is most significant for authors. Indeed, the most salient aspect of the antebellum book market was not its inexorability but the unpredictability and unevenness of its development. I am less interested in authors' alienation from the market than in the forms of their relation to the shifting conditions of literary production. For while a national literary culture may have been incipient in this period, its triumph was by no means inevitable.[17] Transforming a decentralized mass-market into a national one required the dismantling and reorganization of other ways of ordering culture. Antebellum writers were subject to multiple markets and publics, particularly under the system of reprinting, where texts achieved a remarkable mobility across elite and mass-cultural formats. Authors' awareness of the tendency of markets to shift the ground on which they stood was sharpened by the demise of reprinting in the early 1850s as the regional articulation of culture gave way to more centralized methods of dissemination. Thus, while I will be concerned in this book to recover the ways in which Dickens, Poe, and Hawthorne are shaped by the practices and values of reprinting, I will also analyze the kinds of pressure that are put on authors, texts, and authorial personae as literary culture becomes organized on a more steeply hierarchical plane.

Taking their cue from Gilmore's study, most subsequent accounts of the antebellum literary marketplace have portrayed the shift from a patronage system to a market for books as uncontested and incontestable. Typically, they depict the market as a monolithic, totalizing entity, one that generates dissent but yields neither to intervention nor to change. And yet, as Richard Teichgraeber has noted, it has become increasingly difficult to square theoretical claims about the comprehensive transformation of print culture by market forces with scholarship that stresses the antebellum literary marketplace's characteristic heterogeneity and volatility.[18] The antebellum trade in books was not only a remarkably differentiated set of practices, its configuration was the subject of considerable political struggle. The fundamental questions that accompanied the commercialization of literature—What kind of a thing is writing? What kind of labor is authorship, and how should it be remunerated? Is the trade in books compatible with the interests of a republic?—were the subject of heated debate in the courts, in Congress, and in newspapers and literary periodicals.

How we think about the structure and malleability of the book market has consequences for the large-scale narratives we tell about the politics of print. Gilmore's analysis has helped to define the antebellum period as one in which a print culture that was intimately bound up with political power gives way to a cultural and political order that is dominated by the market. Grantland Rice, for example, has argued that the antebellum period witnessed "the gradual but continuous replacement of a political understanding of authorship with an exclusively economic one."[19] For Rice and Gilmore, the republican ideal of a polity in which liberty is preserved by the unhindered circulation of texts becomes at best a nostalgic alternative to the new economic order; the triumph of the market coincides with the fateful withdrawal of politics from the field of culture. Although Gilmore has recently come to question this dimension of his argument,[20] his description of the emergence of market culture as the eclipse of a meaningful politics of print remains widely influential.

I will argue to the contrary that antebellum authors' primary struggle was with the way in which republican values transformed the literary marketplace. The strong half-life of the republican understanding of print as public property sustained the culture of reprinting and involved publishers in the era's defining controversies over the nature and course of economic development. Historians such as Charles Sellers have recently emphasized how thoroughly and fiercely contested were all aspects of the "market revolution."[21] Jacksonian democracy's acute concern with the centralization of political power and the consolidation of capital are richly reflected in the debates over international copyright, linking the defense of reprinting to antidevelopmental measures such as the dismantling of the national bank and the rejection of a national transportation system. In reinforcing the precedence of local over national authority, reprinting also becomes complexly imbricated with the protection of chattel slavery. My aim in elucidating these connections is to return some sense of political conflict and consequence to the story of the explosive growth of antebellum print culture, a story which is most often told solely in economic terms as capitalism's effective harnessing of technological innovation. Due to the implicitly nationalist framework of most Americanist literary criticism and book history, this story is also most often told with an unqualified enthusiasm for national development. In calling attention to reprinting as one means by which the centralization of American culture is forestalled, I will insist both that economic questions are inseparable from political questions, and that in an industrializing society, the circulation of printed texts remained critical to Americans' imagination of state power.

Some of the difficulty of integrating the study of culture and politics in this period is manifest in the divergent terms historians and literary critics use to designate their fields of study. "The Age of Jackson" identifies the keynote of the period as its transformation of partisan politics but doesn't designate a cultural field that extends much beyond the campaign song and party newspaper. With some prominent exceptions, the epithet "Jacksonian" fails to describe either the aesthetic ambitions or the political commitments of authors. And yet, the categories relied on by literary critics to group the period's major texts and movements seem to acknowledge political ferment chiefly by placing literature beyond its reach. From a historian's perspective, "Transcendentalism" can seem too local a phenomenon and "Romanticism" too autotelic to bring literature into contact with the major currents of social and cultural change. Cultural historians' frequent recourse to the adjective "Victorian" captures the transatlantic nature of much of antebellum literary culture but appears to leave domestic politics aside, taking the reign of the British monarch as its point of reference. Even the tag "antebellum" names the period by naturalizing the coming of the war as its telos and significance. These rubrics suggest a provocative nonalignment of culture and politics, a disjunction that our critical approaches reflect but cannot centrally address. Much of the appeal of "Market Revolution" as a conceptual framework has had to do with its ability to interweave political and economic history, and yet its use within literary criticism has for the most part been restricted to the study of authors' attitudes toward market capitalism, attitudes that have been richly traced at the level of figure or theme.[22] What is missing in these accounts, however, is some sense that literature itself was caught up in the period's formative struggles over economic development. A focus on reprinting can help to integrate literary study with historians' representation of the market system as politically contested by training our gaze on readers' modes of access to literary culture. Reprinting will remind us that the politics of culture is played out at the level of form and format as well as in the explicit themes of literary texts.[23]

Literary critics' perception of the market revolution has also been shaped by the discipline's customary reliance on authors to frame and to organize its insights. American literary history is particularly rich in studies of market culture from an authorial perspective. Nicholas Bromell has analyzed the representation of work in antebellum culture through the lens of writers' heightened self-consciousness about the work of writing. Michael Newbury has examined authors' attempts to place writing within hierarchies of labor, while Cindy Weinstein has measured authors' use of allegory against market culture's transformation of labor, agency, and the body.[24] These studies grapple in various ways with the advantages and limitations of taking authors to be representative of the society they seek to represent. Michael Gilmore nicely captures the complexity of this problem when he argues that antebellum writers' alienation from the reading public helps them to reflect the reading public's own alienation from market culture. What an author-centered approach to market culture cannot register, however, is the way in which the shift to a market for books in America places the category of authorship in doubt. Not only does the author-concept hold partial and inadequate sway within the culture of reprinting, literature itself has not yet successfully been harnessed to the task of national representation. To be sure, all of the studies I mention acknowledge American authors' experience of their own marginality, albeit chiefly in the register of authorial anxiety or complaint. But an author-centered critical approach ultimately contains the threat to authorial agency posed by the culture of reprinting. After all, we rehearse the complaints of writers who have become major authors, figures we rely on to represent antebellum culture. The importance of American authors and their centrality to the nation is never in doubt for contemporary literary critics. The ability of a rapidly changing market for print to reconfigure the ground rules of literary culture is not a story that is easily told with the ordinary tools of literary criticism.

In this book, I counteract the foreshortening effect of the author-concept by beginning with legal and political debates over literary property. These debates raise questions about the nature of books as objects, the relation of the circulation of printed texts to state power, and the role of authors in a democracy, subjecting these questions to judicial interpretation and legislative enactment. I have chosen to examine legal and political discourse about literary property because of its efficacy: debates in the Supreme Court and in Congress have the power to shape the development of the publishing system. And yet I am also interested in these discursive contexts because they frame copyright as a matter for debate; they offer competing definitions of literary property, rationales for its protection, and positions on the role of literature in the nation. They also enable me to get beyond the testimony of authors for theories of the author's relation to society. These debates provide access to an exuberant vision of a print culture that could thrive without native authors; they also enable us to perceive the peculiar weight that gets placed upon authors as figures of exemption from market culture.

My chapter on Charles Dickens serves as a hinge between the analysis of legal and political discourse and a series of chapters organized around the writing and careers of individual authors. In treating the work of a popular British author as an American text, I adopt the logic of the reprinters, but I also seek to unfold a mode of reading that could address the question of authorial mastery without being governed by it. Dickens's 1842 tour and his widely reprinted narrative of his travels illustrate some of the practical consequences of the reprinters' theories of democratic authorship and some of the limitations of an author-centered approach to the culture of reprinting. Dickens's absorption into a set of cultural and political controversies that he fails to comprehend shows how unauthorized reprinting can generate a range of meanings that spectacularly exceed the control of authors.[25]

As my interest in Dickens, Poe, and Hawthorne should suggest, I do not eschew authorship as a point of entry into the culture of reprinting. I am not convinced that it is possible or desirable for literary criticism to do without authors. Neither am I persuaded that studying the culture of reprinting requires such a renunciation. After all, in rejecting authorship as a governing principle for the production and distribution of literary texts, the culture of reprinting does not eliminate authors so much as suspend, reconfigure, and intensify their authority, placing a premium on texts that circulate with the names of authors attached. Indeed, it was the fiercely competitive reprint publishers who pioneered American book marketing techniques, trumpeting the names and fortifying the reputations of authors as a means of distinguishing their editions from rival reprints. Even authorized editions, with their engraved portrait frontispieces, prefatory statements, and florid authorial signatures, owe their development in this period to the everyday circulation of unauthorized reprints.

In studying the work of American authors who are formed by the system of reprinting (rather than, like Dickens, briefly subjected to it from outside), I develop two strategies for bringing literary analysis into rapport with reprinting's transformation of the category of authorship. First, I try to avoid presuming that an author unifies or is unified by his published work. The regional and ephemeral nature of most of the periodicals in which Poe and Hawthorne published in the 1830s and '40s, and the availability of their texts for unauthorized reprinting, meant that complete or even coherent bodies of their work were unavailable to readers. Authors themselves had difficulty determining exactly where, in what formats, and how extensively their poems and tales circulated. Returning a sense of the tenuousness of the link between author and work to the scene of antebellum writing and reading, I examine how these authors' conjectures about their profoundly unknowable and unstable audiences shaped formal decisions about modes of address, tone, and genre. Disaggregating the corpus then enables me to reexamine the ways in which authors came into prominence in this culture, a process which is never wholly within the control of authors. I will look carefully at readers' investments in Poe and Hawthorne, the problems to which their works and authorial personae are thought to respond, and will examine how a dialogue with their cultural construction as authors in turn shapes their careers and writing.

In tracing some of the complex textual and social processes through which authors emerge, are recast, and reestablish themselves in this culture, I hope to open up new ways of thinking about the relations of literary texts to their conditions of production. Historicist criticism has generally relied on a language of privation to establish a link between literature and socio-economic conditions. Indeed, it is most often the figure of the author that brokers this connection, his singularity and the finitude of his life narrowing and focusing the seemingly infinite ways in which one might imagine the relation between texts and contexts. Michel Foucault has famously described the author as "the principle of thrift in the prolif-eration of meaning." According to Foucault, the figure of the author pro-vides the grounds of coherence and stands as the source of writing; he also governs the larger interpretive field as "a historical figure" located "at the crossroads of a certain number of events."[26] Historicist critics fre-quently turn to an author's life and times to identify and delimit the range of discourses they will bring to bear on a particular work of literature. Similarly, studies of the conditions of literary production frequently invoke the author's life as a force field on which economic influences, understood as a variety of incitements and compulsions, are clearly inscribed. These influences are imagined to be particularly keenly felt at the point of pro-duction, where the economic motives of both author (the need to write) and publisher (the need to sell) restrict and give concrete form to the boundless imagination.

William Charvat's identification of his subject as "the profession of authorship" in his landmark study *Literary Publishing in America, 1790–1850* provides a classic case in point. Arguing that "Publishing is relevant to lit-erary history only in so far as it can be shown to be, ultimately, a shaping influence on literature," Charvat limits his study to "those writers for whom both art and income were matters of concern, and whose work, accordingly, revealed the often conflicting pressures of the will to create and the need to create for a buying public."[27] Charvat here eliminates both private poets and hack writers from consideration, as well as authors who aspired to but failed to achieve professional status. What most interests me about this formulation is not Charvat's exclusion of some categories of writers in order to focus on others, but his assumption that in restrict-ing his field of inquiry he gains a measure of epistemological certainty. While publishing history might easily be imagined to shape both private poets, who withdraw from the market, and hack writers, who are fully absorbed in it, for Charvat, without a clear struggle between authorial desire and economic constraint there would be no way of tracing how a particular publishing context leaves its mark upon a text. Following Charvat, Americanist literary critics commonly invoke publishing conditions under the sign of privation because it makes economic determination sharply legible. Unfortunately, however, it commits them to endlessly retelling the story of individual desire and market constraint, documenting, for instance, how the publishing industry limits an author's development, or how an author reflects on and compensates for such restrictions within the text, imagined as a space of comparative freedom in which such barriers are potentially overcome.

But invoking the material grounds of literature only insofar as they constrain literary production radically restricts the scope of literary criticism. To return to Foucault's proposition, there is no reason why socioeconomic conditions should not be imagined as a potential site of proliferation as well as a principle of thrift. Certainly, the explosive growth of print in antebellum America radically multiplied the means and modes through which writers could emerge as authors. In this period, men without capital like Poe and Hawthorne, middle-class women, and socially marginal individuals such as demobilized soldiers and escaped slaves all found ways to tell stories in print.[28] Rather than assuming that conditions of literary production come into view only when they offer checks and barriers to individuals, we need to ask how the structure and development of literary markets make possible the emergence of particular kinds of authorial subjects.

This is not to suggest that the culture of reprinting or any other publishing system operates without palpable constraints. Indeed, although Foucault is often misunderstood to project a utopian world in which signification would be freed from the superintendence of the "author-function," he insists to the contrary that all discursive systems pass through "something like a necessary or constraining figure" (119). But what if, in examining the relation of literature to its conditions of production, critics did not decide in advance that this principle of constraint was necessarily the author? In describing the workings of the system of reprinting—a set of publishing conditions characterized by a superabundance of literature that has historically been conjured as a space of lack—I will shift my attention from the privative to the generative aspects of the development of a market for books, looking past the sufferings of authors to identify the social processes and rhetorical structures that allow for the specific forms of their emergence.

*   *   *

How was a distinctive literary culture established and sustained through the circulation of unauthorized texts, and how could subsequent literary criticism largely fail to notice this phenomenon? Looking at three representative reprint vehicles from the 1840s, I will sketch some of the ways in which the uneven disposition of property rights in texts redefined the nature of the literary field. I am concerned here to show both how reprint formats delineate the boundaries of literary culture and how reprinters think about literary value. As we shall see, reprint publishers made complex calculations about their reading publics, perpetually estimating, projecting, and seeking to meet the desires of readers who could be persuaded to buy cheap books and periodicals. Reprinted texts are a rich source of speculation about what kinds of literature were demanded by a democratic public, what counted as literature in this culture, and how high art might be reconfigured for middle-class and working-class audiences. These negotiations have remained invisible to critics, however, because reprinting is at odds with our assumptions about what constitutes a national literature. As a brief look at some of these formats will demonstrate, reprinted texts offer considerable resistance to the conceptual frameworks of author-centered literary nationalisms.

From the perspective of a nationalist literary criticism—one that until recently devoted itself to the writings of a handful of representative authors—the 1830s and '40s were unquestionably a fallow period in American literature, a time of inferior and imitative literary production and of a general disregard for culture that was overcome only by the artistic efflorescence F. O. Matthiessen called the "American Renaissance." Reprising the complaints of authors such as Washington Irving and Nathaniel Hawthorne, critics have sustained the image of a young nation bereft not only of a national literature, but also of the romantic associations—the picturesque ruins and storied places—that would make such a literature possible. And yet the problem for authors, publishers, and readers in this period was not a scarcity or lack of literary culture, but a proliferation of literature that operated according to different principles. As nineteenth-century nationalists repeatedly protested, writing by native authors had to compete with popular foreign reprints that circulated independently of authorial control and national purpose.

Reprinting cannot, however, simply be opposed to the production of a national literature as copy to original. Reprint publishers frequently acknowledged nationalist aims, using foreign texts to refract an image of the nation as a whole that was seemingly impossible to produce by domestic means alone. Likewise, the culture of reprinting does not dispense with authors, but places authorship in complex and heightened forms of suspension. Take, for example, the reprint edition of Charles Dickens's travel narrative *American Notes for General Circulation* that was published as a newspaper "extra" by the New York literary weekly, *The New World* (Figure 1). In Chapter 3 I will discuss at greater length how

Figure 1. Title page, *The New World* (1842). Courtesy, American Antiquarian Society.

this particular text became a centerpiece of the defense of reprint culture, but I want to focus here on the complex double gaze that is created by the relation of masthead to text. The masthead lays claim to "The New World" from a European perspective, deploying the iconography of Columbus's discovery in the service of the nation's imperial ambitions. The new nation's continuation of this inheritance through westward expansion is established by the periodical's motto which is taken from a revolutionary war-era adaptation of a British classic, an American "Epilogue" to Addison's *Cato*: "No pent-up Utica contracts our powers; for the whole boundless continent is ours."[29]

But while the figures on the masthead look expectantly westward, the editors look east for the content of their magazine, reprinting a much awaited account of Dickens's travels along the eastern seaboard and into the western territories. Regarded solely in literary nationalist terms, the reprinting of *American Notes* is an exercise in colonial dependency. And yet Dickens's text is set within a nationalist framework that defies British authority even as it conscripts it for the purposes of national description. Printed in forty-six closely set pages and sent through the mail or hawked by newsboys for 12½ cents, this edition of *American Notes* sells for one-fortieth the cost of the two-volume, 21 shilling, 614 page British original. Moreover, the editors append to their edition an "Appeal to the Reading Public," an extended commentary that defends reprinting as "the unrestrained dissemination of learning among the people" and offers an astute critique of British copyright law and publishing practices.[30] Whereas in Great Britain "a society had to be formed for the diffusion of useful knowledge, and liberal donations made, before good books could be published for a sum within the ability of the poorer classes,"[31] the editors of *The New World* propose achieving the same aims through their "plan of cheap publications," relying on low production costs, small marginal profit rates, and sales in the tens of thousands. Thus they cared less about an author's national origin than about texts that would appeal to a broad readership. Their series of "Extra Numbers" includes works of history, biography, and popular science in addition to domestic and foreign novels. What unifies these diverse texts is the editors' conviction of their value to large numbers of readers, bringing the work of authors such as Dickens and Bulwer, who were extremely popular both in Britain and the United States, into a series that included scandalous texts (Eugene Sue's *Mysteries of Paris*), partisan texts (Epes Sargent's *Life and Public Services of Henry Clay*), reform texts (Walter Whitman's *Franklin Evans: or, the*

Inebriate. A Tale of the Times), domestic texts (Frederika Bremer's *The Home; or, Family Cares and Family Joys*), and reference works (Justus Leibig's *Chemistry, in its Applications to Agriculture and Physiology*).[32] *The New World's* "Extra" series relies on an odd concatenation of usefulness and currency as grounds of literary value. The editors assume that political aims and market mechanisms are mutually enabling, and attach national ideals not to texts or authors, but to publishing formats and methods of distribution. As the left-hand column of their edition of Dickens's text prominently announces, this is a "First American Edition." These are not "Notes by an American," but they are "American Notes" nonetheless.

As I will argue in Chapters 2 and 3, editions such as this one give substance to the reprinters' claim that it is not American authors but American publishers who most reliably promote democratic principles. Reprinting is not simply the antithesis of a legitimately national, original culture, neither are reprinted texts merely passive vehicles for the dissemination of European culture. In this case, reprinting is a sophisticated instrument for projecting an image of a nation that is at once colonial and imperial. Read either in terms of its content or in terms of its format, *The New World's* edition of *American Notes* gravitates too far toward the pole of dependency or toward that of conquest. It is only in the charged relation of text to format that the complex cultural politics of reprinting begins to emerge.

Americans looked to Dickens and to other foreign travelers to represent a nation that was fragmented and rapidly changing, one whose external boundaries and internal fault lines were continually unsettled and redrawn by westward expansion. The uncertainty provoked by these changes and the consequent importance of foreign opinion to Americans' understanding of themselves is richly registered in the hybrid modes of authority that are characteristically produced by reprint formats. For instance, the assumption that the nation could best be seen to cohere from the perspective of foreign shores is conveyed by an editorial note to the first issue of *Littell's Living Age*, an "eclectic" magazine or miscellany composed entirely of unauthorized reprints. Concerned that his move from Philadelphia to New York and finally to Boston might have alienated former subscribers, the editor, Eliakim Littell, jokingly refers to divisive controversies over tariffs, nullification, and the annexation of Texas in order to persuade his readers to stick with the new magazine:

We hope our Southern and Western correspondents will not give us up because we have *annexed* New England. We cannot agree to the dissolution of the union which has subsisted between us for so many years. It is to their advantage that we should have the most favorable post for our army of observation, that is, our printing-office. We shall here receive the foreign periodicals earliest;– we shall have the best communication with western New York, and with the countries bordering on the lakes (north as well as south); and we hope that we shall receive a kindly welcome to many new post-offices in this part of the country.[33]

Reassuring his readers that he can still reach Southern and Western markets through the Erie Canal,[34] Littell proposes that Boston might well serve as the cultural center of a divided nation because of its proximity to Europe. Taking a meliorist position on the admission of Texas to the Union as a slave state, Littell prefaces his brief comments with a surprising aside: "We shall have abundant time and opportunity for treating of the matter of *Texas* in its rebound from Europe in about a month." For the editor of a nonpartisan weekly who aspired to circulate his magazine across increasingly polarized regions, national expansion becomes a legitimate subject only after it is registered in the foreign press. In a version of *The New World's* double vision, Littell imagines an "army of observation" eagerly looking east for the arrival of a steamer with fresh news of the American west.

Reprinted foreign texts carry with them the authority of an older, established, and centralized media, but the process of reprinting also produces authority through its indirection. Foreign texts on American subjects offer the promise of disinterestedness at a time of intense sectionalism. Moreover, reprinted texts can be relied on as the common property of a dispersed and internally divided population. Littell's treatment of pressing domestic issues frequently takes advantage of reprinting's indirection. In the second issue of the *Living Age*, he addresses the tariff question by referring to articles on the "English Factory System" and republishes an article on "Cheap Postage" from the London *Spectator* as a means of encouraging American postal reform.[35] If the most comprehensive and the only disinterested perspective on national issues is a foreign one, foreign texts become indispensable to the nation's self-conception.

The title page of the first issue of *Littell's Living Age* gives a good indication of how the eclectic magazine reconfigures both nationality and authorship (Figure 2). Articles are listed by title with the space conventionally used to designate an essay's author given over to marking its place of origin in a foreign periodical. This form of signature is in part the product of necessity: many of the texts Littell reprints were first published

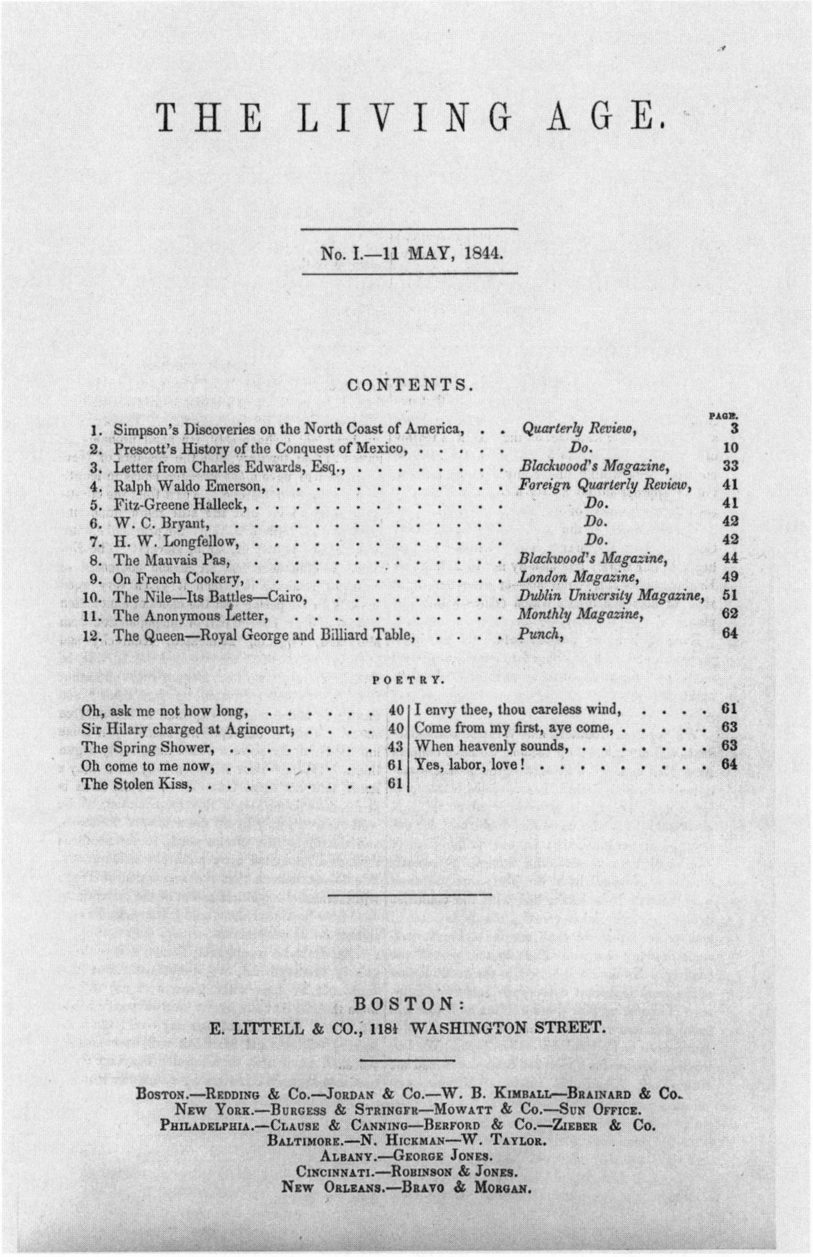

THE LIVING AGE.

No. I.—11 MAY, 1844.

CONTENTS.

BOSTON:

E. LITTELL & CO., 118½ WASHINGTON STREET.

Boston.—Redding & Co.—Jordan & Co.—W. B. Kimball—Brainard & Co.
New York.—Burgess & Stringer—Mowatt & Co.—Sun Office.
Philadelphia.—Clause & Canning—Berford & Co.—Zieber & Co.
Baltimore.—N. Hickman—W. Taylor.
Albany.—George Jones.
Cincinnati.—Robinson & Jones.
New Orleans.—Bravo & Morgan.

Figure 2. Table of contents, *Littell's Living Age* (1844). Courtesy, American Antiquarian Society.

anonymously in Britain. In the context of British publishing, however, these texts possessed a qualified, gentlemanly anonymity. Overwhelmingly concentrated in the print centers of Dublin, Edinburgh, and London, British magazines and reviews tended to sharpen their identities as a way of cultivating readers. If the names of authors remained a mystery to subscribers, the political positions and sectarian affiliations of the periodicals for which they wrote were clearly denominated.[36] Anonymous texts in British journals bore marks of class, religious and political identity by virtue of the centralized and hierarchized periodical culture in which they appeared.

The American eclectic magazine, however, cultivated generality both in its selection of materials and its mode of address to its readers. In the table of contents of *Littell's Living Age*, the right-hand column becomes a switching point where gentlemanly anonymity becomes indistinguishable from republican anonymity, where the namelessness that protects an author's privacy is conflated with the namelessness that signals the *text's* status as common property. The eclectic magazine repeats and reconfigures the effacement of the author's name, reassigning what Foucault termed the "author-function" to the periodical of origin. It also renders much of the cultural freight carried by a particular article largely unrecoverable by removing it from the context in which it signified. While a knowing American reader could certainly weigh the difference between an article that was excerpted from a reform periodical and one that originated in the Tory press, Littell's skimming of "the cream of the foreign periodicals"[37] is designed to transfer authority and literary value from an article's source to the eclectic magazine, a format that is understood not as a place of origin but as a method of distribution.

The testimonials from far-flung newspapers that Littell publishes as a supplement to his first volume testify to the success of this transformation. They emphasize the extraordinary variety that can be encompassed by the eclectic magazine, the sense of up-to-dateness that is achieved by reperiodizing British periodical culture (transforming the "stately" quarterlies and magazines into a fast-moving and adaptable American weekly, the record of a "Living Age"), and most importantly, the value that is produced by Littell's exercise of judgment in selection. These testimonials repeatedly invoke editing as a principle of refinement that sifts out essays of lesser worth and those that are too local in their field of reference. Littell addresses and seeks to produce a general reader, one whose dislocation from any particular place is indicated both by the jumble of articles drawn from the periodicals of numerous foreign cities, and by the list of regional distributors that expands upon the customary title-page reference to his publication's place of origin.[38] Indeed, Littell and other reprint publishers seem surprisingly indifferent to the carefully crafted sensibilities and the political commitments of the journals from which they draw. While in Britain it is highly unlikely that a single household would subscribe to both the high Tory *Dublin University Magazine* and the dissenting Unitarian *Monthly Magazine*, Littell juxtaposes selections from these periodicals with no sense that they might chafe against each other.[39] Littell's extracts from the foreign press are also abstractions of periodical writing itself. Littell trades on the settled authority of foreign journals while driving the texts he reprints towards the radical decontextualization of the lyric poems that he lists, utterly authorless, below them.[40]

For a periodical composed almost entirely of unauthorized foreign texts, however, this issue of the *Living Age* is remarkably preoccupied both with America and with American authors. For example, Littell has an eye to American readers' interest in national history when he renames his lead article, initially published as "Simpson's Narrative of Discoveries by Officers of the Hudson's Bay Company," so as to emphasize the place of discovery rather than the British corporation of explorers. Most striking in a format that circulates texts without reference to their authors, Littell republishes a single *Foreign Quarterly Review* essay on "American Poetry" as if it were four separate articles on individual American literary figures. It is important to note that the strong nationalist emphasis of this premier issue is unrepresentative of the journal as a whole; it reflects less the ethos of the magazine than Littell's canny attempt to woo new subscribers by telegraphing his interest in both Boston and New York literati. Nevertheless, it provides a good example of the way in which reprinted texts can assert authorship and nationality as grounds of value despite their structural refusal of such categories as organizing principles of literary culture.

The New World and the *Living Age* both suggest that the common property status of reprinted texts potentially makes them more national in outlook and in circulation than texts produced by American authors. Reprint publishers exploited the time lag built into the constitutional justification of copyright as an incentive, a means for Congress "*to promote the Progress of Science and useful Arts.*" Designed to facilitate interstate trade in books, American copyright law gave authors and publishers a national monopoly on domestic texts far in advance of the development of a national market for books. In a decentralized marketplace, copyright could be as much a liability as a strength: structurally speaking, where the distribution of printed texts is a challenge, the right to control distribution by restricting copying is a right of limited value. Seeking the broadest possible field of distribution, reprint publishers generally invested in foreign texts for which American demand could be assured. Taking advantage of the attunement of the American press and American readers to the British critical establishment, they seized on texts that had been well received abroad and widely noticed in American newspapers. Nevertheless, they still sought ways to protect their substantial investments in texts that were unprotected by copyright. Indeed, the vulnerability of popular foreign books to reprinting and the uncopyrighted status of newspaper and magazine writing made it all the more imperative for publishers to find ways to distinguish their periodicals and editions. Publishers' attempts to assert property rights in reprinted texts had complex ramifications for literature. I will turn now to the graphic environment of antebellum poetry and fiction to show how reprinting puts literary texts into a new and charged relation with engravings. Looking at the ways in which gift books detach texts and images from their sources and readdress them to a generalized, middle-class reader will show how the dislocation characteristic of reprinting can nevertheless serve as a text's proprietary ground.

The culture of reprinting conferred a new kind of value on illustrations. While type could easily be reset, engravings were more difficult and expensive to reproduce, enabling publishers to secure property in their texts by investing heavily in ornamental plates, a practice that Hugh Amory has called "proprietary illustration."[41] Amory coined the term to explain why British publishers lavished money and attention on illustrations at the moment when a landmark copyright decision instantly transformed many of the English classics from exclusive into public property. Amory's insight that engravings help to mark a text's identity, to ward off wholesale reprinting, and to create a stable sense of value applies with particular force to the American literary marketplace, in which publishers' ability to secure property in their texts was more radically in question.

Some sense of the importance of engravings to American publishers and the peculiar form that "proprietary illustration" took in America, is clear from an extraordinary publishing project such as the Harper's *Illuminated and New Pictorial Bible*, published between 1843 and 1846 in 54 installments and distributed like a periodical, through the mail, accompanied by more than 1600 illustrations. Ordinary publications increasingly relied on illustrations, too, albeit on a much smaller scale. A typical advertisement from a Philadelphia publisher announced an edition of *Shakespeare's Dramatic Works* issued like the Harper's Bible, in parts, with each number containing "a play complete, with a fine steel engraving of its leading female character."[42] *Godey's Lady's Book* ensured a regular, periodic demand for the magazine by publishing hand-colored plates of the current month's fashions, while a whole host of magazines claimed distinction for themselves and for the literature they printed by linking poetry and fiction to the visual arts.

The general graphic environment in which antebellum literature appeared owed its genesis to a particularly influential mode of publication, the gift book or annual. As Stephen Nissenbaum has argued, when gift books burst onto the publishing scene in the late 1820s, they were technologically and commercially cutting-edge products. Gift books were one of the first mass-produced luxury commodities, designed to overcome the uncertain and intermittent demand for books by appearing annually, in time to be purchased and given away for Christmas.[43] With their miscellaneous tables of contents and their emphasis on fine art and other engravings, gift books established the formula that illustrated magazines would exploit in the 1840s and '50s.

What is most striking about gift books in the context of reprinting is the disjunction between word and image that was dictated by their method of publication and reinforced by their aesthetic. The story of a disconnection between word and image is not one that scholars are used to telling. Far more familiar is a story of collaboration, borrowing, or a struggle for domination between "sister arts."[44] And yet, in the decades in which a mass market for books was still developing, a separation between word and image was veritably enforced by the technology to which publishers turned in their attempt to satisfy a middle-class readership. Prior to the emergence in the 1850s of illustrated newspapers, which employed wood engravings that were printed on the same presses as the accompanying text, books and periodicals overwhelmingly employed steel engravings, a method of production that could both handle large print runs and marshal the cultural prestige required for elite publications. Disproportionately valued by readers, hundreds of times more costly to publishers than the poems, tales and sketches with which they appeared, and fundamentally unintegrated with the letterpress, these steel engravings testify to a profound disjunction between word and image even as both words and images were being mass produced, together, on an unprecedented scale.[45]

In a typical gift book, separate tables of contents for the literature and the "embellishments" attest to the fact that most of the literary contributions were solicited independently of the engravings, and that the engravings were given pride of place. It was frequently unclear to the editors which of the eight to twenty engraved plates they had commissioned would serve as the frontispiece to the volume. Indeed, this decision was so often made after the text-block had already been printed that one frequently comes across a frontispiece whose accompanying text is stranded somewhere in the middle of the volume. Despite the general arbitrariness with which images and text are interleaved, most of the engraved plates are accompanied by poetry or a short piece of explanatory prose that was composed for the occasion. And yet these "literary illustrations,"[46] as Hawthorne termed them, are frequently anonymous; the texts that bear the responsibility of connecting word to image are often of the lowest stature in the volume.

The differences in attribution in the tables of contents testify to the prestige the editors hoped the engravings would convey, and to their far lesser confidence in gift book literature. Lists of embellishments frequently include elaborate chains of attribution, naming the painter or designer of the original image, the engraver who transferred the image to the plate, and the patron who was kind enough to lend the unique work of art to the engraver for reproduction. By contrast, tables of contents for the literary matter generally contain a mixture of signed, anonymous, and pseudonymous contributions. Editors who trumpeted the fact that particular engravings were unique to their publications did not evince a comparable concern for the originality of their literature. As the editor of the *Mayflower for 1846* nonchalantly put it: "A great portion of the [literary] contents is original, and that which is not, the editor has selected from the most popular periodicals and other sources little known to the American public, but which he opines will prove more acceptable than a boasted array of entirely original articles of only mediocre composition."[47]

This unevenness in standards of value for visual art and literature in part has to do with the greater susceptibility of literature to mass production, and in part speaks to a pervasive sense of national inferiority. While the editors of gift books and illustrated magazines worried that American painting could not measure up to that of the Europeans, they could still take pride in the craftsmanship of American engravers, valuing not their originality but their fidelity to their object.[48] Gift books frequently included American copies of paintings and engravings whose foreign origins were not obscured by the copyist.

Increasingly, however, American gift books marketed themselves as exclusively American productions, and it was the plate articles that were called on to compensate both for American painters' and engravers' bias toward Europe, and for the potential irrelevance to the middle-class consumer of fine art itself. The poems and prose that accompanied the engravings frequently worked to make European culture safe for Americans. For example, an engraving pointedly titled "Byron, at age 19" is accompanied by an anonymous poem that begins: "Does it not break upon thee now, / The vision of thine after years, / and bid the youthful spirit bow / With misery too deep for tears?"[49] American readers get a Byron both innocent of and condemned for his unnameable transgressions. And yet these often bathetic examples of poetry and short prose provide crucial insight into the crisis of value that inhabited the gift book as a form. Publishers were clearly worried about the value of their investments in engravings insofar as they dislocated their subjects from the contexts in which they readily signified. It is the plate articles and poems that are asked to overcome the distance between fine art and the middle-class reader.

Take for example the 1831 *Token*'s publication of an engraving of a now well-known painting by Thomas Cole, "Scene from 'The Last of the Mohicans': Cora Kneeling at the Feet of Tamenund,"[50] painted in 1827 at the behest of Daniel Wadsworth (Figure 3). While this might seem an easy image to which to append a text—chapter and verse are veritably prescribed by the painting—the anonymous author of the plate article begins defensively, addressing the generic expectations that would have been raised by the *engraving*'s title "American Scenery": "It is not a view of a particular spot, but a combination of sketches from nature, taken in various parts of the country. The design of the artist appears to have been to present in one view the characteristic features of our mountain landscape; and, as not inappropriate to such a design, he has introduced in the distance a scene from Mr. Cooper's tale of the Last of the Mohicans" (55). Charged with a failure to represent a particular place, Cole's miscellaneous rendering of American scenery is redeemed by its nationalist intentions, intentions which are confirmed by the inclusion of a scene from Cooper's novel. Described as if it were an afterthought, the scene from the novel nevertheless bridges the gap that had opened up between painting and viewer, whether through ignorance, indifference, or the radical difference

Figure 3. "American Scenery," *The Token: A Christmas and New Year's Present* (1831). Courtesy, American Antiquarian Society.

in scale between painting and engraving, which renders the engraving's narrative subject nearly invisible. While the gift-book circulation of this image recalls the broader middle-class project of yoking fine art to landscape tourism, the plate article betrays a surprising anxiety about the engraving's field of reference. This is an odd painting indeed to reproach with a failure of nationalism.

It is important to note that plate articles and poems are not critiques of art but rather attempts to bring the experience of the viewer into line with the range of affects that are produced by the volume as a whole. This is particularly evident the further removed the world of the engraving is from the experience of the middle-class woman whom the gift book primarily addresses. Take, for instance the engraving after an illustration drawn by Robert Hood[51] (Figure 4) which was first published in John Franklin's *Narrative of a Journey to the Shores of the Polar Sea* (London, 1823). In its original incarnation it was a portrait of sorts, depicting natives who had played an important role in Franklin's search for the Northwest passage[52] (Figure 5). Hood's drawing included to the right of the girl an image of her father in silhouette overlooking the scene. In the decontextualized world of the gift book, however, this engraving is narrowed in its focus to center on the girl alone, and is glossed by a poem spoken in a voice that approximates that of a gift-book reader:

Go, go away, you foolish man;
You certainly had best
Give up all thoughts of marriage vows,
And let a body rest.
What need to ask for whom or what
This snow-shoe I repair?
You poor old man, your tottering weight
This shoe will never bear.[53]

Figure 4. "The Snow-Shoe," *The Token: A Christmas and New Year's Present* (1831). Courtesy, American Antiquarian Society.

Shaken free of its ethnographic context, as well as from the figure of the
supervising father, this image is positioned so as to address a lover who
never enters the field of representation.

The dislocation of this image from its context and its redeployment
by the poem points to the asymmetrical conditions of gift-book circulation. Generally purchased by men and given to women—often as part of
the courtship process—gift books are situated at a pivot point between
economic and affective systems of exchange. As they pass from purchaser
to receiver, suitor to woman sought, gift books also need to be transformed from mass-produced commodities into another kind of currency,
"tokens of affection" that will be rewarded by a return of the same.
One site for this transformation is the engraved presentation plate that
scripts a relation between purchaser and receiver even as it allows for the

Figure 5. "Keskarrah A Copper Indian Guide and His Daughter Green
Stockings," *Narrative of a Journey to the Shores of the Polar Sea* (1823). Courtesy,
American Antiquarian Society.

personalization of the gift[54] (Figure 6). The work of conjuring female
affective response is also carried out in the body of the volume, primarily
in tales of love and romance, but also through engravings such as "The
Snow Shoe" that have been loosed from their referential moorings and
readdressed to the woman reader. Drawn within the orbit of the gift

Figure 6. Presentation Plate, *The Token and Atlantic Souvenir: A Christmas
and New Year's Present* (1836). Courtesy, American Antiquarian Society.

book's overlapping systems of exchange, this remnant of imperial conquest recalls, instead, the woman reader's affective power in the form of the exoticized, coy refusal of a generic native woman.

The transformation of an image into a figure for female subjectivity is perhaps the gift books' most common strategy for understanding and assimilating the engravings they incorporate. Biblical scenes were popular subjects for gift books, both because of their propriety and because of their ready legibility—these were images with culturally acceptable, didactic purposes. The biblical scenes one finds in gift books, however, frequently center on female consciousness itself, not for the purposes of instruction but to accord with the medium's emphasis on female subjectivity. Gift books jumbled together generic depictions of women's meditation, engravings of figurative paintings that were loosely connected with European literary classics, and images of female historical figures.[55] Portraits were cut off from their representational function and reassigned a generic one. Thomas Sully's "A Portrait"[56] (Figure 7), for example, emphasizes a nameless woman's fashionability and the engraver's skill, relieving the image of

Figure 7. "A Portrait," *The Gift: A Christmas and New Year's Present* (1840). Courtesy, American Antiquarian Society.

its responsibility to represent the subject and to reflect her social position and power. Dislocated from reference, these images are nevertheless assimilated into a signifying system that articulates the gift book's proprietary ground. Looking out at the reader from the title page of numerous gift books—the page that claims property, or title—is the head of a generic woman (Figure 8) gazing directly, if blankly, back at the portrait's new

Figure 8. Title page, *The Gift: A Christmas and New Year's Present* (1840). Courtesy, American Antiquarian Society.

patron, the generalized middle-class reader. These severed heads are only a step away from the remarkable candor of the title page of N. P. Willis's literary weekly, the *New Mirror* (Figure 9) which has abandoned the task of representing women in lieu of presenting a figure for reflection. Here the nonspecificity of the gift book's signature emphasis on female subjectivity is given its most damning gloss: in its very address to its readers, the contents of this illustrated periodical are acknowledged to be mere vanity.

Figure 9. Title page, the *New-Mirror* (1843). Courtesy, American Antiquarian Society.

The title page of the *New Mirror* shows the figural logic of the gift books and illustrated magazines at their most extreme, where the mobility of the image threatens to empty it of content, where circulation produces the possibility of depth and reflection (and not the reverse). This turn to address the reader can be seen as a solution to the crisis of value brought on by the mass production of fine art. In their reliance on dislocation and generality, gift books recall some of the rhetorical strategies of eclectic magazines, which similarly project a placeless, general reader as a means of creating and stabilizing value. Gift books also suggest the significant challenge offered by an aesthetic based on imitation to ordinary modes of historicist analysis. In order to read a literary text drawn from a gift book in the context of its initial publication, one cannot simply return the text to its context; one would have to read it in the context of the radical decontextualization that marked the gift book medium as a whole.

The three reprint formats I have surveyed—newspaper extras, eclectic magazines, and gift books and illustrated magazines—all demonstrate the importance of distribution to the organization of culture under the system of reprinting. The emphasis of reprinters on getting books and periodicals to new groups of readers shifts the locus of value from textual origination to editing and arrangement, placing authorship under complex forms of occlusion. In reprint culture, authorship is not the dominant mode of organizing literary culture; texts with authors' names attached take their place alongside anonymous, pseudonymous, and unauthorized texts.

In placing the category of authorship into question, these formats suggest new ways of examining antebellum print culture along the axes of gender and race. Disentangling antebellum writing from literary critics' dependence on proprietary authorship should open up a wealth of topics for further study, topics that I can only adumbrate here. For instance, there is good evidence to suggest that women authors felt enormously empowered by gift books' organization of miscellaneous images and narratives around female subjectivity. As the title page of the 1832 *Token* suggests (Figure 10), women readers were addressed not only as subjects and patrons, but also as potential contributors. In this engraving, the remoteness and evanescence of women's natural writing is captured and counterbalanced by the sculptural solidity of the frame, its potential permanence suggested by the reflection of the gift-book title on the polished marble of the aristocratic interior. Women increasingly served as gift-book authors and editors, finding ways of recasting their agency within these books' characteristically asymmetrical systems of exchange.[57] The gift books and illustrated magazines of the 1830s and '40s paved the way for women's domination of the market for sentimental fiction in the 1850s. Catharine Maria Sedgwick, Sara Josepha Hale, and Harriet Beecher Stowe all wrote for gift books early on in their careers, suggesting that these books' dislocation and relocation of images and their mix of anonymous, pseudonymous, and authored writing were enabling to women authors denied ready access to publication.

Figure 10. Title page, *The Token: A Christmas and New Year's Present* (1832). Courtesy, American Antiquarian Society.

In addition to studying reprinting's projection of modes of authorship that middle-class women could comfortably occupy,[58] one might also examine how the suspension of authority under reprinting gets marked by gender and sexuality. The theatrical effeminacy of an author such as N. P. Willis, who thrived under the culture of reprinting—even founding a high-toned eclectic magazine brazenly called *The Corsair*—suggests that spectacles of cultural dependency can carry a complex erotic charge.[59] One might also think about the ways in which reprint culture remaps the relation of gender to literary value, rendering the circulation of elite literature dependent on the stable periodicity of women's fashion.

The limited power of the author-concept to organize literary culture under the system of reprinting can be seen as a peculiar kind of advantage for writers who were marked by race and gender, providing access to print while suspending or deferring the question of authorial identity. While in the case of slave narratives, the suspension of authorial identity raised troubling questions of authenticity, the popular circulation of uncopyrighted texts helped to give certain kinds of writing by socially marginal authors a powerful cultural presence. For instance, both women and African-American authors gained broad readerships through the evangelical press, which depended on a combination of market mechanisms and charitable contributions to distribute uncopyrighted tracts and periodicals.[60] Reprinting also played a critical role in supporting the fledgling black press. As Elizabeth McHenry has observed, *The North Star* and *Frederick Douglass's Paper* both eagerly republished British poetry and fiction; the latter serialized Dickens's *Bleak House* in the spring of 1852 in tense proximity with critical commentary on Harriet Beecher Stowe's *Uncle Tom's Cabin*.[61] Attending to reprinting in this context not only would provide literary critics with new collocations of texts, it would also help to define the cultural territory that was shared by mainstream antebellum readers and radical reformers—common ground that is projected in this case through reprinted British fiction.

In order to open up these areas of study, however, we need first to be able to see reprinting as a culture, as something more than an obstacle to the development of an authentic national literature. For both rhetorical and practical reasons, I will focus in this book on the careers and writing of canonical writers. Like the reprinters themselves, I trade on the cachet of major authors, hoping to make the lineaments of reprint culture as visible as possible. But I also depend on these authors' canonical status for the bibliographic research that undergirds this study. The undisputed importance of Dickens, Poe, and Hawthorne to British and American literary history has made it possible for me to begin to recover the patterns of reprinting of their texts. Authors such as Willis and Sedgwick, who were arguably more important to reprint culture than Poe and Hawthorne, have yet to galvanize the kind of interest that would underwrite the formidable task of compiling reliable bibliographies. The importance of the authors of this study to nineteenth-century literary nationalist canons also makes it possible for me to trace some of the ways in which the literary forms and values of the culture of reprinting were reconfigured and misrecognized by the literary regime that began to supplant it in the early 1850s.

*   *   *

Readers from different disciplines will likely trace different pathways through this book. Cultural and social historians, and historians of the book may be most interested in the first three chapters, in which I analyze legal and political debates over literary property and pursue the reprint history of a specific text. Literary critics interested in the relations of literary works to their conditions of production may in turn be drawn to the last three chapters, in which I consider how the culture of reprinting and its displacement by literary nationalism structured the careers and writing of well-known authors. This book follows a rough chronology from the landmark domestic copyright case *Wheaton v. Peters* (1834), which established a narrow interpretation of authors' rights, through the political debates over international copyright, which peaked in the late 1830s and 1840s, to Dickens's, Poe's and Hawthorne's navigation of reprint culture in the 1840s and early 1850s. Although reprinting had long been an important part of American book and periodical publishing, these are the years in which the rapid expansion of a market for print provoked a struggle over the definition of literary property. I offer not a continuous narrative history but an analysis of flashpoints in which political and economic change is made visible in discourse, in which authors and publishers intervene to shape the development of the market for print, and in which authors position or find themselves positioned at the pivot of cultural change.

   In the first three chapters, I argue that the suspension of authorial rights that gave rise to the culture of reprinting was the product of calculated resistance to the model of authorship and the system of publishing that was operative in Britain. Focusing on nineteenth-century case law, my first chapter shows how a Lockean notion of the book as inalienable private property was defeated in the courts by a republican emphasis on the publicity of print and on the political need for its wide dissemination. Through a reading of the landmark copyright case *Wheaton v. Peters* and a consideration of its legal legacy, I argue that in the American courts, going-into-print was imagined not as the moment at which personal property rights were secured, but as the point at which individual rights gave way to the demands of the social. Private ownership of a printed text was defined as the temporary alienation of what was essentially public property.

My second chapter takes up the effect on the publishing industry of this identification of print with public property, detailing the logic behind the century-long resistance to international copyright. Here I examine the defense of a decentralized literary marketplace in publishers' petitions to Congress (1837–53), in popular debate, and as it is embodied in the physical form of reprinted texts. Reading the struggle over international copyright in the context of concurrent debates over economic development, I argue that Congress's apparent failure to respond to American authors' pleas for intervention in the market represents not an indifference to their plight so much as a complex consensus as to the limits of their claims, a consensus that is grounded in a sophisticated analysis of the politics of print.

My third chapter traces the transatlantic publishing history of Charles Dickens's *American Notes for General Circulation* (1842), detailing how Dickens's narrative obliquely registers the conditions of literary production to which he was subject in America. Hailed as the unprecedented encounter of an author with his enthusiastic mass-readership, Dickens's 1842 visit promised to ratify the link between social reform and popular reading. However, Dickens's insistence on speaking publicly in favor of international copyright opened up a rift between author and audience, one that richly reveals the different cultural values that underwrote English and American publishing systems. Analyzing his obsessive recasting of his visit in *American Notes*, his serialized novel *Martin Chuzzlewit* (1843–4) and his 1867–8 reading tour, I take up Dickens's and his American readers' mutual misprision, comparing Dickens's struggle to recapture authority over his texts to American reprinters' theories of the relation of circulation to literary value.

My fourth and fifth chapters examine how Edgar Allan Poe's writing and career are centrally shaped by the culture of reprinting. Poe's career is in many ways exemplary of the dislocating force of the decentralized literary marketplace; his moves from city to city map the shifting importance of antebellum publishing centers, and his poetry and tales are published in virtually all of the formats that were prevalent in this era. In Chapter 4, I will show how a creative engagement with reprinted British texts and with the subjection of his writing to reprinting structures Poe's poetry and fiction. I am concerned in this chapter to demonstrate the appeal to Poe of unauthorized writing and to analyze some of his strategies for claiming property in his texts. Achieving proprietary control over the circulation of his writing largely eluded Poe until he was taken up by an influential group of literary nationalists, the Young Americans. In Chapter 5 I will examine Poe's vexed attempt to reap the benefits of this alliance while repudiating literary nationalist ideas about the cultural role of fiction. I will argue that Poe gets caught in the gears of a paradigm shift, paradoxically losing hold of his creative and critical autonomy when he is invoked as a figure of independent judgment within literary nationalist discourse.

Whereas Poe had perilously little control over the terms of his refashioning by New York literary nationalists, Nathaniel Hawthorne's alliance with the publishing house Ticknor and Fields afforded him the opportunity to recast his writing to meet the demands of a more reliable but increasingly stratified audience. In my final chapter, I examine Hawthorne's transition from an often anonymous tale-writer for gift books and magazines to the nationally known author of novel-length romances. Approaching Hawthorne's early fiction through the history of its reprinting, I argue that his claim to have suffered early obscurity was an attempt to withdraw his magazine fiction from its surprisingly extensive circulation. After the success of *The Scarlet Letter* (1850), Hawthorne's national ambitions ran up against the problem of his investment in suddenly outmoded literary forms. In a reading of his first full-length novel, *The House of the Seven Gables* (1851), I argue that Hawthorne renegotiates his relation to the reading public by reanimating and repudiating the literary forms on which he depended in his early career. *The House of the Seven Gables* provides a particularly rich example of how literary nationalist expectations can transform modes of writing that served different aims and carried different valences under the culture of reprinting.

I

Commerce, Print Culture, and the Authority of the State in American Copyright Law

RECENT WORK ON THE HISTORY OF AUTHORSHIP has looked to the development of copyright law for confirmation of the simultaneous emergence of the property-owning author and the development of a market for literary works.[1] A central premise of this scholarship has been that changes in the law and in the marketplace were reciprocal and mutually enabling. Mark Rose in particular has argued that the modern concept of the author-as-proprietor finds its origin within the domain of law—specifically, in the eighteenth-century British struggle over interpretation of the Statute of Anne—and that the law of copyright, in turn, facilitated the development of authorship as a market phenomenon. For Rose, it is the legal elaboration of the Lockean notion that an author, like any other workman, has a natural right to the product of his labor that enables both the text and authorship itself to become assimilated into the world of ordinary commodities.

However accurate Rose's analysis may be to the terms and conditions of British authorship,[2] his claims cannot easily be translated into the American context without misrepresenting the historical origins and cultural consequences of American copyright law. At the simplest level, to suggest that American law inherits and perpetuates a British concern with individual property rights in texts is to assume a false continuity between these legal traditions. As I will argue, the landmark American copyright case *Wheaton v. Peters* (1834) self-consciously restages the British debate over literary property, reformulates its terms, and rejects both common-law copyright and the Lockean argument that undergirds it. Rather than confirming the author as the owner of a text that was clearly defined as a commodity, *Wheaton v. Peters* establishes going-into-print as the moment

when individual rights give way to the demands of the social and defines
the private ownership of a printed text as the temporary alienation of
public property. It is with the circumscription of individual rights and not
with their extension that nineteenth-century American copyright law is
primarily concerned.

To regard copyright law as the means by which the individual author
and the text are absorbed into market-culture, then, is to ignore what is
centrally at stake in competing definitions of the text as property—the
struggle between commerce and the state to control that market. It is
also to overlook the immense cultural weight that gets attached to the book-
as-object. Recent critics' tendency to treat copyright as a tool of modern-
ization—the means by which an object of elusive origins, produced by
dubious labor, is made amenable to the emergent socioeconomic order—
both reverses the rhetorical polarity of the nineteenth-century debates and
threatens to erase the productive misalignment of legal discourse and the
market. In the American debate over literary property, both sides define the
text as an extraordinary commodity, an exception to the laws that govern
ordinary things. Indeed, it is the resistance the book offers to nineteenth-
century definitions of private property that enables publishers to make an
extraordinary legal claim—that of a property right in books past the point
of sale—and that enables the law, in turn, to claim a federal stake in the
circulation of these commodities. Through a close examination of *Wheaton
v. Peters*[3] and a number of cases that draw on its authority, I will argue that
the extraordinary materiality of the subject of copyright encodes fantasies
about the circumvention of mass-production and provides a vehicle for
exploring the form and limits of state power.

Discontinuities in the Genealogy of Authorship

Mark Rose traces the pedigree of modern authorship to an attempt by the
inheritors of Stationers' Company privilege to maintain the monopoly
publishing rights they had held under the system of patronage. Briefly,
when provincial publishers began to exploit the Statute of Anne (1710), a
law that sought to regulate monopolies in the book trade by limiting the
term of copyright protection to fourteen years, the London booksellers,
who held most of the valuable copyrights, seized upon an author's rights
at common law as a means of questioning the authority and reach of the
statute. Essentially, what the London booksellers argued in the celebrated

cases *Millar v. Taylor* (1769) and *Donaldson v. Becket* (1774) was that the author's perpetual right to his copy under the common law preceded and thus outlasted any statutory limitation of that right. Basing their case on the inviolability of natural rights and the priority of the common law to the dictates of the statute, the booksellers portrayed the Statute of Anne as a kind of secondary protection, a supplementary enforcement of preexisting rights and not the foundation of these rights.

What is intriguing about this argument is that Rose locates the origins of modern authorship not in an embrace of the new socioeconomic order, but as the rhetorical by-product of a retrogressive bid to solidify royal privilege as monopoly power. And yet throughout his account, Rose represents the London bookseller's eloquent defense of authors' rights as an idea whose time had come, one that *despite* its ultimate defeat in the House of Lords, faced little or no substantive resistance:

the Lords' decision [to reject perpetual copyright] did not touch the basic contention that the author had a property in the product of his labor. Neither the representation of the author as a proprietor nor the representation of the literary work as an object of property was discredited. Nor, I suspect, *could* these contentions have been discredited at this point in history: too many and too powerful economic and social and ideological forces were at work. So long as society was and is organized around the principles of possessive individualism, the notion that the author has the same kind of property right in his work as any other laborer must and will recur.[4]

It is this image of the certain triumph of the figure of the author-as-proprietor that a close examination of copyright in the American context disrupts. In *Wheaton v. Peters,* the argument on behalf of common-law copyright is met by a theory of authorship of equal coherence and, given the ideological bent of the new nation, far greater persuasive power. This theory of authorship, grounded in a republican belief in the inherent publicity of print and the political necessity of its wide dissemination, stressed the interests of the polity over the property rights of individuals and maintained that there could be no common-law property in a manuscript "after the author shall have published it to the world" (99).

That the transformation from manuscript to print is imagined here to be instantaneous and absolute—going–into–print is not simply a matter of making a manuscript available to the public, but implies immediate, universal diffusion—gives some indication of the tremendous power accorded to print within republican thinking. Yet it is not simply the diffusionary power of this technology that persuades the court to establish a distinction at law between handwriting and print, limiting the author's common-law right to property in his manuscript and requiring that property in a published work be established by strict compliance with the statute. The debate over literary property cut to the heart of republican ideology. As Michael Warner has argued, republican discourse regarded print as coextensive with the public sphere and relied on the generality of the printed text to represent and legitimize popular sovereignty.[5] The notion that an individual author had a *natural* right to his printed text—a private or personal right that was prior to and in excess of the protection granted by the state—was fundamentally incompatible with a political philosophy that associated the depersonalization of print with a kind of selfless publicity, the exercise of civic virtue. *Perpetual* private ownership and control over printed texts was unacceptable in a culture that regarded the free circulation of texts as the sign and guarantor of liberty. In the American context, the central tenets of republicanism that ally the printed text with the public sphere qualify the impact of the "principles of possessive individualism" on the development of literary property and, in concert with developments in print technology and publishing practice, work to postpone the emergence of the modern property-owning author until late in the century.[6]

If the arguments in *Wheaton v. Peters* provide evidence of a rupture in the genealogy of authorship, demonstrating the resistance a republican theory of authorship can offer to the forward march of possessive individualism, they also expose another kind of discontinuity: that between the available models of authorship and the conditions of publication they attempt to describe. One can plot the debate over literary property in America as a pivot point for a number of interlocking transitions: the transition to a market economy, which enables the shift from a patronage system to a market for books; the ideological shift that reconfigures the relation of the individual to the state, reformulates monarchical legal structures as republican ones, and creates the possibility of a national literature; the federalizing project of the Marshall Court, which consolidates power at the national level by limiting common-law protections at the level of the state; and significant changes in the technology of print and systems of distribution that make possible the mass-publication and mass-marketing of books. This last transition—one characterized by a difference of scale that is nonetheless constitutive—proves least negotiable within the available terms of discourse. The arguments in *Wheaton v. Peters* demonstrate that neither the Lockean nor the republican model of authorship is capable of conceptualizing private ownership in an era of mass-production, suggesting that the discourse of authorship develops not congruently, but at odds with changes in the conditions of production.

Materiality and the Common Law in *Wheaton v. Peters*

The difference that republican culture makes to a consideration of literary property is evident from a simple outline of the case. Whereas the text at the center of the British controversy was James Thomson's *The Seasons* (1730), a long descriptive poem that aspired to the top of the hierarchy of literary genres, the text at the center of the American debate was a series of court reports published by the plaintiff, Henry Wheaton, in the ordinary course of his duties as a Supreme Court reporter. I make this comparison not to remark on the poverty of the American literary scene, but to suggest that a different standard of literary value and of commercial profitability obtained in the new nation. James Gilreath's study of federal copyright records from 1790 to 1800 demonstrates that by far the most frequently copyrighted texts in early America were practical works such as textbooks, manuals, atlases, and directories—books that met a republican standard of useful knowledge, had a broad appeal, and because of their usefulness, were thought to have enduring commercial value.[7] Wheaton's *Reports*, which consisted of texts of the oral opinions delivered in the nation's highest court, complete with abstracts and explanatory annotations, could be considered representative of what was thought to be most valuable in American textual production of this era.

At the time of their initial publication (1816–27), Wheaton's *Reports* were more of a scholarly than a commercial success. Wheaton was the first official Supreme Court reporter under the Reporters Act of 1817, and he relied on profits from the sale of his annotated texts to supplement his modest salary.[8] Because of Wheaton's scholarly thoroughness, however, the volumes' readership was limited to an elite audience; because of their extraordinary bulk, they were priced out of the range of all but the most wealthy consumers. Wheaton's successor as Supreme Court reporter, Richard Peters, envisioned a wider audience for court reports and issued both his own and prior *Reports* in a condensed form—one more accessible to ordinary users—at a fraction of the price. Peters's strategy of opting for high volume sales at a low marginal profit rate was ideally suited both to the republican dream of a universal diffusion of learning and to the American reality of widespread literacy, an increasing need for a knowledge of national law, and expanding Western markets. Not surprisingly, the success of Peters's *Condensed Reports* rendered Wheaton's copyright in his *Reports* virtually worthless and prompted him to seek legal redress.[9]

That the first Supreme Court case to provide a ruling on the nature of the constitutional copyright provision should take up the question of who had the right to publish Supreme Court reports seems uncanny at the very least. While the self-reflexivity of this case raises its stakes by bringing the question of authors' rights to bear on the nature of the court's own authority, it also helps to clarify the ideological conflict at its heart. Because it takes control over the dissemination of federal law, not literature, as its subject, *Wheaton v. Peters* creates a clash of absolutes: the inviolability of private property under the common law is countered by the unarguable virtue (in this courtroom) of a widespread knowledge of the decisions of the federal judiciary. *Wheaton v. Peters* brings into stark relief the potential contradiction between the private ownership of texts and the public interest.

In his analysis of *Millar v. Taylor* and *Donaldson v. Becket*, Mark Rose characterizes the difference between the arguments of the plaintiffs and those of the defendants as one of interpretive emphasis: "The proponents of perpetual copyright focused on the author's labor. Those who argued against it focused on the results of the labor, the work." Rose represents this difference in emphasis as a tactical one: because those in favor of the author's right at common law right pitched their arguments on what was thought to be unassailable moral ground—the right of the individual to the product of his labor—those opposed had to target their opposition at the doubtful definition as private property of the thing in question. Rose sees in the split focus of this debate "a twin birth, the simultaneous emergence in the discourse of the law" of the two concepts most crucial to the operation of the literary marketplace: the author as owner and the text as a commodity.[10]

What is striking about the American restaging of this debate is that the philosophical problem of the nature of the property to be protected takes over the center of both the argument for common-law copyright and the case for its statutory limitation. While Wheaton's counsel follow British precedent in grounding the right to the copy in the author's labor, they devote most of their energies to arguing that literary property is a thing like other things and thus falls under the ordinary protection of the common law. Alternately, Peters's counsel base their defense not on the incorporeality of ideas, but on the publicity of print and the political necessity of its broad dissemination. Relying on the radically performative nature of legal writing—the fact that it both describes and, in the act of its dissemination, promulgates the law—Peters's lawyers shift the characterization of the court reports in question from material objects that can be owned to something like pure circulation. Viewed as a rereading of the British copyright debate and a redistribution of its terms, *Wheaton v. Peters* transforms an argument over writing as either labor or as a commodity into a debate over the materiality or immateriality of the text itself.

On the whole, the argument on behalf of Wheaton's right to his *Reports* is multifaceted in approach and frequently self-contradictory. Strategically, Wheaton's lawyers, Daniel Webster and Elijah Paine, attempt to cover all angles by arguing for Wheaton's right both under the common law and under the statute. While this dual approach needn't be inconsistent, their argument is riddled with contradictions, suggesting a conflicted relationship to the arguments laid out in the British precedents. Typically, their catalog of "general principles on which an author's property is based" includes mutually undercutting appeals to the necessity of this right as derived from natural law, and to the convenience of its enforcement under the statute (23). Throughout, they invoke a Lockean model of property rights, and yet on more than one occasion they rail against those who would derive rights from the state of nature (18, 20).[11] Most strikingly, they repeatedly invoke the name and authority of Lord Mansfield while virtually ignoring his line of argument, building their case instead by engaging the terms of the argument set out by his opponent, Joseph Yates.[12]

Webster and Paine had good reasons to avoid invoking *some* of Mansfield's arguments in favor of perpetual copyright. For instance, Mansfield's pivotal insistence that the common-law rights of authors can be deduced from the King's common-law right to Crown-copies would be decidedly unpersuasive in an American court.[13] What is more perplexing, however, is that they seem to ignore some of Mansfield's most powerful points even in the act of citing them. For instance, Paine begins his argument in support of Wheaton by quoting Mansfield's definition of copyright: "'I use the word copy in the technical sense in which that name or term has been used *for ages*, to signify an incorporeal right to the sole printing and publishing of somewhat intellectual, communicated by letters'" (18). This reference to the incorporeality of the *right* to produce copies is striking because of its potential as a line of inquiry—it promises to shift the grounds of debate from the problematic incorporeality of the thing, writing, to the incorporeality of the right to one's writing (and, implicitly, the incorporeality of the rights to all forms of property).[14]

Yet, far from being prepared to assert the irrelevance of the material status of writing, Paine is bent on determining the precise physical nature of what Mansfield nonchalantly refers to as "somewhat intellectual." Throughout, Paine's argument seems haunted by Justice Yates's proposal that, because what one seeks to protect with copyright is essentially insubstantial, it cannot be considered property. As a counter to Yates's vision, Paine proposes not simply that writing is a material substance just like any other kind of property, but that it possesses a unique kind of materiality, one irrevocably marked by individuality and identity: "Mr. J. Yates, the great opponent of literary property, . . . urges that it is impossible to appropriate ideas more than the light or air; forgetting that books are not made up of ideas alone, but are, and necessarily must be, clothed in a language, and embodied in a form which give them an individuality and identity that make them more distinguishable than any other personal property can be. A watch, a table, a guinea it might be difficult to identify; but a book never" (18).

In attempting to fix the subject of copyright, Paine produces a series of material designations that exist in an unstable relation to one other. Tacitly acknowledging that ideas themselves could not be privately owned, Paine suggests that the object, the book, is the proper ground for a discussion of literary property. "Books" are further subdivided into ideas, which are immaterial, and two types of material manifestation—language and form—which are necessarily related to the appearance of ideas in books and which provide the grounds of any book's claim to uniqueness. In shifting terms, however, Paine invokes a distinction between form and content that is only partially supported by the metaphorics of clothes and body which succeed it. Initially, language seems to serve as the clothing for ideas, their outer shell, that which makes them distinctive and identifiable. Yet, discerning perhaps that the discardable nature of clothing renders it inappropriate to describe the necessary relation of language to ideas, Paine shifts his emphasis from clothes to the body, stressing the corporeality of the form in which ideas appear. This metaphorical slide creates the image of a disappearing body: the clothes of language are stripped to reveal, not content, but the "form" that had occupied the privileged interior space. It is, finally, this repeatedly displaced interior space—whether occupied by the ideas within the book, the body beneath the clothes or the content of the form—that seems oddly cut off from the "individuality and identity" on which the text's definition as personal property depends.

The significance of this grounding of textual identity in a materiality figured as a kind of unrelieved exteriority, and its connection to the extraordinary claim for the text which follows (that books are "more distinguishable than any other personal property can be") become clearer when this passage is read against the section of Blackstone's *Commentaries* on which it is based, a passage Paine cites at a later stage of his argument:

Now the identity of a literary composition consists entirely in the *sentiment* and the *language*. The same conceptions, clothed in the same words, must necessarily be the same composition; and whatever method be taken of exhibiting that composition to the ear or the eye of another, by recital, by writing, or by printing in any number of copies, or at any period of time, it is always the identical work of the author which is so exhibited; and no other man, it hath been thought, can have a right to exhibit it, especially for profit, without the author's consent. (19–20)

Blackstone's well-known definition distributes "the identity of a literary composition" across form and content: identity "consists" in sentiment *and* language, conceptions *and* words. In contrast, in Paine's version, identity is conferred on books solely by language and form. The hypothetical scenarios of detection in these two accounts, and the nature of the authorial project they imagine, reveal much about the assumptions underlying their positions. Blackstone's logic suggests the exposure of a plagiarism or piracy; his deduction stages a comparison of texts that devolve, inevitably, into a single composition. Paine's scene of detection, on the other hand, suggests the identification and reclamation of a lost object. His comparison is not between texts but among seemingly random objects that are comparable only in the degree to which they can or cannot be marked with the identity of their owner. Whereas the threat in the Blackstone passage seems to be that of imposture—the possibility that one author's work might be appropriated and exhibited by another, "especially for profit"—in the Paine passage, the scenario that must be dismissed with an emphatic "never" is something like the utter loss of the signature, the fear that a book could drop back into that group of objects whose owner is unknown and possibly indeterminable. The difference between these passages could be characterized as a shift from a focus on the relation between texts in the market to a narrower concern with the relation between author and text; it could also be characterized as a shift from a fantasy of unerring judgment to one which would make such judgment irrelevant. Whereas Blackstone projects a world in which competing claims to ownership could always be adjudicated, Paine imagines that the text is so imbued with the identity of its owner as to make plagiarism impossible: "A watch, a table, a guinea it might be difficult to identify; but a book never."

What is behind this elimination of the possibility of plagiarism is a desire to escape the market altogether. Here and elsewhere in Paine's argument, the relation between the analogies he uses to justify the author's common-law right and the market for books these analogies purport to describe (and aim to regulate) is a complex one. While Paine insists on the text-as-object, characterizing it as an ideal type of personal property, he short-circuits the process of its production and distribution, permitting a narrative of loss and reclamation to stand in for one of exchange and profit. Blackstone's scenario is conspicuous in its inclusion of scenes of production and reception. While its focus is on the transfer of the text, its rhetorical aim is to insist that the "work of the author" retains its identity despite exchange. For Blackstone, the materiality of the text is largely irrelevant to its integrity. The ordinary objects with which Paine compares the text, however, are notably cut off from a narrative of production or consumption by virtue of their indeterminacy, their *failure* to be marked by the individuality and identity of the persons to whom they belong. They hang in suspended animation, objects that can be neither owned nor exchanged, personal property detached from persons.[15] The excess of materiality Paine ascribes to the text—the distinctive embodiment that makes books "more distinguishable than any other personal property can be"—seems designed to ensure that, should a book become similarly lost, it could easily be restored to its rightful owner. This owner—he or she whose "individuality and identity" is unmistakably inscribed in the language and form of the text—is presumably the author, yet the assurance of this identification conceals a crucial equivocation. The watch, the table, the guinea, and the book have been compared as articles of personal property, not in relation to the history of their production. And, while it is possible that the watch and the table could be owned by those who made them, the addition of the guinea to the list would suggest that what is at issue here is the degree to which these objects can be marked by the identity of those who *possess* them, regardless of their manufacture. Within the narrative of detection set up by this passage, the restoration of the book to its author as rightful owner circumvents the entire system of exchange, making the author the destination as well as the origin of the text.

A comparable collapse of the roles of producer and consumer is apparent in Webster's closing remarks, in which he invokes the self-evidence of the argument from natural rights: "It is a prevailing feeling, and none can doubt that a man's book is his book—is his property."[16] What the force of the tautology would override is the fact of the market, the necessary discrepancy between the man who owns the book as author, and the man who owns the book as reader. Implicit in this repression of the market is the elision of the fact of mass-production. Paine's emphasis on the ability of the author to inscribe his individuality and identity in the materiality of the book places authorship within the field of artisanal production. Paine imagines the book to be a kind of ideal craft-object, one that bears within its material form a trace of the process of production which is absent from ordinary things. Yet, as Roger Stoddard has observed, "Whatever they may do, authors do *not* write books. Books are not written at all. They are manufactured by scribes and other artisans, by mechanics and other engineers, and by printing presses and other machines."[17] As a mainstay of his argument for the author's right at common law, Paine's insistence on the materiality of the subject of copyright—his assertion that "the question is not as to property in *ideas* but in books" (19)—overlooks the entire sphere of production, glossing over the crucial technological and commercial difference between the author's manuscript and the printed book. In Paine's argument, the extraordinary materiality of the book bears the burden of overcoming not only the difference between producer and consumer, but also that between author and producer.

The frequent recurrence in both Webster's and Paine's arguments of the representation of the author as sole producer of the text is a constant reminder of the structural conditions of this debate—that the author and authors' rights serve as shadow figures or place-holders for the publisher and publishers' rights. One might be tempted to conclude that this portrayal of the author-as-producer represents the publishers' skillful making over of the author in the image of themselves. Yet I would argue that the many ruptures in their argument—the logical contradictions, the metaphorical slippages, and the analogies that do not fit—testify to a genuine difficulty in extending the moral reach of natural law to cover mass-production, in stretching the common law to embrace the technology of print. The shortcomings of the argument on the common-law side are better measured as an index of anxiety about the instability of property in the marketplace than they are as proof of its manipulation.

For instance, even though Webster and Paine repeatedly identify the

subject of copyright as a thing, they persist in imagining it to be fundamentally inseparable from its producer, either by comparing the author's
ownership of a book to the ownership of land, by comparing the book to
a moveable good or commodity that always returns to its owner, or as in
the example above, by imagining it to be an autonomous object which has
inscribed within it the history of its production. This desire to return to
the book as personal property the integrity, stability, and continuity of
real property is evident in Paine's response to what he refers to as "One of
the strongest points in Mr. J. Yates's opinion . . . that it is impossible for
an author to have a property in his works after he has published and sold
them" (19). Paine makes his case with a series of analogies that are utterly
inappropriate to the publication and sale of books: "As well might [Yates]
say that a man who leases lands, parts with all his property in them, and
can never claim the reversion; and that the tenant has a right to sell or
waste the inheritance. As well might he say that one who loans a chattel
can never reclaim it" (19). Paine clearly prefers to think in terms of inheritance than in production, leasing instead of sale, and in the reclamation
of an object rather than in profit or exchange. As in the comparison of
the book with ordinary objects, each of these examples presumes a single
owner, and each stages the inevitable return of a temporarily estranged
possession. What is being asserted here, however, is not so much the
coalescence of producer and consumer as it is the substitution of a set
of reciprocal economic relations for the more threatening prospect of
anonymous and multiple sales.

That Paine should invoke the ownership of land as a model for literary property is not surprising, given that the common law was built around
the protection of real property and was thought far better equipped to
defend rights in land than rights in moveable goods and commodities.[18]
The absolute character of the right to land under the common law and the
emphasis on its preservation through an orderly succession were precisely
the attributes that those arguing for perpetual copyright strove to attach
to literary property. What is remarkable, however, is the consistency with
which Paine overextends the analogy to real property, exposing the incom-
patibility, not the similarity between the two. These ruptures in his argument seem to be the product of Paine's contradictory acknowledgment
of the book as a commodity (an acknowledgment made manifest in his
emphasis on the materiality of the text) and his commitment to a Lockean
theory of property, a theory that sees property not as an alienable thing but
as a relation of enclosure.

This contradiction is readily apparent in the most Lockean passage in Paine's argument, one in which he makes a powerful appeal to the self-evidence of natural rights and to the necessity that underwrites private property under natural law:

It would seem needless to discuss those general principles on which an author's property is based. They are the same as give man a title to any species of property. An author acquires a property in his works, because they are the product of his own labour, bestowed with the declared and known intention of appropriating such product exclusively to himself. They are his, because the natural law makes it necessary for man to labour for his subsistence, and therefore secures to him what he thus acquires in obedience to its commands. They are his, because the same law forbids a dependence upon casual acquisitions, but enjoins the duty of providence, and of course protects those stores which by labour he seeks to lay by for the future. (23)

The central features of this appeal are familiar from Locke's "Of Property." Paine justifies the author's private property in his text as an act of appropriation which is necessary for his subsistence. As in Locke's treatise, the circumference of the private is drawn by the author's labor, the moral ground for appropriation is bodily self-perpetuation, and the moral limit to acquisition is suggested by the principle of self-sufficiency.[19] And yet the mismatch between mass-publication and Locke's central paradigms of foraging and subsistence farming becomes evident almost immediately. Paine's anxiety about this discrepancy can be observed as his initial claim that "an author's property" is like "any species of property" gives way to a representation of the text's extraordinary materiality: "An author acquires a property in his works, because they are the product of his own labour, *bestowed with the declared and known intention of appropriating such product exclusively to himself.*"

As in the comparison of the book with ordinary objects, Paine here imagines authorial production to be a solo affair, a drama of separation and return. Once again it is the object itself that bears the material trace of its economic destiny. That the author's product should *need* to be "bestowed" with the author's intention to reappropriate it, however, marks the degree of its fall from the Lockean narrative in which it is set. Locke's model of property is notable for its depiction of the relation between persons and property as one of reciprocal self-constitution. This is nowhere more clear than in Locke's depiction of the primary act of appropriation, that of eating: in the case of the "wild *Indian*" whose only "inclosure" is his mouth, the person and his property become literally indistinguishable.[20] Locke is able to sustain this sense of the interdependence of persons and property throughout his genealogy of property as his dominant metaphor for appropriation shifts from incorporation to annexation, extrapolating from man's ownership of his body to his ownership of whatever he mixes his labor with. It is labor, finally, that Locke relies on to draw the distinction between that which is common and that which has been appropriated from the common for private use. In this context, the suggestion that the product of an author's labor needs to be *marked* for exclusive appropriation becomes a sign of its prior abandonment. The supererogatory materiality of the text gives the clue to Paine's uneasiness about a process of production that involves not solitary, but diversified labor, not exclusive but shared possession, not enclosure, but dissemination.

Dissemination and the State

If the arguments of Wheaton's counsel founder in part because of their dependence on a theory of property rooted in an anachronistic model of socioeconomic relations, the arguments of Peters's counsel could be said to exploit the political and social dimensions of the mass-production and distribution of texts. Peters's lawyers, J. R. Ingersoll and Thomas Sergeant, build their case around the special nature of legal reports, arguing that because of their importance to the state, the texts of Supreme Court decisions could not be made the subject of literary property. Yet they treat these reports less as an exception to the general rule of rightful authorial proprietorship than as a correction to the excesses produced by the private ownership of printed texts. Playing to the vanity and the ambition of the Marshall court, Ingersoll and Sergeant propose judicial reports as the ideal form of republican publishing.

The urgency that underwrites this politics of print is evident in the following passage where Ingersoll argues not simply that the broad dissemination of judicial reports is compatible with republican principles, but that the very survival of the republic depends on their circulation:

Reports are the means by which judicial determinations are disseminated, or rather they constitute the very dissemination itself. This is implied by their name; and it would necessarily be their nature and essence, by whatever name they might be called. The matter which they disseminate is, without a figure, the *law of the land*.

Not indeed the actual productions of the legislature. Those are the rules which govern the actions of the citizen. But they are constantly in want of interpretation, and that is afforded by the judge. He is the "*lex loquens*." His explanations of what is written are often more important than the mere naked written law itself. His expressions of the *customary law*, of that which finds no place upon the statute book, and is correctly known only through the medium of reports, are indispensable to the proper regulation of conduct in many of the most important transactions of civilized life. Accordingly, in all countries that are subject to the sovereignty of the laws, their promulgation is as essential as their existence. (74)

Ingersoll's pun on "reports" as blasts from a cannon underscores the direction in which he wants to push his definition: judicial reports don't so much contain the law as enforce it by enabling citizens to behave in accordance with its strictures; reports don't simply describe the law, the fact of their dissemination insures its efficacy. This shift in emphasis empties the reports of their materiality; they are no longer the vehicle or "means" by which laws get transmitted, they "constitute the very dissemination itself."

This characterization of the reports as a kind of pure circulation is part of a complex devaluation and revaluation of written law. Initially Ingersoll faults the statutory law for its fixity and its incompleteness: the problem with the "productions of the legislature" is that they stand "constantly in want of interpretation." Ingersoll finds a remedy for these defects in the immediacy and fullness of the judicial voice which clarifies by supplementing the written law, giving expression to "the *customary law* . . . which finds no place upon the statute book." The value of the judicial reports, then, is that they are able to extend the range of the *lex loquens*, representing the common law in printed form while escaping the fixity of the singular "statute book" in their multiplicity and contemporaneity. The periodicity and wide dissemination of the judicial reports enable them to represent the "naked written law" clothed in all the positive attributes of the orally transmitted "customary law," while escaping the limitations implicit in the singularity and small compass of the judicial voice. The completeness of the judicial reports, however—their paradoxical status as the written form of unwritten law—requires an immateriality that borders on the sinister: the "sovereignty of the laws" depends on their agentless "promulgation"; though they do not contain rules, they are "indispensable" to regulation.

Ingersoll turns the tables on those arguing for authorial property from the vantage of the common law by claiming that to restrict the circulation of these reports would be to undermine the authority of the common law itself. In a declaration designed to flatter, he elevates the status of judicial reports above that of both the statutory and the common law: "the extended principles of national law . . . are fairly and authoritatively known only as they are promulgated by this bench" (75). Yet his pleas for unfettered circulation have a broader range than the reports alone. In detailing the potentially disastrous consequences of the private ownership of legal texts, Ingersoll suggests that the private ownership of any text is a potential breach of liberty:

If either statutes or decisions could be made private property, it would be in the power of an individual to shut out the light by which we guide our actions. . . . A particular case, or a whole series of cases might be suppressed by a reporter endowed with different feelings from those of the highly respectable complainant in this cause. It might become the interest of such a person to consign the whole edition to flames, or to put it at inaccessible prices, or to suffer it to go out of print before the country or the profession is half supplied. These are evils incident to every publication which can be secured by copy-right. Mere individual works, whether literary or religious, the authors can undoubtedly thus control. During the "limited time," for which they are constitutionally secured in an exclusive enjoyment of them, there is no remedy. . . . Can such a power be asserted, with all its consequences, over the decisions of the highest judicial tribunal in the land? (76)

Far from the just reward of individual labor, authorial control here represents the depredations of personal interest, which, if permitted, would frustrate the disinterested operation of the public sphere. As examples of the deleterious effects of private ownership, Ingersoll cites the overpricing and undersupplying of editions, tactics that would impede the circulation of a book while driving up profits. Even when private ownership is legitimately secured by copyright and these tactics are used to sell "mere individual works," they appear in the guise of "evils" for which, during the time allowed by statute, "there is no remedy."

This depiction of the dangers of authorial control is consistent with other moments in Ingersoll's argument where he identifies judicial reports as a form of inalienable public property comparable to state buildings and public works (76–77). Yet the exaggerated sense of power he accords to the individual manipulator of texts testifies to a persistent asymmetry in Ingersoll's portrayal of the nexus between the public and the private sphere. If Wheaton's counsel finds it difficult to imagine the surrender of the text at the point of sale, Peters's counsel imagines the relinquishment of private property in the act of publication to be so complete as to threaten the very survival of the private. Responding to the plaintiffs' claim that, intermixed with the reports of the judges' opinions was an editorial apparatus which rightfully belonged to Wheaton as the product of his labor, Ingersoll sets out a kind of reverse Lockeanism whereby the mixing of private labor with that which is public causes the individual to lose proprietary control over the entire product:

An individual who thus mingles what cannot be exclusively enjoyed, with what can, does upon familiar principles, rather forfeit the power over his own peculiar work, than throw the chain around that which is of itself as free as air. The inter-mixture . . . must render the whole insusceptible of exclusive ownership. That which is public cannot in its nature be made private, but not *e contra*. (78)

According to Ingersoll, there cannot be any such thing as appropriation from the common. Going-into-print becomes an act of incontrovertible surrender; the consequence of the exercise of civic virtue is irredeemable personal loss.

The absolutism of this claim, however, allies this narrative of dispossession to the fantasy of absolute possession put forward by Paine. As we saw in his definition of judicial reports, Ingersoll doesn't reject the authority of the common law, he redraws the field, invoking its authority from a higher ground. In a similar move, he appeals to the natural-law definition of property in order to redefine the private property of the author as the common property of readers:

Feudal principles apply to real estate. The notions of personal property of the common law, which is founded on natural law, depend materially on possession, and that of an adverse character, exclusive in its nature and pretensions. Throw it out for public use, and how can you limit or define that use? How can you attach *possession* to it at all, except of a subtle or imaginative character? If you may read, you may print. The possession is not more absolute and entire in the one case than the other. (79)

As in his characterization of the judicial reports, Ingersoll's defense of the statutory nature of copyright relies on a shift in the locus of common-law protection: the act of appropriation he seeks to preserve is that of reading, not that of authorship. Yet this endorsement of the reader-as-owner depends on the assumption that the private act of reading could be rendered nonexclusive, that individual appropriation could, by a smooth and easy transition, become public distribution: "if you may read, you may print."

This proposition constitutes an astonishing elision of the sphere of production from the opposite direction than we have come to expect. Whereas Webster and Paine imagine an unmediated relation between author and printed text, casting the author as sole producer, Ingersoll imagines an unmediated relation between reader and text, suggesting that the technology of print is fundamentally no different than the repetition in the mind of the reader of the ideas of the author: "The possession is not more absolute and entire in the one case than the other." However outrageous, this rewriting of consumption as a kind of production is more easily accomplished than the reverse operation due to Ingersoll's repeated insistence on the immateriality of the text in the public realm.

The image of a thoroughly dispersed, individualized mass-production of texts conjured up by the conflation of reading and printing serves a double purpose. Within the terms of the republican fantasy, the multiplication of texts and the conversion of private acts of reading from acts of appropriation into instances of dissemination would seem to render textual production immune from the manipulations of individual interests. In addition, the proliferation of texts created by the shift in the locus of ownership from producer to reader creates the justification for statutory regulation. As Ingersoll argues, "It is an artificial, and therefore arbitrary rule which draws the distinction [between reading and printing]; and in order to render it available, the lesson must be read in the statute" (79). Only statutory regulation of dissemination can guard against the dangers implicit in an "arbitrary rule"; predictably, it does so by making this rule public, or "available."

In a later passage, Ingersoll imagines what would happen should the distinction between reading and printing be enforced without recourse to statutory law. He projects a world in which, due to the mobility of literary property, textual identity is radically unstable:

The inconveniences to the public that would be the consequence of mere common law assertion of [literary property] would be endless. It would lead to perpetual strife. If the mere individual stamp of authorship would afford even a foundation for a claim, originality might be pretended to by numerous individuals, and a test of truth might not be obtained. If the real author give his work the official stamp of originality before it goes forth into the world, most of the questions that would otherwise occur are anticipated. The source of exclusive ownership is therefore found in positive enactments, and not in any unwritten law. (80)

Ingersoll presumes the scenario that Paine so feared, the utter loss of the signature or "individual stamp" of ownership. As if in response to

Paine's assertion that the identity of the author is indelibly inscribed in the materiality of the text, Ingersoll proposes that texts are radically unidentifiable and dangerously subject to imposture: should we rely on the ability of the object to be marked by its maker, "a test of truth might not be obtained." The proliferation of texts, then, and the uncertainty built into the relation between author and text, requires the intervention of the state. With the replacement of the signature with the "official stamp" provided for in the written law, Ingersoll's argument has come full circle: while dissemination is necessary for the existence of the state, the supervision of the state is necessary to ensure proper dissemination.

In arguing for the statutory nature of copyright, Ingersoll associates state power with a special kind of writing, one that is exempt from the problem of authorial indeterminacy. In this account, the written law is the proper source for property rights in texts and the proper instrument for their regulation because it is the only printed text whose authorship is self-evident: it is authored by the public itself. According to a republican theory of authorship, exclusive ownership of texts in the public sphere can only be secured by a writing that is pure publicity.

"Perfect Title":
American Copyright and the Letter of the Law

The arguments of counsel in *Wheaton v. Peters* suggest that the nature of authorship and the legal status of the printed text were genuinely contested issues at the moment when a national market for books first began to be imaginable. What becomes clear from a close analysis of this case is that in America the struggle to define the nature of copyright neither establishes the text as a commodity, nor grounds the right to literary property in the person of the author. As we have seen, the argument from common law sought to define the printed text as an autonomous craft-object, one that had become temporarily estranged from its maker. Rather than an acknowledgment of the profitable trade in books, the plaintiffs' insistence on the materiality of the text became the sign of its noncommodity status, the track or trace of a desire to imagine the mass-produced book as an exception to the rules of market-exchange.[21] Whereas the argument from common law sought to identify the text with inalienable private property, the argument from statutory law sought to establish print as a form of public property that could only be rendered private at the whim, and for the benefit of, the state. In *Millar v. Taylor*, Justice Yates had opposed common-law copyright on the grounds of the intangibility and interiority of thought itself, arguing that "The property claimed is all ideal; a set of ideas which have no bounds or marks whatever—nothing that is capable of a visible possession. . . . Their whole existence is in the mind alone."[22] The defense in *Wheaton v. Peters*, however, rested its case on the publicity of print, shifting the justification for statutory protection from the inaccessibility of the personal, to the visibility of the public realm. This alliance of the printed text with publicity and with circulation itself made it difficult for the defense to acknowledge either that book-making was private enterprise, or that books themselves could be considered articles of personal property. Shifting the locus of textual ownership from production to reception, the defense redefined the act of reading, transforming it from a private into a public act, from individual appropriation into a form of production.

The opposing arguments in *Wheaton v. Peters* not only demonstrate the inability of currently available theories of property to accommodate the phenomenon of mass-production they were called on to describe, they also suggest that the mass-production and distribution of printed texts in America cannot be considered apart from the question of state power. The decision in *Wheaton v. Peters* inaugurates a legal tradition in which the printed text is considered an exceptional commodity, one in which the state has a controlling interest. And while the history of American copyright law is in part a history of the way in which state interests and the interests of commerce are brought into alignment, the peculiar development of copyright law in the wake of this case ensured that the two would remain at odds well into the twentieth century.[23] While enabling interstate commerce in books by establishing federal criteria for their protection, *Wheaton v. Peters* does so by defining the printed text as common property, only temporarily ceding monopoly rights to copyright holders. With its emphasis on print as something that necessarily exceeds the bounds of private property, *Wheaton v. Peters* builds into American law a resistance to individual control over texts. With going-into-print imagined as the transfer point at which an author's individual claim gives way to the public interest, nineteenth-century judges placed all but the most rudimentary definitions of the text-as-object outside the bounds of individual ownership.

The central paradox of the defense in *Wheaton v. Peters*—that the sovereignty of law is dependent on, and constructed in the image of that which it must also regulate—is played out in the majority opinion, which set precedent both for establishing the technical requirements for federal copyright protection, and for clarifying the nature of federal law itself. The majority opinion favored the defendant on three important points of law, ruling (1) that an author's common-law property in his text ceased on publication; (2) that strict compliance with all statutory requirements was necessary for establishing title in a work; and (3) that there could be no common law of the United States. This latter ruling explicitly connects the legal definition of the text with the writtenness of federal law. Both narrowing its jurisdiction and considerably strengthening its power, the Supreme Court determined that the common law did not extend beyond state boundaries, asserting that "There is no principle which pervades the union and has the authority of laws, that is not embodied in the constitution or laws of the union" (100). The court used the debate over the definition and regulation of the printed text to claim for federal law the generality and availability of the print medium itself.[24]

Justices Smith Thompson and Henry Baldwin dissented from these rulings, insisting that an author's common law right to his text existed quite apart from the question of statutory protection. And yet all six justices voted unanimously that "no reporter has, or can have any copy-right, in the written opinions delivered by this court" (108). This final ruling proved most damaging to the prospects of Henry Wheaton, who was left with the expensive option of pursuing a property claim in what amounted to little more than his editorial apparatus.[25]

Writing for the majority, Justice John McLean established the moment of going-into-print as a point of crossing. As McLean explained, an author holds property in his text under the common law up until the moment of publication; thereafter he surrenders his common-law right in exchange for statutory protection. McLean was sympathetic to the plaintiffs' case, but he insisted that an author's property claim was satisfied at the point of sale: "The argument that a literary man is as much entitled to the product of his labour, as any other member of society, cannot be controverted. And the answer is, that he realizes this product by the transfer of his manuscripts, or in the sale of his works when first published" (99). This ruling not only establishes a distinction at law between handwriting and print, identifying the former as personal, and the latter as public property, it provides for state intervention at the point of transfer from one medium to the other—the point at which the manuscript becomes potentially profitable.

In his dissent, Justice Thompson objected that the court sought to restrict an author's rights at the very moment he tried to exercise them. He found it ironic that an author could maintain absolute control over his text only insofar as he didn't attempt to publish it. Yet the majority agreed with McLean that the fact of publication transported the text outside the bounds of private law. Calling for collective assent to the proposition that an author surrendered his private rights upon going into print, McLean asked: "Is there an implied contract by every purchaser of his book, that he may realize whatever instruction or entertainment which the reading of it shall give, but shall not write out or print its contents?" (99). That McLean expected a resounding "no" where we would answer in the affirmative testifies to the powerful, reprivatizing effects of twentieth-century interpretations of the copyright law. Curiously, the distinction at law between handwriting and print depends on an argument that refuses to regard the two, when performed by the *reader*, as substantially different. Thinking along the lines set out by Ingersoll, McLean secures the easy transition between handwriting and print at the point of reception by carefully controlling this relation at the point of production. It is as if the stable, hierarchical relation between original and copy is wholly shattered by mass-production, and can only temporarily be held in place by government decree. Once in the public realm, the text is susceptible to uncontrolled copying because it is, itself, all copy. As public property, it has no necessary connection with the author's manuscript, which is entirely and inaccessibly private. The state grants the author temporary control over the printed version of his handwritten text by severing the connection between the two, and by inserting itself as the principle of their articulation.

The centrality of the distinction between handwriting and print to the court's definition of statutory copyright was not lost on lecturers and playwrights who attempted to prolong their rights under the common law by deferring publication. For instance, in *Ferris v. Frohman* (1912), the Supreme Court ruled that an unprinted play fell under the protection of the common law despite frequent public performances in both America and Great Britain. Even though stage audiences might be as numerous as a book's readership, the fact of live performance and the limited number of viewers in each audience suggested to the court that theatrical exhibitions fell short of the wholesale abandonment to the public signified by the medium of print.[26]

That in American law, going-into-print was imagined to be the definitive moment at which an individual surrendered private rights within the public sphere is perhaps best demonstrated by the late nineteenth-century attempt to convert this loss into a kind of gain. In their influential essay on the right to privacy, Samuel Warren and Louis Brandeis rest their proof of the "general right to the immunity of the person,—the right to one's personality" on the common-law right "to prevent the publication of manuscripts"[27] Warren and Brandeis see the absolute right over the hand-written text conferred by the common law—specifically, the author's right to choose against the dedication of his writing to the public via going-into-print—as the key instance that proves the general rule of the citi-zen's right to privacy. Rather than presupposing the right to property in one's personality, and establishing the right to all forms of writing on that ground, American law infers a property in the self from the differential protection it affords to handwriting and print, deducing the right to pri-vacy from an author's ability to choose between an absolute and a quali-fied right to his productions. What to Justice Thompson looks like a radical and unjust curb on an individual's right to property, at the turn of the century becomes the ground for the assertion of a whole new set of rights. The court's decision in *Wheaton v. Peters* that an author *cannot* maintain "a perpetual and exclusive property" in a text after he has "pub-lished it to the world," becomes proof of the existence of a realm over which *every* person holds rights that are perpetual and exclusive.

The emphasis of the court in *Wheaton v. Peters*, however, was on the limited nature of an author's right to his printed text, and on the fragility of this right. Grounded neither in custom nor in nature, copyright was a grant from the state that could easily be forfeited. The complex status of the printed text as a form of temporarily alienated public property is evi-dent from the procedural requirements that the court insisted were abso-lutely necessary for establishing copyright protection. Like the British statute on which it was based, the Copyright Act of 1790 required that the prospective copyright holder deposit a copy of the title of his book in the clerk's office of the local district court—a sort of regionalized version of the Stationers' Company register. In addition, the author or proprietor was required to "cause a copy of the said record to be published in one or more of the newspapers printed in the United States, for the space of four weeks," and to deliver a copy of the published book to the office of the Secretary of State. A final prerequisite added in 1802 involved giving "information of copyright" on the title page of each edition published during the term in which the book was to be protected.[28]

What is striking about these requirements is both the interplay they set up between public authority and textual authority, and the judges' insistence that the author adhere to them in the order they were pre-scribed or fail to achieve "perfect title" (106) in his work. The prerequi-sites for copyright mark the text's dual status as both personal and public property. While the copyright notice on the title page serves to secure individual ownership, it also implicitly gives notice of the date on which that right expires. This was powerfully the case under the original statute, which limited the author to a fourteen-year term of ownership (renewable for a second term of fourteen years provided that the author, his executor, or his assigns reregistered and republicized this claim). While the initial period of ownership was extended to twenty-eight years in 1831, making the duration of copyright protection roughly approximate that of an author's professional life, the decision in *Wheaton v. Peters* reemphasized the fact that the correspondence between an author and his copyrighted text was fully mediated by the state.

This is nowhere more clear than in the judges' disagreement over the nature of the copyright notice. The 1802 statute defines the title page not as the locus of private right, but as the site on which a copy of the news-paper record should be printed. This published announcement of the intent to publish is in turn defined as a copy of the record that is entered by the author in the district court.[29] Rather than a simple sign of ownership, the copyright notice bears witness to a multistep process by which the pub-lic, which authenticates the book and consents to restrict its distribution, is acknowledged. Through the process of duplication that is its mark, the authorizing public sphere is folded into the book itself.

In the lead dissent, Justice Thompson offered an alternate reading of the title page, arguing that it should be considered an "express contract made with a party who shall purchase a book, that he shall not republish it" (114). Thompson claimed that "the right set up and stamped upon the title-page . . . shuts the door against any inference, that the publication was intended to be a gift to the public" (116). Both dissenting judges strug-gled against the majority's identification of print with a generalized public sphere, arguing that an author's statutory right was simply bureaucratic; it was vested at the moment he registered his title at the district court. But the majority of judges rejected this notion. Maintaining that property in a printed text could not be vested until all of the statutory requirements had been fulfilled, they emphasized the public origins of this right and the dependence of copyright privileges on the performance of a public duty. For the majority, the authority that restricted the distribution of texts could only be a public authority, itself established by recourse to the medium of print. Property rights in printed texts could only be secured by an inter-locking series of printed—and circulating—claims to property.

With its insistence on strict compliance with the statute, *Wheaton v. Peters* inaugurates an emphasis on the letter of the law in American copy-right that is inseparable from the court's conception of the essential writ-tenness, or availability of the rule of law. While the court's primary aim may have been to assert federal control over interstate commerce,[30] the majority justified its decision that "there can be no common law of the United States" (100) with an attack on judicial arbitrariness familiar from the broader movement for the codification of American law.[31] McLean asked sardonically if the minute complexities of British common law were either "brought into the wilds of Pennsylvania by its first adventurers" or were "suited to their condition" (101), suggesting that even American geography militated against common-law authority. As an antidote to its unnecessary intricacy, McLean praised the publicity, clarity, and specificity of the statutory law. In fact, the entire tenor of the decision seems designed to disallow in interpretation of the copyright statutes the kinds of com-plexity characteristic of the interpretation of the common law. In perhaps its most notorious ruling, the majority determined that Henry Wheaton's deposit of eighty copies of his *Report* with the Secretary of State (as required by his contract as Supreme Court reporter) did not satisfy the copyright law's requirement that a single copy be sent to the same address. While it would hardly take great sophistication to argue that, in satisfying the demands of his contract, Wheaton had also satisfied the demand for access required by the copyright statute, the majority still preferred the simple and irrefutable argument that eighty did not equal one. Given the opportu-nity to judge on principle, the court retreated behind the letter of the law.

The judges' discomfort with legal authority that was obscure and sub-ject to interpretation is apparent from their unanimous decision that no one could hold copyright in the written opinions of the court. This dec-laration at once reaffirms the pure publicity of Supreme Court decisions, steering clear of the tyrannical implication that any individual could own the law, and covers for the contingency of the decision-making process. While from the moment of their delivery, Supreme Court decisions carry the full force of law, they are, after all, mere opinions, acts of interpreta-tion that are subject to the whims of individual judges. Susan Stewart's account of the dynamics of identity and difference in the law's regulation of the literary helps to explain how the judges' insistence on the publicity of their opinions works to conceal the operation of the law at the moment of its making. Stewart argues that "the oxymoron of 'literary property' continually appears as the site in which the law works out all that it is *not* as a form of writing; the unlocalizable, the excess of the signifier, the nondeclarative in syntax. The idealized conditions of codification—authority, genealogy, precedence, application, specificity, and transcendence—are established as qualities of a literary realm that it becomes the task of the law—as writing that is *other*—to regulate."[32] According to Stewart, the law projects the literary as an idealized version of its own operations, both doubling itself, and redoubling its authority by serving as the instrument by which an unruly textuality is disciplined and ordered.

In *Wheaton v. Peters*, the court accomplishes the work of idealization and differentiation in two ways: by requiring that copyright law be subject to a literality in interpretation and exacting standards of compliance that will confirm the rationality and inflexibility of the written law; and by defining Supreme Court opinions as the archetypically unowned and unownable text. While the judges vehemently disagreed over whether going-into-print transformed the text from private into public property, they were able to come to the unanimous decision that the as-yet-unprinted opinions of the court were a uniquely inalienable form of public property. Necessarily of one voice on this issue, the court proclaimed both that no reporter could hold copyright in the opinions of the court, and that "the judges thereof *cannot confer* on any reporter any such right" (108; emphasis mine). The social mechanism for monitoring private control over public property could not itself be subject to this transformation. As Stewart argues, the law must exempt itself from its own supervision; the legal attempt to articulate criteria for textual ownership "strengthens that ground upon which the law stands . . . by [deflecting] our gaze from its situated quality" (21).

The court's insistence on the unqualified publicity of their decisions proved problematic for Richard Peters—ostensibly the victor in this case—who was forced to defend his reprinted text against a competing set of reprints within a year of the decision.[33] It is, however, the court's emphasis on the irrevocable publicity of print and its insistence on strict compliance with the statute that prove most consequential for the history of American copyright. The case law that draws on the authority of *Wheaton v. Peters* is marked by an extraordinary literalism in defining what it is that authors own and a readiness to qualify or overturn the rights of authors that often seems excessive. The emphasis on the letter of the law in *Wheaton v. Peters* set the standard for a legal tradition that, for much of its history, was heavily weighted against the rights of authors.

On the authority of *Wheaton v. Peters*, the Supreme Court established dedication to the public upon going-into-print as the general rule, against which an author's temporary right to hold property in his text had to be scrupulously defended. For example, in *Holmes v. Hurst* (1899) the court determined that an author's failure to secure copyright for a single installment of a serial publication was enough to "vitiate a copyright of the whole book."[34] Similarly, the court in *Mifflin v. Dutton* (1901) ruled that an author's copyright was invalid when the rights to the book were taken out in a different name than that of the installments that were serially published in a magazine.[35]

The court's insistence on a narrow definition of the criterion of usefulness—the republican notion that copyright could only be justified insofar as it promoted "the Progress of Science and the Useful Arts"[36]—kept a wide range of published material from being covered by the statute. Up until 1903, when Justice Holmes vastly expanded the purview of copyright by suggesting that the mere presence in a text of marks of personality could afford a ground of ownership,[37] the texts of industry, such as advertisements, market quotations, and even newspaper reports were not thought to be subject to copyright. These texts were uncopyrightable not simply because they were based on facts, which were public property, but because they were *merely* useful works. The texts of industry could not promote learning because they were too ephemeral, exhausting themselves in the course of use. Like the machines protected under patent law, to which copyrighted texts were frequently compared,[38] printed texts were judged worthy of government protection according to a standard of performance. Like a machine, the copyrighted text must continue to perform its service over time, thereby justifying federal protection. It must be a means of production, not a mere object of consumption. While the value of the copyrighted text is linked to its durability, this is not the endurance of the literary masterpiece which, while traceable to a moment of inspired origination, is imagined to exist outside of time. Property in a useful text is conferred not on the basis of its singularity or universality, but on its ability to perform its work through history; it must remain useful past the point at which state protection ceases. As Justice Thompson argued in *Clayton v. Stone* (1829), literary property could not be lodged in "a work of so fluctuating and fugitive a form as that of a newspaper or price-current."[39]

The court's narrow interpretation of the criterion of usefulness comes into conflict with the general intention of the statute in the case of obscene works, which were deemed uncopyrightable because their only imaginable effect was "to corrupt the morals of the people." In *Martinetti v. Maguire* (1867), the court ruled that *The Black Crook*, "an exhibition of women 'lying about loose' [in] a sort of Mohammedan paradise," could not be considered property because of its impropriety. According to the majority, *The Black Crook* was pure spectacle, incapable of promoting anything but "prurient curiosity or an obscene imagination by very questionable exhibitions and attitudes of the female person."[40] Not only is prurience unproductive, the obscene text is virtually content-less. Like the advertisement or the newspaper price-current, which are too intimately bound up with the process of consumption to leave a remainder that can be owned, this spectacle of women "lying about loose" cannot be the subject of property because its subject is too diffuse. According to the judges, this spectacle lacked the coherence of a dramatic composition. The inherent lawlessness of lasciviousness—in form and function—causes it to fall outside the protection of the law.

Tellingly, the judges represented the uselessness of this spectacle in terms of its inaccessibility to print. For all its emphasis on illicit exposure, *The Black Crook* was marked by a kind of opacity: "A play like this has no value except as it is appreciated by the theatre-going public. It cannot be read—it is a mere spectacle, and must be seen to be appreciated."[41] Here, the limited publicity of the spectacle—the fact that what viewers valued in *The Black Crook* was in excess of the printed text, and therefore, in some sense, resistant to mass-production—is not the sign of a uniqueness that confers prestige, but a structural limitation that makes it unworthy of protection as an article of property. That which exceeds the letter of the text also lies outside the bounds of the letter of the law. And yet, as Eaton S. Drone noted in an influential nineteenth-century commentary, far from censoring the obscene, the court's insistence on restricting copyright to edifying texts actually grants vice a form of license: "in declining to interfere with the piratical publication and sale of an obnoxious book, [the court] removes an obstacle to its wider circulation."[42] The republican ideal of an automatically enlightening, propertyless dissemination finds its pathological realization in the unfettered circulation of obscene texts.

The extent to which an author's rights could be undermined by a literalistic interpretation of the copyright law is perhaps best illustrated by the controversial case *Stowe v. Thomas* (1853) in which the court determined that an unauthorized German translation of *Uncle Tom's Cabin* did not infringe upon Harriet Beecher Stowe's copyright in the original. The court's decision in this case turned on the difficulty of finding a material ground for the author's property once she had exchanged her inalienable but unprofitable right to her manuscript, for a qualified right in a printed text that remained elusive in its generality and unreclaimable from the public realm:

Before publication [the author] has the exclusive possession of his invention. His dominion is perfect. But when he has published his book and given his thoughts, sentiments, knowledge or discoveries to the world, he can have no longer an exclusive possession of them. Such an appropriation becomes impossible, and is inconsistent with the object of publication. The author's conceptions have become the common property of his readers, who cannot be deprived of the use of them, or their right to communicate them to others clothed in their own language, by lecture or by treatise.[43]

The German edition of *Uncle Tom's Cabin* posed a problem for the court because it reproduced the text without duplicating either the author's manuscript or the printer's copy. As Justice Robert Grier remarked, "The same conceptions clothed in another language cannot constitute the same composition; nor can it be called a transcript or '*copy*' of the same '*book*.'"[44]

Translation, which insists on textual identity despite material differences, upsets the legal equation of the uniformity of print with the fact of common property. Translation challenges the republican assumption of a unitary public by insisting on the existence of insuperable linguistic differences within the confines of the nation. Translation not only serves as a reminder that the circulation of a text is not instantaneous, inscribing a lag between the appearance of the copy and the original,[45] it introduces a model of circulation that depends on exploiting this difference. Rather than a limitless, lateral extension of the same, translation introduces a rift in the plurality of copies. Struggling to find a locus for the author's property somewhere between the privacy of her manuscript and the publicity of print, the judges ruled that Stowe's copyright in *Uncle Tom's Cabin* secured no more than a property in the words of her text in the order in which they appeared.[46] In this case, the emphasis on the letter of the law meant that the author could own only letters.

The court's problematic attempt to affirm the immateriality of public property in texts while also acknowledging the necessary materiality of the subject of copyright, finds its most apposite metaphor in an extraordinary passage, which represents the public's property in Stowe's text as the freely circulating, naked bodies of her central slave characters:

By the publication of her book the creations of the genius and imagination of the author have become as much public property as those of Homer or Cervantes. Uncle Tom and Topsy are as much *publici juris* as Don Quixote and Sancho Panza. All her conceptions and inventions may be used and abused by imitators, play-rights [sic] and poetasters. They are no longer her own—those who have purchased her book, may clothe them in English doggerel, in German or Chinese prose. Her absolute dominion and property in the creations of her genius and imagination have been voluntarily relinquished; and all that now remains is the copyright of her book, the exclusive right to print, reprint, and vend it.[47]

The unresolved doubleness of the slave who is both person and thing, a subject capable of sentiment and an article of property, serves well as the private-property analogue of the public text. Because Tom and Topsy are subject to use *and* abuse, they are better able than Don Quixote and Sancho Panza to represent both the practical ambitions of republican reading, and the radical diminution of liberty that accompanies the American legal defense of the rights of readers. While in its decision, the court represents going-into-print as an act of voluntary surrender, the cost to Stowe is obliquely acknowledged in the implication that, like the longsuffering Mrs. Shelby, she is helpless in the face of a slave-transaction.

Justice Grier's representation of the statutory limits of authors' rights in terms of the novel's own discourse—his identification of the legal status of Stowe's text with the fate of Tom and Topsy—is especially troubling when one considers the broader historical context in which this decision was reached. In this case, the court uses the figure of the freely circulating slave body to posit a vision of linguistic pluralism and commercial union that would take the place of a nation divided by slavery. Certainly, the dissonance between the republican dream of the steady diffusion of knowledge across the mass—the free circulation of texts in what Philip Fisher has described as uniform, unbounded "democratic social space"[48]—and the bitter moral, political, and economic differences that fractured the nation in the early 1850s, is especially pronounced in reference to Stowe's novel, in which slaves' circulation through an increasingly polarized geography is anything but free.

While by 1870 Congress had reserved to authors the right to dramatize and translate their works, *Stowe v. Thomas* suggests how far a market for books can develop without confirming the rights or promoting the economic interests of individual authors. Indeed, as I will argue in the following chapter, the strength of American resistance to foreign authors' rights, which held off an international copyright agreement until 1891, suggests that the development of a market for literature in America depended less on the institution of copyright than on the suspension of private property rights in texts. Like the defense in *Wheaton v. Peters*, the publishers, printers, and typesetters who opposed the passage of an international copyright law articulated a vision of a literary marketplace that operated according to republican principles—one in which profiteering would be counteracted by the limitless multiplication of editions, radically expanding the number of individuals who could benefit from the sale of any one text. Opponents of international copyright saw the decentralization of the literary marketplace as an important hedge against the tyranny of centralized power.

The court's circumscription of authors' rights in *Wheaton v. Peters* prompts one to ask, as David Saunders has done, what critical desire motivates the erasure of this history, producing in its place a narrative of the triumphant emergence of the rights-bearing author from within the market? Saunders is rightly critical of the tendency to route cultural and legal history through the figure of the author, imagined as the idealized form of human subjectivity. Indeed, the distortions produced by such a subject-centered history seem especially severe when projected onto a copyright system that explicitly rejects individual rights as its ground of value. But we should be equally wary of the explanatory power of the economic insofar as it marks the vanishing point of both rhetoric and politics. To represent the history of authors' rights as the achievement of individual economic freedom is, finally, to relinquish the nineteenth-century belief in the existence of a public sphere that was not coterminous with the market.

2

International Copyright
and the Political Economy of Print

EARLY ON IN HIS CONTROVERSIAL 1842 TOUR of the United States, Charles Dickens fulminated in a letter to his friend and advisor John Forster that the seemingly unaccountable American reluctance to support the passage of an international copyright law was a regrettable instance of the tyranny of the majority, a fear of publicly criticizing the status quo that reduced even thoughtful literary gentlemen to guilty silence. Dickens came to this conclusion after his third attempt to raise the subject of international copyright in an after-dinner speech drew mixed reactions from those who had organized banquets in his honor, and a highly negative response from the newspaper press. Trying to make sense of a tense and difficult social situation and of the unanticipated, *ad hominem* attacks in the popular press, Dickens took refuge in self-aggrandizing oppositions between collective repression and individual defiance, cowardly silence and forceful speech, political paralysis and heroic action. And yet he also obliquely recognized the way in which outrage at his legal disenfranchisement had distorted his perspective. For Dickens, the lack of international copyright was a "monstrous injustice" that made authors monstrous:

I spoke, as you know, of international copyright, at Boston; and I spoke of it again at Hartford. My friends were paralysed with wonder at such audacious daring. The notion that I, a man alone by himself, in America, should venture to suggest to the Americans that there was one point on which they were neither just to their own countrymen nor to us, actually struck the boldest dumb! . . . every man who writes in this country is devoted to the question, and not one of them *dares* to raise his voice and complain of the atrocious state of the law. It is nothing that of all men living I am the greatest loser by it. It is nothing that I have a claim to speak and be heard. The wonder is that a breathing man can be found with temerity enough to suggest to the Americans the possibility of their having done wrong. I wish you could have seen the faces that I saw, down both sides of the table at Hartford, when I began to talk about Scott. I wish you could have heard how I gave it out. My blood so boiled as I thought of the monstrous injustice that I felt as if I were twelve feet high when I thrust it down their throats.[1]

Part of the pleasure of this violent, retributory fantasy is that it is so out of keeping with the elaborate gentility of the occasion and with the American public's embrace of Dickens as a font of edifying sympathy, the gentle defender of "the humble and oppressed."[2] And yet Dickens's account of the rhetorical force of his speech provides an insightful gloss on the power dynamics that are implicit in his sentimental invocation of the death of Sir Walter Scott. Reanimating a deathbed scene that was familiar from John Lockhart's recent biography and infusing it with the pathos of the death of Little Nell, Dickens summoned a Scott who was "faint, wan, dying, crushed both in mind and body by his honorable struggle" to pay off his debts. "Hovering round him," however, were not members of his family, but the most popular characters from his novels, "the ghosts of his own imagination," whom Dickens calls upon to do the work of chastening American readers and pirate publishers. Dickens envisions these characters "fresh from traversing the world and hanging down their heads in shame and sorrow that, from all those lands into which they had carried gladness, instruction, and delight for millions, they had brought him not one friendly hand to help to raise him from that sad, sad bed. No, nor brought him from that land in which his own language was spoken, and in every house and hut of which his own books were read in his own tongue, one grateful dollar piece to buy a garland for his grave."[3]

In imagining that he has "thrust" this vision down the throats of his hosts, Dickens confesses pleasure in his display of vengeful ingratitude, a posture that inverts and is partially obscured by his portrayal of the popular British author as the helpless victim of an ungrateful readership. In fantasy, his performance decisively closes the gap between author and reader that had been opened up by the transatlantic piracy of British novels. If Scott lies immobilized while his characters circulate, unable finally to produce "one grateful dollar piece" for their author, Dickens is able to confront his readership directly, responding to Americans' insatiable appetite for sentimental fiction with a parable about copyright reform that they are fed by force.

What is striking about Dickens's account of his speech is both his attempt to translate authorial control over "the ghosts of his own imagination" into control of the *market* for his works, and the distortions that are necessary for him to perform this act rhetorically. Dickens cannot seem to address the issue of international copyright without resorting to hyperbole. According to Dickens, "not one" American dares to speak in favor of the measure (although the New York dinner included both supportive toasts and a pro-copyright speech)[4]; he is "the greatest loser" by the present arrangement (although this remains unverified and unverifiable); "not one friendly hand" is extended to assist Sir Walter Scott (although both Scott and Dickens had received payments from American pirate publishers).[5] The most grotesque distortions, however, are reserved for the figure of the author himself. Expressing anger at the unauthorized reprinting of his work in a letter to another friend, Dickens turns again to the trope of the author-as-monster: "my blood so boils at these enormities, that when I speak about them, I seem to grow twenty feet high, and to swell out in proportion" (230). Gigantism here is not simply an index of Dickens's superhuman rage, but of a disproportion between the crisis as Dickens perceives it and the resources he can muster to address the problem. Even inflated to twenty times its ordinary size, authorial outrage will prove no match for the clash of political principles, cultural values, and economic interests that converged around the issue of international copyright.

In Chapter 3, I will return to Dickens's frustration at his inability to control the circulation of his texts and to his unsuccessful attempts to persuade Americans to pass an international copyright law. I will approach this episode, however, not as one author's bold call for the international protection of authors' rights, but as an occasion for the intensification of a debate that was well underway before Dickens's arrival. In order to lay the groundwork for a rethinking of Dickens's exemplary failures, I will outline the parameters of the American debate over international copyright and bring into focus what Dickens, preoccupied by injustice to authors and by a sense of his own importance, is unable to perceive—that the question of foreign authors' rights under American law was the vehicle for a domestic struggle over the political economy of print.

Like Dickens, literary critics' ability to understand what was at stake in American opposition to an international copyright law has been obscured by the outsized figure of the aggrieved and indignant author; it is only by recognizing and circumventing this figure that we can begin to account for American resistance. It was neither the moral turpitude of the press nor the cowardice of his hosts that made these after-dinner speeches such a social blunder and strategic error, but Dickens's failure to grasp the political significance that the American public had attached to his visit. In appealing to British and American authors' shared interest in the transatlantic protection of literary property, Dickens betrayed a tin ear for the terms of his welcome as the common property of the common reader, and a costly ignorance of how republican political principles had been mobilized to support the system of reprinting.

I will begin by examining the terms of the American debate as it unfolds before Congress, paying particular attention to the petitions on international copyright submitted by authors, publishers, and members of the print trades to be read before the Senate and the House of Representatives. These petitions provide access to a popular discourse about authorship that is significantly broader than the testimony of authors. As I have argued, critical studies of the conditions of authorship written from an authorial perspective generally remain trapped within the logic of literary nationalism. Even when they show how antebellum authors internalize a sense of their peripheral cultural status, they are able to discern little place for literature outside of the nationalist frame of reference. In these accounts, authors' national ambitions are thwarted by the market or stymied by the self-interest of publishers and readers; authors are not, however, confronted with alternative ways of understanding the relation of literature to the nation.[6] By contrast, the petitions sent to Congress concerning international copyright offer theories of authorship at the pitch of their imagined power to structure the market for print, elaborating competing models of the relation of literature to national authority and identity. These petitions give access to a cultural imaginary in which the cultivation of a national literature is thought to be a hindrance to the development of a political and social order that is nonetheless held together by the circulation of print.

These petitions also place the debate over international copyright in the context of partisan struggles to influence the development of market culture and to imagine a form of national power that was compatible with local authority. The lineage of the right "to petition the Government for redress of grievances" can be traced to the medieval right to appeal directly to the king and was included in the First Amendment to the Constitution along with the rights to freedom of speech, freedom of the press, and peaceable assembly.[7] In the 1830s, petitioning the government was radicalized by abolitionists seeking an end to slavery in the District of Columbia; it was also taken up by laborers agitating for a ten-hour day who saw it as a less confrontational alternative to striking.[8] In directly addressing a legislative body rather than relying on the mediation of elected representatives, citizens' petitions shift attention both to the intimate effects and to the structural limitations of governmental authority. Abolitionists brilliantly exploited the performative power of this mode of address in calling not for an end to slavery *per se*, but for Congress to affirm its jurisdiction over slavery in the District of Columbia, forcing into public visibility the contradictory models of state power that underwrote the "federal consensus"—the widely held belief that the federal government had no authority over slavery in the states.[9] Congressional copyright petitions similarly raise the question of the nature of the federal government's power over the circulation of print. At a time in which struggles over the tariff, transportation and banking, and the extension of slavery into the territories called into question many of the federal government's most fundamental powers—the ability to collect revenues, to regulate commerce, and to protect its citizens' rights to both property and liberty—debates over authors' rights turn the free circulation of print into a test case and model for the workings of state power.

Legalizing Piracy

Section 5 of the Copyright Act of 1790 clearly indicates that, in the opinion of the First Congress, the constitutional mandate to promote "the Progress of Science and useful Arts"[10] did not require the extension of copyright privileges to foreign authors. Indeed, were it not for the double negatives in which it is couched, this provision would read like a ringing endorsement of international literary piracy: "nothing in this act shall be construed to extend to prohibit the importation or vending, reprinting, or publishing within the United States, of any map, chart, book or books, written, printed, or published by any person not a citizen of the United States, in foreign parts or places without the jurisdiction of the United States."[11]

Lyman Ray Patterson has suggested that this unusual clause is based on a misreading of Section VII of the British Statute of Anne (1710), which allowed for the importation of books written in a foreign language as a means of combating censorship.[12] And yet the shift in defining the point at which state protection ceases seems important enough to be a deliberate recasting. By making citizenship and not linguistic identity the cutoff for copyright protection, the American provision underscores the statutory nature of this right while also acknowledging that the identity of the state is not founded on linguistic difference. The American statute allows for political difference alongside cultural continuity by emphasizing the limited reach of national law and by stopping short of bringing British works—foreign texts written in a common language—under its protection. The statute calls attention to the government's limited interest in protecting, and limited jurisdiction over the rights of noncitizens, and yet its overall purpose is to ensure that foreign works would continue to be published and circulated in the new nation. Indeed, Section 5 of the Copyright Act seems motivated by a concern that the rights granted to native authors and foreign residents might be *over*extended, injecting a note of caution or reluctance into this founding document of authorial prerogative. Because it defines copyright as a negative right—that of *preventing* the vending, reprinting, or publishing of a text—the American statute inscribes the citizen's privilege as a prohibition, and portrays foreign piracy as the lifting of such restrictions. The same act that somewhat warily grants authors a limited monopoly in their works bestows upon publishers an extraordinary license: that of the unrestricted republication of foreign texts.

It is important to note the simultaneity of and the countervailing pressure exerted by the establishment of domestic copyright and its denial to foreign authors. Historians and critics have traditionally treated the two as separate issues, regarding domestic copyright as uncontroversial and easily established, while devoting most of their efforts to accounting for the century-long delay in the adoption of an international copyright agreement. This approach has had the effect of making Congress's repeated refusal to extend copyright to noncitizens appear as an oversight or "failure"[13]—a gap in the enforcement of authors' rights—rather than a substantive measure. This depiction of the resistance to international copyright as a form of negligence is remarkable, considering that throughout the antebellum period, Congress frequently reasserted its unwillingness to grant copyrights to foreign authors. Between 1837 and 1854 Congress formally rejected or tabled numerous international copyright bills, denied petitions signed by Britain's and America's most prominent authors, and blocked the passage of an Anglo-American copyright treaty that had been supported by two presidents.[14] In his definitive account of the political struggle over international copyright, James J. Barnes attributes Congress's recalcitrance to the effective lobbying of entrenched publishing interests and to legislative indifference in the face of widespread economic depression. While these factors are undoubtedly crucial to an understanding of congressional action, they fail to account for the unusual strength and

specific form of the resistance to foreign authors' rights. Like the convo-
luted syntax of Section 5 of the Act of 1790, congressional opposition to
international copyright provides strong evidence of an alternate system of
value in tension with the whole notion of authors' rights. Foreign authors'
disenfranchisement under American law was not inconsistent with but
integral to many Americans' understanding of the nature and scope of
domestic copyright protection.

A reexamination of the struggle over international copyright in Congress and in the periodical press suggests not an indifference to the plight
of authors so much as a complex consensus as to the limits of their claims,
not a lack of interest in the allocation of property rights in printed texts,
but a sophisticated analysis of the political consequences of their manufacture and distribution. While it is true that the copyright controversy
drew far less energy and attention from Congress than concurrent debates
over tariff rates, the transportation and banking systems, and the extension of slavery into the territories, congressional resistance to an international copyright law was intimately bound up with these struggles. In
particular, opposition to international copyright drew on the critique of
centralized power that was a constant refrain in these debates, a critique
that had been honed over decades by Democrats who opposed national
funding of internal improvements and the rechartering of the National
Bank.[15] The persuasiveness of the opposition was not simply the product
of publishers' power, but of the way in which they marshaled fears about
concentrations of capital and the consolidation of governmental authority, fears that were heightened by more pressing conflicts over economic
development and the expansion of slavery. Rather than trying to explain
the "failure" of Congress to act on proposed legislation, then, we need to
take better measure of what one critic referred to as "a widely extended
prejudice . . . against the establishment of international copyright."[16]
Rather than chronicling setbacks on the way to the eventual triumph of
the cause of foreign authors' rights, we need to establish the grounds for
one reprinter's confident claim that international copyright was "a most
unpopular measure and can never be carried."[17]

A number of factors have combined to make the resistance to international copyright largely invisible to historians and literary critics. An
authors'-rights bias has been built into scholars' materials as well as their
consciousness: the primary sources for the study of the nineteenth-century
debate were compiled and indexed by copyright advocates who were instrumental in passing an international copyright law in 1891.[18] In addition,

most prominent nineteenth-century authors supported the cause of international copyright. Expecting American literature to flourish once it was relieved from the competition posed by cheap reprints of successful foreign books, American authors actively endorsed the measure in memorials, public declarations, and in the pages of newspapers and literary magazines.[19] Literary critics' bias toward the testimony of authors and the long-standing alliance of literary study with literary nationalism have combined to give international copyright advocacy undue prominence in our histories. Authors' support of international copyright, however, must be weighed against the consistent and organized antagonism of the trade. According to Barnes, memorials to Congress opposing the first international copyright bill outnumbered those of advocates by a ratio of three to one.[20] A handful of influential pamphlets and magazine articles also helped to solidify, coordinate, and popularize positions that found bedrock support in reprint publishing houses, trade unions, and at public meetings of interested tradesmen.[21]

The conceptual outlines of the opposition have also been difficult to perceive because of the political slipperiness of the issue. Initially, positions on international copyright did not divide cleanly along either party or sectional lines, although the fact that the first five international copyright bills were presented to the Senate by Henry Clay inevitably associated the measure with Clay's "American System" of developmental nationalism, the protectionist program that linked high tariffs on imported goods and a strong national bank to federal spending on transportation networks. Party lines were drawn more sharply in 1843 when John O'Sullivan published a lead article in *The Democratic Review* declaring that "The International Copyright so eagerly clamored for is all a humbug."[22] And yet the cause of international copyright continued to be associated with a vocal group of Democrats, the Young Americans, even after O'Sullivan's rejection of this plank of their platform forced them to take their appeals for copyright reform to the pages of the Whig monthly, the *American Review*.[23] Elite literary magazines' general support of the measure was occasionally disrupted, most notably when the *Southern Literary Messenger* followed up William Gilmore Simms's passionate appeal for recognition of foreign authors' rights with an extended rebuttal of his claims.[24] But for the most part, the defense of the system of reprinting took place not in literary or partisan monthly magazines, but in the nonpartisan popular press: in mammoth weeklies, such as *Brother Jonathan* and *The New World*, which relied on reprinted texts for much of their content, and in penny dailies, such as the Philadelphia *Public Ledger*, which cultivated an urban working-class readership.[25] If the antebellum politics of print appear to divide more cleanly along class than party lines, these were emerging differences that both Whigs and Democrats sought to exploit and to appease. Appeals for an international copyright law galvanized a discussion of the dangers and advantages of the circulation of cheap print and brought into focus sharply differing positions on the relation of print to market culture, on the compatibility of the market and democracy, and on the relation of the market for print to the shape of the nation.

In Congress, active support of international copyright tended to be Whig, northern, and avowedly protectionist.[26] The defense of private property rights and the cultivation of American letters were causes that resonated with Whig concern for economic stability, national unity, and national identity. As a political position, however, support for international copyright was confused by analogies to tariff policy and by appeals across sectional lines. For example, in presenting the first international copyright bill to the Senate, Henry Clay famously compared a pirated English book to a "bale of merchandise" that was stolen upon arrival on American shores.[27] As opponents of international copyright were quick to note, however, the coherence of Clay's position depended on whether one thought American authors or American publishers stood most in need of protection. Copyright opponents were thrilled to catch the "Father of the *American System*" in an obvious contradiction, claiming that Clay's support for international copyright was inconsistent with his protectionist policies.[28] To Clay's assertion that "we should be all shocked if the law tolerated the least invasion of the rights of property, in the case of the merchandise" (1), Philip Nicklin, a copyright opponent and free trade advocate replied:

Unhappily we are not *all* shocked, when the law not only tolerates but requires the taking away from the foreign merchant who brings to the United States a bale of merchandise one-fourth, one-third, or one-half of its value without paying for it, in order that somebody, somewhere down east, may be able to make a similar sort of thing; and yet *mirabile dictu!* a law is proposed to prevent us from making books like those imported by the foreign merchant.[29]

In light of concurrent debates over tariff rates, Clay's ambiguous comparison of books to a "bale of merchandise" seems deliberately designed to garner southern support for copyright payments by associating them not with their obvious counterpart, the much-despised tax on finished goods, but with a tariff on raw materials more congenial to southern planters. Similar attempts to build support for the measure across sectional lines produced the oddity of a petition signed predominantly by New York and New England literati that argues for international copyright on the grounds that it would help to preserve America's "peculiar institutions."[30]

While Whigs had trouble reconciling their support of international copyright with their position on the tariff, the largely Democratic opposition[31] seems to have gained strength from the political indeterminacy of the issue. As Nicklin's critique of Clay suggests, denying copyrights to foreign authors could be understood as a lifting of trade restrictions that benefitted American industry. Opposition to international copyright was a protectionist policy that sailed under the flag of free trade.[32] As I will argue with reference to petitions sent to Congress and to influential anti-copyright treatises, the opposition's core defense of the decentralization of the print trades demonstrated a remarkable political flexibility: it allowed for an alignment of the manufacturing north with the anti-development south; it offered a rebuke to centralized capital that was, nevertheless, compatible with small-entrepreneur capitalism; and it employed a rhetoric of self-erasure that was characteristic of the Jacksonian exercise of political power—it was based on a populist appeal to the national legislature to eschew the use of federal power.[33]

Very little of the political and cultural controversy that made international copyright "a most unpopular measure" is discernable if one regards it primarily as an economic matter. Therefore, while much of the debate is conducted on economic grounds, including rival estimates of authors' earnings and tables comparing book prices in the United States and Great Britain, I will not try to determine the accuracy of projections about the effect of international copyright on authors' pay or the availability of books.[34] Instead, I will focus on the way in which participants in the debate articulate theories about the structure of the literary marketplace and about the relation of authorship and literary production to the state. For what is at stake in the struggle over international copyright is not simply authors' and publishers' profits, or the nature of intellectual property, but the place of print in market culture at a moment when the shape and fate of markets was anything but assured.

Given the importance of the print trades to the national economy and the urgency with which the circulation of print was identified both with threats to and with the preservation of the republic, the relation of print to market culture was a deeply political issue. The expanded reach of printed texts, made possible by new technologies of mass production and distribution, coincided with the extension of suffrage to an increasingly literate public and the aggressive solicitation of the popular vote by well-organized political parties. Elites worried about the unmediated access of newly enfranchised citizens to cheap publications, what Charles Lyell referred to as "the indiscriminate reading of popular works by the multitude, when the higher classes and clergy can exert little or no control in the selection of the books read."[35] And yet evangelists, abolitionists, and politicians had also made many Americans highly suspicious of the attempt to *control* what was circulated and read, in particular, the use of the penny press and the postal service to distribute cheap or free publications. The Sabbatarian controversy of the late 1820s, abolitionists' mass mailing of anti-slavery literature in 1835, and the bitterly fought election of 1840 all demonstrated the considerable power that could be wielded through well-coordinated print campaigns.[36] Popular sovereignty made control over the circulation of print seem both acutely necessary and unusually dangerous. Both advocates and opponents of international copyright invoked Congress's power under the Constitution's copyright clause to fashion the trade in books toward democratic ends.

One sign of the insistence with which the circulation of print raised questions about the compatibility of democracy and market revolution is the passionate cultural investment in the foreign reprint itself. As I will argue, the "unbought foreign literature"[37] of which copyright advocates complained represented more than the problematic competition afforded by texts unburdened by payments to authors. The figural drift of this curious phrase suggests that, despite the workings of the market, foreign reprints somehow managed to remain "unbought." The idea of an "unbought literature" is a particularly volatile one because it stands as a point of crossing between aristocratic and republican systems of publishing, neither of which could easily accommodate the idea of authorial profit. Even as the commercial success of pirated foreign texts provoked a partisan battle to shape the expanding market for print, widespread uneasiness about the effects of market culture made reprinted texts the focal point of contradictory, competing fantasies of exemption from market conditions. Among pro-copyright petitioners, British authors' virtuous detachment from the questionable business of reprinting provokes a nostalgic desire to stand outside the very marketplace in which they sought to solidify their rights. Copyright advocates' attempt to equilibrate the market for books becomes confounded with an attempt to insulate authors from the workings of this market. However, the overwhelming popularity of cheap reprints posed a challenge to American authorship that could not be solved by according the author a special status—both inside and outside of the market system. Copyright opponents used the success of these reprints to argue that the author was largely irrelevant to republican publishing, recasting the privileged position of authorial withdrawal as a peripheral one. The flourishing of the reprint trade enabled copyright opponents to imagine a market for books in which the consolidation of capital would be counteracted by the availability of many of the most valuable texts—both popular sensations and standard works—for republication. Anti-copyright petitioners argued for a system of publishing that would offset the danger implicit in the private ownership of printed texts by distributing this ownership as widely as possible.

Representing the Nation: The Campaign for International Copyright

The concerted effort to persuade Congress to amend the Copyright Act began with a petition signed by fifty-six "Authors of Great Britain" at the instigation of the British publishing firm Saunders & Otley. In the spring of 1836, this firm set up a branch office in New York City in a bid to control the reprint market for the books they had first published in England. Soon realizing that their claims were unsustainable without an international copyright agreement, they enlisted the help of Harriet Martineau, who circulated a petition to prominent British authors, gathered signatures, and submitted it to Congress under the lead signature of Thomas Moore. The firm presumed that the eminence of these authors would carry considerable political clout. As Harriet Martineau remarked in a letter soliciting the signature of Henry Brougham: "I rather think both Houses will fall on their knees on the receipt of our petition."[38]

This petition set the tone for the American pro-copyright appeals that followed, characterizing the lack of international copyright as an affront to individual rights. While protesting that unauthorized reprints had inflicted "extensive injuries" on British authors' reputation and property, the petition deemphasized pecuniary loss, calling attention instead to the reprint trade's lack of respect for the author as an individual. Thus the injustice perpetuated by this system had less to do with stolen profits than with the violation of an implicit contract: British books were being reprinted "not only without the consent of the authors, but even contrary to their express desires."[39] This fundamental lack of respect for individual rights manifested itself as a shocking disregard for textual integrity. British books were "liable to be mutilated and altered at the pleasure of [American] booksellers" (1), a possibility that undermined the status of the text as the product of, and proxy for, its author.

Despite this contractual rhetoric and emphasis on individual rights, the British authors' petition ultimately grounds the moral right of the author in hereditary privilege. This is clear from the way in which what starts out as a narrative about stolen goods gets recast in familial terms as lost inheritance and false paternity. Citing the bankrupt Sir Walter Scott as an example, the petition suggests that an "equitable remuneration" from the American public "might have saved his life" or at least provided for his heirs, relieving his "closing years from the burden of debts and destructive toils" (2). While the accusation remains oblique, the "Thomas Moore" petition implies that American reprints were partially responsible for Scott's demise. The negligence and greed of American publishers had substituted a profitless, generalized fame for the literal perpetuation of Scott's line.

Of course, Scott is a volatile figure for the British authors to cite in this context, in that he represents a limit case for the viability of the aristocratic model of authorship. Scott's bankruptcy is a delicate subject precisely because it points to the fragility and superannuation of the very fiction the British authors are trying to sustain. Rather than poignant proof that authors' rights needed to be upheld on Lockean grounds—as if an author, laboring in seclusion, produced a form of private property that was then stolen in the process of its dissemination—Scott's career illustrates both the hope and the fear that authorship in the age of mechanical reproduction might work this process in reverse. The lesson of Scott's success is that the anonymous circulation of texts could produce a profit for their author that could then be translated into aristocratic status (represented by the *faux* castle, Abottsford, and by Scott's acquisition of a knighthood). It is no wonder, then, that the story of Scott's demise should take a central place in the debate over international copyright. Scott's career represents the totalizing ambitions of the aristocratic model of authorship—as if the individual control lost to mass-production could be wholly recaptured by the author—and suggests that this figure is subject to a spectacular collapse.[40]

This threat to an author's ability to sustain himself and to secure his legacy, however, was only half of the problem. The British authors complained that they were continually "made responsible for works which they no longer recognize as their own" (1), a circumstance that left American readers plagued by "uncertainty . . . as to whether the books presented to them as the works of British authors, are the actual and complete productions of the writers whose names they bear" (2). Even the fame British authors received as meager recompense for their labors was tarnished by the possibility of bastardy and imposture. As if to underscore the dissociation of author and text produced by this system, and more firmly to attach one to the other, the "Thomas Moore" petition supplemented its list of signatures with a second, double-columned roster matching each of the signers with his or her most popular books. Although intended to impress, this list stands as a tacit acknowledgment that in America, an author's signature alone was insufficient. In the culture of reprinting, authorial stature remained uncertain without some mechanism for tying author to text.

The moral outrage of the "Thomas Moore" petition reflects both the British authors' sense of wrong and their lack of legal standing: they could appeal to neither law nor custom, and so relied on American pride in the protection of individual rights. By contrast, the American petitions in support of international copyright are a good deal more politic and conciliatory. Acknowledging that an international copyright law might "injuriously affect American publishers," Henry Clay proposed a bill hedged about with safeguards and qualifications.[41] To justify its passage, he took what was essentially an aristocratic appeal for authors' rights and routed it through a defense of national honor. Raising the British emphasis on individual integrity to the level of the state, Clay and numerous petitioners who followed his lead argued that a nation's ability to offer "reciprocal justice"[42] to foreign authors was the sign of its cultural independence. Although all of these petitions worked from the premise that an international copyright law would encourage the development of American literature, their common thread was not a crude nationalism, but a preoccupation with questions of equity. Drawing on arguments familiar from debates on the tariff, they argued that a "copyright tax" on foreign texts would redress the imbalance in the American market, transforming it into a "fair field"[43] for literary competition. Like the "Thomas Moore" petition, which clothes a defense of authors' hereditary estate in the language of liberal individualism, the American petitions in support of international copyright lean so hard on abstract principles of equity as nearly to obliterate the fact that they were calling for government intervention in the market on their behalf—in effect, asking Congress to ameliorate the negative effects of the privileges American authors had been granted under the Copyright Act of 1790. Acknowledging that the restriction of copyright to citizens had limited the circulation of American texts, they argued that comparable privileges should be made available to foreign authors. Requiring payments to foreign authors would thus be an indirect way of supporting American authorship. While these petitions continually circle around the problem of ensuring equal profits for American and foreign authors (neither of whom, it was claimed, were receiving adequate pay under the system of reprinting), they pitch their appeal largely at the symbolic level. Granting the same rights to foreigners as those enjoyed by native authors would not only be good for American letters, it was an act of generosity extended by nations to other nations of equivalent status. Playing off fears of cultural immaturity, these petitions repeatedly allege that the cost of international copyright was something a truly independent nation could easily afford.[44] Allowing the price of British texts to increase would prove that America was no longer reliant on the mother country for its "literary resources."[45] The redirection of the industry toward the production of American texts would remove the stigma of secondarity that was undeniable so long as American publishers remained "mere re-publishers of foreign books."[46]

While they differ in approach, these petitions share a conviction in the centrality of the author to the production and preservation of national identity. To the author devolved responsibility both for representing the nation in the international arena, and for inculcating American principles at home. As one petition argued, "native writers are as indispensable as a native militia"; Americans "must look, for the defense of their habits, their opinions, and their peculiar institutions . . . to their own authors, as to their own *soldiers*, whatever may be the cost *in dollars and cents*."[47] While a number of petitions argued that American "habits" and "opinions" needed to be defended against "misrepresentation in foreign lands,"[48] the comparison of authors to a native militia suggests that the site of battle was primarily imagined to be a domestic one. An influx of foreign texts reflecting monarchical principles posed an internal threat to national security that could be eliminated by the government's active intervention on behalf of American authors. Authors were thus cast into a mediating role between citizen and state, preserving American habits in part by policing them.

The habit that most needed to be policed was reading itself. As one petition argued, "the feverish and unhealthy taste engendered by the perusal of transatlantic novels" could be countered only by the dissemination of "books of real value, teaching republican principles and inculcating American feelings."[49] Representing authors as crucial to the preservation of national identity heightened the urgency of these appeals, and yet it also presumed widespread ignorance of or resistance to the "principles" and "feelings" American authors were charged with upholding. The petitions on behalf of international copyright frequently register anxiety about the dislocating social and cultural effects of immigration, western expansion, and sectional conflict; the nation they seek to protect and preserve is internally divided and urgently in need of reconciliation. In many of these petitions, the work of authorship comes to resemble the work of political persuasion, as if the cost of international copyright "in dollars and cents" could only be justified by a literature which would "explain, defend, and disseminate our principles throughout our borders, [and] cement more strongly our Union."[50]

The extremity of the posturing in some of these appeals is a product of the difficulty of their rhetorical task—to explain how payments to British authors could possibly benefit the American public. This was a daunting assignment in that opponents of international copyright were quick to take any expression of concern for the British authors' plight as evidence of collusion between American and British authors to defraud the American public.[51] Copyright advocates, then, were forced to find justifications for foreign authors' rights that would keep critics from regarding foreign authors as stand-ins and mouthpieces for American publishers and authors. While their depiction of the American author as writing in the service of the state helped to distance the two, transforming the problem of payments to foreign authors into a necessary defense of national security, it also covered for another kind of anxiety: the problem of imagining the role of authors and the stability of culture under a market system. The petitions on behalf of international copyright are riven by a curious contradiction: while nearly all involve some sort of passionate appeal for equality in the marketplace, they repeatedly return to a representation of the author as either indifferent to personal profit, or temperamentally unable to sustain economic relations. Henry Clay, for example, depicts this champion of American independence as extraordinarily vulnerable, both by trade and by disposition: "[authors] are often dependent, exclusively, upon their own mental labors for the means of subsistence; and are frequently, from the nature of their pursuits, or the constitutions of their minds, incapable of applying that provident care to worldly affairs which other classes of society are in the habit of bestowing" (1). Clay is concerned here to justify government intervention in the market with reference to the extraordinary nature of literary labor, describing authors as "among the greatest benefactors of mankind" (1). And yet such special pleading runs counter to his claim that the foreign book, like a "bale of merchandise," needs to be brought under the laws of property that govern ordinary things. Clay's need to insulate authors from the market even as he seeks to classify the product of their labor as ordinary property suggests that the author may have come too much to resemble an ordinary worker, one exclusively dependent on his labor for subsistence. Clay's hope that international copyright will afford the American author and publisher welcome relief from the "dangerous competition" (2) of the reprint trade suggests that the American author's vulnerability stems not from his habitual detachment, but from his subjection to the market. Boston publisher Nahum Capen similarly argues that an author's absorption in his work precludes "skill in protecting his pecuniary interests."[52] For Capen, the importance of the author to national identity, and the necessity of authorial withdrawal from the world, makes it incumbent on the state to secure "a life interest" (6) in the products of his labor. In Capen's account, the author's professional anti-professional status makes him a worthy recipient of government subsidy.

Both Capen and Clay invoke the romantic conception of the isolate artist under the sign of infirmity, not strength. Paradoxically, the author seems susceptible to financial ruin because of his self-reliance. Part of the appeal in agitating for payments to *foreign* authors, then, is that international copyright advocates are able to preserve the American author from the stigma of self-interest while providing for his financial security. The argument on behalf of international copyright comes loaded not only with fears of cultural dependency, but with fears about the dependence of the author upon the very payments it prescribes. The representation of the author as a selfless defender of national values seems driven by the hope that an alignment with the public good could somehow carve out an extra-market space for the author from within the confines of the market. Rather than integrating the writer-as-producer into the economic order, pro-copyright petitioners use the special vulnerability of the author to market fluctuation to justify legislation that would regulate the dangerously speculative market in printed goods. It is the unfitness of authors for market society that provides the pretext for legislation that would discipline the reprint trade through the figure of the author-as-proprietor.

Decentering the Market:
Defending the System of Reprinting

Instead of viewing republication as inevitably consigning American letters to an imitative, secondary position, the petitions opposed to international copyright elaborate what might be called a theory of *republic*ation, constructing the reprint market itself as the locus of national values. They argue that America could prove its independence not by producing a literature that measures up to—and thus in some way merely replicates—British standards, or by assuming the role of Britain's equal partner in trade, but by supporting a radically different system of publishing. While its proponents maintained that this system could coexist with one that paid homage to the rights of native authors, the hallmark of these petitions is a profound distrust of any measure that would consolidate the private ownership of texts.

Like the arguments of the defense in *Wheaton v. Peters*, these petitions draw much of their rhetorical power from the republican equation of national identity and political stability with the wide dissemination of texts. At their simplest, these petitions maintain that international copyright would be inegalitarian in its effects: payments to British authors would "greatly enhance the price and limit the circulation of literature—confining it to the wealthy alone."[53] And yet many make the more radical claim that copyright payments are fundamentally incompatible with the function of literature in a republic. Inverting the advocates' paradigm, they argue that *granting* copyrights to foreign authors could be politically dangerous. Typically, one petition argued that Americans should abandon the "higher walks of authorship" because the national literary vocation lay instead in the "great work of popularizing knowledge." Whereas "the policy of Europe" was "to make the light of science shine brightly in certain focal points, as the university and the institute" (transforming "literature and literary institutions" into "the pillars of monarchical government"), the American "mission" was "to adapt light to the people, and bring it in at the windows of every house and home, and make it burn in every American bosom."[54] Importantly, the democratization of knowledge shifts the work of authorship from origination to adaptation and distribution. Under a republican definition of authorship, it made no sense to uphold the property rights of a foreign literary elite when they clearly ran counter to the "general good" of "a reading people."[55] In fact and in principle, international copyright was "hostile to that general diffusion of intelligence . . . which is the best safeguard of our republican institutions."[56]

As pro-copyright petitioners sardonically noted, this spirited defense of the reprint trade was mounted by those who most stood to gain from its protection. While the appeals on behalf of international copyright were put forward by both authors and publishers,[57] the opposition was clearly identifiable as the voice of the trade, "embracing booksellers, papermakers, printers, bookbinders, type founders and others . . . connected with book making and periodical publication."[58] And yet to dismiss this rhetoric as a mere cover for the interests of manufacturers would be to ignore the complex ways in which these petitions redefine literary value, shifting the locus of literary nationalism from the author to the text-as-object. Rather than establishing the Americanness of a book by reference to its subject matter or to the nationality of its author, copyright opponents argued that national values were instantiated in the process of a book's production. Thus the means by which a British novel in "three handsome volumes"[59] was transformed into an affordable American double-decker carried with it the entire ideological freight of the republican dream of popularizing knowledge. One identified an American book by its physical appearance—by "the compression of bulk, and consequent less consumption of paper," by "the use of smaller type, and putting the lines closer together" (2)—regardless of its content or the provenance of its author.

In these petitions, the resetting of type becomes a powerful point of re-origination, the most important stage in the adaptation of the foreign text for American uses. Not exempt from fears about unfettered circulation, some petitioners maintained that resetting type gave American publishers an important measure of control over content, an opportunity to excise "sentiments offensive to good taste and good morals."[60] There are indications, too, that southern legislators worried that granting copyrights to foreign authors would embolden British abolitionists and encourage the circulation of anti-slavery publications. Reprinting was thus imagined as a local or regional instrument for censorship.[61] And yet what is striking about these petitions on the whole is the degree to which they shift the terms of the debate from the question of content to the politics of the manufacture and distribution of texts. Although it may *also* be read in the plot and characters of British novels, British tyranny is *most* legible in the London publishers' desire to control the American book market on their own terms, accruing economies of scale by printing large editions from "type already standing,"[62] and yet refusing to lower the price of books accordingly, so that reading could be made affordable. Far from a hedge against British dominance of the American literary marketplace, international copyright would solidify their power, allowing British publishers "to supply the American market without risk of competition and underselling" (2). Not only would this monopoly deal a terrible blow to industry, "causing books to be manufactured in England that are now printed in this country" (1), it could alter the distinctive character of American publishing. As one petition predicted with dismay, "English prices and style of publication would soon begin to be *fashionable* here."[63] Granting copyrights to British authors would ensure that nothing but British texts—in form or content—were available in the American market. The American reprint, then, was more than a cheap, degraded version of its British original. Its small type and narrow margins broadcast a defiance of the monopolizing intentions and elitist, enervating products of the "luxurious press of London."[64]

In defining reprinting as the resetting of type, copyright opponents aligned this act with origination and productive labor, redistributing the passivity conventionally associated with copying onto the British original (printed from "types already standing").[65] This defense of the reprint trade bears all the marks of what Isaac Kramnick and Carroll Smith-Rosenberg have identified as the "commercial republican" recasting of "classical republican" values. Grounding national virtue in the labor of the printer, rather than in the inalienable property of the author, the tradesmen who opposed foreign authors' rights shifted the stigma of idleness and self-interest onto British authors, London publishers, and their American allies.[66] Over and against copyright advocates' sentimental tales of the suffering of authors' widows—tales that incessantly rewrite the crisis of copyright as a problem of inheritance—copyright opponents cite the many female laborers who would be "thrown idle by the passage of the bill," arguing that the misery of working women would be "poorly compensated for by any display of ultra sympathy towards those who stand in no need of it."[67] Associating authors' rights with luxury and hereditary privilege, these petitions argue that any extension of these rights would be an irresponsible sacrifice of public good to private interest. In equating international copyright with a threat to American industry, and locating national identity in the process of production, they make the powerful claim that manufacturing, and not literature, is America's true cultural product.

It is, however, not simply this defense of the "national industry,"[68] but the opposition's elaboration of the politics of book distribution that

poses the greatest challenge to the American authors' bid to be acknowledged as the guardians of national identity. In railing against the pernicious influence of a "London literature,"[69] copyright opponents did more
than complain about the importation of British books or the production
of expensive, British-style facsimiles; they agitated against a system of production and distribution that, like the London market, worked according
to a dynamic of center and periphery, metropolis and colony. In this model,
the "diffusion of knowledge and instruction over the whole mass" (1),
which was the guarantor of liberty, always threatened to collapse back
into centralized control. Ceding the power of re-origination in the name
of authors' rights would mean nothing less than ceding independence
itself: "our entire country would be as much a market secured to the London publisher, and the English author, as Scotland or Ireland" (3).[70]

These were highly charged comparisons in the context of American
publishing. As Richard Cargill Cole has shown, the American reprint industry was heavily indebted to Scots and Irish publishers who pioneered the
production and marketing of cheap reprints of English books. The American reprint trade also depended on the provincial British press for much
of its labor, employing large numbers of printers and other tradesmen
who emigrated when the extension of British copyright to Ireland under
the Act of Union (1800) caused the Irish reprint trade to collapse.[71] American reprinters were thus acutely aware of the vulnerability of provincial
trade to centralized capital, and all too familiar with the London publishers' use of authors' rights to extend the reach of their domain. In an influential 1853 pamphlet, *Letters on International Copyright*, Henry C. Carey—a
publisher, economist, and the son of Philadelphia's most prominent Irish
emigré reprinter, Mathew Carey—drew a strong connection between the
unification of Great Britain, the consolidation of capital and political power
in London, and the consequent impoverishment of Scots and Irish letters.[72]
Reanimating the American revolutionary defense of provincial liberties
against the oppressive, centralized authority of Great Britain and counting
on the relevance of this defense to the class and sectional politics of the
1850s, Carey reminded his readers that "centralization tends towards taxing the people for building up great institutions at a distance from those
who pay the taxes" (45). Carey made the cause of international copyright
resonate with the threat of absentee landholders, the dangers of a distant,
unresponsive government, the poignancy of deserted villages, and the flight
of literary talent from provincial capitals to a corrupt metropolis.

Over and against this model of a literary marketplace in which satellite nations tracked in an inevitable orbit around the London publisher and English author, American copyright opponents proposed a system in which decentralization would ensure that free trade operated in the interests of the republic. The suspension of private property rights in texts made possible by the lack of international copyright was crucial to this formulation. The legalization of international literary piracy made it possible for publishers to imagine a system in which editions of any single text could be both limitless in number and thoroughly dispersed. As one petition argued, the surrender of authors' proprietary rights translated directly into the popularization of knowledge: because "no one house [had] the exclusive legal control of publication," prices were "kept moderate from the dread of competition," and books, as well as profits, were distributed as widely as possible.[73] In a culture of reprinting, there would be no center from which authors and "monopolizing publishers"[74] could assert control. Rather, this system would distribute property in the same way and at the same time that it distributed knowledge, multiplying the sites of textual re-origination and maximizing opportunities for virtuous labor. Multiple American editions of foreign works were not a sign of dependency, excess, or inefficiency, but proof of that general diffusion of knowledge that preserved independence. One petition remarked with pride that three different editions of Scott's complete works had been published in America. Establishing a high-water mark for its regionalizing ideal, it went on to effuse: "Of Byron's works, editions have been published in all the principal cities of the Union."[75]

These arguments on behalf of the reprint trade are persuasive both because they bring the fact of the market into alignment with the interests of the state, and because they take into account the difference that the technology of stereotype made to the politics of print. While it greatly increased the cost of book production, the ability to cast and store a plate of type offered publishers a valuable hedge against risk. Whereas books composed from ordinary moveable type were dismantled in the process of production (their pages broken down and the type distributed for use in the composition of subsequent pages), books composed through the stereotype process could be stored indefinitely in plate form, and used for multiple reprintings. Stereotype shifted the locus of publishers' property in texts from unwieldy and fragile printed sheets to durable and transportable metal pages—in effect, a master-copy of the book itself. Crucially, stereotype gave publishers a measure of control over unpredictable consumer demand. It enabled them to print and release books in smaller batches, cutting losses should the book fail to sell, and saving the cost of resetting type in the event that the book turned out to be successful.[76]

It was precisely this measure of control over the market that worried the opponents of international copyright. Stereotype did not in and of itself restrict the supply of books or produce monopolies. Indeed, this technology enabled economies of scale that could theoretically result in cheaper books for the general populace. Producing duplicate plates was relatively inexpensive, radically expanding the upper limit of any single print run. This increase in the capacity of the press and the mobility of the plates themselves meant that stereotype lent itself just as easily to a system based on high volume and multiple sites of production, as it did to one that regulated supply and concentrated publishers' power.[77] And yet stereotype, when combined with copyright, sharpened fears of centralized control. One petition projected that, when secured against competition by international copyright, London publishers would print off large American editions from their London plates, or, more drastically, would ship duplicate plates to America for domestic printing. In this petition, the fantasy of foreign control is so complete that it imagines the British publisher recuperating his entire tariff payment upon shipping the plates back to London. Not only would the American reader be placed in thrall to the British publisher, the government would be deprived of "the trifling importation duty which is justly its due."[78]

It was the argument on behalf of a decentralized literary marketplace that pro-copyright forces had the most difficulty rebutting. Even copyright advocates' willingness to add a manufacturing clause to their bill— one that would ensure that all foreign books would be produced in America—could not answer to opponents' fears about British control over stereotype plates. Neither could their pleas for government support of native authors address the need to maintain decentralization across the national market. In calling for government intervention, pro-copyright petitioners identified the author and the reader as potential sites of national vulnerability—the former dangerously subject to market fluctuations, and the latter to foreign influence. While the American author could be relied on to instill democratic principles and to fortify republican institutions, it was the government's responsibility to protect this figure from a market that favored cheap reprints over original productions. By contrast, copyright opponents welcomed the mass-production and distribution of texts so long as there were structural barriers to the recapture of disseminated property by a central power. Theirs was not an unqualified embrace of the market. Indeed, the threat to political stability posed by print monopolies made it incumbent upon the state to protect the system of dissemination that underwrote its virtue. Luckily, however, this could be done with a minimum of intervention by the central government. The benefit of entrusting national virtue not to authors but to a circulation that preserves and is self-preserving, was confirmed by the fact that supporting the latter system required no exercise of government power. As the committee recommending Senate rejection of Henry Clay's first copyright bill reported, booksellers', publishers', and typographers' interests were "coincident with public policy"; copyright opponents "asked no change of the law."[79] Such logic recasts Congress's "failure" to act on foreign authors' rights as fully ideological. Far from an unaccountable (and thus, invariably self-interested) neglect of individual rights, the legislature's refusal to extend copyright privileges to foreign authors becomes the sign of its virtuous abjuration of the exercise of central power.

The virtue of this refusal becomes more apparent as copyright advocates pursue an international copyright treaty with Great Britain after the failure of Clay's many attempts to pass the measure into law. In 1853, while a privately negotiated copyright treaty was awaiting ratification by the Senate, Henry Carey issued his influential pamphlet, protesting that the treaty represented a dangerous attempt "to substitute the will of the Executive for that of the people as expressed by the House of Representatives" (7–8): "Here we have secrecy in the making of laws, and irrevocability of the law when made," political means that are "better suited to the monarchies of Europe than to the republic of the United States" (6). The American negotiators of the treaty responded to anxieties about the link between international copyright and the consolidation of economic power by adding price-control provisions that required British publishers to produce cheap editions for the American market. But the copyright treaty foundered under the weight of these politically volatile amendments amidst growing public concern over the secrecy of the proceedings.[80]

If the importance of cheap books to American culture was an emerging ground of consensus in this debate, the chief point of contention was how best to protect American authors' rights, which appear in the arguments of both sides as a hindrance to the circulation of their books. Pro-copyright petitioners sought to counter the inhibiting effects of domestic copyright by requiring payments to authors regardless of national origin. They maintained that stabilizing the literary marketplace through international respect for authors' rights (and the publishers who wielded them) would deliver adequate profits without substantially increasing the price of books. Anti-copyright petitioners insisted, however, that it was not the stabilization but the expansion of the domestic market that would most benefit the American author. They argued that the widespread availability of cheap reprints was instrumental to the creation and maintenance of the mass readership on which the prosperity of American authors and American letters ultimately depended. Moreover, they insisted that the restriction of copyrights to American authors accorded them a unique form of property that provided leverage with American publishers: under the system of reprinting, American publishers were able to issue native works without fear of competition, but given an international copyright law, they were likely to invest all their capital in more valuable British texts. Calling attention to the relatively weak demand for American books in foreign markets, they argued that the literary property of American authors could retain its value only in the context of the mass circulation of affordable reprints that elevated the taste of American readers and that sustained the publishing system as a whole. Mainstream opposition to international copyright held that a fledgling national literature was actually protected by a system in which authors' rights and publishers' control extended only as far as national borders.[81]

Some copyright opponents, however, saw in the suspension of foreign authors' property rights an extraordinary national opportunity—the possibility of doing without a literary elite altogether. Harriet Martineau could not have been more mistaken when she assumed a conjunction between the cultural status of authors and political power. Rather than dropping to their knees when addressed by the author-monarch, anti-copyright petitioners argued that authors were ultimately peripheral to the interests of the state. Inverting Jefferson's plan for securing national virtue by discouraging domestic manufacture (confining commodity-production and the corruption that attends it to the other side of the Atlantic[82]), some petitioners suggested that authorship could be delegated almost entirely to the Europeans. By focusing their energies on the reproduction of foreign texts, Americans could acquire all the benefits of elite culture without encouraging the development of authors as a specially protected "class of our own citizens." Like the expensive products of the London press, a literary elite tended in its exclusivity to "widen those distinctions which it should be the policy of a republican Government to discourage."[83] One petitioner argued that, rather than representing the nation or policing culture, American writers should devote themselves entirely to the work of adaptation, translation, and popularization. With this shift in aspirations, all knowledge could be treated as general knowledge, and there would be no barrier to its "diffusion . . . over the whole mass."[84] While the *Democratic Review* dismissed this kind of thinking as "literary agrarianism," stressing the sanctity of authorial property within the confines of the nation, its support for a system in which authors' rights expire at the geographic limits of the state can secure American authors' property only at the cost of foreign authors' rights.[85]

Surrendering rights, however, did not necessarily imply lost profits. Alongside their political defense of the culture of reprinting, copyright opponents delivered a spirited rebuttal to the allegation that the reprint trade was responsible for Scott's demise. Confirming that large sums were paid to Scott by American publishers for early copies or "advance sheets" of his novels, these petitions argued that market competition and breadth of circulation were ultimately more valuable to an author than direct control over his text. They insisted not only that Scott was well paid in his lifetime, but that large sums continued to be paid to John Lockhart, Scott's son-in-law, for his multivolume biography, *The Life of Scott* (1837).[86] According to these petitions, the story of Scott's demise was not one of disrupted inheritance, but one of surplus returns produced by the very system Scott's colleagues were so eager to outlaw. While the system of decentralized mass-production required the surrender of foreign authors' property, it was capable of providing enormous profits for authors—albeit indirect ones. Copyright opponents insisted that in Scott's case, the lack of a direct legacy was more than made up by the success of his son-in-law's biography. Although compensation proceeded by way of mediation and deflection, *The Life of Scott* was adequate recompense for the life of Scott.

It is, finally, the presumption of an inexhaustible demand for books that ensures indirect, but hefty returns for authors within the system of reprinting. In countering the copyright advocates' claim that American books were being edged out by their British competitors, the Senate committee report maintained that "Every book that is read makes a market for more even of the same character. Mind, unlike matter, hungers upon that on which it feeds."[87] According to this report, the excessive demand that drove the reprint trade made direct authorial control over texts unnecessary. Within the terms of the republican fantasy, relinquishing ownership produces profits in such extraordinary amounts that the author is bound to be remunerated far in excess of the figure that would represent an adequate return on his labor. In fact, the large sums sent to foreign authors by American publishers take on an idealized character precisely because they are divorced from any notion of readerly indebtedness or just reward for labor. Payments for advance sheets or for the right to produce "authorized" editions smack equally of patronage and entrepreneurship: they are both market-driven and voluntarily made. Reprinting allowed American publishers to invoke the figure of the author-as-proprietor without requiring that they pay him homage. Indeed, at their most extreme, these petitions imagine the British author to be something of an American creation, an otherwise faltering type who is sustained by the fame and fortune generated by American reprints. As one petitioner argued with reference to Scott: "British authors of high repute have been, and are still paid liberally for their works. Competition among American publishers has caused this."[88]

Maintaining Decentralization:
Reprinting and the Syncopation of the National Imaginary

Given the opposition's vigorous defense of the status quo and their success with the American legislature, it is not surprising that the vision of the literary marketplace put forward by the anti-copyright forces should begin to be registered within pro-copyright petitions as a considerable source of panic. If the chief anxiety driving the opposition was a fear of centralized control, the correspondent anxiety among pro-copyright petitioners was a generalized fear of the disruptive social effects of an industry that produced and sold books "without reference to responsible ownership."[89] As the debate progressed, copyright agitators began to depict the unrestricted circulation of reprinted texts as a threat to all forms of textual possession. In a lengthy petition, Nahum Capen characterized the lack of international copyright as a general crime against property, representing the circulation of reprinted texts as the unjust scattering of valuable goods and the domestic text that had outlived its copyright as a form of instant trash: "when the property of authors becomes public property . . . it is absolutely thrown away" (4). Capen's somewhat predictable attack on dissemination finally gives way to an extraordinary construction of reading itself as a radically nonproprietary act: "Books are reprinted on poor paper, [with] small type, and put into binding that rather serves to hide their blurred pages, than to protect fair ones; and thus millions of volumes of standard works are produced and sold, which serve but to weaken the eyes of the people, or to refill the vat of the paper-maker, from which they had been taken but a few months before" (8). Capen's complaint works an important change on the thematics of ephemerality through which Augustans such as Pope and Swift had condemned mass-produced literature, linking it to the instability of a credit economy.[90] For Capen, cheap, standardized texts are somehow *too* substantial, wearing down the reader's body in the process of their consumption, while at the same time managing to escape being fully comprehended or read. This is, finally, a vision of mass-production without consumption, or rather, without a form of consumption that is able to exhaust the mass-produced object. Both the blurred, unreadable pages of the book itself and the perpetually re-filled vat to which the book returns identify the "standard work" with a kind of pure materiality—a materiality that, unlike the thingness of a commodity, actually *prevents* the book from being subject to individual appropriation. This image of the infinitely recirculating, perpetually trans-formed, yet unapprehended text, seems a nightmare version of the magically self-sustaining circulation that copyright opponents claimed would preserve American independence. While anti-copyright petitioners regarded the mass-production and circulation of texts as centrifugal forces capable of liberating the individual from the tyranny of centralized power, Capen sees mass-produced books as the textual precipitate of the social in its most anti-individualistic, radically dispossessing form.

For Capen, circulation-without-possession is most troubling at the point of reception. The widespread availability of cheap reprints threatens the future of both libraries and serious reading: "To say that good books are worthy of more than one reading, and that they are worth preserving would be an almost unpardonable slight to the understanding of our read-ers . . . and still, one would suppose that our whole nation were opposed to these propositions as being yet doubtful or undecided" (8). Despite the *Democratic Review*'s efforts to distinguish its position from "literary agrar-ianism," Capen perceives the threat to property posed by the system of reprinting to be radically leveling.

Other pro-copyright petitioners worried more about the effect of re-printing on book production. According to John Jay, lack of control over literary property "deranges the regularity" and "impairs the prosperity of the book trade" (7), transforming the respectable business of publishing into something more like gambling:

the publisher who reprints a foreign work cannot in advance form certain calculations as to the result of the enterprise. The work being open to all, other publishers may be printing it at the same time; and the more popular the work, the more numerous the editions: so that neither in regard to the required supply, nor the reasonableness of the price, nor the extent of the sales, can he form any estimate with probable certainty. The publication of books under such circumstances becomes a mere speculation, where the risk of loss counterbalances the chance of profit, and which prudent and cautious publishers are apt to shun, as opposed to safe and correct principles of business, and from which men of small capital are driven by the fear of being ruined. (6)

Like Henry Clay's depiction of the vulnerability of the American author, Jay's appeal for authors' rights reflects not confidence in, but anxiety about market culture. For Jay, an unregulated literary marketplace can only look disorderly and inefficient. Citing "a waste of capital in the multiplied editions of the same book" and "the risk attending this business, when it does eventuate in loss" (6), Jay argues for international copyright on the grounds that it would protect American publishers against the excesses of market competition. Where literary property is "open to all," publishers are exposed to dangerous levels of uncertainty, speculation, waste, and risk. Countering the assumption that the decentralization of the literary marketplace worked to prevent concentrations of political and economic power, Jay argues that the manifold uncertainties of an unregulated market produce the opposite effect, chasing out the small entrepreneurs anticopyright forces intended to protect. By way of proof, Jay notes that "the business of reprinting the new and popular books that issue from the English press is to a great extent monopolized by a few large houses whose wealth and power enable them to crush competition" (6).

Jay's warnings about reprint monopolies and the hypermateriality of Capen's vision raise questions that will prove crucial for the defenders of the system of reprinting. How can a model of circulation that preserves and is self-preserving be prevented from agglomerating? Is the suspension of foreign authors' rights sufficient to prevent the consolidation of publishers' power?

The debate over international copyright plays out in parallel one of the central paradoxes of the Jacksonian model of political power, a contradiction inherent to federalism that shaped pivotal struggles over economic development and the legality of chattel slavery: how can the decentralization of power be sustained when it has to be enforced from the center?

In the case of the large-scale republication of popular foreign novels, the fact that a particular text was officially "open to all" reprinters did not prevent consolidation. Acutely aware of the destructiveness of the kind of market Jay described, reprint publishers developed a system of de facto copyright known as "courtesy of the trade" by which a newspaper announcement of the intent to publish a foreign work informally carried the weight of a property claim. While this kind of gentleman's agreement allowed publishers like the Harper Brothers in New York, and Carey, Lea & Blanchard and T. B. Peterson & Brothers in Philadelphia to invest considerable sums in stereotyped editions of foreign authors' collected works—publishing schemes that often went uncontested by rival printers—"courtesy of the trade" proved unenforceable both in practice and in courts of law. Even when control over the market for a particular reprint was seemingly secured by public declaration and by payments to the author for early proof sheets of his work, delays in the delivery of these sheets, disputes over the priority of claims, and upstart competitors left even powerful reprint houses battling to corner the market for a particular title.[91] As the Harper Brothers explained in a letter to Edward Lytton Bulwer, whose historical novel *Rienzi* (1836) had been reprinted by a rival publisher, neither the intensive capitalization of the larger houses, nor their determination to protect their investments in "uniform editions" of a particular author's work could rule out losses sustained by the need to compete with publishers who preempted them in getting a book to market: "although we have said, and truly, that we could prevent the priority from being any great advantage to any other publisher, we have not said and do not say, that we should not be the losers by the operation."[92] Terry Mulcaire has persuasively argued that the reprint industry's reliance on high volume sales at low prices favored publishing houses with large capital reserves. According to Mulcaire, investments in high-speed presses and in distribution networks enabled the larger houses to survive cut-throat competition and economic depression "while smaller establishments failed in bunches."[93] And yet their control over the market for reprinted books was always more precarious than the scale of their operations would suggest.

Moreover, the system that anti-copyright petitioners sought to protect extended further than the highly visible and controversial reprints of foreign novels that peaked in popularity in the early 1840s.[94] In refusing to extend property rights to foreign authors, Congress protected not only the domestic market for cheap reprints of popular fiction, but also a host of miscellanies, pamphlets, magazines, and newspapers that relied on uncopyrighted texts for much of their material. The system of reprinting was a cross-media phenomenon, in which sentimental tales that were first published in expensively bound gift books reappeared as filler in local newspapers; in which elite British magazines were reprinted in their entirety and mined for essays that were reassembled into regionally published eclectic magazines; and in which evangelical tracts, works of popular science, medical, legal, agricultural, and school texts were freely excerpted, imitated, plagiarized, and reissued. If, in proposing an international copyright law, British authors and publishers chiefly intended to bring order to the transatlantic book trade, they encountered opposition from American publishers who were heavily invested in blurring the lines between books, pamphlets, magazines, and newspapers.

Finally, those defending the system of reprinting were ultimately more concerned with the general availability of texts for republication than they were with the incipient concentration of the reprint trade in New York and Philadelphia. What was important was that a wide range of printed matter remain "open to all"—not only the products of the foreign press, but also magazine writing by American authors, which by custom circulated without copyright protection, as well as government publications, lectures and addresses, and the many genres of newspaper writing, such as court reports, prices current, political commentary, and fugitive poetry, which, by virtue of their appearance in a newspaper, were considered public property by law.[95]

The system of reprinting not only enabled small entrepreneurs to imagine a market for printed goods that would operate without centralized capital or control, it also offered a model of national identity that was particularly congenial to advocates of a loose federal compact, providing evidence of the noncoercive coexistence of national unity and local autonomy. Benedict Anderson has famously argued that the novel and the newspaper were crucial to the production of "that remarkable confidence of community in anonymity which is the hallmark of modern nations."[96] According to Anderson, formal aspects of these mass-produced texts, such as the novel's omniscient narrator and the arbitrary juxtaposition of stories on the newspaper page were instrumental in establishing the consciousness of "steady, anonymous, simultaneous activity" among strangers which is "a precise analogue of the idea of a nation" (26). The modern newspaper also allows for reassuring performances of community-in-anonymity through the spectacle of its simultaneous consumption: "the newspaper reader, observing exact replicas of his own paper being consumed by his subway, barbershop, or residential neighbours, is continually reassured that the imagined world is visibly rooted in everyday life" (35–36).

Adapting Anderson's general insight to the characteristic print forms of antebellum American culture, I would argue that the prominence of reprinted texts in newspapers, literary weeklies, monthly magazines, and periodical miscellanies of all kinds created a sense of near-simultaneity that was crucial to the imagination of the federal form of the nation. Reliance on reprinting was most visible in the cheapest periodicals, declining in frequency as the reader moved from daily and weekly papers to general interest monthlies, to magazines with elite pretensions that conspicuously advertised their publication of original productions. And yet reprinting suffused the antebellum print environment. For instance, both mass-produced urban dailies and small-scale rural weekly papers relied for their news on a system of newspaper exchanges made possible by a law that allowed newspapers sent between printers to travel free of postage through the mails. With little or no provision for reporting outside their own localities, antebellum newspapers were a tissue of items copied from other print authorities, giving credit to the paper of origin at the head of most of the reprinted articles. Alongside the sense of simultaneity produced by the paper's graphic order and its assumption of calendrical coincidence, then, were constant reminders of the complex relays by which information was gathered from and disseminated to scattered commercial and cultural centers. Reprinting allowed for the national circulation of the same, but each iteration marked the distinctiveness of the regional or the local. Although large-circulation, partisan papers headquartered in Washington and in state capitals were able to establish reliable networks of exchange, elevating local affairs to national prominence and getting out the party line to the hinterlands, the selection of items for reprinting ultimately depended on local editors. Given the proliferation of American newspapers, which by 1838 were thought to number between 1300 and 1500, and antebellum printers' rich exploitation of the system of exchange (in 1843 the post office estimated that publishers received on average 364 exchanges per month) the distribution of news could be neither enforced nor supervised by the center.[97] The prominence of reprinting in antebellum newspapers offered a syncopation of the national imaginary that fortified the principles of a states'-rights federalism, providing both the homogeneity crucial to a sense of national belonging and constant reassurances of a saving heterogeneity. Antebellum Americans may have held their news and its mode of presentation in common, but the spectacle of the consumption of exact replicas extended no further than the local.

Similarly, the traffic in essays, tales, and poems copied from British and American periodicals and reassembled into literary weeklies and monthlies served as a constant reminder of the disjointed nature of American literary culture, its suspension between and among distant publishing centers that competed with each other for cultural authority. Though perceived by antebellum Whigs and twentieth-century literary critics chiefly as an obstacle to the development of a national culture, the system of reprinting embodied a central tenet of Jacksonian political philosophy—the commitment to the decentralization of power as the mark of national difference. In establishing a public sphere based on the general accessibility of printed texts but defined by the stutter of locally interrupted circulation, and in its disaggregating response to the challenges posed by economic development, the system of reprinting represents the Jacksonian form of national culture.

3

Circulating Media:
Charles Dickens, Reprinting,
and the Dislocation of American Culture

THE HISTORY OF AMERICAN RESISTANCE to international copyright illustrates the power of the figure of the author to simplify and distort the politics of print. As I have argued, what from the perspective of an author-centered literary culture looks like an unconscionable violation of authors' rights was understood in the antebellum period as a struggle between competing visions of a rapidly expanding marketplace. Although an international copyright law was repeatedly invoked as indispensable to the development of a national culture, the production and circulation of printed texts flourished in the absence of such a law; what was at stake was not the existence but the definition of national culture. The argument that a universal application of the principle of authors' rights would stabilize the volatile trade in books was decisively turned back by publishers and tradesmen who were less concerned with regulation than with the need to preserve decentralization across the market for printed goods.

Literary critics have generally assumed that the expansion of print culture coincided with and reinforced the emergence of commercial nationalism, but debates over literary property suggest instead that the market for print in the 1830s and '40s was shaped by the Jacksonian resistance to centralized development. Andrew Jackson was swept into office on a wave of populist suspicion of the elite abuse of political power and the widespread perception that northern capitalists reaped disproportionate benefits from the extension of market culture. His controversial refusal to recharter the national bank and his commitment to the restraint of credit were a direct assault on the policies of John Quincy Adams and Henry Clay, who promoted integrated plans of national development that relied on centralized finance and oversight. Encouraging economic growth while preventing the consolidation of capital was an explicit aim of Jacksonian democrats, but a long-standing skepticism about the pursuit of development on a national scale is suggested by the refusal of presidents from Madison to Polk to provide federal funding for a national transportation system. The rapid growth of market culture raised intractable questions about the terms of Union and about the nature and legitimacy of federal authority. Antebellum debates over print culture, like those concerning internal improvements and the national bank, were driven by the need for means and modes of circulation that could resist being coopted by a central power.

In this chapter, I will examine Charles Dickens's 1842 tour of the United States and the narratives he published in its wake in order to trace some of the contours and consequences of the decentralized literary marketplace. Dickens's visit not only brought the popular author into close contact with his far-flung American readers, it also brought into sharp relief critical differences between English and American systems of publishing. The culture of reprinting was so alien to Dickens that he had difficulty comprehending why his vocal support for international copyright posed a serious threat to his literary reception. Nevertheless, as I will argue, the shape of Dickens's incomprehension speaks eloquently about what he and we, who are equally estranged from this culture, can neither value nor perceive.

If Dickens's accounts of his travels bear witness to the problematic decentralization of American culture chiefly in the form of violated expectations, American reprints of Dickens's texts will enable us to trace some of the ways in which debates over national credit, internal improvements, and literary property are reciprocally imagined and cross-referred. These reprints will also enable us to mark the imbrication of a decentralized print culture with the protection of slavery. Long before the question of the legitimacy of national law was crystallized by the problematic legal status of the fugitive slave, the debate over slavery was cast as a question of circulation. Not only was the national distribution of texts that discussed slavery regarded by slaveholding communities as a significant threat to their safety, the southern interdiction of abolitionist pamphlets was countenanced and reinforced by a Jacksonian understanding of the limits of federal power.[1] Both the opposition to international copyright and the defense of slavery relied on a weak central government's deference to local authority. In his American narratives, Dickens explicitly links a depraved indifference to slavery to the licentiousness of the American press. The history of the unauthorized reprinting of Dickens's texts will enable us to weigh his insights into the dangers of uncontrolled circulation against American fears about centralized power and against reprint publishers' confidence in the meliorative effect of common property in Dickens.

Property in Dickens: The 1842 Tour

In September 1841, exhausted from the pressures of serial publication, Charles Dickens signed a contract with his publishers that gave him fourteen months' respite from writing in exchange for agreeing to commence a new work in monthly numbers in November of the following year. In the interim he would receive a monthly stipend as an advance on royalties for the novel he had promised and a substantial loan drawn against the profits of a book he would write on his American travels. Logically speaking, then, Dickens's travel narrative precedes and sponsors his American tour. Despite his repeated and no doubt genuine assertion that he traveled to the United States to see "the Republic of [his] imagination,"[2] Dickens is throughout this tour an author, delightedly exclaiming in a letter to John Forster soon after he arrived: "I have a book, already."[3] The problem of the form, format, and mode of distribution of popular literature is with Dickens from the very beginning of his American tour.[4]

Dickens comes to North America as an observer of character and customs, but soon discovers that he is "the observed of all observers."[5] While he initially finds this position thrilling—in a typical moment of grandiosity and expansion, he writes to Forster: "I wish you could have seen the crowds cheering the Inimitable in the streets"[6]—he is quickly discomfited by his extreme lack of privacy. Dickens becomes a traveling spectacle, a mobile figure of authorship. Crowds throng the streets wherever he goes; he is overwhelmed with invitations to public and private functions in his honor. His American secretary records that within days of his arrival, Dickens could be found eating breakfast while dictating replies to an already voluminous correspondence even as a sculptor modeled his bust, running back and forth to measure his head with calipers. While Dickens is still in Boston, the papers are full of plans for a "Boz Ball" and public dinner in New York complete with lavish decorations, fulsome speeches by statesmen and literati, and tableaux vivants illustrating familiar passages from his works.[7]

Some hint of what will go wrong for Dickens is evident from the first official welcome dinner in Boston where his presumptive role as an observer of the new world is met by a series of speeches that invoke the breadth of his books' circulation, Dickens's *already* thorough penetration of American culture and consciousness. Josiah Quincy waxes typically eloquent:

In the empty schoolroom, the boy at his evening task has dropped his grammar, that he may roam with Oliver or Nell. The traveller has forgotten the fumes of the crowded steamboat, and is far off with our guest, among the green valleys and hoary hills of old England. The trapper beyond the Rocky Mountains has left his lonely tent, and is unroofing the houses in London with the more than Mephistopheles at my elbow.[8]

Quincy suggests that Dickens will discover not a society waiting for his appraisal, but a complex reciprocal gaze, a people prepossessed by Dickens to the extent that they no longer seem to inhabit the landscape.

The real trouble comes—and with it, an intensification of negative publicity that makes Dickens extremely uncomfortable—after the public dinner in Hartford at which, for the second time, he speaks up in favor of international copyright. It is clear from his letters that Dickens thought he was speaking nobly and disinterestedly on behalf of British and American authors, speaking as the momentarily empowered representative of a group with common interests. Americans, however, had heralded Dickens's arrival as proof of the power and honor of popular affection. "The occasion that calls us together is almost unprecedented in the annals of literature," Quincy opined, "A young man has crossed the ocean with no hereditary title, no military laurels, no princely fortune, and yet his approach is hailed with pleasure by every age and condition and on his arrival he is welcomed as a long-known and trusted friend."[9] In appealing for payments to foreign authors, Dickens appeared to discount the value of his American reception, in the words of one reviewer, "urging upon those assembled to do honor to his *genius*, to look after his *purse* also."[10] He also threatened rhetorically to exclude the very readers whose enthusiasm had justified these ostentatious (and frequently exclusive) celebrations. As Quincy took care to note, Dickens had captivated Americans across differences of "age and condition." He had not simply included the "humble and oppressed" in his novels as objects of sympathy; cheap reprints of his serialized fiction had enabled them to be drawn into the orbit of literary culture as actual or potential readers. A more savvy Dickens might have been warned off his course by a toast directly following his Hartford speech, a toast that one reporter ridiculed, but made a point of marking as untutored speech:

"[Mr. Miles] commenced with the angels, approximated to the patriarchs, floundered through Republican resolutions, and ended in 'pop'lar literature,' which . . . could not be 'monopolated' by any aristocracy."[11] But Dickens seems not to have understood that his popularity in America was in part a function of the lack of international copyright, the system of reprinting he continued publicly to attack.[12]

Dickens's importance to antebellum American thinking about literary property is clear from how quickly the subject of debate—the question of the need for international copyright—gets transformed into the question of what Dickens was doing in speaking about it. Dickens can't simply voice an opinion, he exemplifies the problem of which he speaks. Dickens characteristically responds to negative newspaper publicity by insisting that he had not *intended* to speak on international copyright, thereby delivering himself from the charge of self-interest.[13] The American press, however, reads Dickens's assertions that he spoke only out of solidarity with other gentleman authors as proof that he was both mercenary and plotting—that he came not voluntarily, to be celebrated by his readers, but as a national emissary on behalf of British trade. This theory gains considerable momentum as Dickens's trip wends south toward Washington, where the last of Henry Clay's international copyright bills is under consideration.[14]

Extremely troubled by "assertions that [he] was no gentleman, but a mercenary scoundrel,"[15] Dickens tries to stage his disinterestedness, placing supportive letters and a pro-copyright petition signed by British authors in American newspapers and magazines, and going out of his way to give the impression that these testimonials have been volunteered and not solicited.[16] Dickens hoped that a display of solidarity from other gentleman authors would insulate him from allegations of unworthy motives, but his efforts to exonerate himself only exacerbate the situation. The publication of these letters looks to many Americans like collusion, further proof that Dickens is the hired agent of British authors and publishers.[17] The newspaper controversy repeatedly grounds to a halt at this impasse of mutual suspicion: Dickens's aristocratic use of gentlemanly anonymity to conceal networks of trade is met by a democratic notion of authorship as subjection to circulation—the American press's insistence that authors are and should be a kind of common property.

The pressure that such a model of authorship places on an author's singular, if circulating, body is apparent from Dickens's often comical letters to friends describing American attempts to parcel him out for distribution:

landing from a steamboat in New York, he is greeted by "some twenty or thirty people, screwing small dabs of fur out of the back of [his] costly great coat";[18] he becomes afraid to get his hair cut "lest the barber (bribed by admirers) should clip it all off for presents."[19] As his tour progresses, however, Dickens becomes increasingly concerned by his inability to control his public appearances, both in person and in print. Despite the fact that after his New York experience, he had firmly declined all invitations to public dinners and receptions, Dickens is manipulated into holding a "levee" by a group of Philadelphia tradesmen who feared that "the *soi disant* magnates" of the city would "monopolize" his visit. Complaining that access to Dickens had become the "*exclusive property* of a self-delegated clique," they forced him to hold a reception in his hotel room by publishing an announcement in the newspaper, transforming a private courtesy into a public invitation.[20] Dickens's awareness of his vulnerability to a mass-public, one whose relation to him and his writing is mediated chiefly or only by the press, causes a shift in his critique of the culture of reprinting. Moving beyond his outrage at the injustice of payments never made, Dickens expresses astonishment and revulsion at the violence done to his texts, and by extension, to himself, when his writing is circulated in newspapers. In a letter to Henry Brougham, he complains that a foreign writer "not only gets nothing for his labors, though they are diffused all over this enormous Continent, but cannot even choose his company. Any wretched halfpenny newspaper can print him at its pleasure—place him side by side with productions which disgust his common sense."[21] Writing to his brother-in-law while awaiting response to the British authors' published letters of support, Dickens is a good deal more explicit about the way in which newspaper reprinting disrupts his sense of social order:

Is it not a horrible thing that scoundrel-booksellers should grow rich here from publishing books, the authors of which do not reap one farthing from their issue, by scores of thousands? And that every vile, blackguard, and detestable newspaper,—so filthy and so bestial that no honest man would admit one into his house, for a water-closet door-mat—should be able to publish those same writings, side by side, cheek by jowl, with the coarsest and most obscene companions, with which they *must* become connected in course of time, in people's minds? Is it tolerable that besides being robbed and rifled, an author should be *forced* to appear in any form—in any vulgar dress—in any atrocious company—that he should have no choice of his audience—no controul [sic] over his own distorted text?[22]

To be subject to reprinting is to be forced into such proximity with the coarse and the obscene that one could easily be mistaken for them ("*forced* to appear" in such "vulgar dress"). Dickens is appalled at a print culture that fails to enforce reliable genre and class distinctions, and at the collapse of the structures of mediation that hold authors at a safe remove from the distribution and reception of their work. Rather than relieving him of agency, Dickens's lack of control over his texts makes him feel personally accountable for their mode of circulation.

In oscillating between scatology and self-righteousness, expressing disgust at and assuming excessive responsibility for the newspaper circulation of his texts, Dickens's letter exemplifies the crisis of agency brought about by unauthorized reprinting. Unable to find his own authority reflected in and buttressed by a hierarchically organized publishing industry, Dickens exaggerates the wealth and power of the "scoundrel-booksellers" and retrospectively projects greater command over his English readers than he actually possesses: does Chapman & Hall's proprietary control over the price and issue of his editions actually give him "choice" over his audience in England? If the figure of the author-as-proprietor provides a useful fiction behind which publishers can consolidate power, it also shields writers from their subjection to the market by exaggerating their sense of agency. The spectacle of Dickens's lack of control over the circulation of his texts in America causes him to fantasize about a mode of relation to his writing and his readers that was never wholly within his grasp.[23] During his travels, Dickens is repeatedly disarmed by his unmediated exposure to the means by which his fiction is popularly distributed. Thus, while he is happy to accept decorous praise at a formal reception from a representative group of his working-class readers,[24] he is shocked at the temerity of an itinerant bookseller who visits him in his rooms and tries to bully him into offering financial assistance on the grounds that he was the first to sell Dickens's books in New York and thus had materially contributed to his renown.[25] A similar astonishment at authors' intimate subjection to the means of distribution is apparent in Dickens's account of his initial landing in Boston when what he takes to be newsboys, leaping on board the boat in an attempt to sell him a paper, turn out to be editors competing to introduce themselves and to circulate news of his arrival.[26]

One index of the stubbornness of the stalemate between the figure of the author as wholly removed from or wholly absorbed by trade is that Dickens's account of his trip in his travel narrative, *American Notes for General Circulation* (1842), deletes all reference to his literary reception — indeed, nearly all reference to the literary itself. A hostile *Blackwood's* reviewer tellingly derided the book as "the play of Hamlet with the character of Hamlet omitted," arguing that Dickens's literary fame had shielded him from "the men and manners of America." Had Dickens desired to be the observer instead of the observed, the reviewer argued, he needed to have traveled incognito; *American Notes* is ultimately little more than the story of a "perpetual and very unpleasant locomotion."[27]

Indeed, one might read the narrative itself as structured by a series of complex displacements: the displacement of the subject of international copyright from its pages; the elimination of the literary itself from *American Notes*, as if Dickens had actually traveled as the anonymous observer that *Blackwood's* chided him for not having been; the elimination of the chapter "Introductory and Necessary to be Read," which explains and attempts to justify this omission;[28] the displacement of the treatment of slavery and the licentiousness of the press—the "peculiar institutions" that Dickens represents as causes of and analogues for his sense of dispossession—from the narrative proper so that they appear as objects of critique outside the framework of the voyage; and, finally, the obsessive repetition/displacement of *American Notes* into the serialized novel *Martin Chuzzlewit*.

Such displacements pose a problem for critics seeking to read *American Notes* in the context of Dickens's tour and the dispute over authorship and literary property that it raised. The lack of direct reference in the narrative to controversial public events that Dickens described in his letters as deeply disturbing[29] causes one to see their ramifications everywhere. For example, Dickens's discomfort at having become a public spectacle seems powerfully to shape his representation of the Perkins Institute for the Blind as a kind of paradise of unselfconsciousness. In Dickens's account, the blind children's inability to return his gaze protects them from invasions of the public eye and from the hypocrisy of self-concealment (81). Dickens's fascination with the moral advantages of disruptions to the exchange of gazes, and his guilty pleasure in his powers of sight (80, 94) suggest relief at the restoration of a stable, hierarchical relation between observer and observed. Likewise, Dickens's revulsion at the compulsory publicity of travel in steamboats and canal boats seems a social correlative of his disgust at the newspaper circulation of his fiction. Dickens's detailed descriptions of his physical discomfort in overcrowded public spaces and his struggle to extricate himself from communal rites such as tobacco spitting and the use of "a public comb and hairbrush" (194) can be read as comic elaborations of his more troubling experience of popular print culture as uncontrolled proximity to the vulgar. Even Dickens's critique of the Solitary System of prison discipline seems inflected by his sense of isolation amid the publicity of his controversial tour. For Dickens, the Solitary System is evidence of the cruelty of a culture of unrelieved publicity, a culture that finds its inverse and culmination in the complete withholding of society from its felons. In *American Notes*, Dickens's sympathetic conjuring of a new prisoner's experience of solitary confinement focuses not on the painful absence of society but on the disturbing presence of companions he can imagine but cannot see. For Dickens, the horror of solitary confinement lies in the illegibility of one's surroundings; his hypothetical prisoner is tormented by visions of neighboring inmates "whose hidden features torture him to death" (154). Dickens's depiction of an agonizing desire for society that will not be fulfilled seems self-reflexive, both in its emphasis on the crushing power of unsatisfied visions and in its sidelong acknowledgment of the presence of others who resist the powers of his imagination.

The trouble with such readings, however, is that they make sense of *American Notes* in piecemeal fashion, unifying a problematically disjointed and episodic text by reference to an absent and omnipresent subject. In transposing Dickens's alienating experience of American culture into the thematic register of his text, we lose track of the ways in which his experience deforms the narrative itself, compensating for the strangeness of the text by assembling scattered evidence of authorial affect. From this perspective, the clash between cultures leaves its mark in the deepening of authorial consciousness; criticism loses hold of the dislocating power of cultural difference as it passes through the figure of the sadder but wiser author.

Similar problems attend critics' attempts to reclaim *American Notes* and Dickens's American tour by identifying them as pivot points for a consequential shift in his career. Alexander Welsh, for example, argues that Dickens's experience of seeing his critique of pirate publishers' commercial self-centeredness return as a characterization of his own motives is the ground of his brilliant depictions of hypocrisy in the later novels.[30] While Welsh offers a convincing account of *Martin Chuzzlewit* as a grab bag of authorial projections, he regards the novel as a space of mastery, a site in which Dickens satirically, melodramatically, and self-incriminatingly transforms his American experience. However, the more we value Dickens's tour, his narrative, and his novel as catalysts for or evidence of authorial metamorphosis, the more distant Dickens's crisis of authorial agency becomes. Translating the unsettling experience of cultural difference into moral fable and Dickens's texts into allegories of authorship, we lose the ability to see how they register aspects of American culture that Dickens cannot master. In order to extract *American Notes* from this interpretive trajectory, I will reapproach Dickens's narrative through the responses of American publishers. The American reprints of *American Notes* not only make prominent what Dickens pushes to the margins of his text, reengaging him in a debate that he has sidestepped and suppressed; they provide a vocabulary for describing what lies beyond Dickens's reach.

National Debt and National Identity: The American Circulation of *American Notes for General Circulation*

It was clear to both Dickens and his American readers that his title, *American Notes for General Circulation*, was intended as a critique of pirate publishers. Dickens initially planned a more explicit attack, withdrawing at the last minute an epigraph taken from the *Old Bailey Report*: "In a reply to a question from the bench, the Solicitor of the Bank observed, that this kind of note circulated most extensively, in those parts of the world where they were stolen and forged."[31] Even without the epigraph, however, Dickens's title links the informality of his observations to his lack of control over their mass-production and reception, hinting at something withheld from the reader (uncensored notes for private circulation?), and condemning the inevitable American piracy of his work by associating it with trade in the spurious currency of defaulting state and local banks.

If Dickens hoped that, failing to control the circulation of his text, he might still dictate how that circulation was perceived, equating successful dissemination with theft and forgery, he underestimated the resourcefulness of American publishers such as the Harper Brothers, who simply changed the running title to "Notes on America" when they reprinted it, disabling Dickens's pun.[32] The Harper edition subtly restores a kind of accountability to Dickens, placing him back in the position of authoritative observer that his studied informality and targeting of the mass press would seem to avoid. The *New World* went further, taking advantage of popular interest in Dickens's narrative to append "An Appeal to the Reading Public" defending its "plan of cheap publications," and questioning the legal basis for support of international copyright. Noting that the English parliament had recently, "by a considerable majority, refused to extend [domestic] copyright to sixty years, on the explicit ground that such a right, without doing much good to an author's descendants and assigns, would do a great wrong to the community by keeping up the price of intellectual productions," the *New World* accused supporters of international copyright of trying to annex the American market to the British market, "creating an expense here which the British legislators refused to create even for a future generation."[33] These are, however, retorts to charges that are never explicitly made within Dickens's narrative, which studiously avoids mention of international copyright. The American reprinters supplement but cannot complete Dickens's text. Nevertheless, the "Appeal to the Reading Public" makes explicit the critique that is built into the physical form of the American editions. The multiple imprints, small type, narrow margins, and low prices of these pirated texts, which sell for $12\frac{1}{2}$ to 25 cents each (and as little as 10 cents per copy if bought in bulk) stand as a reproach to the extravagance of the London press, which produced a single edition of *American Notes* in two volumes of over 300 pages each, and sold it for 21 shillings, 40 times the price of the cheapest American reprint.[34]

The eloquence of pirate publishers' reframing of Dickens's narrative in terms of the very questions that his text would silence is most apparent in the edition published by *Brother Jonathan*, the *New World*'s rival in reprinting foreign novels as newspaper "extras." As a way of advertising their low prices and "respectfully" soliciting bulk orders "from the country," *Brother Jonathan* appended a facsimile $50.00 note to Dickens's text (Figure 11). With extraordinary condensation, *Brother Jonathan* cuts to the heart of the problem that plagued Dickens on his tour and vexed politicians trying to set monetary policy in the wake of Jackson's veto of the charter of the second National Bank: does circulation precede and generate value, or follow and dissipate it? Is the trade in unauthorized books and inauthentic bank notes fatal to or necessary for the expansion of culture and commerce? The editors of *Brother Jonathan* enjoy a joke at the author's expense—they are indeed making money out of Charles Dickens—and yet they also assert that it is the pirate press that has put Dickens into circulation in the first place.

This spurious "American note" offers a more serious challenge to Dickens's representation of the new republic than might at first appear. Had the editors of *Brother Jonathan* merely wanted to respond in kind to Dickens's condescending title or to his description of the American character as marred by the "love of 'smart' dealing . . . [gilding] over many a swindle and gross breach of trust" (286), they might have appended a

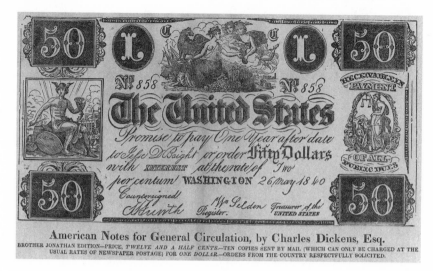

Figure 11. "American Notes for General Circulation, by Charles Dickens, Esq.,"
American Notes for General Circulation (1842). Courtesy, Beinecke Rare Book and
Manuscript Library, Yale University.

copy of a suspicious or clearly inauthentic note—either one drawn on
the now-defunct Bank of the United States, or one of the "wildcat" notes
that flourished in the wake of its dismantling.[35] Instead, the editors of
Brother Jonathan reproduce a facsimile of an interest-bearing treasury note,
an instrument of Jacksonian monetary policy that is neither in "general
circulation" nor complicit with the gross breaches of trust to which Dickens alludes in his narrative: the collapse of the national bank and the repudiation by the states of foreign debts that had been incurred to promote
ambitious and unprofitable schemes of internal improvement.[36] Rather
than flaunting Britons' lack of control over their literary and financial investments, *Brother Jonathan* responds to Dickens's characterization of the
fraudulence of American circulating media with a powerful counterexam-
ple, a representation of Jacksonian caution in dealing with the problem of
national debt.

As *Brother Jonathan*'s illustration should remind us, following Jackson's successful attack on the Bank of the United States, there was no such
thing as an American note. Fiat paper money or bills of credit issued by
local and state-chartered banks had circulated since the Revolution, but

only those notes issued by the federally chartered Bank of the United States, which had branches throughout the Union, approached "general circulation" and representative status. However, Jackson's firm opposition to the recharter of the bank, articulated as part of a principled stance "against all new grants of monopolies and exclusive privileges, against any prostitution of our Government to the advancement of the few at the expense of the many,"[37] produced a shift in the structure of American banking. Concerned about the concentration in private hands of the power to contract or expand the money supply, and about the use of such power to influence elections, Jackson not only blocked the renewal of the bank's charter, he forced the Secretary of the Treasury to remove the federal deposits that underwrote its lending. Unable to get Congressional approval for an independent treasury, which would separate public funds entirely from privately owned institutions, Jackson settled for placing federal deposits in a series of state banks that promised to curb promiscuous lending. While it was by no means clear in 1842 whether Jackson's forced decentralization of the banking industry had halted or accelerated the extension of risky credit, his anti-monopolistic, bank-wary approach to public assets and the public debt was reflected in the periodic issue of interest-bearing treasury notes like the one represented by *Brother Jonathan*.

As Richard Timberlake explains, interest-bearing treasury notes were designed to limit the monetary impact of short-term federal debt. Issued in small quantities "to meet unforseen demands on the Treasury," these notes hovered somewhere in between money and investments: "the high denominations and interest-bearing features, plus the fact that they were receivable for government dues and payments, made them especially attractive to banks who used them as high-powered reserves for the expansion of their own notes and deposits, and as clearing media for adverse balances with other banks."[38] *Brother Jonathan* responds to Dickens's attack on American publishing and American credit by reproducing the closest thing, amid a clamor for a total return to specie, to a representative Jacksonian paper currency, a circulating medium instinct with radical democratic values. The choice of the treasury note resonates with a defense of reprint culture as well as a defense of the Jacksonian economy: this is an American note that is legal tender not for private transactions, but for "Payment of all Public Dues"; it is a vehicle not for wildcat speculation, but for investment—its modest rate of return is limited to a period of time which is inscribed upon its face; and it is a financial instrument designed not to maximize individual profit but to stabilize a system that relied on the dispersal of assets (and liabilities) to counter the "concentration of power in the hands of a few men irresponsible to the people."[39]

Brother Jonathan's parody banknote returns us to a set of questions that are raised, if not explicitly articulated, by Dickens's *American Notes*: how can one represent the progress of a nation in the grips of a states'-rights federalism, a nation whose policies and institutions are arrayed as much against as in concert with the forces of consolidation and development? How can a political, economic, and social order be imagined to cohere when the polity is riven by sectional differences, dislocated by geographical expansion, and officially committed to maintaining cultural and economic decentralization? How can one represent the ghostly force of a strategically weak central government, Jackson's ideally invisible state which "[makes] itself felt, not in its power, but in its beneficence; not in its control, but in its protection; not in binding the States more closely to the center, but leaving each to move unobstructed in its proper orbit"?[40] *Brother Jonathan*'s treasury note does a remarkably good job of representing "The United States" in one of the few forms that a strict constructionist reading of the limits of federal powers would permit.[41]

Though unconstrained by Jacksonian ideology, Dickens seems unable to recognize the ways in which it has structured the society he depicts. Although in *American Notes*, Dickens calls attention to a number of institutional and cultural differences between Great Britain and the United States, praising, for example, the American state's involvement in charitable reform (78) and somewhat irritably recounting the social freedoms exercised by newly enfranchised white workingmen (162, 171, 290), the dislocating force of economic decentralization is primarily visible in the narrative's formal failures, Dickens's unsatisfying struggle to find a way to bring the nation into focus.

Representing Decentralization: The Narrative Structure of *American Notes*

The narrative disorderliness of *American Notes* is a sure sign of Dickens's discomfort with his task. Its episodic structure, the surprisingly long passages interpolated from other sources, and the narrator's uneasy, shifting modes of address to the reader all suggest Dickens's difficulty in establishing a stable perspective from which to describe what he has seen. Dickens tries out a number of solutions to the problem of narrative structure, oscillating between sympathetic proximity to and authoritative distance from his subjects. For instance, he enhances the gravity of his account of the Perkins Asylum by incorporating two long, unidentified passages from Samuel Gridley Howe's "Education of Laura Bridgman" (82–90, 92–94). Resuming first-person narration for two short chapters, Dickens suddenly swerves to address the reader directly as a way of unifying a chaotic walk through the city of New York: "Shall we sit down in an upper floor of the Carlton House Hotel . . . and when we are tired of looking down upon the life below, sally forth arm-in-arm, and mingle with the stream?" (128).[42] Seemingly at a loss for ways to propel his story forward, Dickens inserts section breaks to entertain new topics (94, 103, 140), finally falling back on the itinerary itself as his central structuring device. Unlike Alexis de Tocqueville's *Democracy in America* (1835), which is organized by categories of political analysis, Harriet Martineau's *Society in America* (1838), which proceeds topically, or Captain Marryat's *Diary in America* (1839), which is organized chronologically by destination, *American Notes*'s destination-oriented organizational scheme begins to be confounded with and taken over by modes of transportation. Whether because constant travel provides a figure for his restlessness, or because it releases him from paying sustained attention to any one object, the majority of the narrative after Dickens's visit to New York and his description of the Philadelphia prison system takes place while he is in transit. *American Notes* pays extraordinarily close attention to transportation, not only registering Dickens's revulsion at the forms of publicity that were enforced by American means of conveyance, but repeatedly inscribing the awkwardness of the transition from rail to road, to ferry, to steamer, to horse cart, to canal boat, to another steamboat, and another, and so forth. Even the frequently admired and reprinted set-pieces of the narrative, such as "The Bright-Eyed Little Woman and Her Baby," a sentimental tale of paternity restored, or the low minstrel comedy of "The Black Driver," take place in the interstices of travel as Dickens fills up periods of obstruction and delay with self-contained sketches.

In his conclusion, Dickens turns to the figure of narrative-as-vehicle to absolve himself of the responsibility to have offered a more sustained analysis: "There are many passages in this book, where I have been at some pains to resist the temptation of troubling my readers with my own deductions and conclusions: preferring that they should judge for themselves, from such premises as I have laid before them. My only object in the outset, was, to carry them with me faithfully wheresoever I went: and that task I have discharged" (284–85). Here Dickens tries to make a virtue of his indecision, asserting a fidelity to his itinerary and not to his subjects, and proposing that his obligations to the reader are satisfied by a serial account of his experiences. And yet another kind of polemic manages to inscribe itself through this very seriality, what *Blackwood's* referred to as Dickens's "perpetual and unpleasant locomotion" across a disarticulated landscape. Unlike his reprinted novels which benefited from multiple and dispersed points of origin, Dickens depended for his travel on disconnected and inadequate transportation networks, networks whose failure to extend across state and local lines reflected the radical democratic refusal to provide federal funding for internal improvements. Dickens's attempt to circulate among the Americans was subject to the system of haphazardly linked localities that a strong central bank and a program of federal borrowing were supposed to remedy. Dickens's narrative follows the course of his travels south and west along the "great lines of Internal Improvement" (129), proceeding according to a plan mapped out for him by no less than the architect of the American System, Henry Clay.[43] And yet with each awkward transition between modes of transportation, with each improvised connection between developed but discontinuous canals, roads, and rails, Dickens inadvertently inscribes the disaggregating power of Jacksonian democracy.

The challenge that decentralization poses for a narrative that aims to describe the nation is reflected not only in the relentless seriality of Dickens's account, but also in his frequently reiterated complaints about the repetitive nature of the sights that he sees. Despite Dickens's near-constant dislocation, his trip doesn't seem to get him anywhere. In every town he visits, he is taken to see courts of law, model schools and prisons, and the workings of the local legislature, but "by dint of constant repetition" he loses interest in "constitutional sights" (181). For Dickens, these multiple and dispersed examples of self-government and self-improvement are insufficiently differentiated; the uncanny sameness of widely separated American localities begins to defeat his powers of description. At times, Dickens's very will to narrate buckles under the pressure of repetition, as when he writes grudgingly of a steamboat that transported him from Louisville to St. Louis: "The arrangements of the boat were like those of the Messenger, and the passengers were of the same order of people. We fed at the same times, on the same kind of viands, in the same dull manner, and with the same observances" (214). Dickens's mechanical prose makes it difficult to tell whether the dullness is in his surroundings or in his reporting. At the furthest point of his trip west, Dickens finally manages to stage his disappointment, finding a figure for the fruitless repetition of his journey in his "Jaunt to the Looking-glass Prairie and Back" (220). Prepared for a unique and sublime experience, Dickens arrives at the prairie after arduous traveling only to discover mere lateral extension of the same, a looking-glass devoid of reflection: "Great as the picture was, its very flatness and extent, which left nothing to the imagination, tamed it down and cramped its interest. . . . It was lonely and wild, but oppressive in its barren monotony" (226).

The monotony that unnerves Dickens here and elsewhere in *American Notes* is not the product of simple repetition or doubling, but of seemingly inconsequential horizontal motion. Dickens actually experiences considerable relief upon doubling back over his tracks. Returning east by some of the same routes he took when traveling west, he finds comfort in familiar sights and in the binary motion of departure and return.[44] What troubles him is iteration without apparent aim or origin, the unintended similarities between institutions, landscapes, and personalities that only a traveler circulating among them is able to perceive: "At every new town I came to, I seemed to meet the very same people whom I had left behind me at the last" (289). Uncannily, these similarities appear to be neither enforced nor designed, neither the result of central planning nor of the desire to conform. Unable to impose a hierarchical model of the nation, which organizes geographic and social space into center and periphery, Dickens can find no way to describe frontier settlements' relation to one another without falling back into the language of sameness ("every place is a city here" [204]), or relying on imperceptible and inconsequential gradations of desolation.[45] Dickens's *American Notes* provides a vision of Jacksonian democracy gone terribly awry, the proliferation of isolated, autonomous communities that endlessly, unknowingly repeat themselves across the landscape. In its evocation of the replication of culture without governing intention, Dickens's account of his travels recalls the difficulty of figuring authorial agency and establishing responsibility for the circulation of texts in the culture of reprinting. At moments of blockage, when Dickens is least able to interpret what he sees, his narrative registers in occluded form the political and economic forces that disrupted his triumphal progress and that shaped American cultural development in unfamiliar and unrecognizable ways.

Circulation and Slavery

At the end of his narrative, Dickens tries valiantly to turn this culture of disseminated repetition against itself. In a highly polemical, topical chapter narrated from the vantage point of a successful "Passage Home," Dickens bitterly attacks both the brutality of slave-owners and the hypocrisy of the "false republic" (271) that sustains them through indifference, trusting in the weak supervision of public opinion to protect the slave from cruelty. Dickens strongly condemned slavery within the body of his narrative as his trip took him south as far as Richmond, but while he is traveling, slavery actually offers Dickens a strange kind of reassurance. His moral certainty of its depravity helps to stabilize his narrative perspective, enabling him to read the landscape allegorically. For example, passing through Virginia farmland, Dickens observes that it "was once productive; but the soil has been exhausted by the system of employing a great amount of slave labour in forcing crops, without strengthening the land." Here the slave-owners' use of force is self-condemned; the barrenness of the land testifies to the injustice of the system. For Dickens, the southern countryside offers an ideal coincidence of transgression and retribution: "Dreary and uninteresting as its aspect is, I was glad to the heart to find anything on which one of the curses of his horrible institution has fallen; and had greater pleasure in contemplating the withered ground than the richest and most thriving cultivation in the same place could have afforded me. In this district, as in all others where slavery sits brooding . . . there is an air of ruin and decay abroad, which is inseparable from the system" (180). Slavery makes legible a reciprocity between land and culture that eludes Dickens elsewhere in his narrative. The confidence with which he interprets vistas, buildings, and customs as "tokens" of "things below the surface" (183), and the pleasure he takes in affixing moral judgment to a particular location differentiate the south from the many "dreary and uninteresting," blighted scenes to follow.

Dickens's separate chapter on slavery, however, inaugurates a radical change in both tone and mode. With this chapter, Dickens finally stops circulating, shifting from recounting his disconnected, serial experiences to addressing the nation as a whole from the vantage point of his return to England. From this perspective, the institution of slavery seems maddeningly to elude the "curses" that so decisively settle on the landscape. In order to counter slaveholders' ostensible control over the representation of slavery—their ability to manipulate public opinion so that it protects

rather than censures them—Dickens adopts the familiar abolitionist strategy of turning the testimony of slave-owners against themselves. Quoting
a series of newspaper advertisements for the identification and return of
runaway slaves, Dickens holds Americans publicly accountable for the violence and degradation of slavery, indicting the institution and the print
culture that supports it by capturing ephemeral and scattered newspaper
notices on the single plane of his page:

"Ran away, the negro Manuel. Much marked by irons."

"Ran away, the negress Fanny. Had on an iron band about her neck."

"Ran away, a negro boy about twelve years old. Had round his neck a chain dog-
collar with 'De Lampert' engraved on it."

"Ran away, the negro Hown. Has a ring of iron on his left foot. Also, Grise, his
wife, having a ring and chain on the left leg."

"Ran away, a negro boy named James. Said boy was ironed when he left me."

"Committed to jail, a man who calls his name John. He has a clog of iron on his
right foot which will weigh four or five pounds."

"Detained at the police jail, the negro wench, Myra. Has several marks of lashing
and has irons on her feet."

"Ran away, a negro woman and two children. A few days before she went off, I
burnt her with a hot iron, on the left side of her face. I tried to make the
letter M." (274)

Dickens's passionate experiment in undermining slavery from within
is complicated by his unacknowledged and unresolved struggle with the
politics of print. As M. Giulia Fabi has noted, Dickens's juxtaposition of
advertisements that detail slave-owners' inscriptions on the bodies of their
problematically mobile property not only serves to condemn human bondage, it also recalls the repressed context of the debate over literary property.[46] Dickens focuses attention on the excruciating and ineradicable marks
on the bodies of slaves as a way of forcing Americans to own up to horrors that are too easily ignored. And yet his use of this brutal writing to
ascribe agency and assign responsibility covers for two failures of inscription. As scholars long have known, Dickens's list of newspaper advertisements is itself an unacknowledged borrowing from abolitionist Theodore
Weld's pamphlet *American Slavery As It Is: Testimony of a Thousand Witnesses* (1839).[47] Moreover, it is an act of unauthorized reprinting that hides
the traces of its theft by suppressing the sources of the slave-notices themselves. Weld had authenticated his documentary account of "the *condition
of American slaves*" by indicating the particular issues of the local and
regional newspapers in which these notices appeared and, where possible,

providing the "names and residences" of their authors "as vouchers for the truth of their statements."[48] Dickens, in turn, chooses from among the horrors Weld lists in chapters on "Tortures, By Iron Collars, Chains, Fetters, Handcuffs, &c." and "Brandings, Maimings, Gun-Shot Wounds, &c.," erasing local contexts as a way of making a general point about the ordinariness of these atrocities as they are mediated by the press. But this is a documentary claim that obscures its documentation, one that explicitly disavows "partial evidence from abolitionists" (277) and dislocates torture from its source. The inscriptive violence Dickens records, then, is very much his own signature, reflecting not only slave-owners' attempts to mark and to control the bodies of their slaves, but also Dickens's attempt to exercise his own authority over a disturbingly elusive subject, his struggle to establish national responsibility for slavery from a proliferation of local instances.

Unlike Weld, Dickens doesn't intend for his moral condemnation to redound upon individuals and communities. Dickens's list of atrocities is an intervention in national culture that depends as much on erasure as inscription. Just as his claim to impartiality is leveraged by the suppression of his politically volatile source, so his attempt to place accountability for slavery on a national footing is necessarily detached from the localities in which these atrocities occur, dislocated from reference because the nation as such cannot be reduced to particular places. Desiring to annex the authoritative public voice of the press to his first-person, impressionistic narrative while at the same time holding his own text aloof from the newspapers he deplores, Dickens recirculates fragments of American newspaper culture shorn of its characteristic locality, summoning the sense of simultaneity crucial to imagining the nation by sheer force of parallelism and juxtaposition.

And yet, Dickens's attempt to approximate the authority of the "public prints" (283) while countering their centrifugal tendencies is hopelessly compromised by his reliance on the medium he condemns. Dickens is unable to establish a moral position external to print culture. He can only describe the nation as a whole by recapitulating and denouncing the extraordinary stories that circulate in print. Despite his attempt to rise above partisan politics and to claim the authority of a firsthand witness—"I shall not write one word," he claims, "for which I have not had ample proof and warrant" (269)—Dickens's critique of slavery devolves into to an attack on the representation of slavery, an attack that recirculates horrific descriptions even as it claims that degradation invariably attends their consumption.[49]

Detached from Weld's apparatus of authentication, Dickens's catalogue of "liveries of mutilation" (284) threatens to float free of reference, slipping from moral condemnation into voyeurism, representing not "the condition of American slaves" but the condition of national description, the violence of Dickens's desire to produce a stable referent for the nation. Dickens's self-defeating attempt to transform his text into a site for the redemptive redeployment of a heterogeneous and dispersed newspaper culture suggests one of the exasperating strengths of a strategically weak central government—its ability to dodge accountability by rendering itself too dispersed to be targeted for critique.

Dickens attempts to produce in and through his text some sense of the governing authority that American society lacks, but he repeatedly gets caught between reference and demonstration, trying to point to something his text is performing. For instance, he represents the nation as defined by the omnipresence of its "licentious Press" (287), but his attribution of centralized powers of corruption to this personified figure is belied by his own efforts to assemble scattered evidence of social depravity from newspapers in remote locations. Dickens evokes a world of unremitting and contagious violence by reproducing newspaper reports of brutal acts from settlements in outlying territories, inferring that the cause of this violence is exposure to slavery in person or in print.[50] Here, Dickens's own text stands as a proxy for the central authority he cannot locate, the extravagance of his tone attesting to his frustration with the attenuation of his evidence. For Dickens, only a singular "Press," to which he attributes universal reach and comprehensive political and social power, could possibly be responsible for such degeneration: "while that Press has its evil eye in every house, and its black hand in every appointment in the state, from a president to a postman; while, with ribald slander for its only stock in trade, it is the standard literature of an enormous class, who must find their reading in a newspaper, or they will not read at all; so long must its odium be upon the country's head, and so long must the evil it works, be plainly visible in the republic" (288). In excoriating the press, Dickens grants it the same self-confirming status as both cause and evidence of national corruption that he had ascribed to slavery while traveling though the south. And yet his own rhetorical strategies attest to the maddening fragmentation of American newspaper culture; ironically, only "standard literature" such as *American Notes* and other texts subject to unauthorized reprinting could achieve anything like the kind of circulation Dickens describes.

Mistaking the existence of a mass-readership for the ability to coordinate and control that readership, Dickens leaves himself open to
the charge that, because no such "Press" exists, no such violence does
either. Southern journals in particular were quick to seize on this defense,
claiming that Dickens had "inserted in his work passages from Southern
Papers, which were actually the coinage of lying Abolitionists."[51] Dickens's
attempt to shift accountability for slavery from localities to the national
imaginary ultimately enables southerners to shrug off his charges. For
instance, in accusing Dickens of fraud, the *Southern Quarterly Review* re-
buts his account of a society in which tales of torture are "cooly read in
families as things of course" (277), replacing it with an image of southern
propriety. Sending "a respectable medical friend" to "one of the largest
reading rooms in the Southern country," the editors ask him "to look diligently into every paper published South of the Potomac" for advertisements like the ones Dickens had published in *American Notes*. It is only
because Dickens directs his censure at a nation mediated by print that
three pages of evidence of the lack of *reference* to slavery can hold talis-
manic force:

The Knoxville Register was examined from the 12th of April, to the 17th of May,
    1843, all that were on file, without one runaway slave advertisement of any
    sort.
St. Louis New Era, from April 19th to 13th of May, same results.
The Mobile Advertiser, from 26th April to 20th May, none of the kind paraded by
    Mr. Dickens.
The Mobile Register and Journal, from 19th April to 19th May, same results.
New-Orleans Republican, from 26th April to 20th May, same results.[52]

In response to Dickens's sourceless and sensational allegations, the *Southern Quarterly Review* summons rational "proof" from a reading room in
which a heterogeneous print culture can be assembled and compared. This
is a print culture diversified by place and party, one characterized not by
violence, but by a decorous emptiness.

Dickens is not wrong to perceive a link between the proliferation of
local print cultures and the defense of slavery. Slave-owners' ability to
exert local control over systems of distribution caused the American Anti-
Slavery Society to shift its approach in the late 1830s from sending abolitionist tracts to southerners through the mail, to petitioning Congress for
the elimination of slavery in the District of Columbia. In effect, abolitionists stopped concerning themselves with the national circulation of their

texts and addressed themselves to the nonrepresentative status of the federal center, the inability of a slaveholding capital city to represent the nation as a whole. Dickens is no more successful than were Massachusetts anti-slavery petitioners in forcing his critique of slavery to occupy that center, although in transforming Weld's anti-slavery polemic past the point of recognition he is able to exploit the "general circulation" of his text. The distribution of *American Notes* both exceeded the locality of the newspapers it quoted, and overcame limits imposed on the circulation of abolitionist pamphlets. Submitted by a nervous distributor to a South Carolina vigilance committee, the *New World* reprint of Dickens's text was able to make it past the censors either because of Dickens's fame, because of anti-censorship publicity raised by the *New World*'s editorials, or because, as one local journal claimed, "the ultra opinions of its writer were so ultra, so false, and so utterly incredible to the South, that they concluded that its circulation could do no harm."[53]

Like Dickens himself, Dickens's text is subject to an uneven and contested circulation, a field of distribution that does not exist prior to or independent of his writing, but that is by no means under his control. *American Notes* was quickly absorbed into ongoing debates over the conditions of possibility for a national market for print, debates that the narrative does a far better job of galvanizing than describing. For instance, in the pages of the *New World* under the headline "A Muzzled Press," South Carolina's attempt to arrest the distribution of *American Notes* became part of a larger discussion about the obstacle that slavery posed to the establishment of a national culture. In the pages of the *Anti-Slavery Reporter* and in the abolitionist pamphlet *Facts for the People*, Dickens's text was enlisted in the campaign to use the federal right to freedom of speech to overturn southern communities' claim that local authority over the distribution of print provided a necessary defense against slave insurrection. As in the debate over copyright, however, Dickens's intervention in American culture ends up going against the grain of his intentions. *American Notes* provoked an outcry against local control over the circulation of print—against associations "formed to prescribe what works may safely be read"[54]—and not, as he had intended, against press licentiousness. Taken up into American debates over literary property, the form and advisability of the national debt, the arrested development of the transportation infrastructure, and the relation of the press to the institution of slavery, the cultural significance of *American Notes* is at odds with and in excess of Dickens's narrative.

Martin Chuzzlewit, the Social Order,
and the Medium of Print

Shortly before the publication of *American Notes*, John Forster tried to bolster Dickens's attack on American print culture by publishing an anonymous article on "The Newspaper Literature of America" in the *Foreign Quarterly Review*. Forster singled out for critique James Gordon Bennett's *New York Herald*, a newspaper that, because of its large circulation and network of correspondents "in every chief city of the Union,"[55] could plausibly be taken to be both representative of and central to American culture. As a supplement to Dickens's text, Forster's article calls attention to Dickens's inability to locate just such a center in *American Notes*. It also contrasts American newspaper publishing with the cheap press in England, which Forster acknowledges to be equally scurrilous but less damaging to the nation because its circulation is "wholly restricted to London": "It is a disease, and a rank one; but where it strikes it stops. The poison is nowhere in the system" (198).

Forster's is a failed strategy of containment on a number of levels. While his aim is to discriminate between cultures, his citation of evidence of American newspaper corruption, although largely confined to a series of footnotes, quickly threatens to overtake the critique itself.[56] Moreover, when this article circulates in America, it is almost universally attributed to Dickens himself, subjecting what Forster hoped would appear as an objective, external verification of Dickens's text to the familiar charge of gentlemanly abuse of print anonymity.[57] Although this article failed to enhance Dickens's authority as an observer of American society, Forster pinpoints an important national difference in the relation of print to social and political power, an assessment that he and Dickens share, and that Dickens richly elaborates in *Martin Chuzzlewit* and his later novels.

What shocks Forster most about the scandal-driven American penny press is that it could acquire direct access to political power, a intimate relationship of patronage and protection that is signaled by the *Herald*'s acquisition of government printing contracts to advertise the sale of public lands. According to Forster, just as American statesmen are reduced to defending themselves in print from scandals that are propagated by these very same papers, so the government, which ought to remain above the press's self-interested maneuvering for market advantage, is forced to rely on newspapers in order to raise its revenue. For Forster, there is perilously little separating the highest and lowest forms of American society, a lack of mediation that is epitomized by the lack of hierarchy in the typical American newspaper: the *Herald*, like other American papers, can be identified by its "perfectly ridiculous non-arrangement; its jumble in one hopeless mass, of leaders and police reports, advertisements and abuse and moral reflections; puffings and bankruptcies, comicalities and crimes, politicians at Washington and paupers in England and pickpockets at the Tombs" (200–201).

By contrast, England possesses a capital city with a well-defined social hierarchy that is powerful enough to keep a licentious press in check. Although Forster is chagrined by the existence in England of newspapers comparable to the *Herald*, he believes their distribution and influence to be restricted to the seamier parts of London, and dismisses them as "part of the social dregs and moral filth which *will* deposit itself somewhere in so large a city" (198). In England, scandals do not circulate so much as accumulate in obscure parts of the metropolis. Furthermore, "no one dares to confound" (198) the penny press with the official press. Forster suggests that the difference between English and American print cultures lies not in the products of the press but in a social order that enforces a distinction between legitimate and illegitimate representation.

In *Martin Chuzzlewit* (1843–44), which, according to Forster, Dickens revised to answer the American "challenge to make good his *Notes*,"[58] Dickens's disorienting experience of American reprint culture is visible in his construction of the novel's moral order. In this novel, Dickens recapitulates his 1842 tour, sending the young Martin Chuzzlewit to America to convert him from a life of selfishness to one of virtue. In analyzing the relation of the novel to Dickens's travel narrative and his American tour, critics have most often reacted to the acerbity of Dickens's satire, which was written in response to continued provocation from the American press and under the cover of fiction. Based largely on Forster's testimony, most critics have assumed that Dickens sent Martin to America to boost the sales in England of the flagging serial. Sidney Moss has argued further that the virulence of the American episodes was designed not only to capitalize on anti-American sentiment in England, but also to thwart American publishers by forcing them to abandon their reprinting of the novel in the middle of its serialization.[59] However, what many critics miss in attending to Dickens's vengeful caricatures is the way in which the novel's restaging of the tour is rigorously self-indicting. While it is true that the novel's American episodes offer a reductive and hurried version of Dickens's prior account of the "false republic," they also inaugurate a rethinking of the author's complicity in the failure of both tour and narrative.

Alexander Welsh has most thoroughly charted the way in which Dickens's chagrin at his failed campaign for international copyright ramifies throughout the novel—in Dickens's savage critique of Pecksniff's claim to disinterestedness, in the comic plot in which Moddle learns about the fatal dislocation of property and desire ("I love another. She is Another's. Everything appears to be somebody else's" [914]), and in the melodramatic plot in which Jonas Chuzzlewit is haunted by a crime he hasn't quite committed.[60] Similarly, the American episodes can be read not simply as a self-indulgent, self-exonerating recasting of his tour, but as a structural reconception of his failed travel narrative. For instance, Dickens implicitly acknowledges the anemic narrative perspective of *American Notes* by sending his aristocratic hero to America in steerage, terrified of being recognized. This is a recasting that seems equal parts self-punishment (he should have traveled incognito) and self-ridicule (confessing the narcissism of his desire to conceal himself). So too does the contraction of the scene of American travel into a simple binary motion represent an acknowledgement that the moral authority of *American Notes* was undermined by its constantly dislocated and unlocateable narrator. In *Martin Chuzzlewit*, the hero quickly travels to the figurative center of fraud and despair in swamp-like Eden, endures illness, experiences regeneration, then is ransomed and returns to England. While in many ways, relaunching his critique of American culture from within the confines of a Bunyanesque moral allegory represents a retreat from the complexity and confusion of his unsettling travel narrative, in *Martin Chuzzlewit* Dickens superimposes an overarching moral framework on both traveler and hosts; uncovering the truth of American deception requires the evisceration of his title character.

The most important revision of the tour and narrative, however, is Dickens's discovery of London as a formal solution to the problem of national representation. As Jonathan Arac has argued, Dickens arrives at a principle of organization for the scattered energies of his serialized novel by fastening on the centripetal force of the nation's capital. According to Arac, *Martin Chuzzlewit* marks Dickens's "imaginative apprehension of the city of London as the center of coherence for English life."[61] It also marks his awareness of the novel itself as the key to the "web of hidden connections and obligations" (69) on which national coherence rests. Arac charts Dickens's "increasingly spatializing overview" (69) of London as he shifts from celebrating the labyrinthine complexity of the city to identifying relationships of moral significance that bind together mutual strangers. Beginning with the neophyte's view, in which people, streets, and consumer goods, in Forster's words, "jumble in one hopeless mass," Dickens comes to align narrative omniscience with an impossibly comprehensive knowledge of the city, a mode of understanding that is ultimately personified by the shady detective, Nadgett.[62] It is the city itself that makes possible the connections between strangers that Nadgett will painstakingly trace. The city is an intricate maze that nevertheless allows for an unconscious simultaneity, a sharing of common space and common thoughts that can only be perceived by novelist and reader. In *Martin Chuzzlewit*, two characters lost in thought pass each other on the street unaware of each other's presences, but, as the narrator assures us, "the same private man out of all the men alive was in the mind of each at the same moment; was prominently connected, though in a different manner, with the day's adventure of both; and formed, when they passed each other in the street, the one absorbing topic of their thoughts" (661–62).[63]

Crucial to Nadgett's ability to profit from the strategic disclosure of secrets and to Dickens's confidence in the moral authority of his novelistic disclosures, is the idea of London as a place in which privacy can be maintained in the midst of public spaces. That Dickens arrives at this conception of the city in recoil from his experience of the unremitting publicity of American culture is clear from the episode in which young Martin and his companion Mark Tapley first alight on English soil after their harrowing experience in Eden. Comfortably lodged in an eccentric tavern with a window on the street from which they can watch passersby without themselves being noticed, Mark and Martin happen to see Pecksniff on his way to a ceremony honoring an architectural design that he has plagiarized from Martin. In this scene, the novel's ironic inversion of the copious praise showered on Pecksniff in the ceremony is guaranteed by the invisibility of Mark and Martin who are able to find a space in the crowd where "they could see all that passed, without much dread of being beheld by Mr. Pecksniff in return" (623). The complex articulation of urban space allows for moral oversight and assures that acts of public fraud will be privately redressed.[64]

Both Forster and Dickens imagine London as the synecdoche for a social order that enforces moral distinctions despite the violations of public trust perpetrated by scurrilous newspapers and moralizing Pecksniffs. By contrast, American publishers imagine that reprint culture can ameliorate social inequality by holding potentially divisive differences in a kind of solution. As in their defense of the decentralized literary marketplace, pirate publishers are indebted to Dickens's successful and steady production of popular fiction for the elaboration of their vision. Take for example the series of advertisements tipped into Philadelphia publisher T. B. Peterson & Brothers's late 1850s edition of *American Notes and Pic-Nic Papers* (Figure 12). In these advertisements, the identity of Dickens's

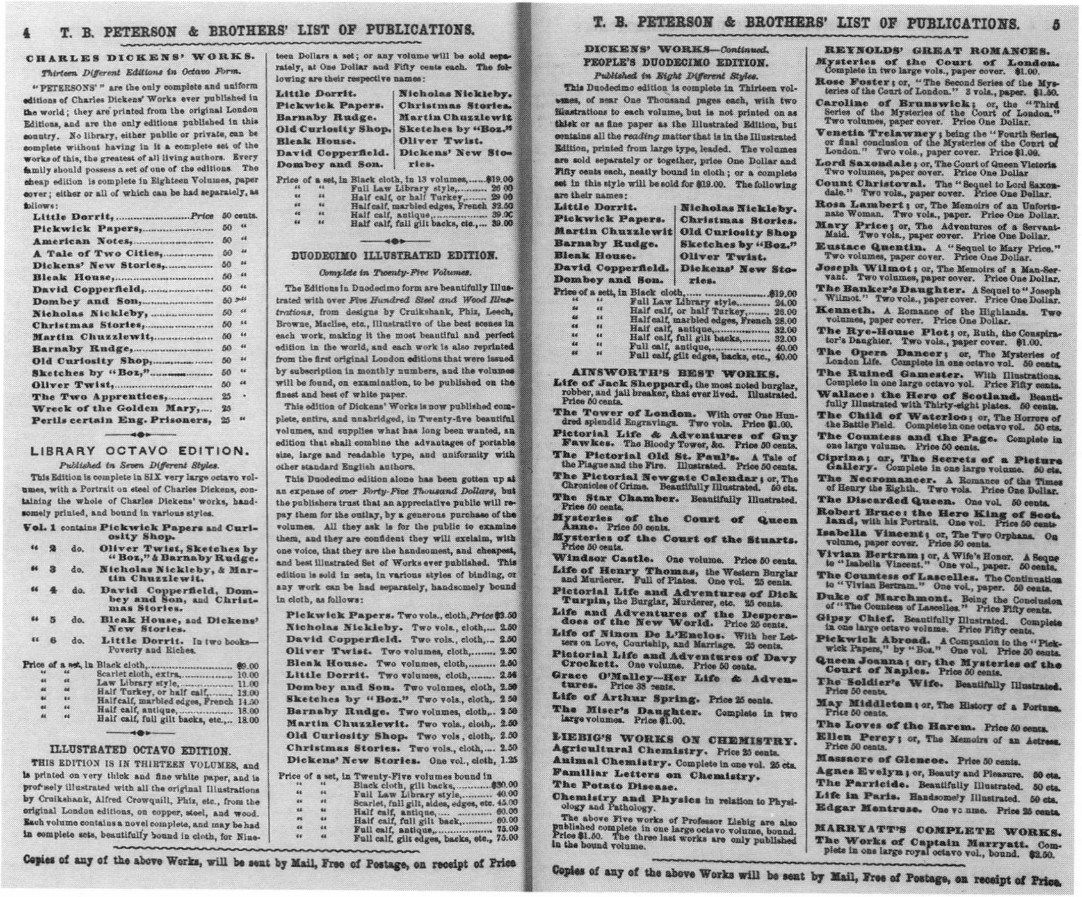

4 T. B. PETERSON & BROTHERS' LIST OF PUBLICATIONS.

CHARLES DICKENS' WORKS.

Thirteen Different Editions in Octavo Form.

"PETERSONS'" are the only complete and uniform editions of Charles Dickens' Works ever published in the world; they are printed from the original London Editions, and are the only editions published in this country. No library, either public or private, can be complete without having in it a complete set of the works of this, the greatest of all living authors. Every family should possess a set of one of the editions. The cheap edition is complete in Eighteen Volumes, paper cover; either or all of which can be had separately, as follows:

Little Dorrit,	*Price*	50 cents.
Pickwick Papers,		50 "
American Notes,		50 "
A Tale of Two Cities,		50 "
Dickens' New Stories,		50 "
Bleak House,		50 "
David Copperfield,		50 "
Dombey and Son,		50 "
Nicholas Nickleby,		50 "
Christmas Stories,		50 "
Martin Chuzzlewit,		50 "
Barnaby Rudge,		50 "
Old Curiosity Shop,		50 "
Sketches by "Boz,"		50 "
Oliver Twist,		50 "
The Two Apprentices,		25 "
Wreck of the Golden Mary,		25
Perils certain Eng. Prisoners,		25 "

LIBRARY OCTAVO EDITION.

Published in Seven Different Styles.

This Edition is complete in SIX very large octavo volumes, with a Portrait on steel of Charles Dickens, containing the whole of Charles Dickens' works, handsomely printed, and bound in various styles.

Vol. 1 contains Pickwick Papers and Curiosity Shop.
" 2 do. Oliver Twist, Sketches by "Boz," & Barnaby Rudge.
" 3 do. Nicholas Nickleby, & Martin Chuzzlewit.
" 4 do. David Copperfield, Dombey and Son, and Christmas Stories.
" 5 do. Bleak House, and Dickens' New Stories.
" 6 do. Little Dorrit. In two books—Poverty and Riches.

Price of a set, in Black cloth,		$9.00
" "	Scarlet cloth, extra,	10.00
" "	Law Library style,	11.00
" "	Half Turkey, or half calf,	13.00
" "	Half calf, marbled edges, French	14.50
" "	Half calf, antique,	18.00
" "	Half calf, full gilt backs, etc.,	18.00

ILLUSTRATED OCTAVO EDITION.

THIS EDITION IS IN THIRTEEN VOLUMES, and is printed on very thick and fine white paper, and is profusely illustrated with all the original Illustrations by Cruikshank, Alfred Crowquill, Phiz, etc., from the original London editions, on copper, steel, and wood. Each volume contains a novel complete, and may be had in complete sets, beautifully bound in cloth, for Nineteen Dollars a set; or any volume will be sold separately, at One Dollar and Fifty cents each. The following are their respective names:

Little Dorrit.	Nicholas Nickleby.
Pickwick Papers.	Christmas Stories.
Barnaby Rudge.	Martin Chuzzlewit
Old Curiosity Shop.	Sketches by "Boz."
Bleak House.	Oliver Twist.
David Copperfield.	Dickens' New Stories.
Dombey and Son.	

Price of a set, in Black cloth, in 13 volumes,		$19.00
" "	Full Law Library style,	26.00
" "	Half calf, or half Turkey,	29.00
" "	Half calf, marbled edges, French	32.50
" "	Half calf, antique,	39.00
" "	Half calf, full gilt backs, etc.,	39.00

DUODECIMO ILLUSTRATED EDITION.

Complete in Twenty-Five Volumes.

The Editions in Duodecimo form are beautifully Illustrated with over *Five Hundred Steel and Wood Illustrations*, from designs by Cruikshank, Phiz, Leech, Browne, Maclise, etc., illustrative of the best scenes in each work, making it the most beautiful and perfect edition in the world, and each work is also reprinted from the first original London editions that were issued by subscription in monthly numbers, and the volumes will be found, on examination, to be published on the finest and best of white paper.

This edition of Dickens' Works is now published complete, entire, and unabridged, in Twenty-five beautiful volumes, and supplies what has long been wanted, an edition that shall combine the advantages of portable size, large and readable type, and uniformity with other standard English authors.

This Duodecimo edition alone has been gotten up at an expense of *over Forty-Five Thousand Dollars*, but the publishers trust that an appreciative public will repay them for the outlay, by a generous purchase of the volumes. All they ask is for the public to examine them, and they are confident they will exclaim, with one voice, that they are the handsomest, and cheapest, and best illustrated Set of Works ever published. This edition is sold in sets, in various styles of binding, or any work can be had separately, handsomely bound in cloth, as follows:

Pickwick Papers. Two vols., cloth, *Price*	$3.50
Nicholas Nickleby. Two vols., cloth,	2.50
David Copperfield. Two vols., cloth,	2.50
Oliver Twist. Two volumes, cloth,	2.50
Bleak House. Two volumes, cloth,	2.50
Little Dorrit. Two volumes, cloth,	2.50
Dombey and Son. Two volumes, cloth,	2.50
Sketches by "Boz." Two vols., cloth,	2.50
Barnaby Rudge. Two volumes, cloth,	2.50
Martin Chuzzlewit. Two vols., cloth,	2.50
Old Curiosity Shop. Two vols., cloth,	2.50
Christmas Stories. Two vols., cloth,	2.50
Dickens' New Stories. One vol., cloth,	1.25

Price of a set, in Twenty-Five volumes bound in		
" "	Black cloth, gilt backs,	$30.00
" "	Full Law Library style,	40.00
" "	Scarlet, full gilt, sides, edges, etc.	45.00
" "	Half calf, antique,	60.00
" "	Half calf, full gilt back,	60.00
" "	Full calf, antique,	75.00
" "	Full calf, gilt edges, backs, etc.,	75.00

Copies of any of the above Works, will be sent by Mail, Free of Postage, on receipt of Price

T. B. PETERSON & BROTHERS' LIST OF PUBLICATIONS. 5

DICKENS' WORKS—*Continued.*

PEOPLE'S DUODECIMO EDITION.

Published in Eight Different Styles.

This Duodecimo edition is complete in Thirteen volumes, of near One Thousand pages each, with two Illustrations to each volume, but is not printed on as thick or as fine paper as the Illustrated Edition, but contains all the *reading* matter that is in the Illustrated Edition, printed from large type, leaded. The volumes are sold separately or together, price One Dollar and Fifty cents each, neatly bound in cloth; or a complete set in this style will be sold for $19.00. The following are their names:

Little Dorrit.	Nicholas Nickleby.
Pickwick Papers.	Christmas Stories.
Martin Chuzzlewit	Old Curiosity Shop
Barnaby Rudge.	Sketches by "Boz."
Bleak House.	Oliver Twist.
David Copperfield.	Dickens' New Stories.
Dombey and Son.	

Price of a sett, in Black cloth,		$19.00
" "	Full Law Library style,	24.00
" "	Half calf, or half Turkey,	28.00
" "	Half calf, marbled edges, French	28.00
" "	Half calf, antique,	32.00
" "	Half calf, full gilt backs,	32.00
" "	Full calf, antique,	40.00
" "	Full calf, gilt edges, backs, etc.,	40.00

AINSWORTH'S BEST WORKS.

Life of Jack Sheppard, the most noted burglar, robber, and jail breaker, that ever lived. Illustrated. Price 50 cents.
The Tower of London. With over One Hundred splendid Engravings. Two vols. Price $1.00.
Pictorial Life & Adventures of Guy Fawkes. The Bloody Tower, &c. Price 50 cents.
The Pictorial Old St. Paul's. A Tale of the Plague and the Fire. Illustrated. Price 50 cents.
The Pictorial Newgate Calendar; or, The Chronicles of Crime. Beautifully Illustrated. 50 cts.
The Star Chamber. Beautifully Illustrated. Price 50 cents.
Mysteries of the Court of Queen Anne. Price 50 cents.
Mysteries of the Court of the Stuarts. Price 50 cents.
Windsor Castle. One volume. Price 50 cents.
Life of Henry Thomas, the Western Burglar and Murderer. Full of Plates. One vol. 25 cents.
Pictorial Life and Adventures of Dick Turpin, the Burglar, Murderer, etc. 25 cents.
Life and Adventures of the Desperadoes of the New World. Price 25 cents.
Life of Ninon De L'Enclos. With her Letters on Love, Courtship, and Marriage. 25 cents.
Pictorial Life and Adventures of Davy Crockett. One volume. Price 50 cents.
Grace O'Malley—Her Life & Adventures. Price 38 cents.
Life of Arthur Spring. Price 25 cents.
The Miser's Daughter. Complete in two large volumes. Price $1.00.

LIEBIG'S WORKS ON CHEMISTRY.

Agricultural Chemistry. Price 25 cents.
Animal Chemistry. Complete in one vol. 25 cts.
Familiar Letters on Chemistry.
The Potato Disease.
Chemistry and Physics in relation to Physiology and Pathology.

The above Five works of Professor Liebig are also published complete in one large octavo volume, bound. Price $1.50. The three last works are only published in the bound volume.

REYNOLDS' GREAT ROMANCES.

Mysteries of the Court of London. Complete in two large vols., paper cover. $1.00.
Rose Foster; or, "The Second Series of the Mysteries of the Court of London." 3 vols., paper. $1.50.
Caroline of Brunswick; or, the "Third Series of the Mysteries of the Court of London." Two volumes, paper cover. Price One Dollar.
Venetia Trelawney; being the "Fourth Series, or final conclusion of the Mysteries of the Court of London." Two vols., paper cover. Price $1.00.
Lord Saxondale; or, The Court of Queen Victoria Two volumes, paper cover. Price One Dollar
Count Christoval. The "Sequel to Lord Saxondale." Two vols., paper cover. Price One Dollar.
Rosa Lambert; or, The Memoirs of an Unfortunate Woman. Two vols., paper. Price One Dollar.
Mary Price; or, The Adventures of a Servant-Maid. Two vols., paper cover. Price One Dollar.
Eustace Quentin. A "Sequel to Mary Price." Two volumes, paper cover. Price One Dollar.
Joseph Wilmot; or, The Memoirs of a Man-Servant. Two volumes, paper cover. Price One Dollar.
The Banker's Daughter. A Sequel to "Joseph Wilmot." Two vols., paper cover. Price One Dollar.
Kenneth. A Romance of the Highlands. Two volumes, paper cover. Price One Dollar.
The Rye-House Plot; or, Ruth, the Conspirator's Daughter. Two vols., paper cover. $1.00.
The Opera Dancer; or, The Mysteries of London Life. Complete in one octavo vol. 50 cents.
The Ruined Gamester. With Illustrations. Complete in one large octavo vol. Price Fifty cents.
Wallace: the Hero of Scotland. Beautifully Illustrated with Thirty-eight plates. 50 cents.
The Child of Waterloo; or, The Horrors of the Battle Field. Complete in one octavo vol. 50 cts.
The Countess and the Page. Complete in one large volume. Price 50 cents.
Ciprina; or, The Secrets of a Picture Gallery. Complete in one large volume. 50 cts.
The Necromancer. A Romance of the Times of Henry the Eighth. Two vols. Price One Dollar.
The Discarded Queen. One vol. 50 cents.
Robert Bruce: the Hero King of Scotland, with his Portrait. One vol. Price 50 cents.
Isabella Vincent; or, The Two Orphans. One volume, paper cover. Price 50 cents.
Vivian Bertram; or, A Wife's Honor. A Sequel to "Isabella Vincent." One vol., paper. 50 cents.
The Countess of Lascelles. The Continuation to "Vivian Bertram." One vol., paper. 50 cents.
Duke of Marchmont. Being the Conclusion of "The Countess of Lascelles." Price Fifty cents.
Gipsy Chief. Beautifully Illustrated. Complete in one large octavo volume. Price Fifty cents.
Pickwick Abroad. A Companion to the "Pickwick Papers," by "Boz." One vol. Price 50 cents.
Queen Joanna; or, the Mysteries of the Court of Naples. Price 50 cents.
The Soldier's Wife. Beautifully Illustrated. Price 50 cents.
May Middleton; or, The History of a Fortune. Price 50 cents.
The Loves of the Harem. Price 50 cents.
Ellen Percy; or, The Memoirs of an Actress. Price 50 cents.
Massacre of Glencoe. Price 50 cents.
Agnes Evelyn; or, Beauty and Pleasure. 50 cts.
The Parricide. Beautifully Illustrated. 50 cts.
Life in Paris. Handsomely Illustrated. 50 cts.
Edgar Montrose. One volume. Price 25 cents.

MARRYATT'S COMPLETE WORKS.

The Works of Captain Marryatt. Complete in one large royal octavo vol., bound. $2.50.

Copies of any of the above Works will be sent by Mail, Free of Postage, on receipt of Price.

Figure 12. "T. B. Peterson & Brothers' List of Publications," *American Notes; and Pic-Nic Papers* (1859?). Courtesy, General Research Division, The New York Public Library, Astor, Lenox, and Tilden Foundations texts across a variety of editions enables the publisher to experiment with niche marketing while also holding out the promise that the elite "Duodecimo Illustrated," the "People's Duodecimo" and even the unnamed "cheap edition" are each in their own way "complete and uniform," alternatives to one another that are essentially equivalent. Just as novels, sketches, and stories of differing lengths, themes, and genres achieve a kind of formal equality at the level of the volume, so the market mediation of social difference is held in check by the essential sameness of the texts across editions. T. B. Peterson's advertisement proposes that differences in wealth or social standing that might be articulated through the purchase of a book in "Full calf, gilt edges, backs, etc." cannot divide a people that holds common property in the works of Charles Dickens. Despite the proliferation of editions and elaborate binding styles, this is a publishing venture that attempts both to meet and to produce a desire for inclusiveness: "No library, either public or private, can be complete without having in it a complete set of the works of this, the greatest of all living authors. Every family should possess a set of one of the editions." In investing in and advertising a wide range of editions, T. B. Peterson aims at representing and containing the field of choices that are available across the system of reprinting as a whole. However, unlike Dickens's world of urban strangers, whose unconsciousness of what they hold in common preserves the moral and novelistic order, this imaginary version of the social requires constant reassurances of identity and inclusion, figured as the ideal completion of the author's body of work. It is an exaggerated consciousness of property held in common that prevents T. B. Peterson's sales strategy from threatening monopoly and the plenitude and variety it describes from sliding into exclusivity.

T. B. Peterson's advertisement suggests that the culture of reprinting doesn't do away with the author in the process of rejecting tight controls over intellectual property; rather, it is capable of raising the author-function to a principle of social coherence. T. B. Peterson's use of Dickens to elaborate a market-mediated social order is profoundly unauthorized insofar as it represents an ideal that Dickens rejects and depends on the author's forced surrender (in the United States) of proprietary control over his works. Like *Brother Jonathan*'s parody treasury note and the American Anti-Slavery Society's championing of Dickens's travel narrative as an abolitionist tract, T. B. Peterson's "Thirteen Different Editions in Octavo Form" demonstrate how easily Dickens's popularly accessible mode of literary authority and his interest in the new republic could be absorbed into the domestic project of imagining the forms of and barriers to national coherence. Not despite but because of their mutual misprision, a rich field of significance comes to occupy the space between Dickens and his American readers.

On his final tour of the United States in the winter of 1867–68, Dickens did much to short-circuit the unauthorized distribution of his work and to close the gap between author and reader that the reprinters had exploited. Rather than allowing his audience to receive him on their own terms, Dickens traveled through the northeast and mid-west performing his authorship, reading selections from his repertoire to sold-out audiences. In these readings, Dickens gave voice to a handful of his most popular characters using a minimalist mode of self-presentation, standing alone on the stage behind a small desk "against a dark background in a frame of gaslight, which [threw] out his face and figure to the best advantage" (Figure 13).[65] In subordinating his authorial persona to the impersonation of his characters—"It was not Dickens, but the creations of his genius, that seemed to live and talk and act before the spectators"[66]—Dickens steers

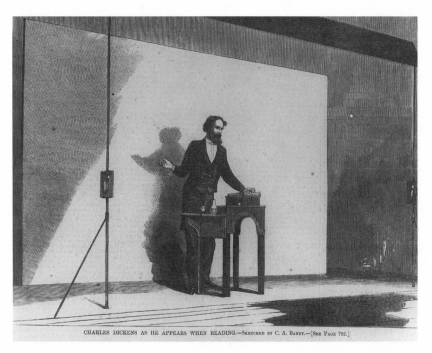

CHARLES DICKENS AS HE APPEARS WHEN READING.—Sketched by C. A. Barry.—[See Page 782.]

Figure 13. "Charles Dickens as He Appears When Reading," *Harper's Weekly* (1867). Courtesy, American Antiquarian Society.

audiences away from a definition of the author as an external guarantor of the nature or quality of a printed book, toward a model of authorship as immanent and evanescent presence, a mode of authentication that is bound up with the notion of authorial voice and that ideally passes through the author's scarce and vulnerable body. This work of redefinition is richly registered in the newspaper coverage of Dickens's second tour as editors divide between cynically calculating the unprecedentedly large sums of money he was earning from his readings, and expressing concern for the author's manifest physical frailty.[67]

During this tour, Dickens tries one final time to recast and redeem the most persistently problematic text of his oeuvre, *American Notes for General Circulation*. In one of the few public events he agrees to attend on the tour, Dickens gives a short after-dinner speech to "two hundred representatives of the Press" offering "honest testimony to the national generosity" in the matter of his reception, and expressing astonishment at the many signs of national improvement he has witnessed: "changes in the amount of land subdued and peopled, changes in the rise of vast new cities, changes in the growth of older cities almost out of recognition, changes in the graces and amenities of life, changes in the Press" (295). As proof of his sincerity, Dickens promises both to publish this tribute "in [his] own Journal" when he returns to England, and to insist that a record of his gratitude and approval be attached to all subsequent editions of *American Notes* and *Martin Chuzzlewit*: "This testimony, so long as I live, and so long as my descendants have any legal right in my books, I shall cause to be republished, as an appendix to every copy of those two books of mine in which I have referred to America" (296).

Dickens's promise to "cause" his speech "to be republished" as an appendix to his texts is a strange concession. It is both an exercise of and an attempt to augment his authority over his widely circulated, wayward texts. His request that his final words on America "be fairly read as inseparable from" his earlier "experiences and impressions" (296) concedes the method but not the victory to his American republishers. And yet even as Dickens speaks, he is far from controlling the troubling resonances produced by his attempt to tighten authorial control over literary property. Dickens's 1867–88 reading tour was financially guaranteed by the Boston publishing firm Ticknor & Fields, which entered into an agreement with Dickens in 1866 to produce a set of authorized editions of his work.[68] As the "only authorized representatives in America of the whole series of [Dickens's] books,"[69] Ticknor & Fields stood to take advantage of the publicity that would be generated from the famous author's visit, and timed

THE BLACK DRIVER.

Figure 14. "The Black Driver,"
*American Notes for General
Circulation* (1868). Courtesy,
American Antiquarian Society.

the release of their edition of *American Notes* to coincide with news of
his imminent arrival. The illustration selected for the frontispiece to this
volume, however, jarringly recalls the highly fraught pre-war connection
between literary property and national development (Figure 14). Striking
the keynote of this authorized edition is "The Black Driver," a thinly drawn
minstrel figure from Dickens's brief sojourn in the south, a Cockney in blackface whom Dickens tellingly describes as "a kind of insane imitation of an
English coachman" (178). It is difficult, finally, to know which edition of
American Notes should represent Dickens's "general circulation" in America. Is Dickens the inadvertent narrator of the disconnected Jacksonian
infrastructure, the provocateur who stimulates a defense of decentralization in finance, government, and print, and who traces the disturbing connection between the proliferation of print cultures and the protection of
the system of slavery? Or is he the tool of a publishing firm that consolidates its authority by deploying the image of a former slave armed with
a whip, a harbinger of northern forces who will subjugate the south in
part through the imposition of federally funded internal improvements?
Dickens himself couldn't possibly tell.

4

Unauthorized Poe

IN THE AUTUMN OF 1844, Kentucky poetess Amelia Welby wrote a letter to the editor of the New York *Evening Mirror*, Nathaniel Parker Willis, seeking to confirm the authorship of a reprinted poem:

Dearest Mirror: I copy the subjoined lines "By Mr. Willis" from an old number of the Jackson (Tenn.) Advocate, where they are evidently out of place, and at all events, so grossly misprinted that I must ask you to re-publish them, the more especially as they do not appear in the late collection by Mr. W. It can scarcely be possible that there are *two Dromios*.[1]

Welby's playful reference to the twin servants who are perpetually mistaken for one another in Shakespeare's *The Comedy of Errors* points to the slapstick logic underlying her request—the assumption that reprinting might be imagined as a corrective to the dislocations of reprinting. A provincial author, Welby looked to a metropolitan center to organize the literary field, trusting in Willis's authority as an editor and as a literary celebrity to restore the integrity of this text and assimilate it to his body of work. And yet her appeal testifies to the structural conditions that militated against bringing textual production and reproduction under the control of authors. The inadequacy of even Willis's well-known name to guarantee the authenticity of this poem attests to the spatial and temporal displacement endemic to the decentralized literary marketplace, the inability of authoritatively published collections to keep up with the periodical circulation of poetry and tales, and the textual corruption that was an inevitable product of literature's unauthorized circulation in magazines and newspapers.

Willis responds to Welby's query by reprinting her letter, sending the poem back into circulation prefaced by the story of its discovery in lieu of an authoritative yoking of text to author:

We thank our friend, *the* "Amelia," for supposing us capable of the authorship of these majestic-paced stanzas. They are not ours—we wish they were! But, (if they

are not "Amelia's["]—and they are very much in the *measure* of the "Step-Son"),—
we do not know whose they are; and we trust that our sail is not filled by *many*
such mis-labelled breezes. (3)

Responding to Welby's play on the duplicity of his authorial signature,
Willis emphasizes the singularity of the poetess's single-name pseudonym,
"*the* 'Amelia,'" as a way of suggesting that these fugitive lines might belong
to the person most concerned about their provenance.[2] Willis hints that
evidence of the poem's authorship might lie in the poem's signature meter,
a ground of identity that is immediately rendered unstable by his reference to one of Amelia's best-known poems, "The Little Step-Son."[3] Initially published in seven-beat lines, Welby's "Step-Son" works a notable
change on common meter, the alternating four- and three-beat lines that
were the standard form of the sentimental verses and popular ballads that
served as ornament and filler in a wide range of antebellum periodicals.
Nevertheless, Welby's choice of meter is not all that distinctive. Not only
is it anticipated by a number of well-known poems by British women,[4]
the template of common meter is visible enough through the architecture
of her lines for the poem to be relineated in ballad stanzas when it is popularly anthologized.[5] The difficulty of owning this all-too-common "measure" suggests that it may be less the meter than the title of Welby's poem
that is useful to Willis insofar as it figures the problem of authentication
of a reprinted poem as the precarious parentage of an adopted child. For
all of their badinage concerning the extent and nature of each other's
poetic reputations, Welby and Willis seem surprisingly accepting of this
poem's fugitive condition. Willis in particular expresses confidence in his
readers' ability to appreciate these poetic lines despite the fact that the
question of their authorship remains unresolved: "if they are not 'Amelia's'
. . . we do not know whose they are."

 While the author of "these majestic-paced stanzas" does not appear to
have been identified within the pages of the *Mirror*, these are no longer
anonymous lines. Thanks to bibliographer Thomas Ollive Mabbott, we
now know that this multiply reprinted poem belongs to Edgar Allan Poe.
Welby's and Willis's flirtatious exchange prefaces the first known printing
of Poe's now-classic poem "Lenore" in its long-line format.[6] This version
of "Lenore" revises the Pindaric ode Poe had published in 1843, putting
it in dialogue with the lineation of popular poems and the tradition of
women's poetry. Pulling the second line of the ballad stanza up as the
tail end of the first, Poe reorganized his poem into seven-beat lines that
intensified the effects of internal rhyme and incremental repetition. Though

Poe could easily have learned this strategy from Welby or from Elizabeth Barrett Browning,[7] this kind of metrical experiment would soon become the hallmark of his style due to the popular success of "The Raven."

Reading "Lenore" in the context of its unauthorized reprinting in the *Evening Mirror* seems paradoxically both to threaten and to strengthen the tie between text and author. On the one hand, Welby's and Willis's failure to recognize the poem places the modern reader rather uncomfortably at the point of Poe's disappearance as an author. It is both a shock to our sense of Poe's cultural status and a threat to the coherence and integrity of his oeuvre that a characteristic work could circulate in misattributed and unattributed form, undistinguished and indistinguishable from the light verse of minor literati. This "lost Lenore"[8] represents not "The Raven's" successful conversion of repetition into a sense of poetic melancholy, but mere recirculation, not Poe's transformation of convention, but conventionality itself. And yet this example of Poe's near-vanishing into the culture of reprinting also suggests that it is the very invisibility of his signature that needs to be recovered. After all, Mabbott first noticed this exchange while working to extricate Poe's poetry and tales from antebellum periodicals and to reissue them in an authoritative variorum edition. It is the mode of circulation and not the poem itself that is alien to us. Both Mabbott's extraordinary labors in assembling the *Collected Works* and the containment of this anecdote of Poe's eclipse within the bounds of his authorized corpus corroborate Michel Foucault's insight into modernity's limited ability to tolerate literary anonymity. Remarking on a transition that was still very much underway in the antebellum United States, Foucault argues that, unlike scientific texts, which in the eighteenth century, began to be "received for themselves, in the anonymity of an established or always redemonstrable truth," literary texts

came to be accepted only when endowed with the author-function. We now ask of each poetic or fictional text: From where does it come, who wrote it, when, under what circumstances, or beginning with what design? The meaning ascribed to it and the status or value accorded it depend on the manner in which we answer these questions. And if a text should be discovered in a state of anonymity—whether as a consequence of an accident or the author's explicit wish—the game becomes one of rediscovering the author. Since literary anonymity is not tolerable, we can accept it only in the guise of an enigma.[9]

In Welby's and Willis's exchange we are confronted not only with antebellum readers' greater familiarity with and toleration of anonymous, pseudonymous, and questionably authored texts, but also with the impossibility of recovering their relation to an unauthorized "Lenore." For readers who come after "The Raven" and "The Philosophy of Composition," Poe's intentions seem to permeate this poem, his authorship signaled by the smallest detail—the mere repetition of a set of "sonorous" syllables:[10]

And, Guy De Vere, hast *thou* no tear?—weep now or never more!
See! On yon drear and rigid bier low lies thy love, Lenore! (ll. 3–4)

As the publication history of "Lenore" suggests, thinking about the ways in which Poe's writing was affected by the culture of reprinting disrupts the stable relation of text to context by returning us to a problem that Poe himself relentlessly dramatized and theorized. There seems nothing more Poe-esque than to find oneself at the charged threshold between insignificance and significance, oscillating between an awareness of the precariousness of authorial identity—its dependence on repetition and the recycling of literary conventions—and the conviction that the author's mark can be detected at impossibly minute levels. In reading the *Evening Mirror* reprint of "Lenore," our experience of the disappearing grounds of textual significance and their reappearance with a vengeance under the sign of an impossibly full intentionality parallels the predicament of the speaker in "The Raven," who fashions devastating personal prophecy out of the "stock and store" (l. 62) of the bird's unthinking speech. It also recalls the method of the poet in "The Philosophy of Composition," who strives to vary "*the application*" of his poem's refrain so that it remains meaningful, aiming to produce "continuously novel effects" (17) through the repetition of a word whose inevitable return threatens arbitrariness and monotony.[11] If, given the way in which authorship has come to organize literary study, it proves difficult to imagine a system in which literature circulated and was read without reliable recourse to the author as originator or principle of coherence, it may be in part because the figure of Poe stands in our way, collapsing a wider range of interpretive possibilities into a volatile binary opposition, writing allegories of authorship that propel us toward the stark alternatives of mastery or its lack.

In Chapter 5, I will argue that Poe's gravitation toward these extremes in his writing and public life was shaped by the demands of an author-centered literary nationalism. What I want to emphasize here, however, is the way in which Poe's immersion in the culture of reprinting continues to trouble the boundaries of his corpus despite our retrospective reauthorization of his texts. There remains a potent instability between the underinscription of the author's name in antebellum periodicals and the overproduction of the apparatus of attribution in twentieth-century criticism, an imbalance that works more as an engine for attribution than as a spur to thinking about the differences between these two literary regimes. The story of the reprinting of "Lenore" with which I began illustrates both the persistence of the problem of attribution and the capacity of the figure of Poe to transform a complex social and cultural field into a simpler, more powerful set of critical alternatives. At the time of the poem's republication, Poe was working for Willis, writing anonymous filler for the *Mirror*—"announcing news, condensing statements, answering correspondents, noticing amusements."[12] Is Poe's presence in the office and his penchant for literary deception enough evidence to suggest that the entire correspondence might have been a hoax, a ruse to generate publicity about a poem to which Poe would soon lay claim in an extended analysis of another of Welby's poems in the *Democratic Review*?[13] Does the unauthorized circulation of "Lenore" point to reprinting as a problem for Poe, or to Poe's successful manipulation of these conditions of publication? How would we be able to decide without access to Poe's signature?

In the case of the reprinting of "Lenore," bibliographers and critics can take comfort in the fact that their intervention completes Poe's intention to be known as the author of a poem that had yet to become identified with his name. And yet, respecting what we presume to be the author's desire can complicate rather than clarify the contours of the Poe canon. If Poe struggled to be credited as the author of a number of his poems and tales, he also had trouble disentangling his name from texts that circulated anonymously but seemed inexorably to point to his authorship. Consider, for example, his response to an anonymous attack on Longfellow that echoed arguments Poe himself had made in a series of articles on imitation and plagiarism he called "The Little Longfellow War." Writing in his capacity as editor of the *Broadway Journal's* Critical Notices, Poe comments on the second number of Thomas Dunn English's magazine, *The Aristidean*:

Some of the papers are exceedingly good—precisely what Magazine papers should be—vigorous, terse, independent. "Travels in Texas" is very interesting. "Richard Parker's Widow" is also admirable; and "Hans Spiegen" is quite in the Blackwood vein. There is a long review or rather running commentary upon Longfellow's poems. It is, perhaps, a little coarse, but we are not disposed to call it unjust;

although there are in it some opinions which, by implication, are attributed to ourselves individually, and with which we cannot altogether coincide.[14]

Singling out for praise a number of titles, all of which were published anonymously,[15] Poe shuttles awkwardly between the protective plurality and formal anonymity of the editorial "we" and the singularity of his authorial persona, wielding his power as an editor to keep the opinions expressed in the review from being "attributed to ourselves individually." Disavowing these opinions, however, only raises more insistently the question of the relation between this review and Poe's *Broadway Journal* articles. Poe describes the review in a way that suggests significant disagreement but also reminds the reader of the plurality of positions he is trying to uphold: these are opinions "with which we cannot altogether coincide."

If the distance between an anonymous text and his authorial name is something Poe tries hard here to preserve, this is a space that has been considerably narrowed by Poe scholarship. Presumably taking their cue from English's eventual attribution of the article to Poe,[16] critics have generally taken this vituperative review to be a part of Poe's oeuvre, speculating as Sidney Moss does, that if Poe did not write the entire piece, the plagiarism charges and the "minute analysis" of Longfellow's poems "indicate that Poe had more than a hand in the article."[17] The awkwardness of Moss's metaphor (what kind of involvement does "more than a hand" imply?) indicates his struggle to preserve Poe's authorship under the sign of an uncertain agency. Concluding that Poe placed this vitriolic attack in English's magazine in order to make his comments in the *Broadway Journal* look "mild by comparison" (177), Moss and others have rescued this text from its anonymous condition and made it proper to Poe.[18] The force of attribution here not only enables this text to be extricated from its context, it stabilizes the relation of context to text. Imitation and plagiarism are cordoned off as the subject of this review, safeguarding literary criticism from the more disturbing possibility that they are an ineradicable part of the conditions of publication, one that renders authorial origin profoundly unknowable. Settling the problem of authorship, even in compromised form, allows criticism to begin, establishing publishing conditions as exterior to a textual problem that is bandied about between individuals.

It is all too evident, however, that the problem of imitation and plagiarism thoroughly saturates the field of anonymous reviewing and perversely and insistently structures English's relation to Poe. Not only are their editorial positions repeatedly and productively confused—the rumor of Poe's editorship of the *Aristidean* is strong enough to call for its own disavowal, and it is English who completes the editorial work for the final issue of Poe's *Broadway Journal*[19]—what begins as a relationship of mutual convenience quickly deteriorates into a series of hostile, public disavowals that are brought to an end only by an acrimonious lawsuit: Poe suggests in print that English is a plagiarist; English accuses Poe of forgery; and Poe, in turn, successfully sues English for libel.[20] The problem with attributing the Longfellow review to Poe, English, or some combination of the two, is not simply that it erases this charged history of identification and denial, but that it obscures the literary system that allowed their relationship to take the forms that it did. Settling the question of authorship shifts attention away from the structures that enable the production of print-authority, making their effects the sole property of individuals. After all, the very strongest case for Poe's authorship of this review would still need to acknowledge that the sound of Poe's voice is produced by imitation, the depersonalization of print, and the traffic in caricatures of Poe's critical positions. If this review is indeed Poe's it is Poe imitating an imitation of himself. Apportioning responsibility for the review closes down consideration of the way in which its vitriol, its license, and the peculiar efficacy of its untraceable ventriloquism is made possible by a literary system that places authorship in complex forms of suspension and that trades on the dislocation of texts from their origins.

My aim in recalling the problematic anonymity of this review is to reflect on the way in which an author-centered criticism necessarily collapses the range of obscured, withheld, projected, and disavowed forms authorship that thrived under the system of reprinting. The herculean task of assembling Poe's anonymous reviews into a canon of critical works provides a case in point. In his definitive study, William Doyle Hull establishes an elaborate system of annotation to reflect his varying levels of confidence in Poe's authorship, signaling the difference between high, moderate, and low levels of probability, recording disagreements among bibliographers, and noting when his opinion remains unsupported by conclusive evidence. Hull repeatedly warns that "Such an attribution may be merely a guess"; "The possibility of imitation must here be considered"; and in some cases, "I merely state my own conviction."[21] Producing a modern reader's edition of Poe's criticism, however, requires that such distinctions be leveled out. For instance, in his edition of Poe's *Essays and Reviews*, G. R. Thompson makes Poe's work commensurate with that of other authors in the Library of America series by narrowing the resonant space of readerly doubt and by minimizing the importance of the variously signifying practices of anonymity that were exercised in reprint culture.[22]

Such editorial interventions produce the expectation of an identifiable, independent critical voice that we may have trouble locating when we return to the magazines and attend to antebellum periodical culture's collaborative and obfuscating editorial practices, its rivalrous recirculation of critical postures, and its often compromised use of anonymity to suggest gentility, multiple authorial voices, critical distance, or indifference. However, enough textual traces of these practices (and the uncertainties they provoke) survive to trouble the integrity of Poe's corpus. The most visible and controversial sign of fracture in the accepted body of Poe's works has been the scholarly debate over the "Paulding-Drayton" review, an anonymous article defending the slave system that bibliographers have long insisted should not be attributed to Poe.[23] Terence Whalen has recently expressed frustration with modern critics' reliance on this review. What bothers Whalen is not simply the fact that this discredited text continues to be included in the canon, but that it has served to anchor critical accounts of Poe's relation to slavery. In his analysis of the author-function, Michel Foucault outlines the process that Whalen decries: attaching Poe's name to an anonymous text establishes relations between and among texts that, in turn, produce a narrative about the author's subjectivity, "a projection, in more or less psychologizing terms, of the operations that we force texts to undergo" (110). Leonard Cassuto, who includes both the "Paulding-Drayton" review and the *Aristidean* attack on Longfellow in his brief selection of Poe's criticism, is forthright about this process: "The Longfellow exchange spotlights the links that bind together Poe's literary theories, his Southern allegiances, and his splenetic attempts to reform the literary business from outside" (xi). In Cassuto's edition, disputed texts become representative texts; the authorial subject, Poe, is more coherent with them than without them. Whalen hopes that his critical intervention will disable a set of arguments based on what he regards as a set of avoidable mistakes, but the historical specificity at which he aims is perhaps better indicated by the persistence of the problem of attribution than by its elimination. Such seemingly ineradicable rifts in Poe's corpus testify to intractable differences between systems of literary production. Texts produced under the aegis of reprinting's peculiar combination of gentlemanly and republican anonymity cannot easily or without distortion be forced to occupy the categories of an author-centered literary nationalism.

In this chapter, I will argue that we produce Poe as a national author and as a name for a unified body of work at the cost of understanding the more complex forms of authorial agency that were practiced in the culture of reprinting. For most of his career, rather than trying and failing to achieve the threshold conditions of national authorship, Poe experiments with the space opened up by reprinting's characteristic dislocation of texts from their sources, its exposure of foreign books and all kinds of magazine and newspaper writing to an open-ended and unknowable field of circulation. Examining Poe's writing can shed light on the rhetorical structures that enable texts to hold their value despite such dislocations. As I will argue, Poe's investments in genre, his adoption of the literary values of the miscellany, and his attempts to establish authorship by disrupting the process of reprinting are authorial strategies made possible by the heterogenous and uncontrolled distribution of antebellum periodical literature.

If Poe's writing can tell us much about the system of reprinting, taking reprinting seriously also changes how we think about Poe's writing, requiring that we disaggregate and reconfigure his corpus. Generally speaking, critics' reliance on the products of bibliographers' labor and their bias toward the form of the book have worked to erase the radical unpredictability of the antebellum field of circulation. For instance, reading Poe's poetry and tales in the chronological order of their composition, painstakingly established by Mabbott in his variorum edition, creates a number of impressions that are at odds with the historical precision of Mabbott's project.[24] The homogeneity of the variorum tends to blunt the specificity of the magazine and newspaper contexts in which Poe's work was circulated and read. The uniformity of presentation tends to minimize the question of the fit between Poe's texts and their periodical formats; it also evens out the geographical range and numerical extent of their circulations. Some of these newspapers and literary weeklies circulated in urban areas only, some weeklies and monthlies had regional reach, and a few, such as *Graham's* and *Godey's*, came as close as any 1840s text to national circulation. Moreover, many of the periodicals in which Poe's texts appeared vastly exceeded the print runs of his published books.

Assembling Poe's widely scattered texts into reliable, standard editions enables critics to make connections across the corpus, but it does so by muting regional differences in Poe's reputation and by erasing the temporal stutter—the odd patterns of repetition and delay—that structured his career. What we tend to think of as single texts circulated in multiple formats in different locations, their existence acknowledged in a spate of exchange-paper notices, only to reappear years later in another set of periodicals, subject to different networks of reception. Much of the staggered circulation and recirculation of Poe's writing can be traced back to Poe, whose poverty forced him to adapt to the regional nature of antebellum literary culture. Moving from print center to print center in search of steady work, Poe reprinted revised and unrevised versions of his poetry, criticism, and tales, repeatedly making them available for circulation to an unpredictable readership.

Recalled from their banishment to bibliographic footnotes, where they are of minor importance compared to the first printings that hold value for collectors, the known reprints of Poe's poetry and tales enable us to chart a career that unfolds in fragmentary, overlapping and multiply articulated form. Recognizing the importance of reprinting to Poe's career has tangible benefits for author-centered study, providing us, for example, with a more nuanced sense of Poe's economic agency. While Poe does not control the reprinting of his magazine writing, his ability to republish his poems and tales provides him with a mobile form of capital. Most often invoked as the victim of a literary marketplace that undervalued American authors' labor, Poe is both subject to and seeks to benefit from the peculiar structure of this market. For Poe, the indirect routes through which reprinted texts appeared in periodicals represented both opportunity and constraint: unauthorized reprints provoke his suspicion that publishing networks are under the control of the elite, but they also offer material proof that work of value could circulate both domestically and abroad regardless of the power of publishing coteries. Allowing reprinting to reshuffle the order of Poe's texts should also provide a way for critics to reintegrate the study of his poetry and tales. From the vantage point of book publication, Poe's career as a poet appears to precede and to be largely superceded by his turn to writing tales and lengthier narratives.[25] However, taking into account Poe's publication and republication of his work in periodicals, it is strikingly apparent that he never abandons his interest in poetry as a mass-market phenomenon. Indeed, Poe experiences remarkable success throughout his career in placing revised versions of what we think of as his early poems in partisan monthlies, gift books, and illustrated magazines.

While we have much still to learn about the shape of Poe's career from the record of the reprinting of his poetry and fiction, the effect of reprinting on Poe's writing cannot be understood by compensating for its effects. That is, to attempt a comprehensive mapping of the sites and significance of reprinted versions of his work would be to recapture unauthorized texts as proper to Poe, rather than to allow them to challenge our sense of the nature of his authorship. Instead of invoking reprinting as an external force—something that happens to Poe's writing—I will ask how the capacity to be reprinted structures Poe's poetry and tales. Looking first at aspects of Poe's writing that have proved obstacles to his assimilation into a literary nationalist canon, I will argue that Poe's allusive appeals to the British literary tradition, the spatial and temporal dislocation of his poetry and tales, and his commitment to an aesthetic of eclecticism all mark his strong engagement with the literary values of the culture of reprinting. Turning more directly to questions of literary property, I will then examine Poe's use of handwriting of a doubtful authenticity to broker the distance between authorial disenfranchisement and editorial ownership. In his early tale "The Visionary," and in a number of nonce magazine genres, Poe cultivates the reader's awareness of the differential iterability of handwriting and print, aligning authorial ownership not with mastery but with the ability to disrupt the system of reprinting.

Embracing Secondarity

If Dickens's American tour and *American Notes* give us an exasperated outsider's perspective on the culture of reprinting, Poe's writing gives us insight into a career charted through the heart of this culture, one in which authors' subjection to the uncontrolled circulation of their writing and the relative scarcity of institutions to mediate the relations of authors and readers were not temporary inconveniences but the rules of the game. The trajectory of Poe's career passes through nearly all the important antebellum publishing centers and his shifts between them chart a progress toward the embattled center of the struggle over a national literature. From his unheralded publication of a slim volume of poems in Boston in 1827, to his disastrous recitation of a juvenile poem before the Boston Lyceum in 1845, Poe's career inscribes a circular path from anonymity to notoriety that encompasses virtually all the forms of publishing that were prevalent in this era. Beginning with his attempt at gentlemanly authorship in the presumptive cultural capital, Poe's attempt to make a living through his writing took him to Baltimore in 1831, where he gained access to print through newspaper contests and subscription publishing, then to Richmond in 1835, where he generated renown as a reviewer in the fledgling southern press. After a brief stint in New York in 1837, where he published his adventure novel *The Narrative of Arthur Gordon Pym*, but was unable to support himself through free-lance reviewing, Poe moved to Philadelphia, which was fast becoming the epicenter of large-circulation, genteel periodicals. In Philadelphia, Poe published in gift books, dollar newspapers, and mammoth weeklies, experimented with lecturing and serializing his tales in cheap pamphlet form, and attempted to launch a high-toned literary monthly, all while editing a successful ladies' magazine. Poe moved back to New York in 1844, where his association with a prominent group of literary nationalists enabled him to publish collections of his poetry and tales and to acquire part-ownership of a literary weekly. Poe achieved considerable fame with the publication of "The Raven" in the spring of 1845, but his journal collapsed by the end of the year and his mismanagement of literary politics caused him to be swallowed up in a regional rivalry. Although after this fiasco Poe would drift from city to city, he died just as he had begun to contemplate reviving his elite literary magazine in the western territories.

The many geographical dislocations of Poe's career and his traversal of mass-cultural and high-cultural formats appear idiosyncratic when viewed through the disciplinary lens of a nationalist criticism. Poe's career and writing resist our critical models in ways that have proved consequential for his status in the canon: he creatively embraces America's cultural secondarity, whereas we have come to expect serious literature to wrestle with the problem of national identity; he remains committed to reprinting's aesthetic of eclecticism, while we are equally committed to sorting this literature according to hierarchies of literary form; and, in moving between and among publishing centers, he recirculates his poetry and tales, frustrating our attempts to construct a narrative of authorial development.

Poe's early poems and tales readily acknowledge their secondarity, suggesting that for Poe, American literature was to take root in the interstices of popular British literature. In typically arch and ironic fashion, Poe concludes *Al Aaraaf, Tamerlane, and Minor Poems* (1829) with a footnote to the poem "Fairyland" that could well apply to the collection as a whole: "Plagiarism—see the works of Thomas Moore, passim."[26] Here, and in the notes to "Al Aaraaf," Poe mimics the lushness, erudition, and self-conscious artifice of Moore's early lyrics and calls attention to his experimentation with the orientalist mode of *Lalla Rookh* (1817). For Poe, awareness of his indebtedness to the popular British poet is a selling point, an index of authorial self-consciousness and poetic ambition. Though these notes betray some anxiety about American readers' ability to pick up on the full range of his allusions, they also suggest that Poe understands literariness to be produced in open dialogue with, not resistance to British models. Poe's notes to "Al Aaraaf" identify him as a sophisticated reader of Shakespeare, Marlowe, and Milton, and as a poet who defends his poems as revoicings of favorite lines and passages from British literature. However awkward they may sound when ventriloquized, Poe's British sources remain too valuable to be elided: "The rhyme in this verse . . . has an appearance of affectation. It is, however, imitated from Sir W. Scott, or rather from Claud Halcro—in whose mouth I admired its effect" (32).[27] In this note, Poe claims a kind of contemporaneity with Scott's fictional bard, invoking the historical romance to justify his own poetic speaking.

Poe's early fiction is similarly dense with references to popular and frequently reprinted British texts. As Timothy Scherman has noted, the stories Poe initially tried to publish as "Tales of the Folio Club" were embedded in a narrative framework that allowed Poe both to imitate popular fictional styles and to insulate himself from the charge of mere copying by appending critical commentary—itself imagined as "a burlesque upon criticism"—to each of the tales.[28] The layers of ironic distance Poe establishes between himself and his fictional experiments reinforce the fact that British popular fiction was a force to be contended with. In "Tales of the Folio Club," the transplanted British fictional types that serve as narrative vehicles and as objects of critique are inherently ridiculous. And yet their foreignness is also indispensable to Poe's conjuring of an American literary elite. Most of the club's members, who in Poe's narrative scheme serve as the tellers of his tales, are caricatures familiar from British periodical fiction, from the Bulwerian aesthete, "Mr. Convolvulus Gondola, a young gentleman who had traveled a good deal," to the mock-gothic Mr. Horribile Dictû . . . who had graduated at Gottingen [sic]," to "Mr. Blackwood Blackwood who had written certain articles for foreign Magazines" (205). Those narrators who are drawn from the world of American letters are notable for their orientation toward the British literary scene: Poe's stand-in for New England author and editor John Neal tells the story "Lionizing," which satirizes N. P. Willis's cultivation of British aristocracy, while the storyteller taken from Washington Irving's *Bracebridge Hall* (1822), is "a stout gentleman who admired Sir Walter Scott" (205).[29] Even when the tales are read as they were eventually published—individually, without narrators who are identified as characters, and without the critical baffling— it is clear that they are not simple parodies but complex redeployments of literary forms that Poe assumes will be recognized by an audience steeped in British poetry, fiction, and criticism.

Poe's knowing address to his reader, which is equal parts ironic self-distancing and eager self-promotion, is apparent from even slight rhetorical gestures such as the epigraphs to these tales. Take, for example, "A Decided Loss," a burlesque of the *Blackwood's* tale of sensation, to which Poe prefixes a partial citation from Thomas Moore's *Irish Melodies* (1821): "Oh! breathe not, &c."[30] Poe's truncated quotation names the parodic subject of his tale, a ludicrous first-person account of a man who has lost his breath, and yet it also identifies the British poet as the common property of American readers. Poe counts on his audience's ability to complete the fragment from Moore's well-known poem: "Oh! breathe not his name." Poe's tale of a man who quite literally has lost his inspiration satirizes the consolations of philosophy by routing the question of the relation of spirit to matter through popular genres such as the predicament-tale and the gallows confessional. Poe's tale takes its bearing toward these genres from what goes unsaid in the all-too-familiar quotation from Thomas Moore. The injunction "Oh! breathe not [his name]," which the knowing reader cannot obey, calls attention to the ironic discrepancy between Moore's poem, in which a nameless, unhonored dead man is commended to common memory, and the conditions of its circulation, the pseudo-anonymity of the mass-produced ballad, which is the vehicle for Moore's considerable fame. Poe addresses a readership alive to the humorous disparity between literary seriousness and the popular media. But Poe does not so much decry as inhabit the space of this contradiction.[31] If the narrator in "A Decided Loss" is passively handed from fictional cliché to cliché, his corpse-like body tossed from a crowded stagecoach, abandoned in a landlord's attic, and mistakenly carted off to be hung for robbery, his lack of animation ultimately works to his advantage: he discovers on the gallows that he cannot be suffocated because he has already lost his breath. In this tale, there is a comic persistence to literary secondarity, which is relentlessly figured as circulation without inspiration. Poe's pleasure in and commitment to the popular genres he nonetheless satirizes is apparent from the subtitle he added to this burlesque when he republished it in the *Broadway Journal* in 1846: "A Tale Neither In nor Out of 'Blackwood.'" This subtitle names both Poe's equivocal narrative position and the indeterminate literary space opened up by the culture of reprinting—the extended influence but unpredictable field of significance produced by the popular American recirculation of British periodical writing.[32]

Dislocating Reference

The strong presence in American periodicals of reprinted foreign texts helps to account for the nature of Poe's address to the reader in much of his writing. Though often taken as a sign of his estrangement from American culture, the elaborate European settings of many of Poe's tales instead mark his engagement with the generic codes of American magazines where foreignness serves to emphasize a story's literary aspirations. "Ligeia's" "dim and decaying city by the Rhine" (320) and the London coffeehouse of "The Man of the Crowd" do not transport readers beyond national borders so much as remind them that they inhabit fictive space, a space clearly marked as such in popular monthly magazines where Germanic romantic tales and Dickensian urban sketches were standard fare.

Poe was on the whole more inspired than distressed by the acute nonreferentiality of a borrowed set of literary norms. While in his criticism, Poe frequently expressed contempt for American writers' slavish copying of foreign texts, he regarded the nationalist attempt to transplant European literary conventions onto American soil and to promote texts with American themes as a continuation of, not a revolt against, colonial "subserviency":

Time was when we imported our critical decisions from the mother country. For many years we enacted a perfect farce of subserviency to the *dicta* of Great Britain. At last a revulsion of feeling, with self-disgust, necessarily ensued. Urged by these, we plunged into the opposite extreme. In throwing off *totally* that "authority," whose voice had so long been so sacred, we even surpassed, and by much, our original folly. But the watchword now was, "a national literature!"—as if any true literature *could be* "national"—as if the world at large were not the only proper stage for the literary *histrio*. We became, suddenly, the merest and maddest *partizans* in letters. Our papers spoke of "tariffs" and "protection." Our Magazines had habitual passages about that "truly native novelist Mr. Cooper," or that "staunch American genius, Mr. Paulding". . . our reviews urged the propriety—our booksellers the necessity, of strictly "American" themes. A foreign subject, at this epoch, was a weight more than enough to drag down into the very depths of critical damnation the finest writer owning nativity in the States; while, on the reverse, we found ourselves daily in the paradoxical dilemma of liking, or pretending to like, a stupid book the better because (sure enough) its stupidity was of our own growth and discussed our own affairs.[33]

Published in January 1842 at the height of international copyright agitation, this preface to the critical notices Poe edited in *Graham's* attacks nationalist critics' and booksellers' attempts to narrow the scope of American writing, trusting that their influence will soon run its course. Though framed as a critique of the nationalists' restrictive political aims, Poe's "Exordium" also serves as a strong defense of writers who understand "the world at large" as "the only proper stage" for literature, writers who aim at a generalized audience by self-consciously choosing a foreign subject. Years later, under the burden of considerable literary nationalist patronage, Poe would be even more explicit: "That an American should confine himself to American themes, or even prefer them, is rather a political than a literary idea—and at best is a questionable point. We would do well to bear in mind that 'distance lends enchantment to the view.' *Ceteris paribus*, a foreign theme is, in a strictly literary sense, to be preferred."[34]

Something like an attempt to transform cultural dislocation into a principle of poetic practice is evident from the elaborate indirection of the opening lines of Poe's ambitious early poem "Al Aaraaf":

O! NOTHING earthly save the ray
[Thrown back from flowers] of Beauty's eye,
As in those gardens where the day
Springs from the gems of Circassy— (ll. 1–4)

As R. C. DeProspo has noted, the negative injunction, "O! NOTHING earthly," with which Poe begins "[removes] the setting of the poem from our space entirely."[35] Poe allows a single exception to this rule, identifying the proper subject of the poem as a ray of light that traces its origin to "Beauty's eye," but this ray is not only minimal but indirect, deflected from "flowers" which are the unearthly flowers of rhetoric itself. In this poem about poetic origins, Poe claims for poetry the territory of rhetoric in all of its artifice and derivativeness. Poe compares the poem's source to gardens in which the day emanates from precious stones rather than being reflected by them; to "the thrill / Of melody in woodland rill" (ll. 5–6), a sound of determinedly indeterminate origin; and to the memory rather than the experience of pleasure: "Joy's voice so peacefully departed / That like the murmur in the shell, / Its echo dwelleth and will dwell—" (ll. 8–10). In "Al Aaraaf," Poe responds to what Harold Bloom has identified as the characteristic poetic predicament of belatedness, not by reclaiming an origin—by Americanizing romantic topoi—but by troping on the situation of belatedness itself. Poe embraces rather than bemoans poetic secondarity, taking a radical dislocation from origins as the condition of writing poetry.

While only a handful of Poe's stories, such as "Siope" and "Eleonora," are similarly allegorical and otherworldly, most of Poe's tales are loosed from temporal and geographic specificity. For example, the "singularly dreary tract of country" through which narrator and reader travel "in the autumn of the year" (397) in order to arrive at the "House of Usher" stakes a claim to an exemplary generality that allowed the tale to achieve extranational status within the culture of reprinting. Republished without acknowledgment in the London monthly *Bentley's Miscellany* eight months after its appearance in *Tales of the Grotesque and Arabesque* (1839), "The Fall of the House of Usher" was subsequently reprinted in the weekly *Boston Notion* under a heading that suggested British authorship: "From Bentley's Miscellany for August." Poe's decision to distinguish his tale generically while stopping short of identifying its location or otherwise marking its national origin not only enables the tale to be absorbed into *Bentley's*, it allows it to be mistaken in Boston for a British text. (That the editors of the *Notion* were unaware that the tale was Poe's is indicated not only by its anonymity, but by the fact that they had published a scathing review of *Tales of the Grotesque and Arabesque* in December of 1839).[36] As the transatlantic traffic in "The Fall of the House of Usher" suggests, British and American periodical culture shared a set of literary norms that were characterized as British by default.

While a strategic generality could not ensure that a particular tale would be reprinted at home or abroad, Poe's minimal use of temporal markers and his erasure or abstraction of spatial location seems a careful attempt to hold open a tale's potential field of address—to be specific enough to set the scene, but elusive enough to keep the reader from tying, or attempting to tie the text to a referent. Many of Poe's tales first invoke and then evacuate temporal or spatial reference, indicating that a narrative takes place "during the reign of _____" ("Bon-Bon," 164), "in the summer months of the year 18____" ("Mystification," 253), or, combining a vague temporality with the projection of a generic setting: "During the autumn of 18____, while on tour through the extreme Southern provinces of France . . ." ("The System of Doctor Tarr and Professor Fether" 699). In the very faintness of its acknowledgment of the world of fact, the opening sentence of "The Oval Portrait" emphasizes that the tale's field of reference is first and foremost the genre of gothic fiction, and only secondarily a spot in an actual landscape: "The chateau into which my valet had ventured to make forcible entrance . . . was one of those piles of commingled gloom and grandeur which have so long frowned among the Appenines, not less in fact than in the fancy of Mrs. Radcliffe" (481).

The opening sentence of "The Oval Portrait" typifies the speed and the economy with which Poe dislocates his tales from reference to the world and relocates them on the grounds of genre. That this maneuver constitutes a response to the peculiar constraints and opportunities afforded by the culture of reprinting is perhaps best elucidated by analogy to Poe's address to his reader in poems such as "To _____" (56), "To the River _____" (56), "To _____" (57), "To F_____" (74) and "To _____ _____ _____" (88). Strikingly, these poems preserve the figure of direct address while simultaneously refusing to delimit it. Poems that employed an open-ended address to their readers were common in antebellum ladies' magazines due to their complex play with intimacy and abstraction, their ability to conjure the private circulation of verse among friends and relatives from within the frame of anonymous mass-production. This mode of address invites the reader to imagine herself as the poet's addressee, but not without also calling attention to the inevitability of the poem's recirculation, whether copied into commonplace books by admiring readers, reprinted by editors filling out the columns of their periodicals, or republished by the author, who, in opening wide the field of reference, retained the right of readdress.

Such poems of intimate, empty address create the fiction of a seamless contiguity between manuscript and reprint practices through their common dependence on repetition and recirculation. Take, for example, the poem that begins "Would'st thou be loved?": Poe initially inscribed this poem in the album of his cousin Elizabeth Herring, then published it in the *Southern Literary Messenger* (September 1835) under the title "Lines Written in an Album," then retitled it "To _____" for its appearance in *Burton's Gentleman's Magazine* (August 1839). This trajectory from specificity to generality, from the delineation of a precise social and cultural location to the empty reflexivity of the act of poetic address itself, marks Poe's recognition of the extended field of the poem's iterability. It also heightens the volatile discrepancy between the structural promiscuity of the poem's mode of address and its call to self-consistency:

Fair maiden, let thy generous heart
From its present pathway part not—
Being every thing which now thou art
Be nothing which thou art not.[37]

This poem succeeds in its prescriptions by invoking in the most general terms the middle-class definition of female virtue as self-identity.

Nevertheless, the duplicitous adaptability that is implicit in the poem's mode of address gets played out in the history of its subsequent uses: this poem is both copied out and signed by Poe's wife, Virginia, in the album of another cousin, and re-published by Poe as "To F____" in the *Broadway Journal* (September 13, 1845) in a somewhat nervous bid to call a cease-fire in his public flirtation with the poetess Frances Sargent Osgood. That the poem comes to rest as the property of a specific addressee, taking as its final title "To F____s S. O____d" in *The Raven and Other Poems* (1845), should not obscure the flexibility Poe acquires by employing an empty figure of direct address, making the uncontrollable circulation of the poem a part of its very form. The conspicuous iterability of this mode of address not only aligns the poem with empty social forms, such as the writing of album verses, through which intimacies are forged, it also helps to protect Poe from the charge of excessive intimacy with a married woman. Although "To F____" teases the reader with the promise of an inside knowledge of Poe's affairs, the poem cannot finally be pinned down to a specific addressee.[38] The space of the blank suspends the poem's delivery, staking a claim to the abstraction and depersonalization that is implied by its appearance in print.

A similar reliance on depersonalization is apparent in Poe's "To the River ____," which conceals an autobiographical pun in its self-conscious echo of Byron's "Stanzas to the Po." In Poe's poem, the identification of the author as the poem's addressee (both the origin and potential terminus of the poem's significations) has to pass through his representation of both river and poem as reflective surfaces in which the *reader's* image is captured and returned. Addressing his unnamed river, Poe writes:

But when within thy wave she looks,
  (Which glistens then, and trembles,)
Why, then the prettiest of brooks
  Her worshipper resembles.
For in my heart, as in thy stream,
  Her image deeply lies—
The heart which trembles at the beam
  The scrutiny of her eyes.[39]

Just as within the poem, Poe depicts the river in trembling subjection to the glance of the reader, so too does authorial self-reference in its title depend on the reader's consciousness of the literary conventions that link Poe's stanzas to Byron's.[40] The emptying out of reference in the title of the poem clears space for Poe's signature, but it does so only through the medium of genre. Hearing the pun on the author's name requires the reader to reflect on Poe's indebtedness to Bryon, while holding open the figure of address as the space of a strategic self-erasure only exposes the poem as a structure for the production and reproduction of readerly narcissism. The space in which Po[e]'s name is delivered up actually directs our attention *away* from the poet as the ground of the poem's authority, sending us instead to Poe's source in Byron's "Stanzas" or to the infinitely replicable, enraptured gaze of Poe's audience of women readers.

I have focused on the dislocation of reference in Poe's poetry both because in antebellum America, the lyric is a tremendously popular technology for the production of print-intimacy, and because the dislocation of reference in these poems is the site of an imagined continuity between modes of circulation. In conspicuously making themselves available for copying, these poems strike the keynote both of the intimate manuscript circulation of polite verse and of the anonymous and unbounded culture of reprinting. The aesthetic and cultural function of the dislocation of reference in Poe's tales is more difficult to plot, chiefly because it marks the space of a discontinuity between the settled authority of the elite British magazines and the more haphazard and shifting field of American periodical culture. Returning briefly to the question of the strategic generality of time and space in many of Poe's tales, I want to suggest that what we have taken to be their placelessness actually serves to locate them within a culture of literary dislocation. The double gesture by which Poe first invokes and then evacuates conventional grounds of narrative authority can be seen as a mechanism for the transfer of authority to the only thing that American readers of magazine fiction reliably hold in common—the territory of genre itself.

Poe has a number of ways of narrativizing his characteristic refusal to locate a tale in a specific time or space, a mode of address to his reader that one narrator describes as a "species of indefinite definiteness" ("The Devil in the Belfry," 298). In "Metzengerstein," the narrator appeals to the universality of human experience: "Horror and fatality have been stalking abroad in all ages. Why then give a date to the story I have to tell?" (134). As the narrator goes on to explain, his choice to set the tale "in the interior of Hungary" at the designedly vague "period of which I speak" is a product of his need to find a suitable locale for a "settled although hidden belief in the doctrines of Metempsychosis" (134). Time and place in this tale are a product of the narrator's solicitation of readerly belief, a feat that is best accomplished by delineating a credulous world from which modern readers can safely distance themselves. Through the medium of his narrator's resistance to telling anything but a universal story, Poe suggests that his tale's elaborate gothic setting is a product of his *readers'* need to align themselves with the disenchantments of modernity, a need that their very desire for absorption in gothic fiction would seem to belie. In this early tale Poe is remarkably candid about the way in which its timeless— because generic—feudal setting is a back-projection of the needs of his skeptical readers.

Other tales psychologize their deracination in the guise of amnesiac narrators: "I cannot, for my soul, remember how, when, or precisely where, I first became acquainted with the Lady Ligeia" (262). As critics long have noted, Poe's mentally suspect narrators function on the level of plot to provide a kind of plausible deniability for the extreme experiences they recount; they act as a framing device that can retrospectively be activated to cordon off the extravagances of Poe's fiction. And yet they also enable Poe to shift the grounds of narrative authority at the beginning of a tale. For instance, Poe's narrators in "MS. Found in a Bottle," "Berenice," and "Ligeia" all gesture toward a genealogy that they withhold from readers, invoking the paternal name under the sign of its omission and satisfying the desire for an account of origins by substituting a history of the narrator's aesthetic or moral education.[41] In "MS Found in a Bottle" the narrator registers the imperative to account for his rootlessness while simultaneously excluding the details of his heritage from the narrative proper: "Of my country and of my family I have little to say. Ill usage and length of years have driven me from the one, and estranged me from the other. Hereditary wealth afforded me an education of no common order, and a contemplative turn of mind enabled me to methodise the stores which early study very diligently garnered up" (189). Shifting explanatory grounds from nationality and heredity to the "stores" of his uncommon education ultimately leads the narrator to reproach himself with excessive rationality, a trait he will identify as "a very common error of this age" (189). Similarly toying with the general availability of what he will also claim as a set of distinguishing traits, Poe's narrator in "Berenice" establishes his aristocratic lineage with reference to a set of "striking particulars," all of which are invoked only in their general and iterable, not their specific or identifiable form:

My baptismal name is Egaeus; that of my family I will not mention. Yet there are not towers in the land more time-honored than my gloomy, gray, hereditary halls.

Our line has been called a race of visionaries; and in many striking particulars—in the character of the family mansion—in the frescos of the chief saloon—in the tapestries of the dormitories—in the chiselling of some buttresses in the armory—but more especially in the gallery of antique paintings—in the fashion of the library chamber—and, lastly, in the very peculiar nature of the library's contents, there is more than sufficient evidence to warrant the belief. (225)

Poe's conspicuous shift from a particular locale to a general grammar of gothic fiction (a grammar he needs only minimal "chiselling" to invoke) makes it clear that his readers are to inhabit the "gloomy, gray, hereditary halls" of fiction itself. Although Poe's narrator will go on to distinguish his own diseased and impoverished attention to detail from the common, luxurious experience of imaginative absorption, his initial description of the pleasures of his arrested development reads like an exaggerated version of the ordinary predicament of the antebellum American reader:

the noon of manhood found me still in the mansion of my fathers—it *is* wonderful what stagnation there fell upon the springs of my life—wonderful how total an inversion took place in the character of my commonest thought. The realities of the world affected me as visions, and as visions only, while the wild ideas of the land of dreams became, in turn—not the material of my everyday existence—but in very deed that existence utterly and solely in itself. (226)

The narrator's disorientation figures the condition of reading gothic fiction in a country without tapestries, buttresses, and antique paintings, where the desire for absorption in this particular "land of dreams" is not continuous with but radically disjunctive from ordinary life, a dangerous detachment from "the material" of "everyday existence."

In "Ligeia," Poe's initial focus on the narrator's confused mental state prepares the reader for a change in register from the details of a particular romance, in which the withholding of Ligeia's paternal name might have been "a playful charge" or "a test of affection" between lovers, to a generic focus on the degree to which "that spirit which is entitled *Romance*" (262) governs the narrative as a whole:

And now, while I write, a recollection flashes upon me that I have *never known* the paternal name of her who was my friend and my betrothed, and who became the partner of my studies, and finally the wife of my bosom. Was it a playful charge on the part of my Ligeia? Or was it a test of my strength of affection, that I should institute no inquiries upon this point? Or was it rather a caprice of my own—a wildly romantic offering on the shrine of the most passionate devotion? I but indistinctly recall the fact itself—what wonder that I have utterly forgotten the circumstances which originated or attended it? And, indeed, if ever that spirit which is entitled *Romance*—if ever she, the wan and the misty-winged *Ashtophet* of idolatrous Egypt, presided, as they tell, over marriages ill-omened, then most surely she presided over mine. (262)

In this passage, the narrator's intermittent recollection and forgetting is interrupted by his sudden, present-tense conviction of the originary erasure of Ligeia's paternity. At first, the narrator's assurance provides some badly needed continuity for the narrative, setting to rights his flickering consciousness and allowing for the unfolding of the romance-sequence: friend, betrothed, partner, wife. And yet the narrator's confident establishment of the threshold condition of his ignorance produces a new kind of uncertainty. His utter confusion as to whether the omission of Ligeia's paternal name was the product of her command or his desire, a matter of submission to her will or indulgence of his caprice, finally provokes a metacritical turn to the established "fact" of its erasure and a projection of authority onto the personified spirit of "Romance" which "most surely" presided over his "ill-omened" marriage. Poe uses his narrator's confusion to raise and to disarm the expectation that he will provide an account of origins, offering in its stead a conviction of generic certainty.[42]

In these tales, deracination and generic self-consciousness operate as a prose-equivalent of Poe's decision in his poems of empty address to make iterability a conspicuous part of poetic form. Like "To the River _____," these tales acknowledge their suspension between the presumptive authority of their British models and the demands of an unknowable mass-readership. Poe creates self-authorizing fictions by staging the often dubious transfer of authority from a settled, hierarchical social order to the more elusive but common territory of genre. While a negative consequence of this maneuver is the readerly identification of Poe with his self-enclosed, deluded narrators, fictions that refer the reader primarily to themselves for their authority are well braced against the prospect of their decontextualization and recontextualization.

It may be structurally impossible, finally, to prove that Poe's detachment of his tales from singular, identifiable contexts is a textual trace that points to reprinting as the context for the circulation of his fiction. After all, these tales are carefully designed to redirect the reader's desire to refer to context in order to stabilize the meaning of the text. It is crucial to note, however, that Poe's relocation of narrative authority represents not a turning away from but a turning toward his audience. Poe's generic self-consciousness is not a mark of his elitism or his disdain for his mass-readership, a claim which has long been used by scholars to secure Poe's inclusion in a high-cultural tradition. Rather, in shifting narrative authority to the common territory of genre, Poe seizes the opportunity afforded by the mass-circulation of fiction in a wide range of periodical formats, building into his tales a kind of portability and creating narrative frameworks that could compensate for the lack of reliable social and institutional structures to authorize his fiction.

Elaboration, Eclecticism, and the Deferral of Authorship

Part of what makes the emptying out of reference in Poe's tales difficult to register is his concomitant elaboration of his generic locales. For instance, in the passage I quoted from "Berenice" above, Poe's careful avoidance of specificity nearly gets buried under the pile-up of clauses he marshals to provide "more than sufficient evidence" of his narrator's aristocratic credentials. In an early letter to Thomas W. White, the editor and owner of the *Southern Literary Messenger*, Poe famously defended exaggeration in "Berenice" as part of a conscious strategy to gain "celebrity" for White's magazine. According to Poe, in "Berenice" he had purposely offered "the ludicrous heightened into the grotesque; the fearful coloured into the horrible; the witty exaggerated into the burlesque; the singular wrought out into the strange and mystical."[43] Only distortions such as these, he claimed, could hope to engender the multiple acts of reprinting that were required for a tale to attract significant public notice. Poe leaves open the question as to whether such generic mutations constitute a violation or a reinscription of aesthetic norms:

You may say all this is in bad taste. I have my doubts about it. . . . But whether the articles of which I speak are, or are not in bad taste is little to the purpose. To be appreciated you must be *read*, and these things are invariably sought after with avidity. They are, if you will take notice, the articles which find their way into other periodicals, and into the papers, and in this manner, taking hold upon the public mind they augment the reputation of the source where they originated. (58)

In this letter, Poe not only calls on White to measure the value of a tale in terms of its effect on readers,[44] he identifies exaggeration as the best way to provoke the necessary chain of acts of reading and republication.

Strikingly, Poe describes a circuit of production and distribution which is influenced but not governed by the author, one in which stylistic extremity is the engine of circulation but where reference to the author is oddly shaken loose from the history of a tale's reception. Just as an effective style is a matter not of originating, but of distorting and augmenting existing genres, so tales like "Berenice" are oddly animate and self-propelled: once published, they "find their way into other periodicals, and into the papers," and "[take] hold" of the public mind." Even when such "articles" prove successful, celebrity does not redound upon the author but enhances the already-existing reputation of the "source where they originated," in this case, White's magazine itself.

In justifying his aesthetic choices to his skeptical editor, Poe had reason to minimize the fact that he stood personally to gain by pressing his tale to "the very verge of bad taste" (58), an aesthetic ambition that, as Joan Dayan and others have noted, finds its most apposite figure in Berenice's brutally violated mouth.[45] But Poe's commitment to the idea that an exaggerated style can stimulate sales carries with it strict limits on authorial visibility. Promising a subtler enactment of his aesthetic principles—"I will not sin quite so egregiously again"—Poe proposes supplying White with a provocative new tale on a monthly basis under the condition that "no two of these Tales will have the slightest resemblance to one another in either matter or manner—still however preserving the character which I speak of" (58). Poe not only fantasizes about the remote and seemingly agentless efficacy of authorial style, he also goes out of his way to refuse the kind of consistency that would enable readers to identify his tales with one another. Poe depicts authorship as a kind of virtuosity that works invisibly, measuring authorial success in editorial terms by "the circulation of the Magazine" (58), while insisting that his corpus can be held together only insofar as it exemplifies his aesthetic theory.

While the self-effacing ambition of this account of the literary marketplace is undoubtedly a product of its rhetorical occasion—Poe is, after all, trying to garner a position as a regular contributor to the *Southern Literary Messenger*—Poe's career-long commitment to the literary value of elaboration and variety is one of the strong signs of the impress of the culture of reprinting on his fiction. Both individual tales and Poe's strategic relation to his expanding corpus demonstrate a sustained engagement with an aesthetic of eclecticism that was fostered by the magazines which were the primary vehicles for the circulation of his fiction. Poe's most explicit statements in defense of this aesthetic occur later on in his career as the culture of reprinting increasingly came under fire from the literary nationalists. And yet his earliest tales bear witness to an aesthetic milieu characterized by a profusion and disarray of national styles. In the over-elaboration of his fictive interiors, Poe celebrates the wide variety of sub-jects and styles that were encouraged by the literary miscellanies, writing his way into the literary field by depicting it in miniature. For example, Poe's description of the poet's palazzo in his early tale "The Visionary" projects in exaggerated and idealized form the aesthetic aims of the ante-bellum magazinist:

> In the architecture and embellishments of the chamber, the evident design had been to dazzle and astound. Little attention had been paid to the decora of what is technically called keeping, or to the properties of nationality. The eye wandered from object to object, and rested upon none—neither the grotesques of the Greek painters, nor the sculptures of the best Italian days, nor the huge carvings of untu-tored Egypt. Rich draperies in every part of the room trembled to the vibration of low, melancholy music, whose origin was not to be discovered. (205)

In describing the nobleman's chamber, Poe evokes a singular space of aristocratic excess. Indeed, the nobleman himself pointedly contrasts his palazzo to his other apartments, which he judges to be "mere ultras of fashionable insipidity" (206). Nevertheless, in this scene Poe defines as the height of taste the juxtaposition of aesthetic objects that are dislodged from their point of origin, their effects intensified by a studied absence of attention to their coordination. In training his gaze on the architecture and embellishments of the room, Poe's narrator recalls both the loose, adaptive structure of the literary miscellanies and their signature jumble of literature, illustrations, and sheet music. In the cultivated disorder of the visionary's chamber, Poe registers the antebellum assumption, evident in the subtitles of so many of what we now reductively consider to be literary magazines, that literary value crucially depends on the association of poetry and fiction with the arts of painting, drawing, sculpture, and music.[46]

Poe's pleasure in describing the extravagance and incongruity of the nobleman's decor frequently seems on the verge of tipping over into self-parody, suggesting an ironic relation to his medium. The nobleman invites the narrator, and by extension the reader, both to admire and to distrust his aesthetic sensibility: "I see you are astonished at my apartment—at my statues—my pictures—my originality of conception in architecture and upholstery—absolutely drunk, eh? with my magnificence" (205). If in this tale, Poe wavers between endorsement and skepticism of the nobleman's taste, he continues to rely on eclecticism as a shorthand for heightened aesthetic effect. Typically, Poe's comic representation of an aesthete's experience of Hell in "The Duc de L'Omelette" requires both the segmentation of space and the exaggeration and intermixing of national styles: "The corners of the room were rounded into niches.—Three of these were filled with statues of gigantic proportions. Their beauty was Grecian, their deformity Egyptian, their *tout ensemble* French" (144–45).

Poe's lovingly detailed description of the "phantasmagoric" (271) bridal chamber in "Ligeia" similarly offers him the opportunity to represent an aesthetic sensibility marked by extravagance, sensory confusion, and the seemingly useless elaboration of particulars, but this description also opens out into metacritical speculation on the relation between eclecticism and narrative order. Poe's narrator initially suggests, as if it were a lost possibility, that the chamber's disarray might once have served as a figure for his disturbed consciousness: "how much even of incipient madness might have been discovered in gorgeous and fantastic draperies, in the solemn carvings of Egypt, in the wild cornices and furniture, in the Bedlam patterns of the carpets of tufted gold!" (270). And yet he also claims that there is a perceptible but unknowable coherence to the room's disorder, linking its decor to the problem of narrative continuity with which the tale begins: "I minutely remember the details of the chamber—yet I am sadly forgetful on topics of deep moment—and here there was no system, no keeping, in the fantastic display, to take hold upon the memory" (270). Poe experiments here with what makes eclecticism an aesthetic rather than simply bad taste or madness, the violation or collapse of sanctioned modes of organizing sensory experience. In "Ligeia," the bridal chamber's extravagant disorder is not the opposite of order, but a figure for the possibility of aesthetic effect without the imposition of a governing consciousness. Poe's narrator wants both to claim that his vision of the room's decor is comprehensive—"There is no individual portion of the architecture and decoration of that bridal chamber which is not now visibly before me" (270)—and to assert that the principle of its organization escapes the grasp of memory. Similarly, though the particulars of the room's design are referred to the narrator's intentions, they begin to take on an eerie autonomy. The Saracenic censer in the middle of the gothic vaulting is "so contrived" that it appears to have its own "serpent vitality," while the arabesque tapestries are arranged so as to provide a figure for narrative progression: "To one entering the room, they bore the appearance of simple monstrosities; but upon a farther advance, this appearance gradually departed; and step by step, as the visiter moved his station in the chamber, he saw himself surrounded by an endless succession of the ghastly forms which belong to the superstition of the Norman, or arise in the guilty slumbers of the Monk." Subjecting oneself to the aesthetic of this room involves surrendering critical distance in exchange for an "endless succession" of images borrowed from somebody else's unconsciousness. Not only is the elaborate "draping" of this apartment fantastically productive, artifice begins to work free of its artificer as the "introduction of a strong continual current of wind behind the draperies [gives] a hideous and uneasy animation to the whole" (271).

Poe constructs a counterpart for his elaborate domestic interiors in the overstuffed hold of the brig *Grampus* in *The Narrative of Arthur Gordon Pym*. As Lisa Gitelman has argued, Poe's fixation on the question of stowage in *Pym* constitutes a complex self-parody of his disorderly narrative. In *Pym*, clumsy stowage both poses a threat to the narrator's survival and turns out to be the saving grace of the ship itself: "it is Poe's joke that the *Grampus*, though its stowage is awful, cannot sink because its cargo is buoyant, empty casks." In the passages on stowage, Poe critiques the loose narrative structure of his own tale and the exploration narratives on which *Pym* was based, but he also acknowledges the ready market for these digressive, miscellaneous collections of firsthand experience, scientific knowledge, and stories of adventure. As Gitelman argues, Poe's is a generous self-parody. Rather than being sunk by its extravagance and slipshod construction, Poe's tale is "buoyed by the expectations of readers accustomed to the conventions of sloppy stowage in the period's habitually eclectic magazines and exploration literature."[47]

In "The Visionary," "Ligeia" and *Pym*, Poe pursues disorderliness and extravagance to the point where they raise questions about the legitimacy of his narratives and their formats. Importantly, however, these moments of textual reflexivity work to accommodate reprint culture's haphazard arrangement of its literary materials rather than to project a desire for an alternative way of organizing culture. To the lasting discomfort of his critics, Poe's fictions participate too enthusiastically in the cultural formations they also appear to critique. Typically, Poe neither produces a stable position within the text from which his fictive world can be assessed, nor does he inhabit his fictions fully enough for them simply to constitute instances of their forms. Poe's tales have too self-conscious a relation to genre; they are both self-authorizing and, in Louis Renza's valuable phrase, "self-distracting artifacts,"[48] repeatedly producing moments of critical self-awareness that disrupt the forward movement of their narratives.

Poe's maddening equivocation between an authorial and a critical relation to his fiction is most often taken to be evidence of his impatience with or contempt for his popular readership. While Baudelaire may be chiefly responsible for the enduring image of Poe as a vengeful hoaxer who designed his fiction to berate his uncomprehending readers,[49] more nuanced accounts of Poe's struggle to come to terms with his audience have been provided by Jonathan Auerbach, who argues that it is only in the late fiction that Poe "seeks to arrive at a mutual understanding" with his readers,[50] and by Louis Renza, who argues that Poe's critical self-awareness works to deprive his audience of the primary pleasures of aesthetic experience. According to Renza, Poe's tales enact a kind of self-encryption, distracting readers by offering them a critical relation to his texts, thereby producing the illusion of a "secretly withheld autobiographical subtext" (82) that only its author is capable of reading.

Jonathan Elmer has most powerfully questioned the assumption of an oppositional relation between Poe and his audience, referring the question of Poe's literary self-consciousness to the general terrain of antebellum culture. Comparing "the notorious tonal instability of Poe's work" (175) to the structure of P. T. Barnum's hoaxes, Elmer argues that the critical turn by which Poe invites his reader to exempt himself from a tale's unmanageable affect marks Poe's engagement with, not his disdain for, an emergent mass-culture. For Elmer, Poe's textual self-consciousness works like a dubious Barnum museum exhibit, attaching the pleasures of skeptical self-awareness to the pleasures of absorption, and folding an ambivalence towards the aesthetic into the mass-cultural object itself.[51]

Elmer's insights into the general cultural currency of what we have come to identify as Poe's signature ambivalence toward his literary medium can help to open up the question of how Poe's texts reflect and reflect on the eclecticism of their formats to more general claims about Poe's articulation of the values of the culture of reprinting. What if we take Poe's seeming failure fully to authorize his fiction as a mode of relation to his writing that is *enabled* by antebellum publishing conditions rather than a disappointing acquiescence to its constraints or an elaborate measure to circumvent them? Can we read both the illocality of Poe's settings and the tonal indeterminacy of his writing—the pleasure he takes in evacuating the position of controlling interpreter—as modes of engagement with the conventions of reprint culture, not as proof of his alienation from his mass-cultural readership?[52] Despite their many differences, New-Critical, Post-Structuralist, and New Historicist critics share a tendency to leverage their accounts of Poe's aesthetic mastery by derogating his nineteenth-century audiences. The forms and formats of reprint culture, however, suggest that antebellum readers were sophisticated about genre, tolerant of generic mixing, and delighted with the unauthorized and parodic mass-circulation of high-cultural texts. The need to resolve generic and tonal instability, and to insist on authorial mastery may indeed be our own.

Consistent with his interest in extravagant and autonomous aesthetic environments, Poe's explicit defenses of American magazine culture suggest not an inability but a refusal to project a coherent authorial persona to which his tales' extraordinary effects can be referred. Poe actively resists both the literary nationalist call to civic authorship and Henry Wadsworth Longfellow's more gentlemanly cosmopolitanism, both models that make the author central to accounts of literary value. Take, for example, Poe's reply to an article "On Writing for the Magazines,"[53] a manifesto of sorts written by Evert Duyckinck, a prominent literary nationalist and patron of Poe's. In this essay Duyckinck argues that magazine writing should offer consistency of tone, channeling a range of observations on contemporary life through a unified sensibility or guiding moral consciousness: "we restrict the magazine article proper to but one species of writing, or rather, one way of thinking or feeling" (456). For Duyckinck, narrowing the compass of the American periodical's tone and scope—"It must," he maintains, "be immediate and local"—would enable it to reconcile readers to the mercurial modern world and to mediate between citizen and state: "We know not what cultivation our statesmen might receive if their measures were ably reviewed by faithful writers, and their speeches commented upon by a body of critics who would be the protectors of manly eloquence" (456).

Over and against Duyckinck's championing of the values of discipline, coherence, and a civic role for literature, Poe defends the magazine's extraordinary ability to produce and contain variety, linking its cultural power to a combinatorial aesthetic that is reflected both in the structure of the magazine and in the composition of individual articles:

We think [Duyckinck] places too low an estimate on the capability of the Magazine paper. He is inclined to undervalue its power—to limit unnecessarily its province—which is illimitable. In fact it is in the extent of subject, and not less in the extent or variety of *tone* that the French and English surpass us, to so good a purpose. How very rarely are we struck with an American Magazine article, as with an absolute novelty—how frequently the foreign articles so affect us! We are so circumstanced as to be unable to *pay* for elaborate composition—and after all, the true invention is elaborate. There is no greater mistake than the supposition that a true originality is a mere matter of impulse or inspiration. To originate is carefully, patiently, and understandingly to combine. The few American Magazinists who ever think of this elaboration at all, cannot afford to carry it into practice for the paltry prices offered them by our periodical publishers. For this and other glaring reasons, we are behind the age in a *very* important branch of literature—a branch which, moreover, is daily growing in importance—and which, in the end (not far distant) will be the *most* influential of all the departments of Letters.[54]

Not only does Poe refuse Duyckinck's suggestion that the magazine take the nation or the national character as its subject,[55] he links the strength of American magazines to the "novelty" of their reprinted "foreign articles" and advises native writers to pursue originality by way of imitation. For Duyckinck, the magazine's projection of a single sensibility safely holds together its contributors' scattered observations, elevating "talk of the day and hour" by passing it through a posture of "negligence and ease, with enthusiasm and refinement" (455). Poe maintains to the contrary, however, that a magazine's capacity to absorb an "illimitable" variety of attitudes and subjects is what keeps it current. For Poe, the magazine does not reflect and manage cultural change, imagined to happen outside the bounds of its refining medium. Rather, it allows for the infinite production of novelty through the unrestrained combination and recombination of extant cultural materials. Whereas Duyckinck calls for the collective fine tuning of the tone of American magazinists, Poe calls for an investment in variety and elaboration. That Poe offers here not simply a postscript to Duyckinck's essay but a radically different vision of the future of American literature is apparent from the fact that he anticipates the imminent dominance of what for Duyckinck, and for the tradition of literary nationalism that follows in his wake, is at best a minor form of literary production.

Poe's rejection of the literary nationalist investment in stylistic unity extends to Duyckinck's 1845 edition of Poe's *Tales*. Poe complained in a letter to poet and critic Philip Pendelton Cooke that Duyckinck's selection of Poe's stories had projected a consistent and controlling literary persona, foreclosing an alternative method of organizing his tales:

The last selection of my Tales was made from about 70 by Wiley & Putnam's reader, Duyckinck. He has what he thinks a taste for ratiocination, and has accordingly

made up the book mostly of analytic stories. But this is not *representing* my mind
in its various phases—it is not giving me fair play. In writing these Tales one by
one, at long intervals, I have kept the book-unity always in mind—that is, each has
been composed with reference to its effect as part of a *whole*. In this view, one of
my chief aims has been the widest diversity of subject, thought & especially *tone*
and manner of handling. Were all my tales now before me in a large volume and
as the composition of another—the merit which would principally arrest my
attention would be the wide *diversity* and variety.

"Book-unity" as Poe imagines it preserves the privilege of inconsistency
which is the stock and store of the eclectic magazine. Poe wants his tales
not to be referred to but to be differentiated from one another. He imagines the book as a structure that allows for "the widest diversity" of thought,
tone, and subject, and for a seemingly endless expansion across time. Poe
takes an additive not a developmental approach to his career; he can solve
the problem of the necessarily partial process of selection (and the logic
of exemplarity it implies) only by projecting forward an edition that would
include all of his tales. Not only does this model of the book elevate variety over stylistic unity, it refuses to produce a stable authorial persona as
its principle of coherence. The author emerges only insofar as he is imagined to be non-self-identical; a book ideally represents his "mind in its
various phases."[56] If Poe imagines the book-publication of his tales as a
constant, unwavering goal, he also defers the moment of completion, which
would shut down the play of "diversity and variety." In Elmer's terms, Poe
arrogates the privilege of self-exemption from the accumulating mass of
his literary corpus. Indeed, merely imagining the consolidation of his tales
into "a large volume" forces Poe to abandon the position of author and to
regard his work from a distance "as the composition of another."[57]

Although Poe defers the moment at which parts-in-succession become
visible as parts-of-a-whole and the author's mind is made equivalent to the
sum total of his work, the virtuosity he champions depends on unity at
the level of the individual tale. Poe's anxiety about the ease with which an
aesthetic of eclecticism could collapse into mere disorder is most evident
in his frustration with Henry Wadsworth Longfellow's comparable experiments with narrative forms that repackaged European cultural riches for
the American market. Although Poe will become infamous in the mid-
1840s for extended diatribes on Longfellow, his early review of *Hyperion*
(1839) is redolent with the disappointment that suggests too close an identification: "we are indignant that he too has been recreant to the good
cause."[58] Longfellow's *Hyperion* is loosely held together by the narrative

device of a melancholy traveler who journeys aimlessly along the Rhine, collecting ballads and folk tales from the people he encounters. Poe's frustration with the book seems to derive from Longfellow's presumption of immediate access to European culture, an impression that is sustained by his refusal to perform the hard work of rewriting and shaping his narrative:

Were it possible to throw into a bag the lofty thought and manner of the "Pilgrims of the Rhine," together with the quirks and quibbles and true humor of "Tristram Shandy," not forgetting a few of the heartier drolleries of Rabelais, and one or two of the Phantasy Pieces of the Lorrainean Callôt, the whole, when well shaken up, and thrown out, would be a very tolerable imitation of "Hyperion." This may appear to be commendation, but we do not intend it as such. Works like this of Professor Longfellow, are the triumphs of Tom O'Bedlam, and the grief of all true criticism. They are potent in unsettling the popular faith in Art—a faith which, at no day more than the present, needed the support of men of letters. . . . A man of true talent who would demur at the great labor requisite for the stern demands of high art—at the unremitting toil and patient elaboration which, when soul-guided, result in the beauty of Unity, Totality, and Truth—men, we say, who would demur at such labor, make no scruple of scattering at random a profusion of rich thought in the pages of such farragos as "Hyperion." . . . without design, without shape, without beginning, middle or end, what earthly object has his book accomplished?– what definite impression has it left? (670)

Longfellow's cosmopolitan eclecticism frees itself from the demand for stylistic unity that characterizes Duyckinck's literary nationalism, but it also refuses integrity at the level of the work, abandoning the commitment to "design" that testifies to invisible authorial or editorial labor.[59] In worrying that "Professor Longfellow" might undermine "the popular faith in Art," Poe contrasts the social and institutional authority on which Longfellow relies with the kind of credibility that can be derived from formal evidence of the work of composition. Although, like Poe's, Longfellow's conception of literature is deliberately transnational, Poe suggests that his spectacular neglect of narrative order all the more presumptuously points to its author as the principle of textual coherence. Poe decries an eclecticism that indicates status and not labor, one that claims the inconsistency after which the magazinist strives as gentlemanly privilege. As Virginia Jackson has argued, Poe is unsettled by Longfellow's enviable assurance that cultural artifacts dislodged from their origins will be credited to him as their source.[60]

Poe's objection to the form in which Duyckinck publishes his tales and his disappointment with Longfellow's weak approximation of his aesthetic ideal suggest not simply dissent from literary nationalist aims or from the cosmopolitan dream of a universalized literariness, but an alternative understanding of the grounds of literary value. It remains exceedingly difficult, however, to recapture these grounds from the vantage point of a criticism that so heavily invests in the positions Poe rejects. Poe's antagonism to Longfellow and Duyckinck reads to us like perversity or failure: a inexplicable lack of interest in the problem of a national literature, an intolerance of the success of his contemporaries, and an incomprehensible resistance to his own good fortune. It is important, therefore, to emphasize what Poe had to gain by holding to an aesthetic that was shaped by and adapted to the culture of reprinting. Some of these advantages include: the richness of writing out of a cacaphonous scene of literary reception; the irreverent pleasures of transforming European cultural forms for popular American consumption; the license to maintain a flexible and inconstant relation to his writing; freedom from the compulsion to yoke literature to a civic or moral purpose and from meta-narratives of artistic development; and a sense of the potential limitlessness of literary experimentation, which, in endlessly deferring the consolidation of the authorial persona, preserves the privilege of self-disavowal. Even Poe's location of "Unity, Totality, and Truth" in the work itself has an adaptive and self-protective feel to it, given the fluctuating demands of his editorial responsibilities and the fugitive nature of his texts. Grounding literary value in an author's "unremitting toil and patient elaboration" places a premium on authorial labor without requiring that the author be identified as a work's origin or source. If the unity of the work serves as a proxy for fantasies of authorial autonomy, it also helps to make it portable and republishable, a repository of literary value that could accommodate "long intervals" between periods of writing. Poe's commitment to diversity and variety at the expense of authorial consistency speaks to his desire to avoid being conscripted to a single mode of writing; it also reflects the currency he trades in as a magazinist, his power to publish (and republish) not the works of an author, but individual poems and tales.

T. S. Eliot's consideration of the difference between Poe's influence in France and his marginality in the United States provides a concise summary of the ways in which Poe's literary values and practices have been misapprehended, construed as a failure to live up to nationalist standards. In Eliot's account, Poe's resistance to the nationalist framework leaves him suspended between cultures: to judge Poe's work from the vantage point of genre would be "to place him in the English tradition, and there certainly he does not belong."[61] Taking into account Poe's national origin, however, only highlights the deracination of his tales, a rootlessness that Eliot ultimately charges to Poe himself: "he seems a wanderer with no fixed abode. There can be few authors of such eminence who have drawn so little from their roots, who have been so isolated from any surroundings" (207). From a modern perspective, Poe's commitment to eclecticism can only be read as dilettantism: Americans tend to "regard Poe as a man who dabbled in verse and in several kinds of prose, without settling down to make a thoroughly good job of any one *genre*" (209). Eliot is exasperated by Poe's additive, serial relation to his writing, seeing not virtuosity but immaturity in his self-exemption from models of writerly development. Eliot's summary of the limits of Poe's achievement reads remarkably like Poe's depiction of the nobleman's aesthetic in "The Visionary" and the arrested development of Egaeus in "Berenice," albeit recast from a position in which taking pleasure in such extravagance has become morally intolerable: "The variety and ardor of [Poe's] curiosity delight and dazzle; yet in the end the eccentricity and the lack of coherence of his interests tire. There is just that lacking which gives dignity to the mature man: a consistent view of life" (212).

In Eliot's account it is only the French who, in their distance from American culture, can perceive any kind of order in Poe's works: "French readers were impressed by the variety of forms of expression because they found, or thought they found, an essential unity; while admitting, if necessary, that much of the work is fragmentary or occasional, owing to circumstances of poverty, frailty, and vicissitude, they nevertheless take him as an author of such seriousness that his work must be grasped as a whole" (209). Here, the unity that would hold variety in solution is produced by estrangement, an exaggerated awareness of cultural borrowing that reprises Poe's self-consciously inauthentic relation to literary tradition. Eliot is finally persuaded that, through the mediation of French poets, he is better able to grasp Poe's aesthetic: "by trying to look at Poe through the eyes of Baudelaire, Mallarmé, and most of all, Valéry I became more thoroughly convinced of his importance, of the importance of his *work* as a whole" (219). And yet the implication of his insight into the history of Poe's reception is far-reaching: Poe cannot, finally, be claimed as a national author if the perception of his work "as a whole" requires the traversal of national boundaries.

The resistance Poe offers to literary nationalist standards has afforded him a secure place just outside the canon of national authors, his exclusion from this tradition most famously providing F. O. Matthiessen with confidence in the cohesion of "the main assumptions about literature" of the central figures of the "American Renaissance."[62] Poe's marginality to this tradition can provide indispensable insights into the terms of its establishment,[63] but for most of Poe's career, literary nationalism was by no means the defining force we now assume it to be. Moreover, although Poe was a man without capital, he was not helplessly subject to market forces. Rather, he found numerous ways to convert cultural secondarity, dislocation, and deferral into forms of literary property. Overcoming authorial subjection to circulation may have required access to the kind of cultural and financial capital that Longfellow wielded, capital that enabled him to maintain a publisher's relation to his writing.[64] Nevertheless, Poe found that he could simulate this kind of power by oscillating between authorial and editorial positions, forms of relation to his writing that he signaled through recourse to the different cultural valences of handwriting and print.

Authentic Facsimiles

In October 1833, the prize committee of the Baltimore *Saturday Visiter* met in the parlor of John Latrobe's house to evaluate the poems and tales that had been anonymously submitted for an award of fifty dollars and publication in the weekly newspaper. According to Latrobe, all three of the judges were taken by a "small quarto-bound book," which stood out from the "bundles of manuscript that it had to compete with" both because of its bulk and because of its handwriting: "Instead of the common cursive manuscript, the writing was in Roman characters—an imitation of printing."[65] Finding the six tales in this volume "far, so very far, superior to anything before us," the judges struggled only to decide which tale deserved the prize, finally settling on one entitled "MS. Found in a Bottle."[66]

This is one of the founding stories of Poe's emergence as an author, useful for its simultaneous depiction of Poe's obscurity and his distinction. In Latrobe's multiple tellings of this tale, the anonymity imposed by the newspaper contest serves to accentuate Poe's difference from his peers. The distinctiveness of his "wonderfully graphic"[67] style produces both financial reward and long sought-after recognition as "MS. Found in a Bottle" becomes the first of Poe's stories to be published with his name attached.

One does not need to know the full story of how this anecdote became a central piece of Poe hagiography[68] to be suspicious of its allegory of the fortuitous encounter of unrecognized merit and just reward, the ideal coalescence of authorship and ownership within an emergent market for literary goods. Indeed, Poe's previous submissions to a newspaper contest had met with a fate more typical of antebellum prose fiction: failing to win the prize, they had become the property of the Philadelphia *Saturday Courier* and were published anonymously, neither profit nor credit accruing to their author.[69] Nevertheless, Latrobe's story of the discovery of the manuscript of the "MS found in a Bottle" offers uncommon insight into the way in which a relation between handwriting and print structured both Poe's and his critics' understanding of the literary marketplace. In this story, an anonymous, handwritten manuscript that gives the appearance of print wins the right to appear in the medium it imitates. Able to publish only one of the tales in this unpublished "Book,"[70] the judges choose a story that grounds its authority in its claim to be handwritten, a story in which the transition from handwriting to print is unnarratable and coincides with the death of the narrating subject. A disjunction between handwriting and print—the modes, respectively, of composition and reception—is foreclosed by Poe in the mode of composition, but opened up in the tale itself, represented by the utmost extremity of the polar abyss.

This heavily invested account of literary origins suggests some of the powerful textual effects that can be produced through the complex co-presence of handwriting and print: both the authority that a relation to printedness can carry in handwriting, and the phantom presence of handwritten forms in print. In the culture of reprinting, where copyright law relied on a distinction between handwriting and print and print-authority often lay in the hands of editors, the difference between writing media also carried proprietary force. Seeking to establish a form of textual property within the culture of reprinting, Poe frequently claims authority through the overlap of handwriting and print. In his early tale, "The Visionary" and in a spoof on celebrity called "Autography," Poe uses handwriting of a doubtful authenticity to negotiate a position between British original and American copy, and between the twin risks of antebellum publishing: the subjection of authors to a propertyless dissemination, and the invisibility of editorial ownership. In both cases, the duplicity of the pen suggests an ability to manipulate the press. By keeping a nearly perfect, but identifiably flawed, facsimile in circulation, Poe claims a privileged relation to decentralized mass-production—importantly, not one of mastery, but of disruption.

Poe's Bryonic tale, "The Visionary," was first published in 1834 in

Godey's *Lady's Book* alongside other anonymous sketches of fictional types such as "The Catholic," "The Fatalist," "The Missionary," and "The Short Gentleman."[71] In this tale, an anonymous Poe imagines he could exert a kind of undercover authority by blurring the difference between himself and Byron, making it impossible to tell British original from American copy. "The Visionary" is remarkable for its canny awareness of the inappropriateness of literary gentility to mass-cultural forms. Indeed, Poe sets out to exploit this discrepancy. In "The Visionary," Poe imagines exerting control over the mass-phenomenon of ladies' magazine Byronism through recourse to a conspicuous anachronism—the indeterminacy of an aristocratic script.

Pitched as an elaborate, fictional defense of Byron who is everywhere invoked, but never named, "The Visionary" sets out to dissociate idleness and speculation from its association with "squandering" (151) and waste.[72] In many ways, the complex plotting of the tale is designed to endorse its hero's final pronouncement: "to dream has been the business of my life" (165). While this narrative aim has obvious bearing on Poe's own attempts to justify his career, the mismatch between Byron's and Poe's predicaments is clear from the lengths to which the story goes to establish grounds for comparison. The story opens with an elaborate and seemingly unnecessary justification for withholding Byron's name from the reader. It soon becomes clear that the purpose of this device is bring to Poe's anonymity as an author into relation with Byron's quite different, generic namelessness. Whereas Byron's namelessness is the product of his extraordinary fame—no one need say his name because everybody knows it—Poe's namelessness is a product of reprint-culture—no one *can* say his name because it has been withheld from readers. Should Poe's Byronic tale succeed, he might, like the Byron in his tale, be everywhere known, but never named, but namelessness for Poe indicates anonymity and poverty, not fame and opulence, or the other kind of withholding that this tale is obsessed with—the aristocrat's delight in concealing his wealth from public view.

Set in Venice by the Bridge of Sighs, "The Visionary" reaches its denouement in a secluded space of aristocratic excess. Invited to a mysterious nobleman's private lodgings after he has witnessed an heroic rescue of a drowning child, Poe's narrator engages the nameless "stranger" in a discussion of his magnificent art collection. As this aristocrat explains, his eclectic assortment of paintings and sculpture has been preserved from the public to guard against imitation. Only the narrator and the nobleman's valet have been admitted to these rooms, because their unusual arrange-ment "has but to be seen to become the rage—that is to say, with those who could afford it at the expense of their entire patrimony" (159).

After a long disquisition on originality, the aristocrat lapses into a reverie, at which time Poe's narrator makes a singular discovery. Written in the margin of an Italian tragedy is a poem that exposes the nobleman's true identity. At the level of plot, these "English" lines (162) confirm the stranger's liaison with the Marchesa Aphrodite, clinching Poe's tale as a romantic rewriting of Byron's affair with the Contessa Guiccioli. And yet, as the narrator explains, these lines were written "in a hand so very differ-ent from the peculiar and bold characters of my acquaintance, that I had some difficulty in recognizing it as his own" (162). The text that follows helps to explain the narrator's difficulty. This homage to Byron has become the vehicle for the anonymous reprinting of Poe's Byronic poem "To One in Paradise." Poe's later title for the tale, "The Assignation," explicitly links the problem of assigning authorship to this doubly-authored poem to the illicit romantic liaison which is the framework for the plot and a hallmark of the Byronic.

In "The Visionary," the indeterminacy of the aristocratic script stands as an acknowledgment of indebtedness and as an attempt at transumption. Poe's insertion of his own poem as the key to unlocking his Byronic hero's identity both declares his poetic dependence—despite Poe's authorship of this poem, these are indeed English lines—and underscores how the Byronic as a cultural phenomenon depends on such acts of imitation. In its neces-sary doubleness, the poetic assignation at the heart of this tale undermines the emphasis on originality that is produced by the nobleman's extrava-gant connoisseurship.

As in "The Fall of the House of Usher," the denouement of "The Vis-ionary" is delayed by a lengthy interlude devoted to aesthetic play—in this case, an explication of the aristocrat's aesthetic preferences more or less lifted out of Thomas Moore's *Letters and Journals of Lord Byron* (1830). What becomes clear from this episode, however, is that Poe is not simply inter-ested in aristocratic discrimination, but in the way in which such taste is vulnerable to exploitation. Poe's tale is itself an instance of such abuse. "The Visionary" takes its place in the eighth volume of the *Lady's Book* alongside a wealth of Byroniana—including a biographical memoir, a re-printed poem, engravings of Byron's residences, an historical essay on Byron's Venice and a poetical address to Byron written in Spenserian stan-zas. Poe's consciousness of the fraudulence of his Byronic posturing can also be traced in the tale itself. The hallmark of the aristocrat in this tale is his ability to tell original from copy and his self-mocking relation to his property, an attitude that serves to double and to expose Poe's self-mocking relation to his medium. Poe's Byron's aesthetic judgments are wickedly self-referential. Commenting on one of his statues this aristocrat remarks: "part of the left arm . . . and all the right, are restorations; and in the coquetry of that right arm lies, I think, the quintessence of affectation" (160). And yet, Poe's narrator's exclusive access to his Byron's "cabinet" (159) and the tale's central scene of poetic misrecognition project an attitude more complex than simple adulation or ironic dismissal. Poe banks on literary aristocracy as a popular phenomenon, yet he also seeks to distinguish his tale from the Byronism that has "become the rage" with a claim of authenticity. Poe hasn't come to praise *or* to bury Byron, but to regulate access to the Byronic. "The Visionary" projects the author's fantasy that, by a single act of doubling that calls attention to its fraudulence or duplicity, Poe's Byron could be protected against mass-duplication.

In thinking through Poe's emphasis on the aristocrat's need to keep his art collection hidden from view, we should recall that Poe's imitation of Byron had indeed cost him his patrimony. In one of his final letters to his stepfather, John Allan, Poe asked for financial assistance in publishing a volume of poems, claiming "I have long given up *Byron* as a model—for which, I think, I deserve some credit."[73] Poe's earliest surviving poetic lines also testify to the fundamentally oppositional relation between Byronic extravagance and a credit economy. Written on the obverse of a page of calculations that represent John Allan's emergency money—an estimation of the liquidity of debts that were owed him—a youthful Poe had written the following:

—Poetry. by . Edgar A. Poe—
Last night with many cares & toils oppress'd
Weary, I laid me on a couch to rest—[74]

Poe's marginal identification with a generic Byron-figure in "The Visionary"—one whose characteristic posture is to recline on an ottoman—represents an experiment in the possible liquidity of the Byronic persona. I would argue that it is finally by giving up modeling Byron *exactly* that Poe is able to generate credit. Poe's Byronic poem and the tale in which it is set hold value because they approximate without exactly reproducing the original. In "The Visionary," and in a whole host of other works that play off the difference between an aristocratic hand and the popular press, Poe's authorial strategy is to place the double or facsimile in a context where the reader is forced to question its veracity.

Poe uses handwriting of doubtful authenticity to establish his authority in a variety of texts, including the "Marginalia," a series of fictional book annotations; the "Autography" series, which, while it began as a hoax, became the basis for two, more serious attempts at criticism; and in "MS. Found in a Bottle" and *The Narrative of Arthur Gordon Pym*. One might also recognize the strategy of keeping a nearly perfect, but identifiably flawed facsimile in circulation as Dupin's signature move at the end of "The Purloined Letter." I want to look briefly however, at Poe's first venture into "Autography" to reinforce the point that it is through disruption of the conditions of reprint culture and not through what we would generally call mastery of them, that Poe imagines he can emerge as an author.

Poe's first "Autography" series juxtaposes printed letters, which purport to be the correspondence of statesmen and literati, with facsimile signatures and a brief editorial comment on the handwriting of each letter's author. Much of the humor of this piece lies in the burlesques of individual authors' styles. For example, Poe makes fun of Washington Irving's fastidiousness through his delicate refusal to read the manuscript "Treatise on Pigs."[75] And yet Poe's "Autography" also sets in motion a more sophisticated play on the way in which the authentic or original derives its authority only in relation to the facsimile or copy. One can see how this works by simply glancing at the format of the piece (Figure 15). While in a print context, the MS-signature is set off as authentic, these are, of course, only *copies* of authors' signatures, facsimiles taken from the business letters that had accumulated on Poe's editorial desk. Similarly, while the parody correspondence is clearly inauthentic, it serves as a reminder that an author can only be said to have established his identity when his style can be imitated and recognized. Poe's witty treatment of this thematic is most evident from the way in which he designs his correspondence to produce the mark of authenticity—the sought-after signature—despite the vehement refusal of the letter writer in question. The concluding letter of the initial series nicely illustrates this triumph of circulation over the subject:

Sir. — Yours of the —— came duly to hand. The fact is, I have been so pestered with applications for my autograph that I have made a resolution to grant one in no case whatsoever.   Yours, &c,

[Wm. Emmons][76]

to hand. If you will be so good as to repeat their contents, it will give me great pleasure to answer them, each and all. The Post Office is in a very bad condition.

Yours respectfully,

JOSEPH W. MILLER, ESQ.

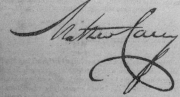

Mr. Carey does not write a legible hand—although in other respects a good one. It resembles that of Neal very nearly. Several of the words in the letter to Mr. Miller are run together. The i's are seldom dotted. The lines are at equal distances, and straight. The paper very good—wafered.

LETTER XXII.

Boston, ———.

Dear Sir,—No such person as Philip Philpot has ever been in my employ as a coachman, or otherwise. The name is an odd one, and not likely to be forgotten. The man must have reference to some other Dr. Channing. It would be as well to question him closely.

Respectfully yours,

JOSEPH X. MILLER, ESQ.

Dr. Channing's MS. is very excellent. The letters are bold, well-sized, and beautifully formed. They are, perhaps, too closely crowded upon one another. One might, with some little acumen, detect the high finish of Dr. C.'s style of composition in the character of his chirography. Boldness and accuracy are united with elegance in both. The paper very good, and wafered.

LETTER XXIII.

Philadelphia, ———.

Dear Sir,—I must be pardoned for declining to loan the books you mention. The fact is, I have lost many volumes in this way—and as you are personally unknown to me you will excuse my complying with your request.

Yours, &c.

JOSEPH Y. MILLER, ESQ.

This is a very good MS.—forcible, neat, legible, and devoid of superfluous ornament. Some of the words are run together. The writing slopes considerably. It is too uniform to be picturesque. The lines are at equal distances, and a broad margin is on the left of the page. The chirography is as good at the conclusion as at the commencement of the letter—a rare quality in MSS.—and evincing *indefatigability* of temperament.

LETTER XXIV.

Washington, ———.

Sir,—Yours of the —— came duly to hand. I cannot send you what you wish. The fact is, I have been so pestered with applications for my autograph, that I have made a resolution to grant one in no case whatsoever.

Yours, &c.

JOSEPH Z. MILLER, ESQ.

The writing of the orator is bold, dashing, and chivalrous—the few words addressed to Mr. Miller occupying a full page. The lines are at unequal distances, and run diagonally across the letter. Each sentence is terminated by a long dash—black and heavy. Such an epistle might write the Grand Mogul. The paper is what the English call silver paper—very beautiful and wafered.

Figure 15. "Autography," *Southern Literary Messenger* (1836). Courtesy, Historical Society of Pennsylvania.

What is perhaps most intriguing about this series, however, is the way in which Poe's insertion of fake signatures in a mass-produced magazine generates profits by disrupting the process of reprinting. Due to the popularity of the piece and the expense of commissioning new woodcuts of the signatures, editors who sought to reprint Poe's extravaganza found it economical to apply to the magazine in which Poe's "Autography" first appeared in order to rent the "originals." It is also likely that Poe's "Autography" produced profits based on other magazines' *failure* to reprint it. One editor praised the series, lamenting "We wish we had the cuts, so that we might transfer it."[77] Calling attention to the magazine while neglecting to reprint its contents could only increase the value of the original. Indeed, the disruption Poe introduces into the system of reprinting actually *produces* this mass-produced magazine as an original. It is not simply the incorporation of handwriting into print that generates this value, but Poe's setting the facsimile signature within a context that raises the question of its availability, alternately asserting and denying its susceptibility to reproduction.

Even late in his career, Poe's image of the ideal coalescence of authorship and ownership involves a complex superscription of handwriting and print. Editing an elite literary magazine was a lifelong, unrealized dream for Poe. He had announced and abandoned an earlier project, the *Penn Magazine*, twice due to lack of funds. When Poe revived the project in 1843, he changed the magazine's title from a pun that was "somewhat too local in its suggestions"[78] to *The Stylus*—the name of a more ancient writing instrument that reflected the seriousness of his national ambitions.

Poe's epigraph to his *Prospectus of* The Stylus reflects the assumption that the image of inscription would counter what he saw as the unreliable publicity of the press. Poe's prospectus begins:

———unbending that all men
Of thy firm TRUTH may say—"Lo! this is writ
With the antique *iron pen*." (1033)

The hyper-rigidity of this appeal to readers is intended as an index of the periodical's promised objectivity. As opposed to ordinary magazines in which anonymous reviewers adjusted their critical commentary to suit a variety of publishing interests, Poe's magazine swore to "[hold] itself aloof from all personal bias" and to deliver "an absolutely independent criticism" (1035). The phallic inflexibility of this goal sets Poe's journal apart from the partisan monthlies and ladies' magazines that would be its close competitors. Poe's "antique iron pen" hearkens back to a mythical

time before print intervened to separate criticism from truth, the hand writing from what is written.

Poe's explanation of his motives for launching his journal clarify what
is at stake in this technological regression. Speaking in the third person of
his dissatisfaction with previous editorial positions, Poe writes:

> Having no proprietary right . . . in either of these journals; his objects, too, being
> in many respects, at variance with those of their very worthy owners; he found it
> not only impossible to effect anything, on the score of taste, for the mechanical
> appearance of the works, but exceedingly difficult, also, to stamp, upon their inter-
> nal character, that *individuality* which he believes essential to the full success of all
> similar publications. (1034)

Here Poe links a periodical's identity to its proprietor's control over the
action of stamping. The magazine's ability to leave a distinctive impression on the reader depends on its direction by "a single mind" (1034), a
relationship that is jeopardized by diversified production. Poe's "iron pen,"
then, takes up the consistency that he sees as potentially inscribed by the
press under the ideal conditions of undivided ownership.

Poe's proposed title page for this magazine, however, undermines the
association of the "iron pen" with identity, continuity, and unwavering
judgment. Rather than securing the *Prospectus*'s promise of objectivity,
Poe's title-page reinstitutes handwriting as the site of duplicity, asserting
control of, not submission to "TRUTH." At the center of the page (Figure 16) is a hand holding a stylus, inscribing *Aletheia*, the Greek word for
truth. Underneath this illustration is a Latin epigraph, which, in the source
from which Poe is likely to have taken it, is rendered "sometimes a pen of
gold and sometimes a pen of iron."[79] Poe's willingness to offer two modes
of address—one bent to flatter and one to tell the truth—seems an astonishing reversal of his claims in the *Prospectus*. Indeed, the hand caught in
the act of inscription seems to have stopped for direction, waiting on the
dictates of its audience to manipulate truth.

Poe's title page and magazine proposal perform a number of complex
relocations: authorial ambitions become editorial, individuality is found
at the press, but control over the press is represented as the maintenance
of a double relation to the reading public, a relation best represented by a
duplicitous pen. This complex model of authorial-editorial agency looks
nothing like the relation to writing we ordinarily attribute to authors.
Not only does "individuality" have more to do with mechanical consistency than peculiarity, the editor's impress on the "internal character" of

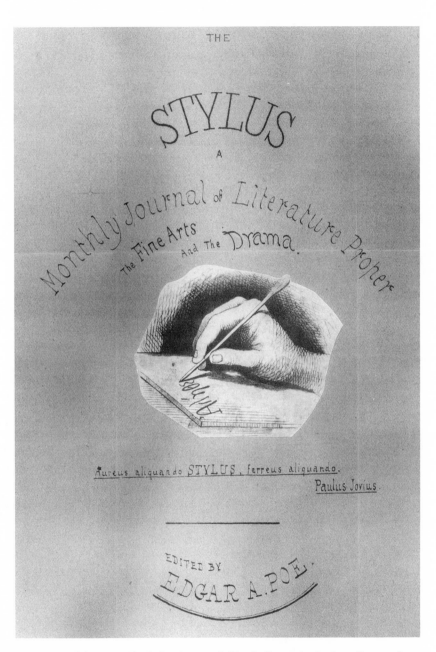

Figure 16. Title page, *The Stylus* (ca. 1848). Facsimile reprint in *Some Letters of Edgar Allan Poe to E. H. N. Patterson of Oquawka, Illinois* (1898). Courtesy, American Antiquarian Society.

the articles he prints remains elusive; it is both the source of their efficacy and, like the quality of paper or typefaces, potentially independent of the writing itself. Likewise, Poe's association of authorial control with duplicity defines authorship not as origination but as manipulation, a practice defined by interruption, inconsistency, and uncertainty, not mastery.

We are, on the whole, made uncomfortable by the fact of an author's subjection to market forces; more unnerving still is an author who is engaged in turning the market to advantage. Among many who have attempted to restore Poe to a version of authorship less threatening than *The Stylus* would suggest is Sara Sigourney Rice who, for the frontispiece to her *Memorial Volume*, altered a daguerrotype of Poe so that a quill pen was placed in his outstretched hand.[80] In using different versions of Poe's signature on their covers—the mark both of originality and standardization—Burton Pollin's *Collected Writings* and Floyd Stovall's edition of Poe's *Poems* have compensated for Poe's subjection to circulation and have provided a corpus for his hand. What we should be aware of, however, is not simply the appropriation of the hand—that these books suggest a relation to print and to authorship that Poe did not and could not have possessed—but our own investment in disguising that appropriation, passing off our own interventions in the reprint market as if they were written in another hand.

Poe, Literary Nationalism, and Authorial Identity

EVEN WHEN THEIR INTENT IS TO PLACE Edgar Allan Poe's career and writings within the context of antebellum publishing, biographical and critical studies generally produce an image of Poe standing apart from the institutions and practices through which authors gained access to the reading public. Characteristically, Poe is depicted in staunch and principled opposition to the coteries that controlled the elite literary periodicals, or in calculated or desperate concession to their demands.[1] Such critiques work to preserve Poe's integrity by insisting that his work remains detachable from the well-orchestrated "puffing" and cliquish favoritism that sought to shape the market for American books. Poe's prominent attacks on this system and his persistent advocacy of an analytic and impartial criticism have enabled literary historians to portray him as a figure of heroic resistance despite the sometimes damning details of his literary and critical practice.

In this chapter, I will argue that the critical investment in Poe as a figure who could remain detached from the conditions of literary production finds its origin in the intersection of Poe's career with the very coteries from which critics have tried to distance him. Rather than isolating him from his milieu, Poe's insistence on critical impartiality enabled him to be taken up as an exemplary subject by an influential group of literary nationalists, the Young Americans. Both Poe's sudden rise to prominence in the early months of 1845 and his spectacular decline in the autumn of that year are crucially mediated by his association with the cause of American literary independence. I will analyze the terms of this alliance as it is forged in an influential biography, tested in the "Little Longfellow War," and fractured by Poe's scandalous performance at the Boston Lyceum. Rather than a story of heroic resistance, unavoidable complicity, and unfortunate psychological collapse, I take Poe's implication with the cause

of literary nationalism to form a crucial chapter in the history of the production of Poe as a subject who stands outside history.

James Russell Lowell and the "Be-Mirrorment" of Poe

James Russell Lowell's biographical essay, "Edgar Allan Poe," not only
serves to announce Poe's arrival on the increasingly important New York
publishing scene, it also marks the incorporation of the figure of Poe into
the discourse of literary nationalism, the public identification of his writings and career as a chief casualty of and possible solution to the problem
of a national literature. Written at Poe's request for an ongoing series in
Graham's Magazine, "Our Contributors," Lowell's essay first appeared in
late January 1845, whereupon it was immediately reprinted in two installments on the front page of the New York *Evening Mirror*, and widely
noticed in New York, Philadelphia, and Baltimore papers. Read in the context of its composition and first printing, Lowell's essay might be regarded
as a friendly critique and informative summary of Poe's life and writings
written for the benefit of the readers of *Graham's*, the popular ladies'
magazine of which Poe had been an editor, and to which he continued to
contribute regularly. Yet Lowell's essay takes on its primary significance for
Poe's career and for the cultural legacy of the figure of Poe, in the context
of its New York reprinting. It is not simply that the republication of the
essay and its endorsement by a group of influential editors and reviewers—N.P. Willis, Margaret Fuller, Charles Briggs, and Evert Duyckinck—
gave this critique added prestige and contributed to its wider distribution.
The embrace of Lowell's version of Poe by these literati, all of whom had
close ties with the literary nationalist program of the Young America
movement, places Poe's New York debut firmly within the context of
the highly politicized struggle to define the terms of American literary
independence.

The publication of Lowell's essay was a pivotal event in Poe's struggle to gain recognition and to profit by his writing. In addition to praising Poe's abilities as a poet, critic, and writer of tales, Lowell reprinted
selections from his poetry and provided a comprehensive list of his uncollected and anonymous tales, marking the first time on the national stage
that a description of Poe had been identified with a body of writing.[2]
The essay, then, represents a significant consolidation of Poe's identity as
an author, and a milestone in the popularization of this identity. It also

enabled Poe to acquire a new form of property in his writing. Lowell's good opinion served as a valuable entrée for Poe into New York literary society and the powerful publishing network of the Young America movement. Charles Briggs, for one, was so impressed by Lowell's essay that he took Poe on as a contributor and editor of the *Broadway Journal*, marking the first time in his career that Poe was able to acquire a proprietary stake in the periodical in which his writing appeared. This was an important achievement in an era when magazine authors were frequently unpaid, and, when paid, traditionally ceded control over publication to the editors in exchange for their pay.[3] Poe took advantage of his new position by performing his own act of consolidation, using the pages of the *Broadway Journal* to print revised versions of a considerable number of his poems and tales, creating a series of authorized texts that continue to form the basis of the Poe canon.[4] In addition, Poe's association with the Young America movement—in particular, the patronage of Evert Duyckinck—opened up the columns of the prestigious *Democratic Review* and *American Review* to his poems and essays, ensured a large crowd and favorable reception for his lecture on "The Poets and Poetry of America," and secured a place for his two volumes, the *Tales* and *The Raven and Other Poems*, in Young America's flagship publishing venture, the Library of American Books.

We must be careful, however, to read this evidence of Poe's increasing self-possession not only against the complicating factor of his dependence on Young America's patronage, but also in the context of the rhetoric of literary nationalism in which the figure of Poe becomes thoroughly enmeshed. As Claude Richard has demonstrated, the consolidation of Poe's authorial identity came at a significant cost to his critical independence: gaining control over his body of writing both in terms of being publicly identified as its author, and in terms of controlling its dissemination as editor and *litterateur*, meant ceding control over the content of his criticism. The period from March of 1843 when Poe began courting their favor, through the collapse of the *Broadway Journal* in late December of 1845, can be read both as a narrative of Poe's long-sought achievement of authorial identity, and as the space of an embarrassing surrender. Within this period, Poe repeatedly compromised his critical principles to curry favor with the Duyckinck circle, sacrificing his independent critical voice to promote the literary and political goals of the Young Americans.[5]

Poe was certainly an unlikely recruit to this cause, which combined the bombastic promotion of a national literature with the vigorous advocacy

of an international copyright agreement. Although he was a lifelong supporter of international copyright, Poe had repeatedly come out *against* the
simpleminded endorsement of books with "strictly 'American' themes,"
ridiculing the critical tendency of "liking, or pretending to like, a stupid
book the better because (sure enough) its stupidity was of our own growth,
and discussed our own affairs."[6] Poe's hostility to the nationalist program
suffused his critical practice and took the New York publishing scene as a
specific target. Not only had he written a scathing critique of "Wakon-
dah," a nationalist epic written by Young America's leading spokesman,
Cornelius Mathews;[7] he had identified the *Mirror* as a primary locus of
the corrupt links between critics and the book trade—in Poe's words, the
"direct system of petty and contemptible bribery" (1006)—that made the
commercial success of such inferior literature possible. The founding editors of the *Mirror* had hoped the journal's name would represent the
democratizing power of print; they saw it as an instrument "for reflecting
back to many, the intellectual treasures of the few."[8] Poe, however, took
the *Mirror* to represent the corruption of the many by the few, the "manufacture" by a coterie of critics of "a pseudo-public opinion by wholesale."
For Poe, "be-Mirrorment" came to signify the entrapment of an author by
the ultimately self-serving power of the press.[9]

How are we to understand the transformation of this resolute opponent of literary nationalism into one of the "merest and maddest *partizans*
in letters" (1027) he had so vigorously condemned? Richard's answer is to
dismiss Poe's conversion as opportunism, depicting his sudden support of
Young America as a calculated move, an unfortunate but necessary step
toward his lifelong dream of establishing his own elite literary magazine.[10]
However, to regard Poe's relation to the literary nationalist movement
purely from the standpoint of Poe's own motives is to overstate his ability to dissociate himself from the terms by which he was embraced by this
movement and through which he gained access to a wide reading public.
For in spite of Poe's motives and his increasingly veiled differences with
the nationalist program, nearly all of his production in this period is put
forward under the aegis of Young America, a point which is graphically
demonstrated by the title pages of the only books written by Poe to
have been widely circulated in his lifetime (and the only books for which
he was paid a royalty): the 1845 *Tales* and *The Raven and Other Poems*.
Both volumes, as part of Duyckinck's nationalist publishing project, the
"Library of American Books," bear on their covers an inscription from the
Address of the American Copy-Right Club: "Sundry citizens of this good

land, meaning well, and hoping well, prompted by a certain something in their nature, have trained themselves to do service in various Essays, Poems, Histories, and books of Art, Fancy, and Truth."[11]

That Poe's writing was widely disseminated under Young America's imprimatur should suggest that his connection with the literary nationalist program was not something he could easily negate. Critics who focus on Poe's duplicity in undertaking this alliance not only mistake Poe's desire to hold himself apart from this movement for his ability to do so, they also misstate the consequences of this alliance. As we will see, the crisis for Poe is not that he is forced to embrace literary nationalist ideals in order to advance his career. Rather, his autonomy is jeopardized when the literary nationalists embrace *his* principles, invoking him as an idealized figure of independent judgment within their discourse. Poe does not abandon his critical ideals so much as lose control over them as they are translated into the literary nationalist idiom. The complex mediations of Lowell's essay will show how Poe's critical independence, the originality of his productions—even the details of his biography—become tied to the problem of American literary independence.

Lowell begins his essay with an analysis of the current state of literary production in America, casting his account of the life and writings of Poe as a polemic on the question of a national literature. This analysis is a particularly volatile one, in that it steers a course rhetorically between nationalist and anti-nationalist positions: it adopts the urgency of nationalist appeals, and is structured as a declaration of crisis and call to arms, and yet its key metaphors imply a powerful indictment of efforts to construct an independent literature out of American materials. This equivocation is not surprising, since Lowell composed this essay at a stage of his career when had fallen out of favor with the Duyckinck circle, due to his failure fully to endorse their cause in his short-lived periodical *The Pioneer*.[12] Writing Poe's biography became an occasion for Lowell to reconceptualize his relation to the discourse of literary nationalism in the light of Poe's increasing influence; it offers a refraction of Poe's critical ideals through the lens of Lowell's disillusionment with the proposals of the Young Americans.

The extent of this disillusionment is apparent from the opening set of images, a description of cultural dislocation which, while it is indebted to the generic pronouncements of Young America, signals a shift from even the muted nationalism of *The Pioneer*. In a rhetorical move common to advocates of literary nationalism, Lowell identifies the failure of American literature as a geographical and political one, a failure to bring culture, politics, and landscape into proper relation:

> The situation of American literature is anomalous. It has no center, or, if it have, it is like that of the sphere of Hermes. It is divided into many systems, each revolving round its several sun, and often presenting to the rest only the faint glimmer of a milk-and-watery way. Our capital city, unlike London or Paris, is not a great central heart, from which life and vigor radiate to the extremities, but resembles more an isolated umbilicus, stuck down as near as may be to the center of the land, and seeming rather to tell a legend of former usefulness than to serve any present need. Boston, New York, Philadelphia, each has its literature almost more distinct than those of the different dialects of Germany; and the Young Queen of the West has also one of her own, of which some articulate rumor barely has reached us dwellers by the Atlantic.[13]

Lowell presents the relation of American literature and nationhood as a series of apparently insuperable disjunctions: publishing centers are detached from each other, and from the seat of government, while the government itself is cut off from "present need," situated at a geographical center that has become peripheral. Read against the conventional proclamations of the Young Americans, this emphasis on detachment and internal disarray becomes all the more pronounced. Nationalist manifestos customarily began with a condemnation of American subserviency to British literary models, and finished with a call for a literature commensurate with the majesty of American scenery and the ideals of republican institutions. Throughout, the emphasis was on independence and self-sufficiency figured as the reciprocity of art, land, and nation. Duyckinck called for "such an image of rural life, of men in cities . . . as the wide area of the land should reflect in the broad shield of the state,"[14] while Lowell himself had declared in *The Pioneer* that he "would no longer see the spirit of our people held up as a mirror to the OLD WORLD;—but rather lying like one of our own inland oceans, reflecting not only the mountain and the rock, the forest and the redman, but also the steamboat and the railcar, the cornfield and the factory."[15] In Lowell's revised account of the national predicament, however, the dislocation between and among geographical, political, and cultural systems is so severe as completely to disable political patronage. Not only does the "isolated umbilicus" of the nation's capital fail to nurture the various centers of literary production, literature itself is rendered incapable of reflecting back either the image of the land or of the state. We are left with the disturbing image of a literary culture cut free and yet unnourished.

Lowell then shifts from this figure of maternal abandonment to a scene of stillbirth, replacing the accusation of a failure to nourish with the charge of a disastrously misplaced affection: "Meanwhile, a great babble is kept up concerning a national literature, and the country, having delivered itself of the ugly likeness of a paint-bedaubed, filthy savage, smilingly dandles the rag baby upon her maternal knee, as if it were veritable flesh and blood, and would grow timely to bone and sinew" (5). While Lowell's ultimate target of contempt seems to be the motherland's deranged approval of its offspring, his disgust at American literary production registers most powerfully as a proliferation of figures for crudity and inauthenticity. The nation's surrogate child is a likeness of a savage, and an ugly one at that; it is filthy, and yet also obscured with paint, a paint that may seek to cover, but which is also the hallmark of the primitive. The figure of the savage is a loaded one for the former editor of *The Pioneer*, as it was for all of the Young Americans who repeatedly called for a literature that would embody the wildness of the American Indian as well as the American landscape. Lowell's emphasis on the lingering horror of maternal approval pointedly shifts the target of his critique from nationalist authors, to the editors and critics who celebrate such grotesque productions. From the materials of a conventional nationalist appeal, Lowell fashions an indictment similar to Poe's attack on the Young Americans for "liking, or pretending to like, a stupid book the better because . . . its stupidity was of our own growth, and discussed our own affairs."[16] Lowell's assessment, however, is more severe than Poe's, whose characterization of literary nationalism as a form of willful self-delusion suggests its eventual dissipation. In the figural logic of Lowell's essay, the nation's delight in her inanimate child-surrogate intensifies his initial emphasis on maternal abandonment by categorically denying the possibility of growth and maturation. Lowell acknowledges the fact of independence but insists not merely on the failure, but on the *impossibility* of America nurturing its literary offspring. He has arrived at an impasse from which it seems impossible to proceed.

At this point, Lowell suggests a reversal of terms. In a dramatic change of registers, he asserts that "before we have an American literature, we must have an American criticism" (5–6). This reversal makes little sense when read against the imagery which has preceded it. Even if it is interpreted as a transposition of nationalist priorities (Duyckinck had insisted in an early review that "It is the office of the critic to follow, not to head. We need authors first, and critics will follow afterwards"[17]), Lowell's insistence on the impossibility of sustenance makes it difficult to place any confidence in the generative power of criticism. It is only when Lowell invokes Poe as a figure of parthenogenesis that it becomes clear that the possibility of a prior, independent criticism offers him a welcome escape from the insoluble problem of maturation.

Lowell's initial description of Poe is oddly anticlimactic: he introduces Poe as "the most discriminating, philosophical, and fearless critic upon imaginative works who has written in America," largely upon the grounds that he is "a man who thinks for himself, and says what he thinks, and knows well what he is talking about" (7). Read in the context of the essay's opening images, however, Lowell's stress on Poe's self-sufficiency seems more important than his superlatives. Indeed, in describing Poe as a man who thinks for himself, Lowell personifies the goals of criticism Poe had set forth in his "Prospectus of *The Stylus*." In this abstract (which he sent to Lowell), Poe expressed the hope that his magazine would "assert in precept, and . . . maintain in practice, the rights, while, in effect, it demonstrates the advantages, of an absolutely independent criticism;—a criticism self-sustained."[18] While his goals are certainly idealist ones—this criticism would "[guide] itself only by the purest rules of Art"—Poe's immediate reference is to his promise that *The Stylus* would be sufficiently capitalized to forswear compromising connections with the book trade, what he referred to in an earlier version of the prospectus as "[reading] through the medium of a publisher's will.[19] For Poe it is ultimately financial independence that guarantees unbiased reviews. In the context of Lowell's analysis, however, the image of self-sustenance takes on a biological resonance. Throughout his exposition of Poe's works, Lowell offers the figure of Poe as a response to the problem of a literature cut free from all sources of support. In the rhetorical economy of the essay, the grounding power of Poe's authorial and critical practice is directly linked to his ability to counter the opening images of impossible growth.

Poe is able to perform this function for Lowell both because of his call for critical self-sufficiency, and because of the contingencies of his own biography. Poe is the type and figure of maternal abandonment; first orphaned, then disinherited, Poe personifies the national predicament. Lowell suggests as much when he locates Poe's turn to authorship at the point when he is "cut off [from] his expectations as an heir" (7) by the birth of a son to his adoptive father, the artificiality of his lineage exposed and displaced by a natural filiation. Poe's biography is both the occasion for Lowell's meditations on the state of the national literature, and his template for understanding it. However, if the details of Poe's biography shape Lowell's literary-political analysis, the idea that Poe is a subject with a history all but disappears from his account of Poe's literary production. Lowell represents Poe not merely as an autonomous critic, but as a figure of impossible maturity, one who seems never to have passed through a state of dependency or incompletion.

This figuration of Poe is most legible in Lowell's long digression on the juvenile poems of famous poets, each of which fails in some regard to anticipate the virtues of the poet's mature verse. After a litany on the failed precocity of Shakespeare, Milton, Pope, Collins, Chatterton, Southey, Coleridge, and others, Lowell praises Poe's early poems as "the most remarkable boyish poems" he has ever read. In "the rudest verses" Lowell finds he can "trace some conception of the ends of poetry," a phenomenon he "can only express by the contradictory phrase of *innate experience*" (10). Lowell has found proof for his maxim which calls for principle to precede practice: before Poe had a mature poetry, he had incarnate in his juvenilia a "conception of the ends of poetry," which renders moot the question of comparative strength or degrees of development.

The source for Lowell's trope of reversal becomes apparent in his account of Poe's prose. In a passage which echoes Poe's nascent theory of the "unity of effect or impression,"[20] Lowell observes that in the composition of his tales, Poe's "mind at once reaches forward to the effect to be produced" (14). This depiction of Poe as the embodiment of his critical ideals bears the marks of Lowell's characteristic overreaching. Poe's version of his poetics of effect recognizes the contingencies of the compositional process even as it seeks to displace its account of origins with the image of a perfectly reproducable effect. For instance, in his early review of Hawthorne, Poe stressed the "deliberate care" (572) required of the artist in selecting an effect, while in his "Philosophy of Composition" he will expand upon the "elaborate and vacillating crudities of thought, . . . the true purposes seized only at the last moment . . . the innumerable glimpses of idea that arrived not at the maturity of full view."[21] Lowell, however, has Poe arrive at his intended effect "at once." Lowell attributes to Poe such control over the reaction of the reader that he redraws self-sufficiency as a kind of self-enclosure. Poe is both author and critic, creator and "spectator *ab extra*"; his autonomy is so complete as to suggest the replacement of the image of biological with that of mechanized production:

[Poe] analyzes, he dissects, he watches,
   —with an eye serene,
   The very pulse of the machine,

for such it practically is to him, with wheels and cogs and piston rods all working to produce a certain end. It is this that makes him so good a critic. (14)

Whatever pulse remains of Wordsworth's "perfect Woman, nobly planned"— the "Phantom of delight" behind the quotation[22]—is all but extinguished by Lowell's emphasis on Poe's careful supervision of his textual machine. The machine *is* a perfect woman insofar as it promises production without dependency. Thus even the creative practice which underwrites Poe's criticism is assimilated to a regulatory function. Lowell's dominant image of Poe is that of effect without cause and without access: "Mr. Poe has that indescribable something which men have agreed to call *genius*. No man could ever tell us precisely what it is, and yet there is none who is not inevitably aware of its presence and its power" (12).

Poe seems to have found the terms of Lowell's praise extravagant and amusing, satirizing this line in particular in his comic tale "The Literary Life of Thingum Bob, Esq."[23] The New York literati who reviewed Lowell's essay, however, reinforced his claims, stressing Poe's extraordinary maturity and the absolute independence of his criticism, and linking him to a powerful, but untraceable effect. N. P. Willis, for example, welcomed Lowell's "biographical and critical sketch of the American Rhadamanthus," asserting that this "*coup d'oeil*, of the position and powers of Mr. Poe . . . is of great interest to the public that *feels* him."[24] Poe's authority is established by the sudden disclosure that it is already in effect.

Willis's notice permits us to trace the trajectory of Poe's critical ideals through the mediating accounts of those who promoted his career. In Lowell's hands, Poe's ambitions for his unrealized magazine were recast as an indictment of American culture for failing to have nourished these ambitions. Lowell saw in the collapse of *The Stylus* a missed opportunity for the instant achievement of a critical mastery which would have rivaled that of England: "Had Mr. Poe had the control of a magazine of his own, in which to display his critical abilities, he would have been as autocratic, ere this, in America, as Professor Wilson has been in England" (7). Taking his cue from Lowell, Willis transforms this complaint into a renewed call for an editorship for Poe, one that he claims would have the power to undergird the New York publishing world: "We wonder, by the way, that, with so fine a critic at command for an editor, some New York publisher does not establish a Monthly Review, devoted exclusively to high critical purposes. Poe has genius and taste of his own, as well as the necessary science, and the finest discriminative powers; and such a wheel of literature should not be without axle and lynch-pin" (491). It remains to be seen why Lowell's portrait of Poe as a critical autocrat should be so warmly received and vigorously promoted by a group dedicated to fostering democratic principles in art.

Removing the Anonymous: Young America and the Control of Dissemination

Evert Duyckinck's favorable notice of Lowell's essay provides a context for understanding how Poe could have appeared to arrive upon the New York scene fully formed, in command of an extensive oeuvre without ever having passed through the process of production. Less than a week after the publication of Lowell's essay, Duyckinck editorialized in the columns of the *Morning News*, "We cordially give welcome to the distinct recognition of Mr. Poe's merits. Whenever his name is mentioned it has been with the comment that he is a remarkable man, a man of genius. Few knew precisely what he had written, his name was not on Library catalogues or any of his books on the shelves. His influence has been felt while the man was unknown. Lowell's article removes the anonymous and exhibits the author of some of the most peculiar and characteristic productions in our literature."[25] It is striking that, given the scope of the essay, Duyckinck should call attention to the role it played in matching the figure of Poe with the texts he had written. After all, at this stage of his career Poe had published three books of poetry, *The Narrative of Arthur Gordon Pym*, a series of gift-book contributions, a school-text on conchology, two volumes of collected tales, a serial issue of prose romances, and, according to Lowell's calculations, fifty-five individual tales and extravaganzas. Yet, given the unpredictability of reprint culture it is not altogether surprising that Poe, who was well known and well respected as a critic, could remain relatively unknown as an author, his writing dispersed, but his reputation indeterminate.[26] Duyckinck celebrates the removal of an anonymity that, though it was frequently manipulated by Poe to his advantage, was an inescapable condition of publishing in this era.

"Precisely what [Poe] had written" could remain a mystery not simply because of the limited circulation of his works, but because of the decentralized publication of his poems and tales, and because many were initially printed or reprinted without his name attached. Although legally possible, domestic copyright of magazine articles was relatively rare, even after *Graham's* and *Godey's* began to seek copyright for their contents in 1845. Magazines such as the *Southern Literary Messenger*, which printed predominantly "original" articles, were the exception, not the rule. Republication without payment and often without attribution was standard practice in newspapers and in literary miscellanies; at the other end of the publishing scale, the editors of prestigious journals such as the *American Review* insisted upon concealing the identities of their contributors as the hallmark of gentlemanly publishing.

Textual integrity and authorial identity were common casualties of the reprint process, as the publishing histories of some of Poe's most famous tales attest. As I have noted, "The Fall of the House of Usher" was reprinted anonymously in the London monthly *Bentley's Miscellany* six months after its collection in Poe's *Tales of the Grotesque and Arabesque*, then reprinted in the *Boston Notion* under a heading that suggested British authorship — "From Bentley's Miscellany for August." "The Purloined Letter" underwent a similar purloining, suffering abridgement—with attribution—at the hands of *Chambers' Edinburgh Journal*, reprinting in its altered state in *Littell's Living Age*, and then a third reprinting in two installments in the *Morning News*, with the head note "From Chambers' Journal, via Littell's Living Age."[27] Given such complex textual itineraries, it is not surprising that all kinds of confusions about authorial identity should arise, misattributions that twentieth-century readers with stable texts might find unimaginable. Poe's career illustrates the difficulty of establishing an authorial identity under such conditions; as Lowell remarked of Poe, "he has squared out blocks enough to build an enduring pyramid, but has left them lying carelessly and unclaimed in many different quarries" (7).

Indeed, it is difficult to overstate the importance of anonymity and pseudonymy as mediating factors in Poe's career. Even bracketing the pseudonymous strategies deployed by Poe relatively successfully for effect— "Arthur Gordon Pym"— or self-protection—"Tamerlane" and "By a Bostonian"—a broad range of his texts and textual practices drift free from the confines of individual authorship. A representative list of these practices might include: a successful newspaper piece such as "The Balloon Hoax" which, in taking the form of report, is necessarily unsigned; a review, such as Poe's of Lowell's *Poems*, which remains unsigned either by editorial fiat or by personal choice; the unsigned reviews, such as C. J. Peterson's of Rufus Griswold or Thomas Dunn English's of Poe's *Tales*, which have been attributed to Poe to his disadvantage; Poe's pseudonymous authorship of *The Conchologist's First Book*, a product of its true author's attempt to circumvent the restrictions of copyright;[28] the unlocatable quotations from non-existent authors used as epigraphs for numerous tales and for the "Prospectus of *The Stylus*"; the anonymous and pseudonymous contributions to the *Broadway Journal* that were Poe's, but were disguised as the work of "††" or "Littelton Barry" to give the impression of a varied authorship; the anonymity of Poe's work as a "mechanical paragraphist," condensing statements and writing announcements for the New York *Mirror*; the implicit pseudonymy of his work for the journals entitled *Burton's* and *Graham's*, magazines for which Poe at times had full editorial responsibility, and which were frequently reviewed by other periodicals issue by issue, as if they were individual books.

The broad range of these practices underscores both the ease with which Poe seemed to inhabit them, and the critical difficulty of finally extricating his persona and his writing from the complex forms of empowerment and disablement they represent. Poe is commonly seen only as a victim or a critic of the publishing practices of his era, imagined to have been crushed by, or to stand somehow outside of these systems looking in. And yet it was from the vantage point of a full participant that he launched his critique of such practices. Poe bitterly attacked the use of anonymity in criticism, as when he complained of the Quarterlies: "Who writes?—who causes to be written? Who but an ass will put faith in tirades which *may be* the result of personal hostility, or in panegyrics which . . . may be laid, directly or indirectly to the charge of the author himself?"[29] Yet he also used it to his advantage, first publishing "The Literary Life of Thingum Bob" anonymously in the *Southern Literary Messenger*, then calling attention to it anonymously in his capacity as paragraphist for the *Mirror*: "A broadly satirical article, oddly entitled 'The Literary Life of Thingum Bob, Esq. . . ?' has been the subject of much comment, lately, in the Southern and Western papers, and the question is put to *us* especially, here in the North,—'who wrote it?' Who *did?*—can any one tell?"[30]

"Can anyone tell?"—a question that still troubles bibliographers of Poe—was a question that horrified Young Americans such as Duyckinck when they confronted the welter of texts produced by the culture of reprinting. A brief account of the anxieties that propelled the Young American platform will help to explain both Duyckinck's relief at the canonizing function that Lowell's essay on Poe performs, and the role that Poe was to play for the movement from his outpost at the *Broadway Journal*. Understanding the shift in rhetoric that occurs as the Young Americans take on the international copyright question will help to clarify why the sudden appearance of Poe as a fully formed author and critical autocrat should seem so appealing.

While the Young America movement was always an elitist undertaking—its founding members a group of affluent *litterateurs* who had formed themselves into an exclusive private association—their rhetoric distinguished itself at the start by its populism, their project drawing strength and gaining prominence from its connection with the radical wing of the Democratic party and with its chief publishing venture, the *United States Magazine and Democratic Review*.[31] As Perry Miller details in his definitive study, this alliance was at first a happy one; the core of the movement— Duyckinck, Mathews, and William A. Jones—joined forces with editor John O'Sullivan to promote a literature that was committed to republican institutions, one that would instill in American youth the proper democratic habits. In terms of literary politics, the Young Americans allied with O'Sullivan against the elitist pretensions of the Whig *Knickerbocker* and the Boston press. According to O'Sullivan, it was the "better-educated classes" who, in "[drinking] in an anti-democratic habit of feeling and thinking" from the "copious . . . fountain of English literature," gave a "tone of sentiment" to "our literary institutions" that was "poisoning at the very spring the young mind of our people."[32] In *Arcturus* and the early *Democratic Review* it was a general maxim that achieving literary independence was a matter of transforming the content of literary works; one established "the true glory and greatness of the democratic principle, by *infusing* it *into* our literature" (emphasis mine).[33] The terms of O'Sullivan's praise for the Democratic party's content-hero, Nathaniel Hawthorne, are broadly indicative of the politics of this position. Reading Hawthorne's literary practices as congruent with a political commitment to domestic manufacture, O'Sullivan commends him for not having "imported his literary fabrics, nor made them after patterns, to be found in either obscure or noted foreign warehouses."[34]

It was, finally, the conflict between O'Sullivan's commitment to domestic manufacture and the adoption of an international copyright law that finally drove a wedge between the Young Americans and the Democratic party. As we have seen, the lack of international copyright was good for American manufacture. In an 1843 declaration on "The International Copyright Question," O'Sullivan concluded that democratic principles lay more with supporting the system of cheap publication than with promoting a literature that was democratic in content alone. O'Sullivan theorized that the adoption of an international copyright law would so raise the cost of books as to create "an aristocracy of readers." Placing his faith instead in the democratizing power of new technologies of print, O'Sullivan speculated that literature with a democratic content would naturally emerge from a system of democratic publishing. If the price of domestic publications were made cheap enough by high-volume printing, the American author, possessing "advantages of national sympathy and patriotic pride on the part of the people" as well as "comprehension of the character and taste of his countrymen" would automatically outsell his British competitor.[35]

O'Sullivan's firm stand against international copyright put Duyckinck and his circle in an awkward position: their own party had abandoned their platform, while the argument in favor of a literature with a discernibly democratic content began earnestly to be taken up by Whig authors and editors as a protectionist measure.[36] The *Knickerbocker*, for example, came out in favor of a national literature on decidedly conservative grounds. Their chief concern was not with republican institutions, but with a possible outbreak of licentiousness. The republication of foreign works exposed the public to a dangerous "sensuality" and "immorality," whereas "Home literature"—of the proper refinement—promoted "good taste, and a sense of fitness and propriety."[37] This new alignment of politics and rhetoric prompted Duyckinck to direct his appeal to a Whig readership in the pages of the newly formed monthly the *American Review*. In an article in the February issue, "The Literary Prospects of 1845" (which appeared, incidently, directly after the "The Raven—by Quarles"), Duyckinck laid out the terms of a regrounding that had already begun to take place, shifting his rhetoric from the promotion of works with American content to an attack on the immorality of the system of reprinting.

Duyckinck's appeal to the Whigs brought out the elitism that had been implicit in the Young American position all along, a condescension toward the masses they were trying to elevate that had been only partially concealed by their association with the radical democrats. In this essay, Duyckinck gives expression to anxieties about the rapid expansion of print culture that had formed a steady background hum in Cornelius Mathews's many speeches on the need for international copyright. Duyckinck's projections for the coming year evince a deep-seated contempt for the popular press, a disgust with the scope and extent of mass-production, and an overriding concern about imposture:

We would fain hope that the literary system which has been distinguished by the epithet "cheap and nasty" is pretty much at an end. . . . Nothing has been too mean or poor-spirited for that system to produce. It was pregnant in nauseous puffs, unworthy of a mountebank. . . . Native authors were neglected, despised, insulted; foreign authors were mutilated, pillaged and insulted besides. Ingratitude was among the least of the current vices. Misrepresentation and falsehood were its companions. The good writers were not only taken possession of, their works altered and thrown upon the public without their just honor and responsibility, but they were made the cover for the circulation of the worst licentiousness.[38]

Read against O'Sullivan's resounding confidence in the liberating powers of the press, Duyckinck's hopes can only be termed reactionary. Toward the end of the passage he draws dangerously close to the position of the *Knickerbocker* Whigs, with an important distinction: it is not the circulation of licentiousness that is the crime here, but the mutilation and misrepresentation of the texts of the "good writers" under whose cover this illicit traffic takes place. On the whole it is *not* foreign sensuality or even the foreign itself that troubles Duyckinck. What the reprint trade threatens to produce in American readers is an inability to discriminate. The popular press is all-encompassing; nothing is "too mean" for it to publish. Like Lowell, Duyckinck figures American publishing in terms of a monstrous female reproductive power, but his focus is on restraining rather than subverting or replacing this power. Duyckinck sees the regulation of the reprint trade as the remedy for the press's grotesque overcapacity; he longs for a press that "will bear the natural and just fetters of order, benevolence, refinement" (150).

Duyckinck's generalized fear of the indiscriminate can be seen in his fervent hope that an international copyright agreement will remove this state of uncertainty: "the line will in future be more strongly drawn between honesty and fraud in publishing" (148). Here Duyckinck's tone is restrained and his prognosis hopeful, but Cornelius Mathews's widely circulated "Appeal to American Authors and the American Press in Behalf of International Copyright" demonstrates how easily the Young American defense of literary property could slide into epistemological panic. In a characteristically dramatic and inconclusive passage, Mathews proclaims: "This— an invasion of property—is only one of the external evils growing out of a false and lawless state of things. Of others, which strike deeper; which create confusion and error of opinion; which tend to unsettle the lines that divide nation from nation; to obliterate the traits and features which give us a characteristic individuality as a nation—there will be another and more becoming opportunity to speak."[39] Duyckinck's preoccupation with textual uncertainty—the inability in an age of cheap republication to tell a book by its cover—manifests itself in Mathews' prose as a more fundamental anxiety about cognition, individual difference, and the instability of national identity.

It is a persistent irony of this rhetoric that those who agitate most fiercely for international copyright should find national identity in writing so precarious as to be hardly worth protecting. And yet what Duyckinck's and Mathews's rhetoric exposes is the crisis of judgment that attends the rapid expansion of the trade. The Young Americans are not simply troubled by the importation of foreign values but by the possibility that citizens might no longer be able to tell the difference between domestic and foreign. It is not so much dependency that concerns them, but indistinction.[40]

Duyckinck's "Literary Prospects" essay announces a shift in strategy and serves as a call to action, a call for renewed efforts to make discriminations among texts. This was the year, after all, in which he was to launch both his "Library of American Books" and a companion series of reprints, the "Library of Choice Reading," which somewhat nervously advertised its selections under the slogan "Books Which Are Books."[41] As both the series-title and the slogan suggest, Duyckinck had become less concerned with pretense than with indiscrimination. This was also the year of Poe's spectacular emergence on the New York literary scene, his access to the nationalist publishing machine paved by the fulsome praise of Lowell's biography.[42] The terms of Lowell's praise and the shift in Young American rhetoric should explain why this essay was persuasive. Given their opposition to the unchecked productivity of the press and their fears of the indiscriminate, one can see why the Young Americans might fail to read the opening of the essay as an attack on their policies. Indeed, the proliferation of images of inauthenticity in Lowell's critique could have been enough to convince them that he was actually on their side. The shift in their rhetoric from a support of democratic content in literature to an attack on the reprint trade perfectly positioned them to receive and to replicate the kind of coterie-critique that Poe had been honing in his struggles with various editors. In fact, Duyckinck echoes this critique in a passage in "Literary Prospects" in which he alludes to the arrival of Poe on the New York literary scene. After a lengthy discussion of the way in which a misguided "feeling of nationality" had prompted editors to praise works with an American content without regard to their merit, Duyckinck suggests that these "false defenders of mediocrity" are actually puffing plagiarisms: "A pungent and rather startling essay might be written on this prolific theme; and such we are given to understand by a hint in a late number of our contemporary, the 'Democratic,' is already prepared, by a writer whose pen 'hath a taste to it,' under the pleasant title of 'American Cribbage!'" (149).

Duyckinck's response to the "overproduction" (148) of the press is technologically reactionary: it is a return to the pen, and to one that "hath a taste to it"—both courage and cultivation. The resort to the pen is a necessity, given the thorough corruption of the practice of puffery and its links to the system of republication; the resort to Poe's pen represents an attempt to get outside of the system by enlisting the help of someone long known as its critic, someone who appeared to have produced a large corpus of work without its assistance, someone who had promised to provide a "criticism self-sustained."

Poe's relative anonymity as an author was indispensable to his construction by the Young Americans as a figure with redemptive power. While advocating a literature with American content their rhetoric had often taken on an extravagant, messianic tone, invoking the truly native author as one who, like Christ, was in the world, but not of it. The Young Americans' rhetorical assumption of the role of prophet and precursor gave expression both to their sense of the nation's urgent need for salvation, and to their own need to be legitimated as the sole critics capable of recognizing this author-savior. Lowell's representation of Poe as a figure of parthenogenesis, one whose works demonstrated impossible, instant maturity, played directly into this formation. Lowell's reversal of the priorities of the literary nationalist program—his insistence that a literary criticism with integrity would necessarily precede the advent of the Master Genius—reinforced Young America's newfound commitment to discrimination and to the restraint of the system of republication, and placed Poe in a difficult position—in Willis's words, as a possible "axle and lynch-pin" for their entire system.

Narratives of Absolute Possession and Dispossession: Authorial Identity in "The Little Longfellow War"

As we have seen, Lowell invoked the figure of Poe as a solution to a series of insoluble cultural problems: the problem of national integrity and political authority in a culture characterized by decentralization; the problem of the growth of a literature mapped onto these fragments, and thus detached from centralized support; and the problem of literary production in the context of a criticism that would celebrate inauthenticity rather than pass through a period of unbearable dependency. Lowell's depiction of Poe as a self-originating poet and self-sustaining critic promised to neutralize and contain the centrifugal forces that threatened Lowell's own fledgling career as poet and editor. Poe's instant maturity eliminated dependency by obviating the need for growth; his critical self-sufficiency seemed capable of serving as a ground for American literature insofar as it embraced the condition of detachment which was inevitable in the disjointed universe of American literary production.

Duyckinck's celebration of Poe's emergence from anonymity and invocation of Poe's powers of discernment fulfill a similar function within his narrative of national crisis. For Duyckinck, Poe's achievement of authorial identity is not a process, but a sudden unveiling, the differentiation and consolidation of texts out of a field of indifference. Within the logic of his essay on the "Literary Prospects of 1845," Poe's proposal for a "Chapter on American Cribbage" stands in for the principle of differentiation itself; the ability to distinguish between original and copy is appealed to as a kind of interim regulatory measure in lieu of the passage of an international copyright law. And yet what is perhaps most striking about Duyckinck's essay is the incommensurate nature of this substitution, the inadequacy of individual judgment (no matter how unimpeachable) as a solution to the problem of uncontrollable production. To begin with, Duyckinck has no clear idea how the regulation of the circulation of texts in the literary marketplace will produce an original genius. In a characteristic gesture of obfuscation he exclaims, "We cannot say of genius, it will be here or there, but the spirit of God breathes it, and lo! a Homer, a Shakspeare [sic]" (150). He can only reassure himself, by insisting upon the making of distinctions, that he has taste enough to recognize a work of genius when it comes along. Poe's proposed "Chapter on American Cribbage" is indispensible to him in this regard, in that it projects a generalized posture of absolute judgment, one of extraordinary accuracy and dependability.

It is, however, unclear how the ability to adjudicate between texts can keep in check the overproduction of the press, how Poe's promise to expose the derivative nature of American literary production will succeed in drawing the line more clearly between "honesty and fraud in publishing" (148). Duyckinck's hope seems to be that Poe's exposures of the fraudulent relations between pairs of texts will disarm the system of puffery by drawing attention from the suspect texts themselves, to the corrupt practices of those who promote them. Yet not only does this model gloss over vast differences in scale, proposing to address the problem of mass-production by the exercise of subtle differentiations at the point of reception. It also represents a retreat from the problem of scale to the simpler terrain of authentic and derivative, an imposition of absolutes of honesty and fraud, guilt and innocence, on what Duyckinck repeatedly acknowledges to be a vast, undifferentiated middle ground of textual production. Duyckinck is attracted to Poe's proposal because it promises a systematic and irrefutable exposure of textual fraud: "The beauty of these *exposés* must lie in the precision and unanswerability with which they are given—in day and date—in chapter and verse—and, above all in an unveiling of the minute trickeries by which the thieves hope to disguise their stolen wares."[43] And yet he invokes Poe's powers of discernment as a means of wresting American literature from the hands of the "false defenders of *mediocrity*," those critics who fall into "paroxysms of admiration" over what is essentially a "minor literature" (148–49). Duyckinck proposes addressing the delicate problem of recalibrating the inflated claims for American texts with the sledgehammer distinction of original from copy.

Poe's proposal for a "Chapter on American Cribbage" answers to Duyckinck's rhetorical needs because of the posture of absolute judgment it projects, and because of the self-authorizing strategies of the fiction of which it is a part. Poe suggests this project in the context of his "Marginalia," a series of fictional book annotations that purport to be the work of a gentleman of excessive leisure and impossible erudition. Poe's preface to the series suggests that these notes derive their authority from their status as handwritten adjuncts to printed texts. This idle scribbling exceeds the immediacy of speech in its utter privacy and inutility; paradoxically, it is the aimlessness of these marginal notes that grants them value. In his *Marginalia*, Poe opens up a textual space that seeks to exempt itself from the corrupting forms of self-interest that suffuse the world of print. The fact that these are *printed* marginalia circulating in a popular magazine, however, belies their claim to represent the pure exercise of judgment performed within the confines of the margin, the virtuous space of gentlemanly seclusion. As Stephen Rachman has argued, Poe exploits the equivocal status of his published "Marginalia," both posing as a literary gentleman, and self-consciously exposing this posture as masquerade. Poe's "Marginalia" serve to parody as well as to exemplify gentlemanly discernment.[44]

However, as Lowell's misreading of Poe's theory of effect makes clear, Poe's characteristic deflationary gestures do not prevent his fictions from being taken up by others; irony is an insufficient defense against appropriation. Although it seems implausible, a false aristocrat was precisely what literary nationalist rhetoric demanded. Poised between a condemnation of the literary elite, and an attack on the popular press, the Young Americans required discrimination of a pedigree that could not be traced back to Britain. Only a performance of literary judgment that was cut off from the historical grounds of its authority could be certifiably American.

The promotion of Poe's late-February lecture on "The Poets and Poetry of America" graphically demonstrates that he was cast in this role. Willis's announcement of the lecture transforms Duyckinck's enlistment of Poe's critical pen into the acquisition of an even sharper instrument: "The decapitation of the criminal who did not know his head was off till it fell into his hand as he was bowing . . . conveys an idea of the Damascene slicing of the critical blade of Mr. Poe."[45] Duyckinck's review of that same lecture makes it abundantly clear that this blade was employed in direct support of the principles he had laid out in the "Literary Prospects" essay:

In the exordium [Poe] gave a great and cutting description of the arts which are practised, with the aid of the periodical press, in obtaining unmerited reputation for literary worth. His observations upon this division of his subject extended also to the pernicious influence of coteries, and he did not hesitate to point to the Capital of New England as the chief habitation, in this country, of literary hucksters and phrase mongers. Mr. Poe's manner was that of a versed and resolute man, applying to a hideous sore a keen and serviceable knife.[46]

Here Duyckinck celebrates Young America's assimilation of Poe's coterie-critique, newly deflected from New York to Boston. Poe's retargeting of his critique demonstrates more than his expedient embrace of local antagonisms; it marks his incorporation into the regional struggle to control national literary culture, a struggle largely fought over the proper terms of literary assessment. And yet it was as much the performance of judgment as the judgments themselves that Duyckinck and his circle welcomed; it was the fact of the cutting that got most of the attention. Poe had become an icon of the act of literary judgment itself, in Willis's words, the "statuary embodiment of Discrimination."[47]

Poe's extended attack on Longfellow both confirms and tests the limits of this appropriation. Longfellow was not only a key member of the Boston literary elite, he had become the standard-bearer for a literary culture that rejected the proposals of the Young Americans. As Perry Miller has noted, Boston and New York conservatives saw in Longfellow's "ever-widening popularity a proof of the 'universality' which is the mark of genuine poetry, . . . [a poetry] which has nothing to do with nationalism."[48] In one sense, then, Poe's attack on Longfellow constitutes the strongest proof of his loyalty to the Young Americans: it represents both a strategic strike on behalf of their critical authority, and an act of courageous discrimination. Yet even a cursory look at the texts which make up the "Little Longfellow War" suggests that this debate is not a straightforward display of personal or regional rivalry. In spite of Poe's title, his antagonist in this debate is not Longfellow himself, but a pseudonymous interlocutor who personifies and defends common property in writing. Poe's rebuttal is not an attack on Longfellow per se, but an elaborate defense of the grounds on which a charge of plagiarism may be made. Poe's position within literary nationalist discourse as a personification of absolute judgment helps to account for the odd, abstract terrain on which most of the Longfellow War takes place. Poe uses this debate to examine the grounds of literary judgment itself. And, while he renews the call for making discriminations between texts, he ultimately undermines the role he had assumed as absolute judge. In the Longfellow War, Poe's most vehement assertions of the undeniability of literary theft slide into a subtle awareness of the dispossession of the subject by the circulation of texts.

What most critics consider the opening salvo of this war was issued in mid-January in a short critique of Longfellow's *The Waif* (1845) that was published anonymously in the *Evening Mirror* a week before the publication of Lowell's biography, and two weeks before the appearance of "The Raven." While this initial review created a minor sensation, resulting in a series of letters to the editor and editorial responses, it was six weeks until Poe recommenced the battle in the pages of the *Broadway Journal*. The gap between this initial, anonymous critique and Poe's full-fledged five-part excursus marks the space in which the figure of Poe as original author and independent critic is delivered up. The *Waif* review, then, serves as an important pretext for the concerns of the Longfellow War; it provides a commentary on the construction of authorial identity that will haunt the later production.

Poe's chief target in this review is what he sees as Longfellow's strategy of anonymity in publishing *The Waif*, a collection of fifty "fugitive" poems, seventeen of them anonymous, prefaced by a proem that is identified as Longfellow's. Poe's odd response to this volume is to insist that all of the unsigned poems were written by Longfellow. The volume thus constitutes both a powerful act of consolidation, and an unaccountable ambiguation, a failure on Longfellow's part to speak in the fullness of his poetic voice. In the context of Poe's review, all suspensions of identity are suspect, conspiratorial. For instance, in commenting on the structure of the volume, Poe asks suspiciously "How does it happen . . . that the name of each author in this volume is carefully omitted from its proper place, at the head of his poem, to be as carefully deposited in the index?"[49] Poe accuses Longfellow of attempting to author all of the poems in the volume simply by making it difficult for the reader to determine their "paternity" (698). He implies that *The Waif* is a false orphan, a text which exploits the condition of namelessness to which he and other lesser poets are subjected.[50] Poe's anxiety about the deployment of anonymity as a textual effect stretches to his assessment of formal aspects of the volume. According to Poe, Longfellow's book is assembled "purposely at random," and the meter of his proem provides the perfect counterpoint for this controlled surrender of control—it is a model of "dexterously executed *slip-shod-iness*" (696).

It is in the context of an obsessive circling around questions of anonymity and identity, surrender and control, that Poe raises the question of Longfellow's imitation. It is not the derivative nature of Longfellow's poetry that initially irks Poe, but Longfellow's emergence as an author against a backdrop of undifferentiated and unacknowledged fellow poets. Here Longfellow's crime isn't theft, but a crucial act of erasure figured as theft: "there does appear, in this exquisite little volume, a very careful avoidance of all American poets who may be supposed especially to interfere with the claims of Mr. Longfellow. These men Mr. Longfellow can continuously *imitate* (*is* that the word?) and yet never even incidentally commend" (702). Poe's coy play on the imprecision of "imitate" as the word for the phenomenon of which he speaks reaches forward to the palpable crime of plagiarism even as it reaches backwards towards the murkier scenario of an undifferentiated field, the repression of which constitutes the grounds of the poet's emergence.

If Poe in the *Waif* review seems to be working out the problem of his own obscurity in relation to Longfellow's maddeningly empowered use of anonymity as a literary device, he will transform this scenario into an accusation of direct theft in the five installments of the Longfellow War. Poe emerges as a full authorial subject in this series, throwing off the editorial "we,"[51] while insisting unconditionally on the existence of plagiarism. The example Poe repeatedly resorts to in order to make good on this unwavering claim, however, is the frequent theft by "authors of established reputation" of "recondite, neglected, or forgotten books" (718), an example that, rather than substantiating his claim, points to the difficulty of a subject's coming into ownership of a text in the first place. Poe's repeated toying with the limits of literary property finally transforms his absolute insistence on the crime of plagiarism into a startling defense.

The Longfellow War is structured as an elaborate response to a letter challenging Poe's judgments in the *Waif* review. This letter, signed "Outis"— Greek for Nobody—was first published in the *Evening Mirror*, but Poe reprinted it in its entirety as part of his step-by-step refutation of its claims.[52] Speaking as a representative of the generalized public (nobody in particular) as well as No-Body, a personification of the depersonalized medium of print, Outis stands up to Poe's insinuations, undermining the critical project of separating original from copy by suggesting that plagiarism simply does not exist. According to Outis, "Images are not created but suggested" to authors by events (710); similarities between poems are coincidental, the product of poets' shared language and shared experience. Recognizing that this attempt to undermine the grounds of the charge of plagiarism also threatens the grounds of authorial identity, Poe attacks Outis's claim that images are common property as an evasion of responsibility and insists upon an author's relation to language as a taking of possession. In a mock courtroom scene designed to return the debate to the question of individual responsibility, Poe suggests that defending Longfellow from a specific charge of theft "by way of showing the abstract impossibility" (721) of the crime would be an absurdity in a court of law. Although his tone is often flippant, Poe's courtroom analogy indicates the authority and finality that he would claim for literary judgment. Poe portrays Outis's appeal for common property in writing as a refusal to perform the adjudication between texts that is required of criticism.

At such moments Poe seems clearly to be performing the work of discrimination set out in the "Chapter on American Cribbage" and endorsed by the Young Americans. He provides an item-by-item comparison of the similarities between contending poems (732–35) and establishes a general formula for the weighing of evidence generated by such comparisons (736). His concern throughout the debate is to distinguish his own careful unfolding of critical principles from Outis's anonymous and unsubstantiated assertions, insisting on the exercise of judgment in the face of unidentified and undifferentiated aggression.[53] Yet Poe's position in this debate drifts from the idealized posture of "Discrimination" not only through his resort to personal invective, but also as a consequence of his broader argument. Describing the vector of literary theft, Poe insists that "Of the class of wilful plagiarists nine out of ten are authors of established reputation" (57) who plunder the work of "poverty-stricken" and "neglected" men of genius (59).

This allegation has the power to unsettle the Young American agenda not because it transforms an attack on the popular press into an attack on the elite, but because it reveals beneath the narrative of a struggle between authors, a counternarrative of the struggle of the author to emerge in the first place, to distinguish himself out of an indistinguishable mass of texts. Poe's insistence that plagiarism is most often the work of the "gentleman of elegant leisure" calls attention to the unstable grounds of literary property, and implies that literary judgment is consequently unreliable. In a series of melodramatic narratives, Poe asserts that in spite of his careful explication of the nature of this crime, the plagiarist can operate with impunity. According to Poe, the author of established reputation "pilfers from some poverty-stricken, and therefore neglected man of genius, on the reasonable supposition that this neglected man of genius will very soon cut his throat, or die of starvation . . . and that in the meantime he will be too busy in keeping the wolf from the door to look after the purloiners of his property" (720). For Poe, the immorality of plagiarism is linked to the invisibility of the theft; the confidence and self-possession of the author of established reputation is a byproduct of the virtual nonexistence *as property* of the texts of the neglected author, which are the targets of the theft. Poe situates his account of literary crime at the vanishing point of the subjectivity of its victims, suggesting the tenuousness of the poor author's attachment to his texts, and the precariousness of considering plagiarism as an intersubjective relation. Far from an "American Cribbage" fantasy where thefts can be exposed with the precision of chapter and verse, day and date, Poe constructs a narrative in which the absorption of one text into another is done with ease, and the detection of the crime seems all but impossible.

Poe's concern with the vulnerability of the authorial subject to the circulation of texts is most evident at the moments when he invokes the act of plagiarism and the accusation of plagiarism as intersubjective struggles. For instance, at the beginning of the third installment of the debate, Poe cites Outis's text in order to demonstrate the emergence of a personal threat out of the apparent impersonality of his prose. Calling attention to Outis's strange capitalization of "THE DYING RAVEN," Poe suggests that the title of Dana's poem was "so printed for the purpose of safely insinuating a charge which not even an Outis had the impudence openly to utter" (67). Yet as soon as he has conjured personal impudence out of the impersonality of Outis's typography, Poe withdraws the charge, claiming that he cannot be sure that "any such thoughts as these ever entered the brain of Outis," that such a charge must remain "purely suppositious," and that, should he insist on the allegation, he would "furnish ground for a new insinuation of the same character, inasmuch as [he would] be employing Outis' identical words" (67). This is undoubtedly lighthearted word play, yet it is also an acknowledgement of the dangerous indistinguishability of their positions. Insofar as Poe's principled stand is constructed as a rebuttal to Outis's letter, and is interlaced throughout with quotes from this anonymous text, it is dependent on the very anonymity it eschews. And what is worse, because the form of Poe's rebuttal involves a repetition of the charges of his opponent, the very antagonism which marks their difference is capable of disappearing in the reiteration of "identical words."

It is not altogether surprising, then, that in the final installment of the Longfellow War, Poe should construct an alternate context for understanding plagiarism, one in which authorial identity is linked not to the forcible taking of possession, but to a form of radical dispossession. In this installment, Poe shifts from his attempt to prove the legitimacy of the grounds of the *charge* of plagiarism to an attempt to construct a narrative in which the *practice* of plagiarism could be considered legitimate.

This shift in emphasis is motivated not only by the internal contradictions of his argument, but also by intervention from without. Concerned by the direction of Poe's analysis, Duyckinck published a warning in the guise of an endorsement, observing nervously that while Poe's impulses were undoubtedly honorable, there is a "great danger that the thing may be carried too far." Duyckinck stops short of naming this danger, but he is troubled both by the tone and by the direction of Poe's analysis. Calling for "more discrimination" and "greater nicety of apprehension," Duyckinck attempts to reroute Poe's critique from a meditation on the difficulty of establishing authorial identity to a depiction of authorial overproduction. Poe's interest in the threshold conditions of authorship is of no use to Duyckinck, who is alarmed by a surfeit of authors. Declaiming instead on the legion of undeserving writers who flood the literary marketplace, Duyckinck exhorts Poe to continue policing the line between the false and the genuine.[54]

In the context of this quasi-disciplinary prodding, Poe's recuperation of the practice of plagiarism in the final installment of the debate is all the more remarkable. In what appears to be a dramatic reversal of his position,

Poe argues that plagiarism can be viewed not as malicious theft, but as the product of a heightened sensitivity to beauty which is the hallmark of the true poet:

What the poet intensely admires, becomes . . . a portion of his own intellect. It has a secondary origination within his own soul—an origination altogether apart, although springing from its primary origination from without. The poet is thus possessed by another's thought, and cannot be said to take of it, possession. But, in either view, he thoroughly feels it as *his own*—and this feeling is counteracted only by the sensible presence of its true, palpable origin in the volume from which he has derived it—an origin which, in the long lapse of years it is almost impossible *not* to forget—for in the meantime the thought itself is forgotten. But the frailest association will regenerate it—it springs up with all the vigor of a new birth—its absolute originality is not even a matter of suspicion—and when the poet has written it and printed it, and on its account is charged with plagiarism, there will be no one in the world more entirely astounded than himself. (759)

What is perhaps most striking about this defense of plagiarism is the utter passivity of the offending poet. He is not only fully possessed by another's thought in the act of reading, he is subject to a kind of hair-trigger reproduction of this thought—"the frailest association will regenerate it." While Poe's emphasis on the helplessness of the plagiarist completely absolves the true poet of responsibility for literary theft, the absolute terms in which he casts his apologia indicate that this is not a retraction of his initial position, but its inversion. In this passage, authorial possession appears as its gothic opposite—the haunting by another—and yet these states are curiously reciprocal. Dispossession is experienced by the author as proprietorship up until the moment of going-into-print: the thought may be another's, but the poet "thoroughly feels it as *his own*." In the absence of the book that secures the textual origin of the poet's thought, its derivation is convincingly restaged as biological origination: it "springs up with all the vigor of a new birth." Poe identifies the poet as wholly deluded (the "absolute originality" of his thought is "not even a matter of suspicion"), and yet the extent of his deception bestows upon him a paradoxical uniqueness. At the moment of exposure there is "no one in the world more entirely astounded" than the plagiarist himself. Poe's representation of the poet wholly overtaken by another's thought enables him to maintain his initial insistence on the fact of possession as the ground of authorship, while at the same time acknowledging the constant vulnerability of the author to self-loss. His model of legitimate literary theft works to contain the threat posed by anonymity, recasting the displacement of the authorial subject that Outis advocates and represents within the domain of personal property. In his narrative of authorial possession, Poe identifies the circulation of texts with a surrender of autonomy (the loss of the "sensible presence" of the book, and the moment of going into print are the twin sites of the poet's betrayal). And yet he seeks to convert this lack of agency into a mark of identity, suggesting that a helpless subjection to iteration is the condition of true poetry.

This redefinition of plagiarism as the provenance of the true poet, however, utterly jeopardizes Poe's commitment to adjudicating between texts. Far from his promised digest of the techniques by which authors perpetuate textual fraud, Poe leaves the critic with no means of distinguishing the debased practice of plagiarism from the inspired one, except perhaps by the frequency of its occurrence. As Poe suggests in his closing argument, the true poet is actually *more* apt to plagiarize: "the liability to accidents of this character is in the direct ratio of the poetic sentiment— of the susceptibility to the poetic impression" (759). Despite the promise of mathematical precision conveyed by Poe's "direct ratio," the true poet's mark of distinction is ultimately inaccessible to the critic and to the poet himself: it is a primary vulnerability to imprinting.

Disowning Ownership: Poe's Evasion of Identity at the Boston Lyceum

In the Longfellow War, Poe defends the author as a proprietary subject by portraying him as subject to a primary appropriation. Poe relies on the convertability of these states, and yet his relentless and recessive logic ultimately collapses the distinctions he sets out to enforce: plagiarism and true poetry become indistinguishable. Given his gravitation toward interchangeable models of authorship as absolute possession and dispossession, Poe's controversial performance at the Boston Lyceum seems an extraordinary attempt to undo the tyranny of these options, to step outside the realm of literary property altogether. Poe's acceptance of an invitation to deliver an original poem before the Lyceum represents the authorial correlative to his attempt to perform an act of absolute critical judgment in the Longfellow War. Reportedly unable to compose an original poem for the occasion,[55] Poe commits an act of self-plagiarism, delivering his early poem, "Al Aaraaf," as if it had been expressly written for this event. According to Poe, the initial reception of the poem was cordial, if reserved, and the affair only erupted into a scandal after he admitted "over a bottle of champagne" that he had written the poem in his youth.[56]

What is remarkable about this violation of decorum is both Poe's drive toward self-exposure, and the intensity of public reaction to reports that the poem had been written "*before its author was twelve years old*."[57] While Poe's arrogance and longstanding antagonism towards Boston certainly fueled the scandal, public outrage over the impropriety of his performance exceeded the offense, spilling over into criticism of Poe's inclusion of juvenilia in *The Raven and Other Poems*. In the newspaper and magazine commentary that followed the affair, Poe was repeatedly decried for permitting immature and fragmentary verses to circulate in the public sphere.[58]

James Russell Lowell's careful elimination of all traces of incompletion and dependency from Poe's biography enables us to read Poe's embrace of the juvenile as a significant threat to the mandate for American originality with which he had become identified. In the words of a critic who wrote in Poe's defense, the Lyceum had called on Poe to "deliver himself in poetry":[59] he was expected not only to present his work for their judgment, but to perform an act of autogenesis that would support the claim to literary autonomy that had been made on his behalf. Instead, Poe recited a poem that he insisted was the work of a nonproprietary subject, a juvenile poet—one in the midst of a process of development. Like "Al Aaraaf" itself, which represents a mythical middle ground between Heaven and Hell, salvation and damnation, Poe's recitation of a juvenile poem eludes the absolutist imperatives of the rhetoric through which his identity as an author had been forged. Neither fully formed, nor belated, the trope of juvenility hovers somewhere in between the impossible alternatives of original and copy.

While one may doubt Poe's intention to have performed precisely this kind of disruption, the intensity and breadth of public reaction, and the far reach of the figure of the juvenile for understanding what is inassimilable about Poe, are less easily dismissed.[60] The degree to which the trope of the juvenile was a threat to existing models of authorship is best indicated by its rapid conversion in the public sphere into the opposing forms of authorship it would deny. Appalled by his lack of respect for their commission of an original poem, Poe's enemies credited his performance to drunkenness or insanity, recasting the intrusion of the juvenile into the discourse of originality as the total surrender of authorial control.[61] Seeking to regain authority over a situation that threatened to undo him, Poe shifted to the pole of absolute self-possession, insisting that he had intended all along to recite an obviously inferior poem. In Poe's account, it was the Boston audience's much vaunted powers of discrimination that had been thoroughly discredited by "the soft impeachment of the hoax."[62]

Poe's claim to have hoaxed the Bostonians has been regarded as self-aggrandizing and foolishly self-incriminating, a perverse confession of his own incompetence.[63] Yet in light of Poe's exemplary status within the discourse of literary nationalism, his attempt to shift attention from his performance to that of the Boston audience seems a remarkably clever retrenchment. Poe's revised account not only places him in complete control of the event, it also places him squarely back within the terms and aspirations of the literary nationalist project. According to Poe, his recitation of a juvenile poem did not display his lack of originality, it exposed the Bostonians lack of judgment. In effect, Poe claims to have been doing the work of the Young Americans all along.

While it is not surprising that Poe's explanation failed to satisfy the Bostonians, it is odd that critics and biographers continue to view the Boston Lyceum affair almost exclusively from their perspective. Poe's performance is most often cited as evidence of his psychic instability, with little or no mention of his circumvention of the cultural demand for originality, or his attempt to shift attention to the struggle over literary judgment that was bound up with this demand. The illegibility of the cultural significance of Poe's performance can be traced to the specific form of his transgression. While Poe disclaims property in his poem by asserting that it is the work of a minor—a self who cannot own—this assertion is undeniably a proprietary gesture. At the Lyceum, Poe challenges his portrayal as a figure of instant maturity by insisting on placing his poem within a developmental narrative; he attempts to shatter his status as an exemplary subject by aggressively reasserting the contingent facts of his biography. While from Poe's perspective, such a fracture might look like reclamation, it represents an unforgivable breach of contract to anyone invested in the cultural fantasy of his autonomy. In a report that reads remarkably like the standard critical interpretation of this event, the Board of the Lyceum described the impropriety of Poe's performance as the irruption of his person onto the field of their expectations. The board explained apologetically that they had invited Poe "on the strength of his literary reputation, and were not aware of his personal habits or the eccentricities of his character."[64] In this account, the difference between the cultural construction of Poe and his self-presentation is refigured as the product of ineradicable and inexplicable aspects of Poe's personality—his habits and eccentricities.

Rather than a complex struggle over originality, authorial identity, and the standards of literary judgment, the Boston Lyceum disaster becomes the scandal of Poe's person.

What this critical dynamic regrettably obscures is the deeply equivocal nature of Poe's proprietary claims. Reciting "Al Aaraaf" may have released Poe from the impossible task of performing his exemplary originality, but this strategy stops short of full flight: a juvenile poem is something Poe needn't fully own, and yet it cannot be fully disowned. Rather than an act of senseless self-sabotage, Poe's exposure of his poem as a juvenile one is an extraordinary attempt to claim legitimacy for his poem in the absence of a legitimating authorial subject. Poe's is an act of defiance that nevertheless seeks approval. Ironically, this act of defiance recapitulates the structure of the literary standard it presumes to repudiate. In reading a juvenile poem rather than a work written for the occasion, Poe exploits the moral indeterminacy of self-plagiarism, which, while undoubtedly a borrowing, also stands as a parodic counterpart to the demand for self-creation. In attempting to circumvent and to challenge the terms of his invitation, Poe performs an all-too-literal fulfillment of the Lyceum's demands.

Even Poe's later claim to have hoaxed the Bostonians inscribes a comparable double-movement of evasion and self-assertion. Lurking behind Poe's disparagement of his poem and his description of his performance as a "soft impeachment" of the Boston literati, lies a powerful proprietary claim that, however brazen, cannot finally be pinned on Poe himself. For Poe's attempt to regain authority over his performance is cast in borrowed speech. His triumphant declaration of absolute self-possession is a partial and unacknowledged citation from Richard Brinsley Sheridan's *The Rivals*: "I own the soft impeachment."[65] Simultaneously signifying proprietorship and confession, that which is held, and that which is released from one's grasp, the unvoiced assertion "I own" resonates despite its detachment from any speaking subject. On the model of Poe's definition of true poetry, this is either empty possession, or a full haunting.

6

Suspended Animation: Hawthorne and the Relocation of Narrative Authority

EDGAR ALLAN POE REACHED THE HEIGHT of his fame as the culture of reprinting was beginning to be challenged by literary nationalism, but well before the coordinated, national distribution of books by American authors had been achieved. Most of Poe's readers encountered his work in newspapers and magazines despite the appearance of his *Tales* (1845) and *The Raven and Other Poems* (1845) in the "Library of American Books." Even the celebrity Poe enjoyed as the author of "The Raven" was largely the product of the poem's unauthorized reprinting.[1] Although in his later years, Poe tried to resuscitate his elite magazine *The Stylus* as a vehicle for recapturing the authority he had lost in the wake of his performance at the Boston Lyceum, he died before he could find a means by which to address a national audience.

Unlike Poe, however, Nathaniel Hawthorne was offered a rare opportunity for self-refashioning through the patronage of Boston publisher James T. Fields. The unexpected success of *The Scarlet Letter* (1850)[2] convinced Fields that he could "sell a good many thousand" volumes of "whatever" Hawthorne wrote, and he promised Hawthorne that he would "apply the publishing steam" to a new book "with the confident assurance that it will run like a locomotive."[3] With Fields's financial backing and strong encouragement, Hawthorne began to transform himself from a moderately successful writer of short fiction for gift books and magazines into a national novelist. To accomplish this metamorphosis, Hawthorne had to navigate shifts in genre and format as well as changes in the larger literary culture that was in the process of transition to a more centralized and stratified publishing system.

As Richard Brodhead has argued, in the early 1850s publishers like Fields began to forge a national market for American literature through organized and far-reaching advertising campaigns. Responding to the lit-erary nationalist clamor for native writers and deploying some of the same techniques that publishers used to promote popular women's fiction, Fields sought to market a handful of regional, New England male writers as a national cultural elite.[4] Of course, the culture of reprinting did not disap-pear overnight. As Jeff Groves has noted, the signature binding style by which the firm of Ticknor and Fields demarcated its group of select Amer-ican authors was first used in 1849 for a reprint of Tennyson's *In Memo-riam*.[5] Moreover, Ticknor and Fields relied on authorized reprints of texts by Tennyson, DeQuincey, and other British authors to raise the profile and secure the high-cultural status of their list of American classics. Nev-ertheless, Fields's patronage of Hawthorne signals a set of incipient changes in the book industry that would spell an end to the culture of reprinting, among them the coordination of regional markets to create a broader and more predictable field of distribution, and the reorganization of American literary culture on "a more steeply hierarchical plane."[6]

Recent scholarship has looked to Hawthorne's career as a primary example of the institutional creation and perpetuation of literary value. As Brodhead has shown, Fields's promotion of Hawthorne as the quintessen-tial American writer required an "interlocking network of literary agencies,"[7] including publishers, editors, and reviewers, as well as means of promo-tion such as the advertisement, the literary salon, and the elite periodical. While it is clear that Hawthorne never could have achieved representative status without such well-organized assistance, accounts of Fields's success run the risk of foreshortening Hawthorne's career and overlooking the author's own role in the process of canonization. Hawthorne was not ele-vated into national prominence ex nihilo; he had to be extricated from one publishing system and repositioned within another. Moreover, this process forced Hawthorne to confront a changing hierarchy of literary gen-res, requiring him to establish and project a narrative voice that would be commensurate with a new set of expectations for literature. While pub-lishing history can offer us benchmarks for the eclipse of reprinting by the rise of a centralized, national culture, what was at stake in the transition between these two regimes can be more richly traced through textual analy-sis of Hawthorne's struggle to reauthorize his fiction.

Hawthorne's status as a major author has made it difficult for critics to perceive his many years of publishing anonymous, pseudonymous, and authored tales and sketches as anything but an extended apprenticeship for his brief career as a novelist. Critical access to the breadth of the circulation of Hawthorne's writing in formats as diverse as gift books, ladies' magazines, partisan magazines, newspapers, and children's periodicals has also been blocked by Hawthorne's own insistence on his early obscurity, his claim that this fiction was almost entirely neglected by the reading public. Following Hawthorne's lead, critics have shied away from what cannot help but look like minor writing from the vantage point of a hierarchical literary culture. In this chapter, I will argue that Hawthorne's autobiographical account of early neglect works to obscure his relative success as an author within the terms offered by the culture of reprinting. Although it is cast as a humble confession of his insignificance, Hawthorne's fiction of obscurity is a nationalizing tool, part of a larger attempt to rid his writing of the taint of the feminine, the childish, the regional, and the foreign. Shifting attention from the meager sales of his books of tales and sketches to the history of their circulation in periodicals, I will argue that Hawthorne's sketches provide evidence of his complex engagement with the status of fiction in the culture of reprinting. What Edgar Allan Poe identifies in a series of reviews as Hawthorne's characteristic tone of repose represents not a withdrawal from the literary marketplace, but a set of careful calculations about the marketability of his fiction.

I then turn to Hawthorne's first full-length novel *The House of the Seven Gables* (1851) as evidence of the extraordinary labor that was required for Hawthorne to produce himself as a major author, reading its characteristic narrative impasses as proof of the difficulty of moving from one set of cultural expectations to another. Focusing on the vexed presence of the genres of reprint culture within the novel, I argue that Hawthorne is riven by his need to disavow his early career and by his inability to do so. Attempting to move beyond short fiction into the territory of the modern novel, Hawthorne is troubled by his dependence on literary forms that suddenly appear to him to be minor and insignificant. In *The House of the Seven Gables*, Hawthorne's veiled acknowledgment of his career as a children's book writer and his redeployment of the sketch form and the gothic tale are occasions for the unleashing of a contempt that the novel struggles hard to master. Looking closely at moments of generic self-consciousness, narrative rupture, and scenes of humiliation, I will show how *The House of the Seven Gables* depends on the literary forms it tries to disavow, arguing that reprinting is carried forward into the national culture that replaces it by the force of its repudiation. Recalling his early commitment to the value of repose, Hawthorne's obsessive return in the novel to figures of suspended animation will give us some sense of what authorial power looks like in the space of transition.[8] Resonant with narrative paralysis and a humiliating powerlessness as well as the equilibrium of power-in-restraint, Hawthorne's violent re-imagination of his narrative authority is part of his bequest to the national literary culture he comes to represent.

Concluding this book by looking at the culture of reprinting through the lens of Hawthorne's mid-century disdain will have taken us some distance from the expansive enthusiasm for unauthorized reprinting that I charted in the opening chapters. But the contempt that drives Hawthorne's minoritizing account of his many years of publishing in uncopyrighted periodicals is a sign of this culture's powerful hold on Hawthorne's imagination. It can also provide some measure of the cost to literary criticism of unthinkingly joining Hawthorne in casting this period of literary history into a dubious obscurity.

The Uses of Obscurity

As he was completing the manuscript of *The House of the Seven Gables* in January 1851, Nathaniel Hawthorne sent his publisher a short preface for a new edition of his first collection of tales and sketches. Republishing *Twice-Told Tales* (1837, 1842) was part of Fields's aggressive campaign to keep Hawthorne's name before the public following the extraordinary success of *The Scarlet Letter* in the spring of 1850. Taking the opportunity to reflect on his writing, Hawthorne begins this gently ironic description of his early literary failures with some comically exaggerated assertions. Pressing the modesty topos to the point of inversion, Hawthorne claims to have been "for a good many years, the obscurest man of letters in America," and credits this "distinction" to the conditions of his tales' publication: "These stories were published in magazines and annuals, extending over a period of ten or twelve years, and compromising the whole of the writer's young manhood, without making (so far as he has ever been aware) the slightest impression on the Public."[9]

One need not be familiar with Hawthorne's penchant for self-deprecatory prefaces to be suspicious of this series of superlatives. Although he goes on to admit that "one or two" of these tales "had a pretty wide newspaper circulation," Hawthorne is too interested in drawing connections between aesthetic failure and readerly neglect to qualify the claim substantially, crediting the slightness of his early production to a "total lack of sympathy at the age when his mind would naturally have been most effervescent" (1150). Alternately accusatory and self-blaming, Hawthorne uses the fiction of readerly neglect to control the terms of his reception, stepping in to criticize his early work for the benefit of his current readers. While for the most part, this self-critique is an exercise in diminished expectations, consisting of warnings as to form and tone ("Instead of passion, there is sentiment;" "in what purport to be pictures of real life, we have allegory" [1152]), Hawthorne concludes his "Preface" with a sly turn that ought to be taken a good deal more seriously. Hawthorne remarks that "on the internal evidence of his sketches," readers have confused the author with his authorial persona, regarding him as a "mild, shy, gentle, melancholic, exceedingly sensitive and not very forcible man" (1153). Self-effacing to the last, Hawthorne flatters the reader by suggesting that he has formed his sense of self on the pattern of his texts' reception: "He is by no means certain, that some of his subsequent productions have not been influenced and modified by a natural desire to fill up so amiable an outline and act in consonance with the character assigned to him" (1153). What has too often gone unnoticed or unsaid is that Hawthorne's disclaimer extends to his "Preface" and to the fiction of obscurity itself. What could be more melancholy than an author who is unable to distinguish himself from his readers' projections and who has come to regard his name as a pseudonym (1153)? What better history of an "exceedingly sensitive and not very forcible man" than one who vacillates in assigning blame between authorial seclusion and readerly neglect?

I dwell on the self-confirming fiction of Hawthorne's obscurity because it has exerted a tenacious and distorting hold on critical accounts of his career. Despite Hawthorne's subtle disclaimer, critics have tended to perform precisely the operation he warns against, taking the "Preface" as a candid explanation of the motives for his seclusion, and as an accurate account of his early reception. Stephen Nissenbaum has long since provided the tools for unpacking what was immediately at stake for Hawthorne in perpetuating this fiction. In his essay "The Firing of Nathaniel Hawthorne," Nissenbaum recounts Hawthorne's struggle to protect his patronage post as a Custom House surveyor by defining his appointment as literary and apolitical. Turned out by the Whig administration in the summer of 1849, Hawthorne found himself the focal point of a virulent debate on the spoils system. Because much of the success of *The Scarlet Letter* was initially due to its topical "Custom House" introduction, Hawthorne had even more of a stake in the following year in perpetuating the fiction of a "young manhood" spent in a shadowy "Dream-Land" (1153), detached from worldly concerns and responsibilities. Like the letters and newspaper articles written in his defense, in which Hawthorne was described as a "retired, quiet and inoffensive" man who strived to live "above the prejudices of the time," Hawthorne's "Preface" seeks to write the prehistory of an author too timid and withdrawn to have engaged in the petty political maneuvering with which he had been publicly charged.[10]

Nina Baym, too, has done much to explode the fiction of Hawthorne's writerly isolation, arguing that far from "the productions of a person in retirement" (1152), much of Hawthorne's early fiction was composed with practical assistance from, and intellectual exchange with his mother, uncle, and sisters in the midst of the busy Manning household.[11] Certainly, Hawthorne's short stint as editor and chief writer for the Boston eclectic *The American Magazine of Useful and Entertaining Knowledge* (March–September 1836) was in every sense collaborative. His letters from the time are full of pleas to his sister Elizabeth to send extracts and "concoctions" to him in Boston, along with his laundry, by the family stagecoach line.[12] Moreover, Hawthorne's careful angling for a succession of political appointments following the first publication of *Twice-Told Tales* suggests both the possession of and a willingness to exploit his considerable political and literary connections. Hawthorne's failed attempts to be named historiographer of Charles Wilkins' expedition to the South Seas (1837) and postmaster of Salem (1840, 1843–44), and his successful appointments as a measurer of salt and coal in the Boston Custom House (1839–40) and surveyor in Salem (1846–49), suggest not a writer in self-defeating, melancholy withdrawal from the world, but one actively engaged in the pursuit of a sinecure that would allow him to write without forcing him to depend on a literary career for sustenance. Indeed, the biographical and bibliographical evidence suggests that Hawthorne's problem was not that his tales and sketches failed to make "the slightest impression on the Public," but that the form of their circulation in newspapers, periodicals, and annuals left him possessed of a reputation that he could not easily turn to profit. As Hawthorne wrote to Horatio Bridge in 1843, "It is rather singular that I should need an office, for nobody's scribblings seem to be more acceptable to the public than mine, and yet I shall find it a tough scratch to gain a respectable support by my pen."[13]

Nevertheless, the fiction of Hawthorne's obscurity has proved too useful, both to Hawthorne and to his critics, to be easily dislodged. Despite ample evidence of the broad circulation of his early tales and sketches in a variety of periodicals, modern critics, who by and large share Hawthorne's bias toward the form of the book, have tended to take Hawthorne's depiction of his neglect at face-value, regarding the twenty-year period in which he wrote more than seventy works of short fiction as a prolonged and unheralded apprenticeship for his "Major Phase,"[14] the concentrated three-year period in which he achieved national fame as the writer of novel-length romances. I have suggested above some of the reasons why Hawthorne himself might have eagerly, if ironically, claimed the distinction of early obscurity: the still-pressing need to position himself as detached from the world of politics in the wake of the Custom House firing; the desire to distance himself from his participation in mass-cultural and feminized forms such as the eclectic magazine, the gift book, the children's book, and the women's periodical; and the remarkable opportunity for self-fashioning provided by his newfound alliance with Ticknor and Fields's increasingly national and high-cultural publishing juggernaut. Republication in book form allowed Hawthorne imaginatively to withdraw these tales and sketches from prior circulation. The absolutism of his insistence on their wholesale rejection by the public gives the clue to his ambition: if Hawthorne can succeed in identifying this fiction with the admittedly distended, but suddenly remote period of his minority ("the whole of the writer's young manhood" [1150]), this minor fiction can be superceded and redeemed by the success of his later work.[15]

It is less clear, however, why modern critics should concur with Hawthorne's self-deprecatory assessment. Most broadly, the presumption of Hawthorne's rejection by the public has enabled critics to regard his early fiction through a highly selective lens. Critics have tended to value particular tales for their historical irony, a hallmark of literary value that places Hawthorne at a critical remove from both his Puritan heritage and his immediate cultural context. When his writing from the 1830s and '40s has been evaluated more comprehensively, it has most often been made sense of by being retrospectively assembled into the novel-like structures that Hawthorne projected, then abandoned as the tales and sketches were published in various periodicals. Perhaps overly comfortable in the role of rescuer and restorer of the author's intention, literary critics have paid significantly more attention to authorial wish than to cultural fact, focusing on the failure of Hawthorne's ambitions—the collapse of his narrative designs—rather than evaluating the forms in which these fictions circulated and were read. For instance, while there has been a great deal of speculation about the precise makeup of the unpublished sequences "Seven

Tales of My Native Land," "Provincial Tales," and "The Story-Teller," there exists no treatment of the early tales that groups them according to pseudonym, the elaborate naming system that establishes networks of affinity across tales and periodicals, distinguishing the stories "By the author of the Gray Champion" from those "By the author of Sights from a Steeple" and "By the author of the Gentle Boy."

Contributing to the occlusion of much of Hawthorne's early work has been the presumption of a consensus as to the aesthetic value of individual tales and sketches. One of the most careful readers of Hawthorne's historical tales, Michael Colacurcio, frankly asserts what is simply implicit in most major studies—that there is a radical dropoff in quality in much of this writing, that only a select group of tales are properly Hawthorne's: "For though it has been possible to fold [a number of sketches] into a pseudo-historical recipe for 'the Hawthornesque,' no one (I think) should want to whip up a counterformula out of ingredients mixed equally from 'Sir William Pepperell,' 'Little Annie's Ramble,' 'A Rill from the Town Pump,' 'The Toll-Gatherer's Day,' 'Mrs. Bullfrog,' and 'The Lily's Quest.'"[16] And yet many of the tales that Colacurcio would place beyond the pale of the "Hawthornesque" circulated more widely in Hawthorne's day than the historical tales that critics have justly come to value.[17] To give but a very few examples, "The Wives of the Dead," which was initially published anonymously ("by F . . . . .") in the popular Boston gift book *The Token* (1832), was reprinted with Hawthorne's name attached in the New York mammoth weekly *Brother Jonathan* in December 1839, and with a change of title (as "The Two Widows") in the partisan monthly *The United States Magazine and Democratic Review* in July 1843, from which it was copied into the temperance newspaper *The Hampden Washingtonian* (10 August 1843), and the Philadelphia literary weekly *Alexander's Messenger* (22 July 1846)—all while the tale remained uncollected in book form.[18] "David Swan," which was anonymously printed in the *The Token and Atlantic Souvenir* for 1837, saw its circulation take off after it was printed in the small edition of one thousand copies of *Twice-Told Tales* in the spring of that year. It was reprinted in Boston and Salem newspapers, in the Philadelphia monthly *Atkinson's Casket* (November 1837), in miscellanies of pirated fiction published in Boston, New York, and London, and as a representative example of Hawthorne's writing in Rufus Wilmot Griswold's anthology *The Prose Writers of America* (1847).[19] If scholars have struggled to understand why Hawthorne failed to include "My Kinsman, Major Molineaux" and "Alice Doane's Appeal" in his early collections, what are we to make of the London piracy of *Twice-Told Tales* (1849), which reprinted "Foot-prints on the Sea-Shore," "Sunday at Home," "David Swan," and "Sights from a Steeple," but *omitted* "The Minister's Black Veil," "The May Pole of Merry Mount," "The Gentle Boy," and "Endicott and the Red Cross"?[20] The evidence of the wide reprinting of these sketches, combined with early reviewers' enthusiastic embrace of Hawthorne's "sedate, quiet dignity," his "easy grace and delicacy," his "calm, meditative fancy," and his lack of "dramatic pretension," suggests that we have been overlooking a literary phenomenon of substantial, if baffling significance.[21]

The enthusiastic reprinting of much of Hawthorne's early work indicates that he was in possession of a significant, if uneven and unpredictable reputation—a reputation from which he could not be assured to profit and which neither he nor his critics could confidently measure or describe. The uncontrolled circulation of Hawthorne's early fiction raises questions about authorial and critical mastery and suggests a final rationale for the collusion of literary critics in the fiction of his obscurity. Taking their cue from Hawthorne's self-characterizations, critics have come to read Hawthorne's novels of the early 1850s as allegories of this neglect. Michael Gilmore in particular has examined *The Scarlet Letter* and *The House of the Seven Gables* across a thematic axis that opposes the artist and the marketplace, an opposition that draws its interpretive charge from Hawthorne's early failure to be recognized and remunerated by the reading public. Gilmore ratifies Hawthorne's desire for detachment when he reads *The House of the Seven Gables* as dramatizing both its author's estrangement from and complicity with the market. According to Gilmore, in this novel Hawthorne was "unable to suppress his misgivings that in bowing to the marketplace he was compromising his artistic independence and integrity."[22] What becomes invisible to a critical narrative that presumes a history of neglect is that the fiction of obscurity itself is one of the means by which Hawthorne, who is thoroughly, and in many ways successfully embedded in the literary marketplace, *renegotiates* a relation to the reading public.

If the tendency of recent criticism has been to trade on Hawthorne's investment in his obscurity, imagining that his early failure in the market is at least partially redeemed by the sophistication of his later thematizations, Poe's approach to Hawthorne's early fiction is decidedly less heroic. In the three reviews he published in *Graham's Magazine* and *Godey's Lady's Book* between 1842 and 1847, Poe is determined to uncover the reasons for Hawthorne's success and to trace the precise limits of his popularity. For Poe, however, the limit to Hawthorne's popularity does not simply lie either inside or outside of his fiction—it is neither a question of his abilities as a writer, nor a matter of injustice in the history of his reception. Rather than positing literature as a site in which market conditions are confronted and potentially mastered, Poe suggests that what is exhilarating and frightening about the literary marketplace is the way in which it can make forms of literary value both appear and disappear. For Poe, it is a shift in the conditions of writing and reading that threatens radically to recast what readers most value about Hawthorne's sketches.

"Sleeping Beauty in the Waxworks": Monotony and Repose in Early Hawthorne

Poe's reviews of Hawthorne are important not only because they helped to forge a critical consensus on Hawthorne's first two collections of short fiction, *Twice-Told Tales* (1837; 1842) and *Mosses from an Old Manse* (1846), but because the problem of Hawthorne's popularity so troubled Poe that it proved the catalyst for the theory that has made these reviews famous—Poe's elaboration of his poetics of effect. What interests me here, however, is the interpretive problem that provokes Poe's fantasy of absolute authorial control, and the terms of analysis he derives from his study of Hawthorne. In these reviews, Poe struggles to define precisely what is distinctive about Hawthorne's fiction, and why it is that Hawthorne's originality has left him with a curiously uneven reputation, "the example, *par excellence*, in this country, of the privately-admired and publicly-unappreciated man of genius" (578).[23] Poe begins to theorize his own writing practice while speculating on the relation between success in the literary marketplace and subtle tonal differences, generating his poetics of effect from his perception of the disarmingly short distance between the narrative quality he associates with commercial and aesthetic failure—monotony—and the tone he ascribes to Hawthorne—that of repose.

Hawthorne's early fiction raises for Poe the question of the relation of style to sales in part because Poe had initially assumed that in Hawthorne's case, there was no relation whatsoever between the two. Poe remarks that before he undertook to write his reviews, he had inferred that Hawthorne owed his literary success to "one of the impudent *cliques*," a regional coterie of publishers and literati who promoted each other's work regardless of quality.[24] Poe's elaboration of the precise nature of Hawthorne's originality, then, is hedged about with anxiety over what it takes to succeed in the literary marketplace *without* the intervention of the coteries.

Poe's concern about the suitability of Hawthorne's characteristic, intimate mode of address to conditions of mass-production is evident from his opening gambit which appears at first to be nothing more than a strange sort of pedantry: "In the first place, they should not have been called 'Twice Told Tales'—for this is a title that will not bear *repetition*. If in the first collected edition they were twice-told, of course now they are thrice-told" (568). Poe calls attention to the discrepancy between the oral context invoked by Hawthorne's title, in which "telling twice" is potentially a ground of value,[25] and the printed form of the collected tales, the fact of their publication and republication, which, in Poe's eyes, threatens to undermine Hawthorne's claim to uniqueness. Why this is so becomes apparent as Poe struggles to define the tonal distinctiveness on which Hawthorne's claim to originality rests. Poe insists that Hawthorne's "essays"—what we would call his "sketches"—are significantly different both from the "Rosa-Matilda effusions" (568) that filled the gift books and magazines in which many of Hawthorne's early tales were first printed, and from the sketches of his nearest high-culture precursors: Washington Irving, Charles Lamb, Leigh Hunt, and William Hazlitt. As Poe explains,

A painter would at once notice [the] leading or predominant feature [of Hawthorne's sketches] and style it *repose*. There is no attempt at effect. All is quiet, thoughtful, subdued. Yet this repose may exist simultaneously with high originality of thought. . . . At every turn we meet with novel combinations, yet these combinations never surpass the limits of the quiet. We are soothed as we read; and withal is a calm astonishment that ideas so apparently obvious have never occurred or been presented to us before. (570)

Hawthorne's ability continually to produce novelty distinguishes his sketches from those of *The Spectator* and Washington Irving, in which, Poe claims, "repose is attained rather by the absence of novel combination, or of originality, than otherwise" (570). Repose, then, is a tricky stylistic marker in that it can signal both a high degree of originality and its lack, a notable authorial achievement or a kind of generic, unremarkable writing, what Poe refers to as "the calm, quiet, unostentatious expression of commonplace thoughts" (571).

It is, in fact, the all-too-easy collapse of this difference, the transformation of the admirable tone of repose into its unremarkable double, that concerns Poe in his final review of Hawthorne. The publication of *Mosses from an Old Manse* in 1846 gave Poe yet another opportunity to consider the effect of republication on the reception of Hawthorne's tales, an opportunity to reflect on the peculiar resistance they offer to mass-acceptance. In this review, Poe is tougher on Hawthorne, arguing that the novelty of combination that distinguished his writing has all but disappeared under the force of repetition. In part through the republication of his tales, Hawthorne has reached that point at which "novelty becomes nothing novel," a point-of-no-return in this system, since, as Poe remarks, "the artist, to preserve his originality, will subside into the common-place" (580). Hawthorne's ultimate failure, then, is a product of his success: his persistent reassertion of his powers of novel combination only serves "to deaden in the reader all capacity for their appreciation" (580).

Toward the end of this review Poe comes up with a figure for the kind of artistic failure he has been describing all along: the collapse of repose into monotony, the transformation of the "natural ease" that he has associated with Hawthorne's style into conspicuous artificiality. Describing what he considers to be the unfortunate, unchanging manner of the majority of American writing, Poe remarks, "The author who . . . is merely at *all* times *quiet*, is, of course, upon *most* occasions, merely silly or stupid, and has no more right to be thought 'easy' or 'natural' than has a cockney exquisite or the sleeping beauty in the waxworks" (582). Poe's first figure for this writing, the "cockney exquisite," aligns it with artificiality, foreignness, and an unconsciousness of its absurdity; the cockney only reinforces his provinciality by his attempts to transcend it. Poe's second attempt to represent the relentless dullness of generic American prose, the "sleeping beauty in the waxworks," more subtly performs the collapse of difference it seeks to represent. What initially registers as a distinction between the object of representation (the sleeping beauty) and its location (the waxworks), and, by way of a quick metonymic slide, its medium (wax), starts to look like repetition or refiguration. If at first we are disillusioned to find that the sleeping beauty is an artificial, man-made thing, we are doubly disillusioned to find a reflection of this disillusionment in the subject of the wax-statue itself. After all, should we be lulled by the excellence of the artist into suspending our disbelief, the sleeping beauty would still be unconscious. This is a figure for a difference that ultimately makes no difference at all, the meaningless slide of novelty into predictable readerly expectation, the collapse of a distinction between the suspension of activity that is characteristic of repose, and the lifelessness of sheer materiality.

Poe's exasperation with the inability of Hawthornian novelty to *stay* novel prompts him to speculate on the difference between "absolute" or "metaphysical" originality and what he terms "true originality"—an originality that could survive under conditions of mass-production. "Absolute novelty," Poe argues,

tasks and startles the intellect, and so brings into undue action the faculties to which, in the lighter literature, we least appeal. And thus understood, it cannot fail to prove unpopular with the masses, who, seeking in this literature amusement, are positively offended by instruction. But the true originality—true in respect of its purposes—is that which, in bringing out the half-formed, the reluctant, or the unexpressed fancies of mankind . . . thus combines with the pleasurable effect of *apparent* novelty, a real egoistic delight. (580)

According to Poe, fiction that aims at absolute originality runs the risk of introducing a sense of inadequacy and cultural hierarchy into the experience of reading. "True originality," on the other hand, is marked by the readerly delusion of a unique form of intimacy with the author, in effect, the mass-production of an unconsciousness of the conditions of mass production:

[In the case of absolute novelty] the reader . . . is excited, but embarrassed, disturbed, in some degree even pained at his own want of perception, at his own folly in not having himself hit upon the idea. In the [case of true originality], his pleasure is doubled. He feels and intensely enjoys the seeming novelty of the thought, enjoys it as really novel, as absolutely original with the writer—*and* himself. They two, he fancies, have, alone of all men, thought thus. They two have, together, created this thing. Henceforward there is a bond of sympathy between them, a sympathy which irradiates every subsequent page of the book. (581)

Poe scholars commonly read this passage as a precursor of his more fully developed account of his writing practice in "The Philosophy of Composition." And yet it is useful to ask what Poe's definition of "true originality" suggests about the writing against which it is measured and from which it borrows many of its concerns. Just as we have come to understand Poe's poetics of effect as a market-aesthetic—one that takes the problem of mass-reception as a point of departure for composition—so too do we need to attend to the "poetics of repose" as a series of aesthetic choices that, rather than being made negligible by their mass-market appeal, are important by virtue of a self-conscious relation to the market.

A full treatment of the antebellum "poetics of repose" would need to examine Hawthorne's work in relation to his numerous contemporaries who wrote "Tales and Sketches," including Theodore S. Fay, Lydia

Sigourney, Sara Josepha Hale, and Catharine Maria Sedgwick.[26] But Poe's critique of Hawthorne's tone and some of the common characteristics of Hawthorne's most popularly reprinted sketches provide substantial insight into the cultural value of repose. In thinking about the "poetics of repose," it helps to remember that Hawthorne's tone bothered Poe insofar as it attained a high level of originality, or distinctiveness without meeting any of his other criteria for excellent prose writing. As he noted, "There is no attempt at effect" (570). And yet Poe's admiration of and patience with Hawthornian repose dramatically lessens across the years. He concludes the series of reviews with the exhortation: "Let him mend his pen, get a bottle of visible ink, come out from the Old Manse, cut Mr. Alcott, hang (if possible) the editor of 'The Dial,' and throw out of the window to the pigs all his odd numbers of 'The North American Review'" (588). Despite its tendency, through repetition, to devolve into mere monotony, the tone of repose, which Poe also associates with "conservatives, hackneys, and cultivated old clergymen" (579), was clearly a cultural force that a poetics of effect would have to contend with. The outlines of some of Hawthorne's sketches begin to suggest why. True to the eschewal of effect, they are either eventless or are built around narratives that are pared to the bare minimum. "Sights from a Steeple" and "Foot-prints on the Sea-Shore" feature speakers who move quietly through the landscape, choosing a series of objects to subject to aesthetic attention. In "The Wives of the Dead," the action is limited to the staggered delivery of the news that the premise of the tale—the tragic deaths of the husbands of two sisters—is entirely mistaken. In a move that must have exasperated Poe, Hawthorne draws the sketch to a close before either sister tells the other what she exclusively knows. The narrative point of this story, which dramatizes the sisters' isolate, interior dramas of consciousness restored, is that nothing changes. So too for what can only be called the center-of-unconsciousness in "David Swan," a story of what might have happened had its protagonist not slept through the entire story. Like Poe's sleeping beauty in the waxworks, David Swan remains wholly closed off to the series of romance-possibilities, the fragments of aborted stories, that pass by him while he is sleeping. To take liberties with a phrase of W. H. Auden's, Hawthorne's sketches make nothing happen. And yet their marked simplicity and narrative restraint give us a clue to their cultural value. In one of the most overwrought sections of his review, Poe works hard to distinguish Hawthornian repose from the idleness that characterizes the light writing of *The Spectator* and Washington Irving, arguing that in these sketches "by strong effort, we are made to conceive the absence of all" (571). Addison's and Irving's is a tone of studied idleness that works to reinscribe the difference between labor and leisure. Poe suggests by contrast that Hawthorne's sketches function as a kind of metacommentary on this process: in Hawthorne "the absence of effort is too obvious to be mistaken" (571). The too-conspicuous effortlessness of Hawthorne's tales suggest that they no longer perform the aristocratic transaction by which the labor of reading works to confirm the idleness of authors. Poe suggests that by making his sketches accessible and commonplace, Hawthorne produces a tone of "ease" that is really easy—that the "cultural work" of these sketches is to perform no work at all.[27] Perhaps, then, these sketches are popular because they do the work of legitimating fiction by allowing, but not requiring, that it be either moral or useful.

Poe's fascination with the characteristic tone of Hawthorne's sketches recasts their very insignificance as the product of careful calculations about the cultural place of the literary in the 1830s and '40s. Indeed, when successful, Hawthornian repose seems to approach perilously close to Poe's definition of "true originality," establishing a "bond of sympathy" between author and reader while appearing maddeningly free of the dynamics of domination and control which will be a hallmark of Poe's elaboration of his poetic method in "The Raven" and "The Philosophy of Composition." If Hawthorne's sketches avoid, in their structure, tone, and scale, the problem of an aspiration toward "absolute novelty" that is implicitly self-destructive, they are, nevertheless, exceedingly fragile—subject to erasure under the force of repetition and unable to withstand sustained critical attention.

Hawthorne's "Preface" to the Ticknor and Fields edition of *Twice-Told Tales* bears witness to the seriousness with which he read Poe's characterization of his predominant tone and his implicit warnings about masking his literary ambition. Tucked away between an invitation to precisely the kind of biographical speculation that Hawthorne disclaims[28] and a dreary passage that proposes to compensate for readerly neglect through nostalgia, is a self-description of his early fiction in startlingly Poe-esque terms. This passage is suddenly legible as genuinely analytic once we've shaken off our melancholy conviction of Hawthorne's neglect. Indeed, given the terms of Poe's grudging praise, it can actually seem like boasting:

The sketches are not, it is hardly necessary to say, profound; but it is rather more remarkable that they so seldom, if ever, show any design on the writer's part to make them so. They have none of the abstruseness of idea, or obscurity of expression, which mark the written communications of a solitary mind with itself. They never need translation. It is in fact, the style of a man of society. Every sentence, so far as it embodies thought or sensibility, may be understood and felt by anybody, who will give himself the trouble to read it, and will take up the book in a proper mood. (1152)

The "proper mood," however, is precisely what the "Preface" discourages, tempting us with fantasies of obscurity, not clarity; seclusion, not society; and the spontaneous disappearance of the tales and sketches, instead of their ready accessibility.

Poe's critique enables us to understand Hawthornian repose as an anti-dramatic balance of narrative energies that brokers a powerful compromise with his middle-class readers, offering them fanciful speculation that is tempered with but not overwhelmed by didacticism. Repose suggests that fiction can provide a break with ordinary life that renders it enchanting, a defamiliarized but potentially edifying perspective on the everyday. Repose signifies Hawthorne's productive restraint on narrative development, his strategic use of unconsciousness to invoke plot lines that he nevertheless holds in check. While it exasperated Poe, who sought to produce dramatic responses in his readers, Hawthorne's sketches successfully exchange plot development and sensational effects for the suggestion of unfathomable and unspecified inward depths.

In writing *The House of the Seven Gables*, Hawthorne will return to the tone and narrative principle of repose but with a strong sense of its tendency toward monotony, a trajectory that he will signal by the use of the word "torpor" to describe a variety of narrative dead ends. If repose calms in part because it promises to be lifted, monotony marks the potential death of narrative. Numerous characters in *The House of the Seven Gables* and Hawthorne's novel itself will have to be shocked out of an inclination toward a lifeless state of torpor.

Monotony and Declension:
The Properties of Narrative in *The House of the Seven Gables*

Hawthorne's attempt to reauthorize his writing through the fiction of early obscurity and his newfound interest in claiming clarity and accessibility as hallmarks of his style mark his awareness that he had achieved a new kind of status in the literary world. Hawthorne's alliance with Ticknor and Fields gave him access to Fields's innovative marketing strategies; it also gave him a new way of thinking about his writing. It was Fields, after all, who suggested that Hawthorne transform the group of short stories he had provisionally called "Old-Time Legends: Together with Sketches, Experimental and Ideal" into the combination of politicized sketch and extended tale we know as *The Scarlet Letter*.[29] Hawthorne approached writing his first full-length novel under the pressure of a sudden change in prospects that held out the possibility of lasting success but also served as a reminder of the tenuousness of this opportunity. Six months after the publication of the novel he was uncertain as to whether he had achieved his aim. In a letter to Horatio Bridge, Hawthorne reports that initial sales of the book had exceeded those of *The Scarlet Letter*, leading him to believe that *The House of the Seven Gables* was "more sure of retaining the ground it acquires." And yet he also worries about the consequences of his success, speculating about what he would have to do in his next book to keep from "losing ground."[30] As Hawthorne's use of real estate metaphors suggests, the architecture of the eponymous "House of the Seven Gables" comes to carry the considerable weight of his literary ambitions. The house's signature "second story, projecting far over the base"[31] most obviously comes to stand for the novel's gothic concern with the overhang of the past onto the present. And yet it also serves as a figurative nexus for other anxieties about prolongation: both the formal problems Hawthorne faced in shifting from writing short fiction to longer narratives, and the opportunity this particular text afforded to extend the success he had achieved with *The Scarlet Letter*.

In taking up the question of how *The House of the Seven Gables* reflects changing conditions of literary production, I will not focus, as others have done, on Hawthorne's thematic preoccupation with a problematic property claim,[32] but on his struggle to take possession of the novel in formal terms. Training my gaze on the narrator's posture toward his evolving tale, I will argue that Hawthorne's conjectures about shifts in literary value emerge more clearly in his text's performance of a relation to its form than in his attempts to capture and control social forces at the thematic level. But I also turn to the question of form in *The House of the Seven Gables* because recent critical accounts of the conservatism of Hawthorne's treatment of property contrast sharply with the novel's astonishing and exasperating formal experimentation. Walter Benn Michaels has richly delineated the dead end of the novel's structuring opposition between the aristocratic Pyncheons's dubious hereditary title and the disenfranchised Maules's right to the land under natural law. Michaels persuasively argues that for Hawthorne, these are, finally, equally unsatisfactory alternatives. According to Michaels, Hawthorne's awareness of the vulnerability of both wealth and labor to market fluctuation causes him to idealize the Romance as a territory free from appropriation. Unlike the novel, which depends on "a very minute fidelity not merely to the possible but to the probable and ordinary course of man's experience," the Romance as Hawthorne defines it in his "Preface" claims "a certain latitude" (1) with regard to reference. Michaels reads this claim as resonant with a variety of antebellum fantasies of inalienable title, arguing that for Hawthorne, Romance becomes a refuge from the market at a time when industrialization and slavery assured that "the possession of one's own body could not be guaranteed against capitalist appropriation."[33]

Michaels's account of the novel's expression of a powerful desire for escape from the market seems in many ways indisputable. Critics have long puzzled over the novel's unsatisfying ending, in which characters who have eloquently critiqued the system of hereditary property speedily reverse their positions and accede to an inheritance. *The House of the Seven Gables* far too easily resolves the intractable property dispute it sets up between the two families; even the novel's main characters abandon the house in the final chapters. And yet identifying this novel as a space of retreat fails to account for the way in which Hawthorne grapples in its pages with the problem of the fluctuating value of literary genres. If in his "Preface" Hawthorne offers his romance as a remedy for social instability, in the body of the text he aggressively courts the kind of novelty that might secure its value. Despite the relentless backward pull of its thematics, Hawthorne works hard in this novel to imagine a mode of writing that would be commensurate with the demands of a changing literary marketplace, putting the narrative strategies he developed under the system of reprinting to new and troubled uses. I will argue that in *The House of the Seven Gables*, illegitimate and uncertain property claims stand in for modes of narration that seem equally problematic and untenable. Looking closely at the modulation of narrative voice in the novel, and the way in which the narrator turns back with a vengeance to address the work that he has done, I will describe how Hawthorne, like the Pyncheons of his story, constructs a new literary edifice by incorporating prior modes of writing.

Hawthorne associates property with narrative modes from the very beginning of the novel, invoking the House of the Seven Gables as the setting of and the justification for his story. The narrator's initial depiction of the house seems promising, even hopeful: "the aspect of the venerable mansion" appears to provide ample material for atmosphere and plot, "bearing the traces not merely of outward storm and sunshine, but expressive also of the long lapse of mortal life, and accompanying vicissitudes, that have passed within" (5). Although the house appears to be an ideal field for inscription and source of expression, the narrator immediately recasts these virtues as problematic, even paralyzing for his narrative. The House of the Seven Gables threatens the unfolding of narrative both in its autonomy and in its capaciousness, an expansiveness conveyed less by the size of the house than by its duration through history. Of the "vicissitudes" of the ordinary lives that have "passed within" the house, the narrator explains:

> Were these to be worthily recounted, they would form a narrative of no small interest and instruction, and possessing, moreover, a certain remarkable unity, which might also seem the result of artistic arrangement. But the story would include a chain of events, extending over the better part of two centuries, and, written out with reasonable amplitude, would fill a bigger folio volume, or a longer series of duodecimos, than could prudently be appropriated to the annals of all New England, during a similar period. (5–6)

"Worthily" telling a story about ordinary life raises problems both of scale and of narrative order. The "remarkable unity" of a mere "chain of events" can give a false impression of "artistic arrangement," and yet the "vicissitudes" of "mortal life" also desperately call for another kind of order. Understood as mere sequence, Hawthorne's narrative material threatens to take up more space than official histories. Stories of ordinary life endanger the art of literary narrative through their sheer repetitiveness, a cheapening that is figured as a potentially unending series of small duodecimo volumes. For Hawthorne, the ordinary possesses both an autonomy that potentially makes fiction irrelevant and a repetitiveness that makes it unwieldy. The only hope for narrative seems to lie with reconceiving it as a mode of abridgment. Faced with the specter of an endless series of duodecimos, the narrator proposes "to make short work" of the voluminous "traditionary lore" that has already gathered around "the old Pyncheon-house" (6).

The threatening autonomy of ordinary life (understood as a chain of events that does not seem to need an author) and its fundamentally repetitive nature (its tendency to accumulate in a way that defies order and arrangement) get translated into the novel's plot as the struggle between the Pyncheons's illegitimate hereditary claims and the Maules's perpetual grievances. The generational antagonism between these two families, which is thematized as a problem of rival claims to property, also carries the burden of Hawthorne's thinking about intertwining and mutually arresting problems of narrative form. Narrative order, understood as mere sequence, gets taken up into a thematics of decline, while the representation of ordinary life as simple mimesis gets figured as compulsive repetition.

These are intertwining problems in this narrative because each seems, at least momentarily, to offer a solution to the other. Take for example the problem of the Pyncheon inheritance. Although the Pyncheons's illegitimate claim to the house is founded on a crime—Colonel Pyncheon, the family patriarch, seizes the land after opportunistically accusing Old Matthew Maule of witchcraft—Hawthorne makes it clear that the durability of the Pyncheon claim depends on the social convention of heritable property, "a line marked out by custom so immemorial, that it looks like nature" (23). Mere sequence has given the Pyncheons an authority they ought not to possess; moreover, their social rank and possessions produce "so excellent a counterfeit of right, that few poor and humble men have moral force enough to question it" (25). If heritable property asserts a powerful, because invisible, authority, inheritance understood as mere sequence also brings with it a more threatening kind of invisibility, one located where property claims intersect with biological inheritance. Because the Pyncheons's illicit possession of the House coincides with their loss of a deed conveying property in "an unmeasured tract" (18) of land in Maine, their claims to aristocratic status are doubly ungrounded. The Pyncheons's consciousness of their "impalpable claim" (19) produces a steady declension in the line, a remitting of industry and an inclination towards poverty despite their aristocratic pretensions. This inevitable slide of distinction toward ordinariness—a movement that should remind us of Poe's critique of Hawthornian repose—is remedied only by the periodic reappearance in the Pyncheon line of a forceful man who manages to resecure the family's status and finances:

In almost every generation . . . there happened to be some one descendant of the family, gifted with a portion of the hard, keen sense, and practical energy, that had so remarkably distinguished the original founder. His character, indeed, might be traced all the way down, as distinctly as if the Colonel himself, a little diluted, had been gifted with a sort of intermittent immortality on earth. At two or three epochs, when the fortunes of the family were low, this representative of hereditary qualities had made his appearance, and caused the traditionary gossips of the town to whisper among themselves:—"Here is the old Pyncheon come again! Now the Seven Gables will be new-shingled!" (20)

At the moment in which the vividness of the Pyncheon inheritance and the social power it conveys is in danger of disappearing into the indifference and monotony of mere sequence, a Pyncheon comes along who refigures inheritance not as sequence but as repetition. Importantly, Hawthorne invokes repetition not as a rupture or break with sequence, but as a principle of continuity. Repetition answers the problem of inevitable decline—this is a family that is so attenuated that it needs a "representative of hereditary qualities"—but the interruption of repetition cannot offer anything like substantive change. The limited power of inheritance understood as repetition is signaled by the Colonel's "intermittent immortality" and by the way in which the Pyncheon family is discontinuously, punctually identified, not by the perpetuation of property or status through the line, but by the periodic exclamations of "traditionary gossips": "'Here is the old Pyncheon come again!'" In the Pyncheon inheritance, Hawthorne models narrative as an illegitimate but unending sequence, one that is made visible by a form of repetition that cannot arrest it. Threats to the sequence, such as the violent death of the patriarch, do not check its power; rather they get converted, through repetition, into the principle of its legibility.

Considered as a Pyncheon family problem, the ebbing of extraordinary into ordinary lives and the tendency of sequence toward monotony call for a mode of narrative rupture that Hawthorne cannot seem to imagine. Unfortunately, the rival claims of the Maules do not offer an effective solution. If the Pyncheon claim carries authority because law and custom have made it powerfully invisible, the disenfranchised Maules come to stand for a principle of continuity that lacks both power and visibility. In terms of the generational plot, they represent the loss of inheritance—both because of the Pyncheons's dubious land grab and because they lose track of their posterity. The Maules are "always plebeian and obscure, working with unsuccessful diligence" (25) at a variety of trades, condemned to repetition without accumulation.

In terms of the novel's property-thematics, the Maules embody the weakness of natural rights claims in an industrializing society,[34] but in terms of its worrying about principles of narrative order they are associated with mimesis understood as compulsive repetition. Reminding the reader of the disproportion between lengthy family histories and the smaller confines of literary narrative, Hawthorne's narrator invokes a looking glass in the Pyncheon household, which is "fabled to contain within its depths all the shapes that had ever been reflected there; the old Colonel himself and his many descendants." Both entertaining and dismissing the possibility of transforming his own narrative into an instrument for faithful, comprehensive reflection, the narrator avers "Had we the secret of that mirror, we would gladly sit down before it and transfer its revelations to our page" (20). But the Maule family possesses a way to make "short work" of this forbiddingly capacious narrative: "by what appears to have been a sort of mesmeric process they could make its inner region all alive with the departed Pyncheons; not as they had shown themselves to the world, not in their better and happier hours, but as doing over again some deed of sin, or in the crisis of life's bitterest sorrow" (21). The Maules's animation of figures in the mirror produces insights into character at the significant cost of range and variety. These images might appear as items in a series, but they quickly devolve into a mode of repetition that gets aligned with the monotone of unthinking vengeance. Faithful imitation can be dangerously repetitive, producing a radical reduction in the field of vision; it offers a kind of truth, but one that is unvaried and unrelieved. If the authority-in-sequence represented by the Pycheon inheritance creates an unsatisfiable desire for rupture, the problem of repetition as figured by the Maules calls out for a novelty that cannot be produced by the means of representation available to them.

I have sketched here what is already by the end of the first chapter of the novel a stifling convergence of sequence and repetition, declension and monotony. Indeed, there is only one moment in this chapter in which an alternative to these patterns seems at all possible. The illegitimate authority that is the Pyncheons's inheritance comes close to being toppled by the novel's first disappointing radical, an "eccentric and melancholy" (22) bachelor uncle who has inherited the estate. The old bachelor's exteriority to the chain of biological reproduction raises the fear that he will transfer the House of the Seven Gables to the Maules in restitution for the family crime. The disapproval of his relatives has "the effect of suspending his purpose" (23), raising the possibility that he might yet act after a space of delay. The laws of inheritance permit him to break the line of descent in his will, but when the bachelor dies under suspicious circumstances it is discovered that even he has succumbed to custom and kept the property in the family. Hawthorne's treatment of the bachelor uncle recalls his poetics of repose, grafting a figure for subdued or withheld agency onto a moment of narrative restraint, an attempt to imagine the terms under which his story might not need to be written. Hawthorne's careful delineation of this alternative, rejected plot suggests that he craves the kind of deviance and rupture with the past that the old bachelor represents without being able to put into action. Like the curse of the Maules—"God will give him blood to drink!" (8)—which is intended as a form of retribution but is converted into a sign of Pyncheon identity, a "gurgle in the throat" (21) that suggests a hereditary disposition toward apoplexy, Hawthorne suspects that even moral conscience can be overtaken by the convergence of monotony and decline. In the Pyncheon family, consciousness of the family crime does not allow for a rupture with the past but becomes a principle of continuity, renewing the unbreakable sequence of Pyncheon privilege. Hawthorne's recasting of inheritance as a moral problem suggests the diminution that goes along with thinking about great crimes in a minor, modern key: "we are left to dispose of the awful query, whether each inheritor of the property—conscious of wrong, and failing to rectify it—did not commit anew the great guilt of his ancestor, and incur all its original responsibilities" (20). Phrased as a rhetorical question, this "awful query" allows for a simple conclusion—that inherited fortune is "a great misfortune" (20), a perpetuation of family crimes—and for a more complex reading that aligns Hawthorne's own narrative with the Pyncheons's hereditary illegitimacy. Rather than constituting something he would like "to dispose of," moral turpitude is indispensable to Hawthorne. Being "conscious of wrong, and failing to rectify it" rejuvenates the narrative, keeping alive in the ordinary, modern world the "great guilt" of legendary ancestors that is in danger of slipping into obliquity.

I have linked the property-thematics of the novel with problems of narrative order because I am convinced that Hawthorne is a good deal more interested in the representation of ordinary life than his defensive identification of his text as a Romance in his "Preface" would suggest.[35] Hawthorne's letters to Fields while he was writing indicate that he understood the book to be a modern novel ("all but thirty or forty pages of it refers to the present time"[36]); that he was drawn to realistic modes of representation ("Many passages of this book ought to be finished with the minuteness of a Dutch picture"); and that he struggled with his bearing toward his materials, aiming for a variety of postures and tones ("I find the book requires more care and thought than the 'Scarlet Letter'; . . . The Scarlet Letter being all in one tone, I had only to get my pitch, and could then go on interminably").[37] The novel itself offers ample evidence of

Hawthorne's often unsuccessful attempts to define narrative subjects that are commensurate with his ambitions, and his struggle to devise rhetorical strategies that are adequate to the representation of modern life. The novel is full of derogatory references to its setting, beginning with Pyncheon street itself: the House of the Seven Gables is "surrounded by habitations of modern date" which are "mostly small, built entirely of wood, and typical of the most plodding uniformity of common life." While the narrator admits that "the whole story of human existence may be latent in each of" these modern houses, he insists that there is "no picturesqueness, externally, that can attract the imagination or sympathy to seek it there" (27). One frequently gets the sense that, like the dust that has gathered on the scales of the Pyncheons's antiquated shop, Hawthorne regards the modern world with calculating skepticism and detachment, "as if it were of value enough to be weighed" (35). Each of his major characters is visibly limited in ways that are unredeemed and unredeemable: the narrative centers on a few days in the life of an "ancient virgin" (243), a "half-torpid" (218) aesthete, a hopelessly corrupt judge, an ineffective reformer, and a virtuous young maiden who, though she is repeatedly invoked as a remedial force within the narrative, is also unable to perceive much of what goes on around her. Given this cast of characters it is perhaps not surprising that at crucial moments the narrator veers off into the subjunctive, using the third person to conjure a hypothetical figure who is more adequate to his musings than the characters at hand.

At a macro-level, the unfolding of the narrative of *The House of the Seven Gables* is beset by a paralysis that resonates with the novel's thematic focus on an intractable property dispute. Numerous characters undertake forward motion only to be stalled upon a threshold; the novel proliferates examples and figures of abortive flight. But small advances in the telling of the story are also frequently disrupted by narratorial intrusions, including introjections and exhortations, sudden shifts in diction and register, swerves to address individual characters, and complex disruptions of narrative sequence in which the narrator turns back with a vengeance to indict the work that he has done. I will examine some of these scenes in which the forward progress of the narrative is stalled in order to bring the problem of narrative order into relation with Hawthorne's concerns about the changing literary marketplace. Hawthorne's attempt to find a way to write about threateningly monotonous, modern life is shot through with anxiety about prior modes of writing. Lacking ready tools for the task of realist description, Hawthorne turns with great ambivalence to forms that had served him well in the culture of reprinting: the sketch and the gothic tale. Like Colonel Pyncheon, who compromises the value of his acquisition by digging the foundation of his house too deeply into a natural spring, Hawthorne's first full-length novel dramatizes a struggle between his ambition and his sources. Hawthorne's fraught relation to his narrative materials will, however, enable us to trace the lineaments of literary forms that thrived under the system of reprinting at a point of transition to a new way of organizing literary culture.

"Time-Stricken": Narrative Disruption and Self-Indictment

As Michael Gilmore and Gillian Brown have observed, Hawthorne locates his novel at the threshold of a belated transition to market culture by beginning the narrative action with the aristocratic Hepzibah Pyncheon's opening of a "cent-shop" (47) within the precincts of the venerable House of the Seven Gables. Noting the homology between Hepzibah's long seclusion from the world and Hawthorne's claim to early obscurity, critics have come to identify her reluctant encounter with the realities of commerce as an allegory of Hawthorne's predicament as a writer.[38] Although Hawthorne certainly courts this identification, reading the opening of the novel under the sign of this equivalence threatens to erase the surprisingly aggressive work of disidentification that Hawthorne also undertakes in representing Hepzibah's decision to sell "toys and petty commodities" (46) to her Salem neighbors. In reexamining these opening scenes, I will argue that they are marked by a complex crossing of narrative purposes. Hawthorne melodramatically stages the elderly Hepzibah's confrontation with modern society in order to shift his narrative focus from Puritan historical allegory to the territory of the modern novel, and to renegotiate a relation to his past. Hawthorne uses the shock of Hepzibah's initial exposure to commercial transactions to exorcize what he has come to regard as a problematic career of seeking to profit from the writing of minor fiction.

That Hawthorne identifies Hepzibah as an author-surrogate is clear from his description of her as a figure of withdrawal, "the recluse of half-a-lifetime, utterly unpractised in the world" (48). Hawthorne will multiply scenes and figures of withdrawal in this novel, most notably in connection with Hepzibah's wrongly imprisoned brother, Clifford. And yet Hepzibah most nearly approximates Hawthorne's fiction of early obscurity. Unlike Clifford, she has voluntarily withdrawn from "sordid contact with the world" (39). In his treatment of Hepzibah's ancestor, who scandalously cut "a shop-door through the side of his ancestral residence" (29), Hawthorne's narrator prefigures her reluctance to market her wares, maintaining a scrupulous distance from this event in family history even as he seems to speak in Hepzibah's voice. Pleading compulsion, the narrator unfolds the story of "the dead shopkeeper" as if to an equally aristocratic, squeamish reader: "The matter is disagreeably delicate to handle, but since the reader must needs be let into the secret, he will please to understand, that, about a century ago, the head of the Pyncheons found himself involved in serious financial difficulties" (28). Later on, when the narrator abandons the omniscience of the opening chapter, synchronizing the time of his narrative with Hepzibah's movements, he continues to acknowledge "an invincible reluctance to disclose what Miss Hepzibah Pyncheon was about to do" (34).

As these examples of belabored narratorial self-consciousness suggest, the narrator's attempt to distance himself from Hepzibah's going-to-market only identifies him more closely with her aristocratic perspective. In the second chapter, which invokes the "pitifully small" (29) scale of Pyncheon enterprise in its title "The Little Shop Window," the narrator repeatedly turns to elaborate third-person constructions in order to buffer his dangerously close identification with Hepzibah. After itemizing the contents of the shop from the perspective of what a hypothetical "curious eye . . . would have discovered" (35), the narrator unleashes a series of rhetorical questions that seem coyly designed to allow for a muted form of authorial self-reference:

In short, to bring the matter at once to a point, it was incontrovertibly evident that somebody had taken the shop and fixtures of the long retired and forgotten Mr. Pyncheon, and was about to renew the enterprise of that departed worthy, with a different set of customers. Who could this bold adventurer be? And of all places in the world, why had he chosen the House of the Seven Gables as the scene of his commercial speculations?

We return to the elderly maiden. (36)

The slippage in the gender of the pronoun does complex work in this passage. It intensifies the incredulity with which we will regard the old woman's attempt at commerce, magnifying the distance between entrepreneurship conceived of as a bold adventure and her pathetic attempts to sell toys and household staples. Hepzibah will prove to be a grammatically and culturally inappropriate subject for this particular fantasy. And

yet the narrator's projection of an alternative world in which a man boldly
speculates on the House of the Seven Gables allows Hawthorne both to
invoke his novel as a commercial venture and to insulate himself from failure by calling attention to the inappropriateness of this vision. Many of
the narrator's sudden bursts of sympathy for Hepzibah similarly solidify
the connection between her aims and Hawthorne's, while also articulat-
ing conditions to which she alone will be subjected. For instance, the narrator's attempt to justify Hepzibah's shyness drifts into a general defense
of the desire of "sensitive persons" to conceal the creative process from
public view: "she was well aware that she must ultimately come forward,
and stand revealed in her proper individuality; but, like other sensitive
persons, she could not bear to be observed in the gradual process, and
chose rather to flash forth on the world's astonished gaze, at once" (40).
If the narrator here endorses Hepzibah's desire to be preserved from oversight, the narrative itself will subject her to just the kind of excruciating
exposure it disavows. The painstakingly slow and inconsequential second
chapter details Hepzibah's every movement as she prepares to open her
shop, mocking her both for her reluctance to face the public and for her
desire to profit from this encounter.

Throughout this exposition, Hawthorne's narrator is careful to maintain a measure of distance from Hepzibah. With a formality that aims at
the comic, he initially places himself where he can overhear but not directly
observe her movements: "Far from us be the indecorum of assisting, even
in imagination, at a maiden lady's toilet!" (30). Insisting on the invisibility of his presence as narrator—"the old maid was alone in the old house"
(30)—he reduces his role to that of a "disembodied listener" (30), track-
ing her movements according to the sounds they make while preserving a
sense of narratorial privilege by insisting that these noises and movements
remain unwitnessed: "Inaudible . . . were poor Miss Hepzibah's gusty
sighs. Inaudible, the creaking joints of her stiffened knees as she knelt
down by the bedside" (30). Of course, in chronicling her movements in
meticulous detail, the narrative itself necessarily takes on the "spasmodic"
(31), jerky quality of her ambivalence. The time of narrative exposition in
this chapter is brought into equivalence with the time narrated through
the periodic use of deixis and indirect address: "Will she now issue forth
over the threshold of our story? Not yet, by many moments"; "Now, she
is almost ready" (31); "here comes Miss Hepzibah Pyncheon!" (32). Hawthorne plays out his own reluctance through Hepzibah's, studding his
narrative with interruptions while repeatedly insisting that the unfolding

of his story waits on her anxious preparations. And yet, Hawthorne's narrator aggressively withdraws his sympathies from Hepzibah the closer he comes to occupying her perspective. Describing her vain attempt to arrange her goods so as to appeal to prospective buyers, the narrator attributes Hepzibah's awkwardness to "the nervousness of the juncture" (47), but this phrase could easily apply to Hawthorne's own attempt to tell his story without getting tangled up by his identification with her predicament.

Take for example, the narrator's insistence on Hepzibah's irremediable ugliness. The opening of the novel reprises the familiar, misogynistic literary scene of a woman at her toilet[39] marked by a fussy formality of diction that intensifies the ludicrousness of her vanity: "Is all this precious time to be lavished on the matutinal repair and beautifying of an elderly person, who never goes abroad—whom nobody ever visits—and from whom, when she shall have done her utmost, it were the best charity to turn one's eyes another way!" (31). The narrator's elaborate, self-protective aversion and his attribution of the temporal delay of the narrative to her mistaken judgment is of a piece with his general reluctance to speak from her point of view. Not only does he launch into rhetorical questions instead of detailing her motivations, the narrator slips into the subjunctive when giving her a voice ("'How miserably cross I look!'—she must often have whispered to herself" [33]) and even spins out a fantasy of commerce as benevolence that he ultimately refuses to attribute to her consciousness: "It might have been fancied, indeed, that she expected to minister to the wants of the community, unseen, like a disembodied divinity, or enchantress, holding forth her bargains to the reverential and awestricken purchaser, in an invisible hand. But Hepzibah had no such dream" (40). Hepzibah provides an occasion for the articulation of a fantasy about the meliorative role of commerce and an instrument for repudiating it. Incapable of such a fantasy, she becomes responsible somehow both for foolish daydreaming and for the privations of demystification.

At the end of the chapter the narrator breaks the exposition of the plot one more time to address Hepzibah as a source of and figure for his narrative discontent:

Our miserable old Hepzibah! It is a heavy annoyance to a writer, who endeavors to represent nature, its various attitudes and circumstances, in a reasonably correct outline and true coloring, that so much of the mean and ludicrous should be hopelessly mixed up with the purest pathos which life anywhere supplies to him. What tragic dignity, for example, can be wrought into a scene like this! How can we elevate our history of retribution for the sin of long ago, when, as one of our most prominent figures we are compelled to introduce—not a young and lovely woman, nor even the stately remains of beauty, storm-shattered by affliction—but a gaunt, sallow, rusty-jointed maiden in a long-waisted silk-gown, and with the strange horror of a turban on her head! (41)

Like the dull modern houses on Pyncheon street, Hepzibah comes to represent the incommensurability of Hawthorne's ambitions and his narrative materials. What is surprising is not simply that he holds her accountable for the "mean and ludicrous" light in which he has portrayed her, but that he associates his own resistance to the demands of the realist mode with his aristocrat's reluctance to appear before the public. Conflating the compulsions of the market with the compulsions of mimesis, Hawthorne returns to Hepzibah's ridiculous appearance in order to recuperate the realist project, defining "poetic insight" as "the gift of discerning, in this sphere of strangely mingled elements, the beauty and the majesty which are compelled to assume a garb so sordid" (41). Both a drag-weight on his ambition to raise modern historical narrative to tragic heights and a figure for the transvaluation of the everyday that is the hallmark of realist fiction, Hepzibah carries a heavy load of expectation and abjection.

That Hepzibah's nervous entry into the modern world is freighted both with Hawthorne's anxiety about the demands of realist fiction and with his uneasy backward glance at his early career is clear from the dramatic moment of narrative suspension when, finally opening the exterior door to the shop, Hepzibah suddenly retreats to the "inner parlor" of the house and collapses, weeping, into the "ancestral elbow-chair" (40). We have encountered this chair before in this narrative: it is the same chair in which Colonel Pyncheon is discovered, dead, in the midst of writing. In the narrator's depiction of this scene from family legend, a large group of the Colonel's guests gathers at the door of his study, which was broken open when the Colonel failed to respond to the knocks of the impatient Lieutenant Governor. While the adults remain frozen in the doorway, the fact of the Colonel's death is left for a child to discover: "A little boy— the Colonel's grandchild, and the only human being that ever dared to be familiar with him—now made his way among the guests and ran towards the seated figure; then, pausing half-way, he began to shriek with terror" (15). Hawthorne's dramatization of the child's approach identifies this "oaken elbow-chair" (15)—without naming it as such—as grandfather's chair, the title and principle of narrative continuity of Hawthorne's first foray into children's book writing.

According to an extant fragment of a letter to Horace Connelly, "Grandfather's Chair" was the solution suggested by Hawthorne's spinster second cousin, Susan Ingersoll, to one of Hawthorne's early writing impasses. After thoroughly exploring Ingersoll's house in March 1840, familiarizing himself with the structure that would become the model for the House of the Seven Gables, Hawthorne apparently complained that he had "no subject to write about," to which Ingersoll responded: "Oh, there are subjects enough,—write about that old chair in the room; it is an old Puritan relict and you can make a biographical sketch of each old Puritan who became in succession the owner of the chair."[40] Whether or not this episode actually occurred, Hawthorne employed the device of an antique chair to organize the historical tales for children he published in three volumes as *Grandfather's Chair* (1841), *Famous Old People* (1841), and *Liberty Tree* (1841)[41]—the only sequence of Hawthorne tales set within an overarching narrative framework that were actually published according to his plan. In this sequence of tales, the chair is the locus of storytelling as well as the principle of historical and narrative continuity. Hawthorne relies on the intersection of the grand events of Puritan, provincial, and revolutionary-era history with "the substantial and homely reality of a fireside chair" (5) to galvanize and sustain the interest of the restless children who are "Grandfather's" fictive auditors. Grandfather's insistence that figures as diverse as Roger Williams, Anne Hutchinson, the persecuted Quaker Mary Dyer and Sir William Phips all sat in "this very chair" (27) enables Hawthorne to conjure the immediacy and enduring importance of the past, while also loosely connecting the stories he tells, maintaining "a distinct and unbroken thread of authentic history" (5). That many of the characters who people these histories are also central to tales aimed at adult readers suggests that Hawthorne's writing for children was thematically as well as temporally continuous with his writing of more ambitious fiction.[42] Although in his letters, Hawthorne frequently speaks of writing for children as "drudgery,"[43] he most often regards it as a reliable way to generate income. From 1838, when he excitedly proposed to Longfellow that they collaborate on a book of fairy tales that might "entirely revolutionize the whole system of juvenile literature,"[44] through 1851, when Fields solidified Hawthorne's celebrity by republishing the Grandfather's Chair series along with his *Biographical Stories for Children* (1842) as *True Stories from History and Biography* (1851), Hawthorne repeatedly tried to interest public figures with connections to local school boards, such as Horace Mann, John O'Sullivan, and Evert Duyckinck, in publishing his writing for children.

Although none of Hawthorne's books for children were financially successful until Fields solicited and marketed *A Wonder Book for Girls and
Boys* (1852) and *Tanglewood Tales* (1853), throughout the 1840s Hawthorne
regarded writing for children as a shorthand for writing for money. As he
noted in a letter to Longfellow, the demand for textbooks created by the
rise of the common schools meant that children's books stood "a very fair
chance of profit."[45]

If in Hawthorne's books for children, grandfather's chair represents
historical and narrative continuity, serving as a point of transfer between
of the great events of public history and more humble, domestic concerns,
in *The House of the Seven Gables* the old oaken chair is transformed into a
site of deathly stasis and narrative paralysis. With a violence that seems
directed at both author and audience, Hawthorne, who referred to himself
as "occupying Grandfather's chair"[46] while writing his children's histories,
introduces the chair into a scene of forcefully interrupted seclusion. The
chair is the site both of Colonel Pyncheon's bloody death while writing and
of the unprotected exposure of a child to the gruesome spectacle. If this
scene represents a violent return to the gentle didacticism of his minor fiction—the Colonel's fixed forward gaze, pen in hand, suggesting a gothically
re-imagined, blood-drenched frontispiece portrait—Hepzibah's collapse
into the same chair at the end of the second chapter brings this disrupted
scene of writing forward into a differently violent, mock-gothic present.

One of the reasons that Hepzibah cannot move forward into the modern world, then, is that Hawthorne uses her as an instrument for turning
back to castigate the compromises he has made in a long career of writing
for profit. Her exaggerated innocence of commercial relations enables her
to represent what Gillian Brown describes as the "bodily risks" of subjection to "the publicity of economic processes";[47] it also enables her to
operate as scapegoat and surrogate for Hawthorne. The narrator's carefully maintained distance from Hepzibah transforms her encounter with
market culture into a complexly self-protective form of self-indictment.
Hepzibah sells both toys and household staples, "commodities of low
price" which are "constantly in demand" (35), but the novel's most insistently dramatized scenes of consumption involve the problem of meeting
the impossible demands of children. Hebzibah's first customer and most
frequent visitor is a generic child, a "little devourer" (67) whose frequency
of appearance eventually prompts Hawthorne to give him a name and the
status of a minor, comic character (81).

David Anthony has argued that the gingerbread "Jim Crow" figures this child ingests connect Hawthorne's anxieties about going-to-market with the encroachments of popular culture. According to Anthony, the insatiability of the child and Hepzibah's attempt to satisfy him by selling him one Jim Crow cookie after another forges a link between iterability, minstrel performance, and Hawthorne's troubled conflation of class mobility and racial difference.[48] Anthony traces this logic through Hawthorne's later depiction of an itinerant organ-grinder, an episode that turns on the racialized depiction of the exchange of money for a mechanical form of entertainment. Well-attuned to the novel's gravitation toward scenes of selling to children, Anthony nevertheless represents Hawthorne as an outsider to popular culture, as anxious as Hepzibah is about the threat to aristocratic status signified by "the sordid stain" (51) of the child's copper coin. And yet the other cookies Hepzibah sells point to Hawthorne's own participation in popular culture, his history of trying to satisfy the consumer desires of children. The locomotive, the elephant, and the dromedary to which Hepzibah turns to quell the child's "omnivorous appetite" (67) are all icons of world history that appear in the frontispiece and title-page engravings of the *Universal History* (1837), a geographical survey of world civilization that Hawthorne and his sister ghost-wrote for Samuel Goodrich's Peter Parley series.[49]

Like the third-person references to a speculative "bold adventurer" and to "sensitive persons" who withdraw from public view, these allusions to Hawthorne's own career remind us that he maintains a conflicting set of investments in the story of Hepzibah's debasement by commerce. While Hepzibah's prospective fear of a long-delayed contact with the public serves as a caricature of Hawthorne's account of his early obscurity, it also serves his retrospective need to cast off his own extended period of dependency. Hawthorne demonstrates in these scenes not only an anxiety about degradation, but also a need to degrade. Indeed, the narrator magnifies Hebzibah's humiliation by calling attention to his inability to treat her more sympathetically. Describing her failed endeavor to "tempt little boys into her premises" by rearranging her stock of toys, the narrator transforms an intimate moment of direct address into a justification for maintaining a punitive narrative distance from his subject: "Heaven help our poor old Hepzibah, and forgive us for taking a ludicrous view of her position! As her rigid and rusty frame goes down upon its hands and knees, in quest of the absconding marbles, we positively feel so much the more inclined to shed tears of sympathy, from the very fact that we must needs turn aside and laugh at her" (37). Must we? Sympathy here can proceed only through ridicule as the compulsion to take pleasure in her ineptitude and the need to excuse himself for so doing overtakes the narrator's intercession on her behalf. Such oscillations between contrition and contempt suggest that Hawthorne is not wholly in control of his attempt to siphon off anxieties about his narrative situation onto the figure of Hepzibah. Hepzibah will become a mobile signifier of genre trouble in the novel, the question of the sound of her voice reappearing at moments in which Hawthorne struggles to establish an appropriate tone, while her personification of a rupture in narrative time will return to postpone the arrival of the novel's central crisis.[50] Her involuntary scowl comes to represent Hawthorne's reluctant self-positioning within the novel's binary system of polar moods—somewhere between the mandatory smile of domestic fiction, which is associated with her country cousin Phoebe, and the aggressive, property-hungry scowl incarnated by the Pyncheon portrait. For all the work she does for Hawthorne in helping him to define a relation to his narrative, Hepzibah is asked to absorb a heavy dose of self-recrimination: "drawing on a pair of silk gloves, to [reckon] over the sordid accumulation of copper coin" (81), she is ridiculed for her ineptitude and her success, for her subjection to market forces and her presumption that her station lies above them, for her pleasure in and her disdain for profit.

Hawthorne's compulsive humiliation of Hepzibah, his depiction of her desperate responsiveness to the sound of the shop bell, and his reduction of the child to a figure for voracious consumption are all the more surprising when measured against the confidence and composure of his earlier strategies for accommodating minor writing. The opening chapters of the novel suggest that diminution is newly a problem for Hawthorne, that the relationship between the details of ordinary life and their larger significance has been unsettled by his attempt to write a longer, more important narrative. As recently as the "Custom House" introduction to *The Scarlet Letter*, Hawthorne had introduced the child's toy as a limit or test case for the power of romance, represented by "moonlight in familiar room," to transform "domestic scenery" into "things of intellect": "Nothing is too small or trifling to undergo this change, and acquire dignity thereby. A child's shoe; the doll, seated in her little wicker carriage; the hobby-horse;—whatever, in a word, has been used or played with, during the day, is now invested with a quality of strangeness and remoteness, though still almost as vividly present as by daylight."[51] In this famous description of the "neutral territory" of romance, the child's toy not only illustrates the power of romance to invest "small and trifling" objects with significance, it also justifies the work of the imagination through its blurring of the categories of use and play. In *The House of the Seven Gables*, however, the enchanting defamiliarization of romance is replaced by a different kind of estrangement, an incomprehension of the world of childhood that is figured by Hepzibah and registered by the equally estranged narrator: "It seemed a queer anomaly, that so gaunt and dismal a personage should take a toy in hand;—a miracle, that the toy did not vanish in her grasp" (37).

In representing Hepzibah's concern with the desires of children as reluctantly and ineptly taken up, Hawthorne surrenders what had been a useful narrative device as well as a tool for accommodating writing for profit. As Karen Sánchez-Eppler observes, Hawthorne's narrators frequently enter the public sphere with a child in hand.[52] For example, in the sketch "Little Annie's Ramble," which Hawthorne published in a children's gift book, *The Youth's Keepsake* (1835), the child serves as an enormously productive vehicle for the enchantment of the ordinary, enabling the narrator to present mundane village sights to the reader as he encounters them with Little Annie, with all the novelty of first sight. In this present-tense narrative, which is loosely held together by the seriality of their "ramble," the sober, moralizing narrator provides a constant foil to the giddy enthusiasms of the girl, whose curiosity provides the occasion for a day of wandering and window-shopping. As Elizabeth Freeman has argued, Hawthorne subtly shifts responsibility for the progress and direction of the narrative onto the child; it is Little Annie who leads the narrator to "commercialized pleasures and legitimates his interest in them" (880). And yet he also uses the child as an excuse to launch inferences about the modern world that are full of adult significance but presumably unintelligible to Little Annie and his child-readers. Childhood innocence provides the spur and the limit to narrative in this story, allowing Hawthorne both to indulge in a variety of transgressive fantasies and to temper them with restraint, to bring the pleasures of voyeurism and speculation into equilibrium with culturally acceptable, didactic purposes.[53]

In turning against the complex compromises of sketches such as "Little Annie's Ramble," Hawthorne will struggle to come up with a substitute for the figure of the innocent child. Little Annie provides Hawthorne with an entry into modern consumer culture and an alibi for taking pleasure in it; she offers both a covering fiction for his circulation through the town and a playful means of imagining his text's exemption from circulation. In their visit to a bookstore, the narrator imagines Little Annie incorporated into the gift book that contains this sketch, "her sweet little self bound up in silk or morocco with gilt edges" to be given as a holiday present and to remain in the family until she "become[s] a woman grown, with children of her own to read about their mother's childhood" (230). If early in his career Hawthorne could take pleasure in imagining this modest form of posterity, subsuming the uncertainties of the book trade within the restricted economies of gift-giving and familial inheritance,[54] in *The House of the Seven Gables* his "time-stricken virgin" (34) is mercilessly subject to market forces and hopelessly cut off from both her posterity and her ancestry (51). Replacing the chaste pleasures of Little Annie's "imaginary feast" (230) with the insatiable desires of a "little cannibal" (58), and the endlessly moralizing narrator of his sketch with a hopelessly reluctant narratorial proxy, Hawthorne oversteps the boundaries of his customary restraint, tipping the balance of narrative energies from "repose" to "torpor," the inclination of the Pyncheons and the narrative itself toward a deadly form of suspended animation. Viewed through his narrator's vexed identification and disidentification with Hepzibah's limited vision, the modern world appears pitifully small, degraded by commerce, and badly in need of a dignity that fiction seems powerless to confer.

Hawthorne will work hard to extricate his narrative from the impasse into which he has driven it with his treatment of Hepzibah, introducing characters such as Phoebe and Clifford through which he can reapproach and revalue the modern world. But, as with Hawthorne's "time-stricken" attempt to redefine his relation to the literary marketplace, turning forward to the territory of the modern novel will require turning back to reanimate the literary forms he is attempting to supersede. Hawthorne will reevaluate the cultural place of fiction as he redeploys shorter forms such as the sketch and the gothic tale, forms that proved popular in the magazine-centered culture of reprinting. And yet Hawthorne's persistent yoking of moments of formal self-consciousness to scenes of humiliation suggests that *The House of the Seven Gables* is very much a liminal text, a narrative stuck on the threshold of a transition to a new set of expectations that Hawthorne cannot seem to master.

"Sordid Contact": Addressing Ordinary Life and the Disenchantments of Address

Hawthorne frequently shifts tone and genre as his novel unfolds, introducing characters who enable him to move beyond the sense of exhaustion and stasis that overtakes the opening chapters. Hawthorne's acute self-consciousness about questions of genre and his uncertain commitment to the choices he makes—what Richard Gray has described as the "shifting and equivocal idiom" of the novel as a whole [55]—gives the impression that he is jockeying for position among narrative options, none of which seems fully adequate to the task at hand. All of the characters who take up residence in the House of the Seven Gables conspicuously carry with them the trappings of genre. As Joel Pfister and others have noted, Phoebe rather abruptly steps into the novel from the pages of popular domestic fiction, turning around the fortunes of Hepzibah's shop and dissipating the gothic gloom of the house, "as nice a little saleswoman as [she is] a housewife" (78).[56] Returning to the house after his release from prison, Hepzibah's brother Clifford takes up a post of observation on the street below that recalls the distanced vantage point of a number of Hawthorne's sketches, while the reformer Holgrave, who has published tales in ladies' magazines, interrupts the narrative to read a story that he intends to send to "Godey or Graham" (212). This ensemble cast enables Hawthorne to experiment with writing in a variety of narrative modes while also exploring their limits. Critics have understood the scattered energies of the novel—its tendency to break into set-pieces and its failure to coalesce around a single character or issue—as Hawthorne's Dickensian attempt to satisfy a range of readerly desires, a sign of his awareness of the potential breadth of his readership.[57] As the novel shifts between and among characters and modes of storytelling, however, the work of narrative exposition is frequently interrupted by both subtle and strident reflections on these narrative experiments. The narrator's passionate apostrophes to individual characters lend an urgency to Hawthorne's experiments with narrative form. If the novel's variability of tone and genre suggests cautiousness or indecision on Hawthorne's part—an attempt to deploy without fully inhabiting a variety of narrative modes—the ruptures of apostrophe indicate his struggle to clear the ground for another kind of writing.

Phoebe's arrival at the House of the Seven Gables breaks the spell cast by Hawthorne's vexed identification with Hepzibah, reversing the aristocrat's fall into market culture through the "magnetism" of her "innate fitness" (76) for domestic and commercial labor. Transforming work into play and spiritualizing commerce, Phoebe's skillful housekeeping and shopkeeping rescue Hepzibah from her predicament, shifting the narrative focus from the old lady's incompetence to the young girl's redemptive domesticity. As Gillian Brown has argued, introducing Phoebe at this critical juncture puts the novel in conversation with mid-century fiction and advice books which similarly "image the rise of domesticity and commercial culture as a return to aristocracy" (78). It also permits Hawthorne a bravura turn, demonstrating his ability to write in the domestic idiom, the success of which can be gauged by critics' approval of his treatment of Phoebe, and by the unauthorized reprinting of a passage on "The Breakfast-Table" in a Boston family almanac.[58]

And yet Hawthorne is careful to distance himself from the conventions of domestic fiction and to qualify his approbation of Phoebe. Phoebe's exteriority to the logic of the narrative is crucial to her ability to break the impasse of the opening chapters. Phoebe is market-savvy without manifesting the desire or the need for acquisition; she is exempt from the Pyncheons's ambition and hereditary uselessness, deriving her domestic competence entirely from her mother's side. Like Hebzibah, who recognizes with pride and relief that "Phoebe is no Pyncheon" (79), the narrator's admiration of her skill at "practical arrangement" (71) betrays a sense of superiority that is rooted in the assumption of fundamental differences. Indeed, read outside of domestic fiction's characteristic affirmation of spontaneous affection, the terms of Hawthorne's praise of Phoebe sound awfully condescending. Phoebe represents aesthetic sensibility without "preliminary design" (72) or "conscious effort" (76). While her sense of "propriety" (69) grants her an enviable autonomy, her benevolence is the product of her adherence to convention: she is "obedient to common rules" (68), thinks the "thought [that is] proper for the moment" (137), and sympathizes with others—"to such depth as she could"—with "facile adaptation" (137). Phoebe may personify a middle-class domestic ideal that is vastly superior to Hepzibah's obsolete gentility, but she also exhibits a crucial lack of understanding, suggesting that Hawthorne finds the domestic idiom inadequate to the task of representation he has set for himself. For instance, the "inscrutable charm" of her innocence, which transforms the interior of the house, erases sexuality along with the gothic overhang of the past onto the present. As the narrator explains, the room in which she sleeps "was a chamber of great and varied experience, as a scene of human life; the joy of bridal nights had throbbed itself away here. But . . . it was now a maiden's bed-chamber, and had been purified of all former evil and sorrow by her sweet breath and happy thoughts" (72). That this purification might be understood as a troubling form of repossession is signaled by the persistence of the gothic metaphor: Phoebe's cheerful dreams "had exorcised the gloom, and now haunted the chamber in its stead" (72).

It quickly becomes clear that Phoebe's limited perception is an imped-
iment to the unfolding of the narrative. Expanding on the "fruitful subject"
of Judge Pyncheon's resemblance to his sexually "remorseless" ancestor, the
narrator is forced to conclude that "[s]carcely any of the items in the above-
drawn parallel occurred to Phoebe" (123). Discussing the effect of Phoebe's
beauty on Clifford, the narrator demonstrates the power of her artlessness
to call a halt to speculation: "Phoebe, it is probable, had but a very imperfect comprehension of the character, over which she had thrown so benef-
icent a spell. Nor was it necessary" (140). Phoebe becomes an instrument
of and figure for a reduction in the field of vision, defining the domestic
idiom as the exercise of power without understanding.

Hawthorne successfully recasts the genre of *The House of the Seven
Gables*, shifting from a mock-gothic treatment of Hepzibah's cent-shop to
a sentimental account of Phoebe's transformation of the domestic interior,
but his main characters intensify rather than resolve his narrative predicament, leaving him with a pair of opposed and unsatisfying figures for the
work of fiction: Hepzibah's impotent complicity with market forces and
Phoebe's innocent efficacy. Hawthorne desperately needs a character who
can take in more of modern Salem than Phoebe can, one who will not be
hamstrung by obedience to the "common rules" of the canons of domestic
fiction. But he also needs a figure who, like Phoebe, can restore a measure
of enchantment to a world that has been devalued by the ugliness, insignificance, and compulsion that surround the figure of Hepzibah. Clifford
and Holgrave each provide Hawthorne with a way to redefine the territory of fiction and to re-imagine authorial agency. But both characters also
draw Hawthorne back to the narrative forms of his early career in highly
charged scenes of humiliation. Rather than dispelling the shadow cast by
Hepzibah's embodiment of narrative paralysis, Clifford and Holgrave provoke Hawthorne to re-imagine authorship as a different kind of suspended
animation.

Clifford's release from his long imprisonment offers Hawthorne yet
another opportunity to recommence his novel by introducing a figure from
outside its narrow precincts. Clifford's return to the house is foreshad-
owed early on by Hebzibah's gazing at a "miniature" portrait (32) and his
approach to the parlor is announced to Phoebe in reverential, messianic
tones: "Hush! Hush! He is coming!" (102). The complexity of Clifford's
narrative position as a belatedly arriving founding figure, the "master" of
the house (75) who nonetheless remains an outsider, is indicated by the
novel's elaborate ways of naming him. Hepzibah and Phoebe both refer

to Clifford as "the original of the miniature" (32, 105), suggesting both a longed-for authenticity and the promise of an expansion in scale and importance, while the narrator preserves an atmosphere of suspense by giving Clifford a distanced, generic title, "The Guest" (98). Clifford's actual crossing into the space of the House of the Seven Gables is shrouded in mystery; significantly, the first threshold he traverses is an internal one (103).

As critics have noted, the character of Clifford is loaded with references to Hawthorne, from the faded "damask dressing gown" (105) that recalls Hawthorne's own elaborate "writing-gown"[59] to the initials Clifford has carved in the doorway of the house (252), a kind of interpolated signature. More important to the progress of the novel, however, is the fact that Clifford absorbs and embodies many of the attitudes we have come to associate with the narrator, giving the scenes in which he plays a part a heightened sense of reflexivity. Clifford maintains both an "invincible distaste" (135) for Hepzibah's appearance and an aesthetic appreciation of Phoebe's domesticity, allowing Hawthorne retrospectively to stabilize and justify his narrative choices. Clifford's flickering consciousness, the product of sensory deprivation during his imprisonment, gives Hawthorne a gentler alibi for narrative rupture than Hepzibah's tortured reluctance to face the public. Describing the multiple pauses that slow Clifford's entrance into the parlor, the narrator explains that although "the delay seemed to be without purpose," it stemmed "rather from a forgetfulness of the purpose which had set him in motion" (103). Characteristically, the narrator excuses rather than exacerbates Clifford's lack of agency. An offhand justification of Clifford's aversion to his sister succinctly captures the larger shift in narrative strategy from blame to exemption: "It was Hepzibah's misfortune; not Clifford's fault" (109). Clifford's forced, unjust rupture with society frees him from knowledge of and responsibility for changes that have transpired during the period of his imprisonment, allowing Hawthorne to return with a clean slate to the task of representing the modern world. A device for regrounding the narrative, Clifford will spend much of his time trying to bring the world of the novel into focus, "seeking to make himself more fully sensible of the scene around him" (109).

The exemptions from social norms that the novel claims for Clifford on account of his forced seclusion are both idealized and pathologized, serving as the occasion for passionate pleas for the privileges of art,[60] and a more subtle chafing against social constraints on narrative. Clifford's feebleness liberates him from responsibility to his family and to society; he can neither work nor "contract debts" (109) of the sentimental or material kind. His faulty memory frees him from accountability to the past and from an orientation toward the future that would compel productivity: "He had no burthen of care upon him; there were none of those questions and contingencies with the future to be settled, which wear away all other lives, and render them not worth having by the very process of providing for their support" (170). His long imprisonment also preserves him from sexual desire. Clifford is invoked early on as an exception to the aggressive masculinity of the Pyncheons, but his incarceration for thirty years ensures that his effeminacy is safely translated into a generalized aesthetic sensibility. Like his sister, Clifford is an "ancient virgin" (243): although "naturally endowed with the liveliest sensibility to feminine influence," he "never had quaffed the cup of passionate love" (141). Gifted with sensibility but denied sexual experience and power, Clifford becomes the repository of a safely intellectualized eroticism. Sexual desire for Clifford is "rather a perception, or a sympathy, than a sentiment belonging to himself as an individual" (142).[61]

Clifford's lack of orientation toward the future, his nonreproductive, intellectualized relation to sexual pleasure, and his forgetfulness of purpose make him a figure for the possibility of nondidactic art, a medium for an idealized mode of aesthetic perception cut free from the coercive norms of domestic fiction. That Hawthorne has difficulty imagining the conditions of possibility for such an art is suggested by the extravagance of the conceit that governs Clifford's character, the intermittency with which his liabilities are conjured as strengths, and by his physical, aesthetic, and emotional dependence on Phoebe. It is, after all, only when Clifford is illuminated by light reflected from Phoebe's youth and beauty that he is capable of idealization by the narrator's transfiguring glances (104, 139, 146). Nevertheless, Clifford is permitted a strained but silent dissent from the novel's domestic plotting. For instance, the narrator insists that, despite his "fits of miniature enthusiasm" (148), Clifford does not fully share in the domestic pleasures of the Pyncheon garden: he "lay darkly behind his pleasure, and knew it to be a baby-play, which he was to toy and trifle with, instead of thoroughly believing" (149). In this scene, Clifford carries what we might think of as the narrative's unconscious, an awareness of a broader, darker world that Hawthorne allows to be registered by but not to disrupt his domestic pastoral. Indeed, the chapter set in the Pyncheon garden concludes with a passionate apostrophe in which the narrator harangues Clifford, reminding him of his feebleness ("You are old . . . You are partly crazy, and partly imbecile; a ruin, a failure") and urging him to

accept this simulacrum of happiness for "the thing itself" (158). Despite
the urgency of the narrator's intervention, however, Clifford hardly seems
capable of threatening the domestic order, embodying only barely articulated resistance and unrealized rebellion. As a proxy for the narrating consciousness, Clifford's habitual forgetfulness offers only a minimal advance
on Phoebe's ignorance, an incrementally richer mode of unawareness that
hardly seems worth the elaborate preparations for his arrival.

What is at stake for Hawthorne in introducing an aesthete who is
afflicted with discontinuous cognition finally becomes clear when he har-
nesses Clifford to the task of realist description. Clifford's acute loss of
memory and consequent attunement to the present not only frees him
from the demands of didacticism, it also solves the narrative problem of
"the monotony of every-day occurrences" (160). Seated at a second-story
window, looking out at the street below from behind "the comparative
obscurity" (159) of a curtain, Clifford provides Hawthorne with a vehicle
for the reenchantment of the ordinary, safe from the dullness of repetition
and the degradation of contact. Clifford's long seclusion makes the world
outside "the arched window" delightfully unfamiliar, but more importantly, the loss of the "proper gripe and retentiveness" (160) of his mind
keeps these village sights perpetually new. As if in response to Poe's critique of his characteristic tone of repose, Hawthorne invokes Clifford's
forgetfulness as an instrument for keeping novelties novel despite the
monotony of modern life. Clifford is drawn to sights that repeat themselves, allegorizing an omnibus as "that vast rolling vehicle, the world"
(160), then promptly forgetting its appearance and importance. Routine
itself becomes an aesthetic object for Clifford, typified by the regular reappearance of the water cart, with which he "could never grow familiar;
it always affected him with just the same surprise as at first" (160).

Hawthorne characterizes Clifford's perpetually renewed but unchanging mode of aesthetic attention as "suspended animation" (161), associating
it with a pitiable powerlessness, an inability to keep up with "the swiftness
of the passing moment" (161). This is paradoxical, because Clifford does
nothing *but* attend to the passing moment; what he cannot do is master
it. Clifford's forgetfulness transforms him into a machine for metaphor-
making, but one that is disturbingly inconsequential. His uncommon ability to invest the ordinary with significance, and his tendency to lapse into
repetitiveness despite himself powerfully recalls the strengths and weak-
nesses of Hawthorne's sketches. It is not surprising, then, to find Hawthorne using Clifford's monitoring of the street below to import a wealth

of material from his early magazine writing, reanimating the sketch form from within the more expansive framework of his novel. In a series of self-contained vignettes, Hawthorne uses Clifford's enchantment with ordinary life to expand on his description of an organ-grinder from "Little Annie's Ramble," to recast the multiple parades of "Sights from a Steeple" as a political procession, and to reprise the descriptions of going-to-church that are the focus of "Sunday at Home."

Incorporating material from these sketches within his novel enables Hawthorne to stretch the limits of the sketch form, expanding its purview and tonal register, questioning the mandatory uplift at the close, and testing the idealizing distance between observer and observed that the sketches scrupulously maintain. For instance, after pressing the mechanical figures of the barrel-organ into service as an allegory of the uselessness of love and labor, the narrator somewhat flippantly puts his conceit under erasure: "rather than swallow this last too acrid an ingredient, we reject the whole moral of the show" (163). Pushing past the "humble" (162) appeal of the self-contained world of the barrel-organ—an all-too-easy machine for metaphor-making—the narrator permits us to glance at the sociopolitical underpinnings of his allegory, depicting a grotesquely sexualized, racialized scene of commercial exchange. Although Clifford remains at a remove from the scene below, someone has to pay for this entertainment; when Phoebe throws down a handful of pennies, the organ-grinder's monkey, onto which an "excessive desire" for "filthy lucre" has been displaced, scoops up payment in his "black palm" "with joyless eagerness" (164). The narrative gains a considerable charge by forcing Clifford and the reader to attend to the vulgarity that it projects onto the organ-grinder and his monkey. Expanding the range of vision of the sketch, and investing its narrator's slight, prurient distance from middle-class culture with more dangerous sensations, Hawthorne indulges in a gothic amplification of traditional sketch material.

Novelizing his sketches enables Hawthorne to re-imagine sketch writing as a self-indulgent play of projection and revulsion, but he stops short of abandoning the constraints of the form. While Hawthorne pushes these interpolated sketches toward a demystification of their processes, he does so at a safe remove from the narrating consciousness; if he is able to jettison the edifying moral in novelizing his sketches, he is unwilling or unable to cede the protected position of the observer. Indeed, Clifford's thwarted attempts to merge with the crowd and join the worshipers at church only reinforce his sense of isolation: "We are ghosts!" he exclaims to Hepzibah,

"We have no right among human beings" (169). Clifford personifies the sketch-writer's privilege, concretizing the desire for narrative transparency that Hawthorne articulated in "Sights from a Steeple."[62] In this early sketch, the narrator acknowledges an unrealizable wish to "[hover] invisible round man and woman, witnessing their deeds, searching into their hearts, borrowing brightness from their felicity, and shade from their sorrow and retaining no emotion peculiar to himself" (43). The erasure of Clifford's life experience and his loss of the power of mental retention justify this desire to observe without being subject to observation, rendering it innocent of voyeurism and parasitism.

But Clifford's discontinuous perception also marks the limits of this form. Hawthorne characterizes his narrative problem in developmental terms when he redefines Clifford's mental state as a reversion to his adolescence rather than an interruption of his adulthood: "Just as, after the torpor of a heavy blow, the sufferer's reviving consciousness goes back to a moment considerably behind the accident that stupefied him," so Clifford's trauma has left him "standing still at a period little in advance of childhood" (170). What Hawthorne defends against in his depiction of Clifford is the demand for maturation, a process that has been embarked upon but hopelessly thwarted. Representing Clifford's mode of perception as a problem of arrested development justifies the seriality of the sketch form, its inability to move beyond mere sequence into narrative progression. It also enables Hawthorne to rationalize the limitations of his own response to the market's unbearable demand for generic transformation.[63]

At the end of the chapter, Hawthorne finally performs rhetorically what he cannot seem to narrativize, turning on the character he has done so much to protect. In probing the limits of the sketch form, Hawthorne comes close to giving Clifford a measure of visibility. For instance, while watching a political parade, Clifford hovers on the brink of leaping from the window, a possibility Hawthorne invokes not only as a suicidal wish to merge with the masses, but also as a reversal of the positions of observer and observed: "As it was, the whole procession might have seen him, a wild, haggard, figure, his gray locks floating in the wind that waved their banners; a lonely being, estranged from his race, but now feeling himself man again, by virtue of the irrepressible instinct that possessed him" (166). While Hepzibah and Phoebe restrain him from jumping and attaining a manly, if deathly, visibility, the threat of exposure ultimately keeps Clifford and Hepzibah from leaving the House of the Seven Gables: "They pulled open the front-door, and stept across the threshold, and felt, both of them, as if they were standing in the presence of the whole world, and with mankind's great and terrible eye on them alone" (169).

Given these dramatic scenes of forced withdrawal from the public gaze, it is striking that Hawthorne interrupts his concluding sketch with a form of direct address that insists on the exposure from which Clifford shrinks. In describing Clifford's pastime of blowing soap bubbles from the arched window, Hawthorne interlaces his narrative exposition with a series of apostrophes that call the reader's attention both to Clifford's protected position and to the incongruity and inconsequence of his activity: "Behold him, therefore, at the arched window. . . . Behold him, with his gray hair. . . . Behold him scattering airy spheres abroad" (171). Using Clifford to set his sketches within the framework of the novel enables Hawthorne to point to them, potentially remedying their insignificance; after all, only the narrator of a novel can call attention to these acts of aesthetic creation, commanding the reader to "Behold." But these apostrophes also disrupt the elaboration of the soap bubbles as figures for the precious insubstantiality of art, "little, impalpable worlds" that make "the dull air imaginative about them" (171) but dissolve upon contact with a skeptical public. The narrator's direction of our gaze to the conditions of their making and the disruptions of apostrophe become associated not with the preservation of these "brilliant fantasies" (171), but with the kind of attention that would destroy them. In his "Preface," Hawthorne cautions against "[exposing] the Romance to an inflexible and exceedingly dangerous species of criticism by bringing [the author's] fancy-pictures into positive contact with the realities of the moment" (3). But Hawthorne's narrative does just that, both describing and performing this kind of rupture. The narrator's present-tense command to the reader to "Behold" quickly gets embodied by Judge Pyncheon who, when a bubble bursts against his nose, looks up from the street at Clifford "with a stern, keen glance, which penetrated at once into the obscurity behind the arched window" (172).

In this scene, Hawthorne stages a subtle but consequential alignment of the narrative voice with the Judge's perspective. Hedging his bets, the narrator intimates that the Judge's response to Clifford—"Still blowing soap bubbles!"—while "meant to be kind and soothing. . . had a bitterness of sarcasm to it" (172). The Judge's tonally indeterminate response invites us to consider the narrator's apostrophes as similarly rife with sarcastic accusation as well as idealization. Are we to "behold" Clifford as childlike in his simplicity or as ridiculously childish and embarrassingly unmanly?

Are we to understand his "scattering airy spheres abroad" as carefree creation or ineffectual dissemination? Is he pitiably powerless or cursed with
a pathetic lack of ambition? However we choose to read these disruptive
moments of direct address, it is clear that Clifford experiences the Judge's
piercing glance as utterly humiliating: "an absolute palsy of fear came
over him" as he feels "that native and original horror of the excellent
Judge, which is proper to a weak, delicate, and apprehensive character"
(172). Although readers know to read the phrase "the excellent Judge" as
drenched with irony, it is difficult not to shudder as the narrative voice
intertwines itself with the Judge's sense of propriety.

In this scene, Hawthorne activates our desire to shield Clifford from
attack, reminding us of the fragility of his own fiction. And yet he also
aggressively undertakes the anti-romantic work of demystification, repeatedly forcing both his characters and his figures for the work of fiction
into "sordid contact with the world" (39). Critics have been drawn to
Hawthorne's allegories of authorial vulnerability, repeating the story of his
desire to withdraw from the world while glossing over his camouflaged
investment in the voice that humiliates, his wish to exchange Clifford's
effeminate tears for "the fiercer, deeper and more tragic power of laughter" (164). In this episode, Hawthorne's cageyness about tone insulates
his narrative from the act of shaming that he nevertheless insists has taken
place. But critics' tendency to read Hepzibah and Clifford as figures for
Hawthorne's vulnerability and not also as instruments of self-repudiation
also testifies to the efficacy of his fiction of early neglect. If there is no past
to repudiate, no curtain of obscurity that can and should be penetrated,
these characters serve only to articulate the author's need to be protected
from a hostile public. In considering Hawthorne's relation to a changing
literary marketplace, however, we need to move beyond attributing to
him a powerlessness like Clifford's that is imposed and inescapable. As I
will argue, Hawthorne is much more interested in modeling authorship
as a suspension of power that is freely chosen.

Authorship and the Power of Humiliation

Hawthorne makes the greatest strides toward redefining his authority in
two narrative experiments that move the novel forward by interrupting
its plot. Invoking Holgrave as an artist figure and proxy narrator, Hawthorne suspends his narrative in order to reproduce a tale that Holgrave

has written for the magazines, a tale he hopes will discharge or "throw off" (186) his obsession with the inhabitants of the House of the Seven Gables. The story Hawthorne needs to tell through Holgrave is a story he has already told—the story of the humiliation of an aristocratic woman—but through the device of the interpolated tale, Hawthorne is able to disentangle his narrative from the object of humiliation. In a similar yoking of a rupture in narrative time with a scene of abasement, Hawthorne turns the tables on Judge Pyncheon, merging the present tense of apostrophe with the Judge's own voice in a remarkable chapter that exhaustively belittles the dead Judge. These two attempts to transform suspended animation into a mode of power suggest that Hawthorne is nowhere more clear about the extent of his ambition than when he figures authorship as a spectacular renunciation.

The inset magazine tale, read aloud by Holgrave to a reluctant Phoebe, pries open the space that gets collapsed by the novel's interest in modeling inheritance as repetition, its charting of the reappearance of the characteristics of the founding father in the Pyncheons "of To-day" (115). Setting Holgrave's tale at two generations' remove from Colonel Pyncheon allows Hawthorne to return to the novel's original scene of trauma, but at a distance. The property struggle at the heart of the inset tale features Gervayse Pyncheon, the child who first discovered his grandfather dead in the ancestral chair. Hawthorne uses Holgrave's tale to reimagine the relation between founders and moderns, the colony and the nation, recasting it as a story of development that depends on the dismissal of provincial culture.

The provincial world depicted in Holgrave's tale is rife with the cultural values of the system of reprinting. Both Gervayse Pyncheon and his daughter Alice have been educated abroad, which accounts for their disregard for New England, in which "nothing beautiful had ever been developed" (192). This generation of Pyncheons has filled the House of the Seven Gables with marble statues, paintings, and elaborate furniture that could easily have been borrowed from the House of Usher. Under their possession, the house becomes "an emblem of a mind, industriously stored with foreign ideas and elaborated into artificial refinement" (193). Hawthorne's depiction of Gervayse Pyncheon's aesthetic preferences suggests his own vulnerability to reprint culture's disregard for native authors: Gervayse's "familiarity with many of the castles and ancestral halls of England, and the marble palaces of Italy, had caused him to look contemptuously at the House of the Seven Gables." The literary nationalist echoes of this version of the Pyncheon story of unjust possession are magnified by the fact that this tale is initially told from the perspective of Matthew Maule's grandson. Holgrave begins his tale by dramatizing a local craftsman's entry into a house that is falsely occupied by a foreign aristocrat.

As critics have noted, the inset tale explicitly depicts economic transactions in sexual, racial, and class terms, connections that are significantly more subdued in the narrative proper.[64] The inset tale revels in its transgressiveness in a way that is appropriate to sensational fiction, but it does so at a formally and historically safe remove from the novel. Renewing the struggle over property in the house through the vehicle of mesmeric possession, Matthew Maule places Alice Pyncheon in a trance in order to discern the whereabouts of the missing deed. But the recovery of property becomes secondary to revenge; Maule's mesmerism of Alice Pyncheon becomes a means for dispossessing her father through the sexual subjugation of his daughter. Alice's submission to Maule's mesmeric gaze will ultimately result in her humiliating loss of self-control, but its more immediate purpose is to transform the aristocratic Pyncheons's attitude toward the craftsman. While Gervayse Pyncheon insults Maule by condescending to him, Alice's eroticized and admiring gaze, her "glow of artistic approval . . . of the remarkable comeliness, strength, and energy of Maule's figure" (201), objectifies and emasculates him, recognizing his allure without honoring his power. Maule's revenge, then, will focus on breaking the Pyncheons's pride, forcing both Gervayse and Alice to attend to his authority. "Behold your daughter!" (204), Maule declares upon successfully entrancing her, taking on the narrator's deictic function. Releasing Alice from her trance, Maule ominously warns "she shall have occasion to remember Maule, the carpenter" (208). Mesmeric power becomes an instrument for visibility and compensation for neglect, a means of reversing American cultural secondarity and of redressing the author's marginal social position.

As an allegory of authorship, Maule's casting of Alice into "an attitude of profound repose" (205), revises Hawthorne's relationship to his prior mode of writing, invoking the power of the author to produce sensational effects through scenes of humiliation. Maule's spiritual possession of Alice throws the "reserved and stately" (205) Gervayse Pyncheon into a "convulsion of rage, terror, and sorrow" (206) at his inability to wake his daughter. Gervayse's disregard for Maule is repaid by his experience of the powerlessness of ineffective speech: "It is indescribable what a sense of remote, dim, unattainable distance, betwixt himself and Alice was impressed on the father by this impossibility of reaching her with his voice" (205). Similarly, Alice is transformed into a kind of sexual slave as a consequence of her disrespect. Maule releases her from her initial trance but retains remote control of her actions. He is able to "wreak a low, ungenerous scorn upon her" (209) by causing her to violate the sense of restraint that preserves her aristocratic status, forcing her to "break into wild laughter" or a "high-paced jig" at inappropriate occasions, and to travel through the mud in her satin slippers to the laboring section of the town. That Maule's retention of the power to humiliate Alice constitutes a sexual violation is indicated both by the fact that it keeps her from marrying and by Hawthorne's adoption of the densely suggestive tropes of feminist-abolitionist fiction: "while Alice Pyncheon lived, she was Maule's slave, in a bondage more humiliating, a thousand-fold, than that which binds its chain around the body" (208).

Setting this tale within the framework of the novel enables Hawthorne to release and to contain the transgressive energy of popular fiction, to indulge in and to moralize on the subjection of aristocratic pretension to the whims of the vulgar. Both Holgrave's tale and the narrative in which it is set significantly revise the trope of suspended animation, transforming it from a sign of powerlessness before the demands of the public to the exercise of a mode of authorial power. Within the confines of the tale, the story of Maule's mesmerism of Alice enables Hawthorne to restage humiliation as the product of consent. Not only does Gervayse Pyncheon agree to risk his daughter for the possible recovery of the deed, Alice herself twice consents to her own subjection, wagering her "unsullied purity" (203) against Maule's powers before he begins, and interrupting the trance to reprove her father for trying to stop the mesmeric process. In the inset tale, Hawthorne both revels in the vengeful exercise of authorial power and explores the complex imbrication of domination and consent. The tale closes with the image of Maule's anguished and unwilling conscription to Alice's funeral procession, emphasizing his own subjection to the powers he has chosen to exercise. Through his compensatory dependence on the exercise of power-at-a-distance, Matthew Maule is brought closer than we might initially suspect to Alice's subjection to circulation.

In Holgrave's tale, the dependence of the mesmerist on the woman he exploits and the failure of his mesmeric abilities to produce the authority he desires constitute a warning about the exercise of authorial power. Hawthorne emphatically marks the difference between the magazine tale and the novel that contains it. Discovering that Phoebe has drifted into a mesmeric state as a consequence of his oral performance, Holgrave is suddenly conscious that he has the power to "establish an influence over this good, pure, and simple child, as dangerous and perhaps as disastrous, as that which the carpenter of his legend had acquired and exercised over the ill-fated Alice" (212). But Holgrave, Matthew Maule's heir and modern-day counterpart, declines to "complete his mastery" (212) over Phoebe. Holgrave's coming into an awareness of his abilities coincides with his principled refusal to use them. For the first time in the novel we encounter a willed but benevolent suspension of animation. In shifting from tale to novel, Hawthorne defines the legitimate exercise of authorial power as a form of self-restraint.

Hawthorne clearly intends Holgrave's "reverence for another's individuality" (212) to become the moral and tonal signature of his novel. Holgrave's renunciation of his powers triggers a sudden gleam of moonlight by which the "common-place characteristics" of the Pyncheon garden are "transfigured by a charm of romance" (213). These beams of moonlight temporarily resolve the problem of mimesis and banish the narrative's discontent with its setting, provoking Holgrave into an outburst of approving declaratives: "After all, what a good world we live in! How good and beautiful! . . . Could I keep the feeling that now possesses me, the garden would every day be virgin soil" (214).[65] This outpouring of moonlight and sentiment, which Holgrave invokes as "the greatest of renovators and reformers" (214), prefigures the romance ending to the novel in which he will renounce his radical views and resolve the property dispute by marrying Phoebe and abandoning the House of the Seven Gables. But all is not necessarily well in this new Eden. As Matthew Maule's double and heir, Holgrave retains the power to humiliate that he so deliberately chooses to hold in reserve. Similarly, although Hawthorne conspicuously claims for his romance the power of self-restraint, he can do so only in contradistinction to the violent excesses of magazine fiction. Hawthorne's novel carries along with it the genres it disavows, depending on them both to advance the narrative and to define the proper territory of romance. In *The House of the Seven Gables*, only spectacular renunciations can keep romance from subsiding into the disenchantments of modernity. Hawthorne's adoption of a posture of humility toward ordinary life—one that, like Holgrave's, is resonant with possibility—depends on his repeated indulgence in and forswearing of scenes of humiliation.

Critics interested in Hawthorne's redefinition of authorship under the pressures of market culture have gravitated to the problematic ending of the novel, reading Holgrave's renunciation of his radical views as emblematic of Hawthorne's own predicament. For instance, Michael Gilmore interprets the jarringly happy ending as Hawthorne's capitulation to the demands of his readers, an act of submission that is full of self-reproach and that demonstrates Hawthorne's "growing alienation from the process of exchange."[66] Using the novel as a measure of the disappearance of "an embattled Puritan tradition of civic authorship," Grantland Rice similarly reads Holgrave's renunciation as Hawthorne's "lament" for his loss of "socio-political agency."[67] But, as I have argued, Hawthorne's novel does not simply register his reluctant complicity with market forces, it serves to reposition him in relation to the market for fiction. We should recognize in the novel's ending yet another one of Hawthorne's ambitious self-descriptions in terms of resignation, withdrawal, and restraint. In order to put some pressure on the idea that the novel mourns or enacts Hawthorne's surrendered agency, I will return to the chapter that threatened to terminate and not to resolve the novel, a seemingly unrestrained indulgence of the desire to humiliate that models the kind of power Hawthorne wants to claim for fiction. In "Governor Pyncheon," a chapter that brings the narrative to a halt in order to ridicule the political ambitions of a hopelessly dead Judge Pyncheon, Hawthorne seeks to redefine authorship as a powerful form of intervention in modern culture that could nevertheless remain unsullied by it.

"Governor Pyncheon" gives us an anti-romantic version of authorial power as a form of suspended animation, one in which structural limitations on the act of narration free the author from the constraints imposed by "reverence for another's individuality." Hawthorne carefully prepares for this chapter earlier on in the novel when the Judge, insisting on a confrontation with Clifford, seeks "repose" in the "capacious arms" of the "great ancestral chair" (238). Holding his watch so that he can measure "the interval" between the time of his command and the time of its fulfillment (239), the Judge dies in this position, releasing Hepzibah and Clifford into a frenzied attempt to flee the House of the Seven Gables. Returning to observe the dead Judge, alone in the house, the narrator hovers over his immobile body, feigning ignorance of his death and using interjections, direct address, and indirect address to mock the Judge for failing to fulfill his obligations.

This chapter is an apotheosis and recapitulation of the novel's many scenes of humiliation. Recalling his painstaking introduction of Hepzibah, Hawthorne slows the time of narration until it is equivalent with the time narrated, collapsing fictive time into the timeless present. Through multiple acts of surrogation, however, Hawthorne has successfully detached the narrator's voice from his object of humiliation and installed a man more worthy of scorn in the ancestral chair. Hawthorne also stages this scene as Clifford's revenge, reversing the episode at the arched window by granting Clifford the narrator's deictic power. On the verge of abandoning the house, Clifford points to the Judge in joyful "scorn and mockery" (249), while in the "Governor Pyncheon" chapter itself, the narrator delivers what might be thought of as Clifford's long delayed retort: "Still lingering in the old chair!" (270). In addressing the would-be "Governor Pyncheon," the narrator takes extravagant pleasure in reproving the Judge for his unachievable ambitions, and yet he also invokes the pathos of his immobilization, reprising Gervayse Pyncheon's desperate, unheard attempts to awaken his mesmerized daughter.

In this extraordinary condensation of the novel's scenes and figures of suspended animation, Hawthorne reimagines the constraints on the exercise of authorial power. A revision and extension of the sketch form, the "Governor Pyncheon" chapter seeks to produce sensation without narrative action, but in this case Hawthorne's text is full of explicitly political content. Detailing the dead Judge's plans for the coming day, Hawthorne launches into an extended critique of Jacksonian society, not only satirizing the avarice, negligence, and gluttony of the rich, but also indicating their corrupt control over banking and the popular vote. Unlike the sketch, however, this chapter is maliciously violent. Shifting from narrative restraint to narrative arrest, from repose to torpor, the narrator persistently, perversely exhorts the dead Judge to take part in events that unfold in an inaccessible, parallel, present-tense universe. The violence that is implicit in forcing the "Judge of the passing moment" (120) to inhabit the stop-time of the narrator's apostrophes is metaphorically rendered by the Judge's slow defacement in the advancing darkness and by the chapter's closing image of the helplessness of the dead. Failing to respond to the narrator's exhortations to rise to face the coming day, the Judge is forced to suffer the indignity of a fly "creeping over the bridge of his nose, towards the would-be magistrate's wide open eyes!" (283). Hawthorne here combines the grotesqueness of mere embodiment with the violation of perception, intensifying the humiliating reduction of the Judge with the bathetic force of a literalized cliché: "Art thou too weak, that wast so powerful? Not brush away a fly!" (283).

The narrator's arrogation of what had been the Judge's power to humiliate, and the unbridled pleasure Hawthorne takes in inhabiting this position is secured by a set of narrative conditions that protect the novel from the violence it delights in imagining. The immobility and insensibility of the Judge insulate the narrative from the consequences of these exhortations, allowing Hawthorne to give voice to corrupt ambitions that cannot be achieved and to indulge a desire to punish that cannot be felt by its object. These, I would argue, are the "immunities" (2) that Hawthorne desires for his romance: ambition without the compromises entailed by achievement, and passionate speech without an accountability for its effect. This chapter models suspended animation not as powerlessness or even power-in-restraint, but as a privileged lifting of the constraints imposed on ordinary speech, producing the author as a figure of exemption from a culture it nonetheless is empowered to critique.

Given this vivid attempt to align his fiction with a mode of political intervention, critics' emphasis on Hawthorne's powerlessness at the hands of market forces becomes all the more perplexing. It may be that it is difficult to gaze for very long at the contempt that marks the displacement of one cultural order by another. It may be that critics themselves desire the exemptions that Hawthorne claims for his fiction, the release from literary ambition and palpable forms of power that is enacted with every telling of the story of Hawthorne's swift transition from undeserved obscurity to a set of compelled and unfortunate compromises. Looking closely at Hawthorne's struggle to project and assume a new kind of power in *The House of the Seven Gables* can give us some sense of the extraordinary privileges we automatically extend to national authors and of the cost to both authors and critics of judging writing produced under different conditions according to literary nationalist standards. We need to reexamine the assumptions about literary value that enable Hawthorne's narrative investments in humiliation to be redeemed by his humility, the reduction in our field of vision that enables us to ignore the dead judge in the house of fiction. And yet, one of Hawthorne's most important legacies to national culture may indeed be his ability to make strategic withdrawal look like powerlessness before the market, the price of composure rather than the exercise of authority. In the antebellum period, as in the present day, the special vulnerability of authors to market forces has served as a compelling pretext for the consolidation of publishers' power. Hawthorne's elaboration of the author as a figure of market exemption serves as a harbinger of the combination of cultural, political, and economic forces that would reduce the power and the significance of the system of reprinting.

Coda

IN THE EARLY 1850S, structural changes in the book trades began to put an end to the culture of reprinting. The characteristic decentralization of American publishing slowly gave way to the integration of regional markets, which were linked both through innovative publishing practices and through the development of a reliable network of railways and roads. Changes in the ways in which publishers managed their businesses were crucial to this transformation. For instance, in 1852, New York publisher Charles B. Norton traveled west to Cleveland and Cincinnati, south to New Orleans, and back north along the eastern seaboard, visiting bookstores, publishers, and libraries, and selling subscriptions to a new trade periodical *Norton's Literary Gazette and Publishers' Circular*, in which he reported on the progress of his tour. While it was still necessary for Norton to circulate bodily in order to assess the current state of the trade, his travels laid the groundwork for a journal that would circulate in his stead, bringing distant print centers into closer working relations.[1] Changes in systems of distribution also promoted cooperation between publishers and altered the marketing of their books. As Ronald Zboray has argued, the ability to ship books across a linked system of railways enhanced communications between publishers at the same time as it extended their reach, encouraging publishers to sell on commission rather than to rely on older, more cautious systems of barter and exchange.[2] The shift in the nature of western publishing serves as a good index of the effects and pace of market consolidation. In the late 1840s and early 1850s Cincinnati publishers successfully competed with eastern houses, publishing expensive reprints of Gibbon and Byron, ten-cent pamphlet editions of Dickens, popular European and western romances, and eclectic magazines with a regional focus on western history and fiction. But as Walter Sutton details, by the mid-1850s railway shipments of eastern books forced Cincinnati publishers to shift from general to specialized publishing and to transform their reprint operations into distribution houses for more powerful eastern publishers.[3]

The increasing commercial viability of American fiction also served as a sign of and spur to consolidation. A new confidence in the marketability of American writing was signaled by George Palmer Putnam's founding of *Putnam's Magazine* in 1853 as an answer to the Harper Brothers' extra-ordinarily successful reprint miscellany, *Harper's Monthly Magazine* (1850). Both publishers' periodicals were designed to build demand for their books through serialization, advertising, and the cultivation of a loyal readership. Differences between the two magazines, however, suggest diverging esti-mates of the desires of the reading public. The prospectus for *Harper's* boasts the familiar virtues of the culture of reprinting, championing the absorptiveness of the magazine as a format and promising to cull through the wealth of European and domestic periodicals for articles that exceeded "merely local and transient interest." *Harper's* is expansive its address: it is "not intended exclusively for any class of readers, or for any kind of read-ing." Its melange of scientific articles, literary criticism, political speeches, illustrations, and popular fiction seeks to please and to produce a general reader.[4]

Putnam's, by contrast, appeals to national pride, promising to provide access to foreign topics through the perspective of American authors who can be relied on to judge the world "by a standard common to ourselves." Not only does it invoke authors as representative citizens who lend order to miscellany, *Putnam's* recasts the cosmopolitanism of the eclectic maga-zine as urbanity, emphasizing New York as an American city that rivals the interest of Paris and London. Nationalism for Putnam is an aesthetic sensibility, a political commitment, and a device for controlling literary property. Putnam takes a risk by publishing only American writing that is original to his magazine, and yet he also stands to profit by retaining exclusive hold on these properties. Making a point of doing "justice to authors," Putnam yokes his publishing prospects to the cause of authors' rights. Arranging for the simultaneous publication of his magazine in New York and London, he banks on Americanness as a transatlantic bill of goods.[5] While the circulation of *Putnam's*, which reached a peak of 35,000, remained dwarfed by that of *Harper's*, which averaged more than 100,000 copies per issue throughout the 1850s,[6] Putnam's editorial gamble heralds a sea-change in publishers' and readers' estimations of the value of Amer-ican writing. The Harper Brothers also seem to have registered this change. Although they continued to promote their miscellaneous magazine, the list of works on hand at the time of the disastrous Harper's fire in December 1853 indicates a shift toward investment in "original" productions which nearly equaled the firm's output of reprinted texts. Indeed, works copyrighted by the Harpers outnumber reprints in the genres of "Travel and Adventure," "Theology and Religion," "Educational," and "Dictionaries and Gazetteers." Only in the category of "General Literature" do reprints vastly exceed original productions.[7]

By 1853, the promise of a coordinated, national market for print had begun to alter what reprinting meant, both in the United States and abroad. In closing, I will look briefly at two texts from 1853 that bear witness to significant changes in American conceptions of literary property, the politics of print, and the relation of the circulation of literature to national identity. Both texts were written in the wake of the extraordinary success of Harriet Beecher Stowe's *Uncle Tom's Cabin* (1852), the book that catapulted its author to fame and fortune when it was transformed from a magazine serial into a best-selling novel. In the United States, Stowe's novel was praised for its evangelical piety and galvanized readers with its compelling anti-slavery sentiment, but it also opened publishers' and readers' eyes to the potentially enormous market for American fiction. Recognized as an unprecedented event in the history of publishing, the novel's success tested the norms of domestic copyright and redrew the terms of debate over an international copyright agreement.

Control of the market for *Uncle Tom's Cabin* was explicitly at stake in *Stowe v. Thomas*, the federal copyright case in which Stowe and her publisher attempted to suppress an unauthorized German translation of the novel. As I argued in my first chapter, the court's narrow definition of Stowe's property in this case reaffirmed that under American law, an author's rights were limited by the act of publication. Writing for the court, Justice Robert Grier emphasized that going into print hopelessly compromised an author's "exclusive possession" of his manuscript, transforming his "conceptions" into "the common property of his readers, who cannot be deprived of the use of them, or their right to communicate them to others clothed in their own language, by lecture or by treatise."[8] *Stowe v. Thomas* literalized Stowe's property in her text; the court decided that copyright protection extended to typographical but not to fictional characters. In explaining that under American law, copyright entailed not simply the assertion but also the surrender of authorial rights, Grier draws a striking parallel between property in ideas and property in slaves by figuring Stowe's lack of control over her "conceptions" as the promiscuous circulation of her popular slave characters:

By the publication of her book the creations of the genius and imagination of the author have become as much public property as those of Homer or Cervantes. Uncle Tom and Topsy are as much *publici juris* as Don Quixote and Sancho Panza. All her conceptions and inventions may be used and abused by imitators, playrights [sic] and poetasters. They are no longer her own—those who have purchased her book may clothe them in English doggerel, in German or Chinese prose. Her absolute dominion and property in the creations of her genius and imagination have been voluntarily relinquished, and all that now remains is the copyright of her book, the exclusive right to print, reprint and vend it.[9]

In this passage, Grier's ruling on the property status of translations and adaptations gravitates irresistibly toward figures that recall the novel's attack on slavery, in particular, its passionate denunciation of the Fugitive Slave Law (1850). Grier's comic invocation of Tom's and Topsy's unrestrained circulation evokes the threat to Union and to theories of "absolute dominion and property" posed by the contested legal status of fugitive slaves. The mobility of slave-property across state boundaries made painfully clear the limitations of a federal government that ceded sovereignty over slavery to individual states. Public seizures of northern blacks and critiques like Stowe's heightened Americans' awareness of intractable differences between the states and called into question the nature and legitimacy of federal power. While southerners had long and bitterly complained that the anti-slavery movement undermined the principle of state authority over slavery, the Fugitive Slave Law's insistence that slave-property be remanded to the south provided northerners with a vivid demonstration of what it might mean for the states to be more tightly bound under southern conceptions of federal law. The hardening of regions into sections divided against one another in a struggle for power had consequences for the ways in which textual circulation was imagined and invoked, unsettling the outmoded symbiosis between the culture of reprinting and the decentralizing ideals of a states'-rights federalism.

Justice Grier's asymmetrical analogy between property in slaves and property in books provides one account of how reprinting's emphasis on the free circulation of texts is drawn into the orbit of the tense political compromises of the early 1850s. The palpable threat posed by *Uncle Tom's Cabin*'s intensification of sectional strife helps to explain the decision's peculiar grafting of a literalistic definition of Stowe's property onto what is also a tribute to the uncontrolled dissemination of her ideas. Grier's insistence that Stowe's text could be freely adapted by imitators, playwrights, and poets recalls the reprint trade's contention that loose control over literary property holds potentially dangerous monopolies at bay. His emphasis on the use and abuse of Stowe's fiction suggests that he may also have hoped that the threat to Union posed by this novel would be diffused by its treatment at the hands of admiring and disparaging readers. As Melissa Homestead has noted, Justice Grier was well known to abolitionists for taking a hard line in enforcing the Fugitive Slave Law; he was appointed to the bench by Millard Fillmore expressly to uphold the provisions of the Compromise of 1850.[10] In light of her research it becomes difficult not to hear in this passage an attempt to balance a heterogeneous and uncontrollable scene of textual reception with an emphasis on the federal judiciary's strict enforcement of property rights. In *Stowe v. Thomas*, as in the Fugitive Slave Law, the incompatible claims of a diverse and divided public are brokered by adherence to the letter of the law. Grier's analogy between property in slaves and property in books suggests the attenuation of the terms of Union that is implied by the Compromise of 1850. This is a nation linked by the circulation of goods in lieu of a consensus about more fundamental freedoms.

The reaction of the *Democratic Review* to the success of *Uncle Tom's Cabin* similarly demonstrates the power of Stowe's novel to provoke a rethinking of the grounds of literary property and to realign the politics of print. For many publishers and readers, the most salient fact about *Uncle Tom's Cabin* was that it was a pirated book. Reviewers focused not only on the breadth of the novel's circulation within the United States but on its phenomenal success abroad, particularly in Great Britain where "millions of copies" were reportedly sold within a year of publication.[11] *Putnam's* provided a lengthy description of the many formats in which Stowe's text had been reprinted in Britain, France, and all across Europe, offering these editions as proof of the reversal of the subserviency of American letters and of "what may be accomplished by American authors who exercise their genius upon American subjects" (101–2). Stowe's 1853 tour of Great Britain was recognized as a rejoinder to Dickens's 1842 visit to the United States and a rebuttal of his attack on American culture. A speaker at a public meeting in Scotland soon after Stowe's arrival struck a note that reverberated in the American press: "We have long been accustomed to despise American literature—I mean as compared with our own. I have heard eminent *litterateurs* say, 'Pshaw! The Americans have no national literature.' It was thought that they lived entirely on plunder—the plunder of poor slaves, and of poor British authors. . . . Let us hear no more of the poverty of American brains, or the barrenness of American literature. Had it produced only Uncle Tom's Cabin it had evaded contempt."[12]

While for this speaker, Stowe's success brings with it some of the pleasures of symmetry, repaying American originality with British piracy, the popularity of *Uncle Tom's Cabin* at home and abroad caused the *Democratic Review* to drop its long-standing resistance to international copyright and to come out in favor of a reciprocal treaty with Britain. A number of factors contributed to this influential journal's decision to abandon its support for the culture of reprinting. Pragmatically speaking, Stowe's success made it newly plausible that American writers stood to benefit from access to the British market, while the development of cheap publishing in Britain made it seem less likely that British publishers would use their copyrights to drive up the price of American books.[13] And yet, in a lengthy defense of their editorial position in August 1853, financial concerns pale before political ones. One clear liability of the culture of reprinting was its vulnerability to changes in the European press. Noting the conservative backlash against the revolutions of 1848, the *Democratic Review* worried that press censorship had turned European journals into the organs of repressive monarchies. Unlike the Whig polemics of the 1840s in which American literary independence was intertwined with elite aspirations for a national equivalent of British letters, the *Democratic Review*'s call for international copyright is wedded to a thoroughgoing class-critique of British culture.[14] Outlining the principles of republican governance, the editors argue that the popularity of British fiction threatens to erase crucial differences between British and American "ideas of the limits of authority and obedience; the relative position of the different classes of men; the source from whence power is derived, and the conditions on which it is exercised."[15] And yet these are obviously national differences that precede the *Democratic Review*'s reversal of its position on international copyright. What makes political difference newly salient and dangerous is the transatlantic popularity of anti-slavery fiction. The success of Stowe's novel and her warm reception by British aristocrats indicate that a decentralized literary marketplace is no match for the superior organization of transatlantic abolition. The *Democratic Review* hoped that an international copyright law would arrest abolitionists' growing influence over American readers. It calls for a "republican school of literature" (112) to defend white male liberties against a "vitiated, effeminate" (112) sympathy for slaves, and while it exhibits considerable nostalgia for "the great republic of letters, in which all nations freely shared" (115), the choice now seems clear:

it is either "international law" or a tyrannical, extralegal code of "universal philanthropy" (III).

These examples of the imbrication of theories of textual circulation with the politics of slavery suggest that at mid-century, the possibility of popular sovereignty continues to be imagined through recourse to the dissemination of print. The development of a national market for books in the antebellum period is not simply an economic but also a political event. The *Democratic Review*'s anxious call for federal protection of a press that is dangerously open to abolitionist influence, and Justice Grier's difficulty in finding a figure for readers' "common property" in Stowe's text point to a disjuncture between the consolidation of national markets and the stability of national culture. I take this to be a constitutive irony of the period of American literary emergence: a national market for literary works becomes possible at a moment in which the nation is on the verge of disintegration. That the conditions of literary production and the framework for American literature's conceptual coherence are disruptively and productively at odds has consequences for the study of the classic works of the "American Renaissance." The unsettled nature of the ground of American literature is not simply a context for antebellum texts; projecting and stabilizing such a ground is part of the work of literature in this period. Instead of studying how antebellum texts embody national values, we need to attend to the ways in which they take up the question of the cultural coherence of the nation.

The politically charged history of the culture of reprinting also has consequences for how we think today about the relationship between authors and copyright. Antebellum struggles over the right to reprint domestic and foreign texts demonstrate that literary property is never simply or only a matter of individual property rights, but rather of systems of circulation in which persons, corporate bodies, and the state have complicated and often conflicting interests. Recognizing that authors are proxies for struggles over property that others fight in their names makes literary criticism an especially rich field for thinking about the relation of what Roger Chartier has called "the order of books" to larger systems of political and economic organization. Reprinting usefully estranges us from the normal protocols of literary analysis, calling our attention to the multiple acts of categorization and framing we undertake in order to perceive a literary object. In demonstrating both the power and the limits of the author-concept to organize the literary field, reprinting can also open up critical reflection on contemporary attempts to extend the reach and the duration of rights that we conventionally presume are held by "authors." The antebellum culture of reprinting gives us access to a long history of American skepticism about tight controls over literary property, and leaves us with a warning about the poverty of reducing the national stake in intellectual property to the ever more vigilant protection of its circulation.

Notes

Introduction

1. Book history conventionally traces its origins to Lucien Febvre and Henry-Jean Martin's *L'Apparition du livre* (1958), tr. Geoffrey Nowell-Smith and David Wootton as *The Coming of the Book: The Impact of Printing, 1450–1800* (London: New Left Books, 1976). The classic essay defining this field for American scholars is Robert Darnton, "What Is the History of Books?" first published in *Daedalus* 3 (Summer 1982) and reprinted in Cathy N. Davidson's important anthology surveying book history in American studies, *Reading in America: Literature & Social History* (Baltimore: Johns Hopkins University Press, 1989). William Charvat's *Literary Publishing in America, 1790–1850* (Philadelphia: University of Pennsylvania Press, 1959) and *The Profession of Authorship in America 1800–1870* (Columbus: Ohio State University Press, 1968) are often retrospectively placed at the origins of American book history. Recent studies of the antebellum literary marketplace include Ronald Zboray, *A Fictive People: Antebellum Economic Development and the American Reading Public* (New York: Oxford University Press, 1993) and Michael Winship, *American Literary Publishing in the Mid-Nineteenth Century: The Business of Ticknor and Fields* (New York: Cambridge University Press, 1995). The first volume of a collaborative, multivolume study of the history of the book in America has been published as *The Colonial Book in the Atlantic World*, ed. Hugh Amory and David D. Hall (New York: Cambridge University Press, 2000).

2. Samuel Goodrich's impressionistic history, *Recollections of a Lifetime, or Men and Things I Have Seen: In a Series of Familiar Letters to a Friend, Historical, Biographical, Anecdotal, and Descriptive*, 2 vols. (New York: Miller, Orton and Mulligan, 1856) offers the only statistical approximation we have of the ratio of reprinted texts to "original" publications in this period. Goodrich charts a suspiciously steady progress from 1820, when, he estimates, seventy percent of American book production was devoted to the works of foreign authors, to 1856, when he projects that this proportion has dropped as low as twenty percent. See vol. 2 of his *Recollections*, 380–93. A more thorough statistical accounting would measure changes in the ratio of reprinted to domestic texts across each of the major antebellum publishing genres Goodrich lists: school books, classical books, theological books, law books, medical books, and "all others." It would also consider the shifting ratio of reprinted to original texts in periodicals, and chart the rising circulation of magazines devoted solely to original productions. Ideally, such a study would also take into consideration changes in the volume of imported books, which was influenced both by trends in domestic manufacture and by fluctuating tariff rates. For an overview of patterns of import and export in mid-nineteenth century British and

American publishing, see Michael Winship, "The Transatlantic Book Trade and Anglo-American Literary Culture in the Nineteenth Century," in *Reciprocal Influences: Literary Production, Distribution, and Consumption in America*, ed. Steven Fink and Susan S. Williams (Columbus: Ohio State University Press, 1999), 98–122.

3. Even as sophisticated a historian and theorist as Roger Chartier describes his subject in this way, opening *Forms and Meanings: Texts, Performances, and Audiences from Codex to Computer* (Philadelphia: University of Pennsylvania Press, 1995) with the question: "How are we to understand the ways in which the form that transmits a text to its readers or hearers constrains the production of meaning?" (1).

4. Book history has arguably achieved its greatest institutional strength and disciplinary credibility in mediating the concerns of social and cultural historians. Foundational books in this tradition include Robert Darnton, *The Business of Enlightenment: A Publishing History of the* Encyclopédie, *1775–1800* (Cambridge, Mass.: Harvard University Press, 1979) and David D. Hall, *Worlds of Wonder, Days of Judgment: Popular Religious Belief in Early New England* (New York: Alfred A. Knopf, 1989). For recent studies that place the history of the book at the nexus of social and cultural history, see Adrian Johns, *The Nature of the Book: Print and Knowledge in the Making* (Chicago: University of Chicago Press, 1998) and James A. Secord, *Victorian Sensation: The Extraordinary Publication, Reception, and Secret Authorship of Vestiges of the Natural History of Creation* (Chicago: University of Chicago Press, 2000). Pioneering studies of the relation of literary forms and genres to book production, circulation, and reception include Janice A. Radway, *Reading the Romance: Women, Patriarchy, and Popular Literature* (1984; reprint, Chapel Hill, N.C.: University of North Carolina Press, 1991); D. F. McKenzie, *Bibliography and the Sociology of Texts* (London: British Library, 1986); and Chartier, *Forms and Meanings*.

5. Barthes argues, for example, that "The work is concrete, occupying a portion of book-space (in a library, for example); the Text, on the other hand, is a methodological field"; "whereas the work is held in the hand, the text is held in language, it exists only as discourse"; "the Text cannot stop, at the end of a library shelf, for example; the constitutive movement of the Text is a *traversal*: it can cut across a work, several works" (74–75). See "From Work to Text," in *Textual Strategies: Perspectives in Post-Structuralist Criticism*, ed. Josué V. Harari (Ithaca, N.Y.: Cornell University Press, 1979), 73–81. Derrida famously associates the "Beginning of Writing" with the "End of the Book" in *Of Grammatology*, trans. Gayatri Chakravorty Spivak (Baltimore: Johns Hopkins University Press, 1974). For a history of the theorization of the text as a critique of disciplinary knowledge, see John Mowitt, *Text: The Genealogy of an Antidisciplinary Object* (Durham, N.C.: Duke University Press, 1992).

6. For a critique of the way in which the concept of *écriture* "runs the risk of maintaining the author's privileges under the protection of writing's a priori status," see Michel Foucault, "What Is an Author?" in *The Foucault Reader*, ed. Paul Rabinow (New York: Pantheon Books, 1984), 101–20, 105. Important deconstructive studies of antebellum American literature include John T. Irwin, *American Hieroglyphics: The Symbol of the Egyptian Hieroglypics in the American Renaissance* (New Haven, Conn.: Yale University Press, 1980); John Carlos Rowe, *Through the*

Custom House: Nineteenth-Century American Fiction and Modern Theory (Baltimore: Johns Hopkins University Press, 1982); and Joseph Riddel, *Purloined Letters: Originality and Repetition in American Literature* (Baton Rouge: Louisiana State University Press, 1995).

7. For descriptions of the theoretical underpinnings of New Historicism and examples of New Historicist critical practice, see H. Aram Veeser, ed., *The New Historicism* (New York: Routledge, 1989) and Catherine Gallagher and Stephen Greenblatt, *Practicing New Historicism* (Chicago: University of Chicago Press, 2000). Important New Historicist treatments of antebellum literature include Walter Benn Michaels, *The Gold Standard and the Logic of Naturalism* (Berkeley: University of California Press, 1987); Gillian Brown, *Domestic Individualism: Imagining Self in Nineteenth-Century America* (Berkeley: University of California Press, 1990); and Lora Romero, *Home Fronts: Domesticity and Its Critics in the Antebellum United States* (Durham, N.C.: Duke University Press, 1997).

8. For a book history approach to this period that focuses on formats, see Isabelle Lehuu, *Carnival on the Page: Popular Print Media in Antebellum America* (Chapel Hill: University of North Carolina Press, 2000). In drawing connections between formats and communities of readers, Lehuu juggles contradictory claims: that print culture in this period is richly unstable, and that it establishes hierarchies of reading sharply marked by gender and class. In focusing on reprinting, I will cover some of the same ground as Lehuu, but with an emphasis on the mobility of texts across formats that Lehuu associates with increasingly rigid social categories.

9. This special status under the law is clearly coveted by the manufacturers of all kinds of objects. The history of copyright law in the nineteenth century can be told as the broadening of the law, by legislation and judicial interpretation, to cover a wide range of things not initially included in the Copyright Act of 1790's spare reference to "maps, charts, and books." Musical compositions, engravings, and etchings were added to the list in 1802, performance rights in dramatic compositions in 1856, photographs in 1865, commercial prints and labels in 1874, and molded decorative articles in 1882. See Thorvald Solberg, ed., *Copyright Enactments of the United States, 1783–1906* (Washington D.C.: U.S. Government Printing Office, 1906).

10. Section 8 of the U.S. Constitution grants Congress the power "To promote the Progress of Science and useful Arts, by securing, for limited Times, to Authors and Inventors, the exclusive Right to their respective Writings and Discoveries."

11. James Madison, Alexander Hamilton, and John Jay, *The Federalist Papers*, ed. Isaac Kramnick (New York: Penguin Books, 1987), 279.

12. Quoted in Bruce W. Bugbee, *Genesis of American Patent and Copyright Law* (Washington D.C.: Public Affairs Press, 1967) 130. Madison seems to be proposing a licensing provision similar to those which were included in a number of revolutionary-era state statues. These provisions allowed a complainant to reprint a book should a copyright holder fail to make enough copies available to the public at a reasonable price. For an extended discussion of the origins of federal copyright law, see Bugbee and my overview essay "Copyright in Early America" in *A*

History of the Book in America, ed. Robert A. Gross and Mary Kelley vol. 2 (New York: Cambridge University Press, forthcoming 2003).

13. The "Act of May 31, 1790" is based on the British "Statute of Anne" (1710), although it rewrites some of its key provisions. I will discuss the way in which these revisions explicitly provide for the reprinting of foreign works in Chapter 2.

14. One touchstone for this idea would be Bentham's *Principles of the Civil Code*: "Property is only a foundation of expectation—the expectation of deriving certain advantages from the thing said to be possessed. . . . Property and law are born and must die together. With respect to property, security consists in no shock or derangement being given to the expectation which has been founded on the laws of enjoying a certain portion of good. The legislator owes the greatest respect to these expectations to which he has given birth." *Works of Jeremy Bentham*, vol. 1 (Edinburgh: William Tait, 1843), 308–9.

15. James Boyle gives a particularly striking example of such reasoning in his analysis of *Moore v. The Regents of California* (1990), in which the court determined that property in a cell line derived from a man's spleen belonged to the doctor who extracted it. Grounding the property right in the doctor's heroic labor, the court construed the public interest solely in terms of society's need to provide an economic incentive for medical research, failing to consider that the public interest might militate against privatizing property in genetic material. See *Shamans, Software, and Spleens: Law and the Construction of the Information Society* (Cambridge, Mass.: Harvard University Press, 1996).

16. *American Romanticism and the Marketplace* (Chicago: University of Chicago Press, 1985), 3.

17. While the general outlines of his study run in parallel with Michael Gilmore's, Michael Davitt Bell usefully calls attention to the uncertain future of a national literature in 1845, warning that "We should be careful about reading our own ideas of literary value and the literary canon back into the pattern of literary history; in 1845, it would seem, the nature and future of American fiction were as unclear as they had been in 1830." See his "Conditions of Literary Vocation" in *The Cambridge History of American Literature*, vol. 2 (New York: Cambridge University Press, 1995), 9–123, 71.

18. As Teichgraeber argues, recent historical scholarship has confirmed both the diversity and the inconsistent development of antebellum print culture, revealing "not the appearance of a single literary marketplace, in which professional writers for the first time came to confront a new mass audience of readers, but rather . . . the emergence of an open and pluralistic culture" (168). See his *Sublime Thoughts/Penny Wisdom: Situating Emerson and Thoreau in the American Market* (Baltimore: Johns Hopkins University Press, 1995), 155–74.

19. *The Transformation of Authorship in America* (Chicago: University of Chicago Press, 1997), 11.

20. In a recent essay, Gilmore notes the regrettable marginality of politics within Americanist criticism: "The marketplace, the rise of domestic ideology, the institutionalized culture of letters—we have all read, indeed, many of us have written, studies that specify *these* factors as having been instrumental in shaping

major artists." But, he continues, "Politics is seldom granted the weight of systemic consequence. Its very nature is assumed to be reactive, not causative. It has small power to shape, we think, because it is itself the product of other forces" (199–200). See "Politics and the Author's Career: Two Cases," in *Reciprocal Influences: Literary Production, Distribution, and Consumption in America*, ed. Steven Fink and Susan S. Williams (Columbus: Ohio State University Press, 1999), 199–212.

21. See his *The Market Revolution: Jacksonian America, 1815–1846* (New York: Oxford University Press, 1991) and the useful volume of responses, *The Market Revolution in America: Social, Political, and Religious Expressions, 1800–1880*, ed. Melvyn Stokes and Stephen Conway (Charlottesville: University Press of Virginia, 1996).

22. See for example Gillian Brown, *Domestic Individualism*.

23. Not surprisingly, the critical studies which best capture both the heterogeneity of antebellum culture and its political volatility are treatments of the popular theater in which questions of access are paramount. See Lawrence W. Levine, *Highbrow/Lowbrow: The Emergence of Cultural Hierarchy in America* (Cambridge, Mass.: Harvard University Press, 1988) and Eric Lott, *Love and Theft: Blackface Minstrelsy and the American Working Class* (New York: Oxford University Press, 1993). For a reading of Emerson's and Thoreau's texts through the lens of their popular appropriation, see Teichgraeber, 175–266.

24. See Nicholas K. Bromell, *By the Sweat of the Brow: Literature and Labor in Antebellum America* (Chicago: University of Chicago Press, 1993); Michael Newbury, *Figuring Authorship in Antebellum America* (Stanford, Calif.: Stanford University Press, 1997); Cindy Weinstein, *The Literature of Labor and the Labors of Literature* (New York: Cambridge University Press, 1995). In the last chapter of his book, Newbury gives an overview of the legal and political territory I examine in detail in my first two chapters, but, as its position in his argument suggests, his analysis of antebellum debates over literary property does not disrupt his focus on authors. Newbury considers how the conceptions of literary property he abstracts from the law are reflected in literary texts. See Newbury, 158–99.

25. Martha Woodmansee's and Mark Osteen's use of the example of Charles Dickens to describe the parameters of what they call "economic criticism" can serve as a shorthand for the distinction I draw here. All of the modes of analysis they enumerate fan out from the author's individual subjectivity, imagined as the instrument or ground of economic activity. They suggest that "to make adequate sense of Charles Dickens's depictions of money, class, and bourgeois subjectivity, one might investigate: how his father's imprisonment for debt affected his attitude towards money and work; his manipulation of the market for his own works; how he responded to and incorporated public relations and advertising to become a kind of recognized brand name; the relationship between mass marketing and his seemingly obsessive industriousness; his labors to revise copyright statutes. One would also need to place Dickens and his work within the rapidly expanding industrial and imperialist economy and shifting class structures of Victorian England." "Taking Account of the New Economic Criticism: An Historical Introduction," in *The New Economic Criticism: Studies at the Intersection of Literature and Economics* (New York: Routledge, 1999), 3–50, 35. By contrast, my treatment of the relation of literature to the economy will question the primacy of the

author's perspective, showing how Dickens becomes a dense point of reference within American culture and how his texts become a means for the articulation of positions on economic development that exceed the compass of his understanding.

26. "What Is an Author?" 118, 111.

27. *Literary Publishing in America, 1790–1850* (1959; reprint, Boston: University of Massachusetts Press, 1993), 7–8.

28. For the emergence of women's authorship in this period, see Ann Douglas, *The Feminization of American Culture* (New York: Knopf, 1977), Mary Kelley, *Private Woman, Public Stage: Literary Domesticity in Nineteenth-Century America* (New York: Oxford University Press, 1984), and Michael Davitt Bell, "Conditions of Literary Vocation." For the publishing arrangements and rhetorical codes governing the production of "pauper's books" (3), the narratives of convicts, beggars, soldiers, and slaves, see Ann Fabian, *The Unvarnished Truth: Personal Narratives in Nineteenth-Century America* (Berkeley: University of California Press, 2000).

29. See Merle Montgomery Hoover, *Park Benjamin, Poet & Editor* (New York: Columbia University Press, 1948), 121. Jonathan Mitchel Sewall's "Epilogue to Cato" (1778) is most easily found in Evert A. Duyckinck and George L. Duyckinck, *Cyclopedia of American Literature*, vol. 1 (Philadelphia: W.M. Rutter & Co., 1875), 300–301.

30. *American Notes for General Circulation*, *The New World* Extra Series (November 1842), 47.

31. The editors refer here to Henry Brougham's Society for the Diffusion of Useful Knowledge. See Richard D. Altick, *The English Common Reader: A Social History of the Mass Reading Public* (1957; reprint, Columbus: Ohio University Press, 1998).

32. For a complete list of *The New World*'s "Extra Numbers," see Hoover, 201–6.

33. "Correspondence," *Littell's Living Age* 1 (May 11, 1844).

34. Littell is likely referring to Massachusetts' completion of the Western Railroad, which gave access to the Hudson through a link with Albany in 1842. See George Rogers Taylor, *The Transportation Revolution, 1815–1860* (New York: M.E. Sharpe, 1951), 92.

35. "Correspondence," *Littell's Living Age* 2 (May 25, 1844).

36. Walter E. Houghton observes that the sectarianism of the major British magazines and reviews remained strongly marked until the mid-1850s. See his "Periodical Literature and the Articulate Classes," in *The Victorian Periodical Press: Samplings and Soundings*, ed. Joanne Shattock and Michael Wolff (Toronto: University of Toronto Press, 1982), 3–27.

37. This phrase is frequently used to describe the advantages of the eclectic magazine as a format. It is repeatedly applied to Littell's magazine in the newspaper excerpts he publishes as an advertising supplement. See "Notices of Littell's Living Age," *Littell's Living Age* 1 (April 11–August 3, 1844): 3–6.

38. That generality in the 1840s United States can itself carry substantial political weight is illustrated by a testimonial Littell reprints from the *Mobile Daily Advertiser*. In an anonymous letter to the editor of the Alabama paper, a correspondent notes that the *Living Age* is "cheaper than the cheapest of those brochures

which come to us in cart-loads every week from the north" (6). Eclectic magazines projected a cosmopolitan worldliness and detachment that stood out against the increasingly incendiary politics of one rival source of cheap reading, the tracts produced and distributed by northern evangelicals.

39. This particular issue of the *Living Age* tilts heavily toward the Tory press, although this bias is unrepresentative of Littell's general practice. The first volume of the *Living Age* takes the bulk of its articles from apolitical, liberal, or reform weeklies such as *The Atheneaum*, *The Spectator*, *The Examiner*, and Littell's British counterpart *Chamber's Edinburgh Journal*. Extracts from Tory magazines and reviews are, however, consistently represented in its pages.

40. Transatlantic differences in periodical culture have carried over into the bibliographic tools for the study of periodicals. While *The Wellesley Index to Victorian Periodicals*, 5 vols. (Toronto: University of Toronto Press, 1966) reprints title pages of individual issues and indexes articles according to author, *Poole's Index to Periodical Literature*, first published in New York in 1853, indexes only according to subject, reflecting the abstraction that characterized American magazinists' approach to periodical writing—their tendency to regard articles in terms of topic rather than point of origin. Strikingly, while the *Wellesley Index* confines itself to British magazines, *Poole's* indexes both American and widely read British periodicals, keying its index to the page numbers of American reprints of the major monthlies and quarterlies. See William Fred Poole, *An Index to Periodical Literature* (New York: Charles B. Norton, 1853). While a compensatory author-index to a later edition of *Poole's Index* was published in 1971 (Edward C. Wall, ed., *Cumulative Author Index for Poole's Index to Periodical Literature, 1802–1906* [Ann Arbor, Mich.: Pierian Press, 1971]), the placeless, generalizing medium of the internet may have made the subject-logic of the eclectic magazines more acceptable to twenty-first century American readers. The editors of Cornell University's "The Making of America" chose *Littell's*—a magazine comprised almost entirely of foreign texts—as one of the first ten antebellum periodicals to be included in their digital library of primary sources for the study of American culture. See <http://cdl.library.cornell.edu/moa/>.

41. "Proprietary Illustration: The Case of Cooke's *Tom Jones*," *An Index of Civilisation* (Victoria: Centre for Bibliographical and Textual Studies, 1993), 137–47.

42. *Sartain's Union Magazine of Literature and Art* (November 1849): 320.

43. For a discussion of the importance of gift books to the development of the book trade, see Stephen Nissenbaum, *The Battle for Christmas* (New York: Vintage Books, 1997), 140–55.

44. Examples of collaboration and competition between word and image in this period would include the dependence of Washington Irving's sketches upon picturesque travel, the intimacy of graphic caricature and social critique in Dickens's serialized novels, and the study of the narratives that are entailed by landscape, history, and genre painting.

45. A typical print run for a book in the period is 1,500–3,000 copies, but gift books were already being printed in the tens of thousands in the early 1830s; *Graham's Magazine* had over 40,000 subscribers when Poe resigned as editor in 1842.

46. See Hawthorne's statement of resignation from the editorship of the

Boston miscellany, the *American Magazine of Useful and Entertaining Knowledge* (August 1832), 520.

47. *The Mayflower, for MDCCCXLVI* (Boston, 1846).

48. For example, *Graham's Magazine* sent W. E. Tucker to Europe to engrave the Old Masters in the late 1840s. Literary magazines of the period frequently reported on the European travels of American painters and engravers, demonstrating a nationalist sponsorship of copying that seems unthinkable in the literary realm.

49. *The Token: A Christmas and New Year's Present* (Boston, 1832), 347.

50. "American Scenery," *The Token* (1831), facing page 55.

51. "The Snow Shoe," *The Token* (1831), facing page 285.

52. "Keskarrah a Copper Indian Guide and His Daughter Green Stockings," *Narrative of a Journey to the Shores of the Polar Sea* (London: J. Murray, 1823).

53. *The Token* (1831), 285.

54. Presentation Plate, *The Token and Atlantic Souvenir: A Christmas and New Year's Present* (Boston, 1836).

55. For instance, "The Raising of Jairus's Daughter," a little-known episode from the Gospels, appears as a subject in a number of gift books, dramatizing the moment at which a young woman's consciousness is restored. See Theodore van Holst, "The Raising of Jairus's Daughter," *The May Flower* (1846), facing page 105, and John Gadsby Chapman, "The Daughter of Jairus," *The Opal: Pure Gift for the Holy Days* (New York, 1844), facing page 173. For the representation of women's meditation in different genres, see for example "Invisible Serenader," *The Token* (1832), facing page 189, "Beatrice," *The Token* (1836), facing page 105, and "Isabella," *The Gift: A Christmas and New Year's Present for 1840* (Philadelphia, 1840), facing page 34.

56. *The Gift* (1840), facing page 228. Susan S. Williams discusses this image in *Confounding Images: Photography and Portraiture in Antebellum American Fiction* (Philadelphia: University of Pennsylvania Press, 1997), 77.

57. I am indebted here to Purvi Shah, who spotted poet and editor Elizabeth Oakes Smith renaming an engraving titled "Confidence and Protection" "Confidence and Affection" both in an accompanying poem and in the table of contents she controlled. See *The Mayflower, for MDCCCXLVIII* (Boston, 1848), facing page 139.

58. In her dissertation, "Imperfect Title: Nineteenth-Century American Women Authors and Literary Property" (Ph.D. dissertation, University of Pennsylvania, 1998), Melissa Homestead argues that as nonproprietary subjects women more easily adapted themselves to unauthorized reprinting.

59. For a rich account of Willis's career, including his sycophantic courting of British aristocracy, see Thomas N. Baker, *Sentiment and Celebrity* (New York: Oxford University Press, 1999).

60. For the provocative argument that the idea of the mass-media or "general supply" was first imagined in the 1830s by evangelical Christians, largely outside the market for literary goods, see David Nord, "The Evangelical Origins of Mass Media in America, 1815–1835," *Journalism Monographs* 88 (May 1984):1–30.

61. See her *Forgotten Readers: African-American Literary Societies, 1830–1940* (Durham, N.C.: Duke University Press, forthcoming 2002).

Chapter 1

1. With a few exceptions, recent scholarship has generally sought to confirm Foucault's perception that a modern notion of authorship emerged simultaneously with the consolidation of capitalist market relations. See Martha Woodmansee, "The Genius and the Copyright: Economic and Legal Conditions of the Emergence of the 'Author,'" *Eighteenth-Century Studies* 17, no. 4 (1984): 425–48; Mark Rose, "The Author as Proprietor: *Donaldson v. Becket* and the Genealogy of Modern Authorship," *Representations* 23 (1988): 51–85 and *Authors and Owners: The Invention of Copyright* (Cambridge, Mass.: Harvard University Press, 1993); and Peter Jaszi, "Toward a Theory of Copyright: The Metamorphosis of Authorship," *Duke Law Journal* (1991): 455–502.

2. Two important challenges to Rose's line of argument merit prominent mention. In *Publishing and Cultural Politics in Revolutionary Paris, 1789–1800* (Berkeley: University of California Press, 1991), Carla Hesse contests Rose's chronology, reaching back prior to the development of a market for books to locate the roots of French authors' rights in an attempt by the Royal Administration to curb the power of the Publishers' Guild. Far from a figure who is representative of bourgeois individualism, the author for Hesse is the instrument of the absolutist police state and the site of competing revolutionary attempts to control the circulation of texts. Most importantly, Hesse counters Rose's contention that copyright was "essentially a commercial struggle" (*Authors and Owners*, 4) by insisting that commercial arrangements are politically contested. In *Authorship and Copyright* (New York: Routledge, 1992), David Saunders offers an excellent corrective to what he characterizes as a "subject-centered schema of cultural history" (235). Saunders argues that the critical tendency to view the history of copyright through a naturalizing lens—one that celebrates the achievement of authors' rights as the apotheosis of individual subjectivity—has all but erased the historical specificity of legal systems. While I am in strong sympathy with Saunders's interpretive focus, his distinction between copyright systems and moral rights systems, and his call for increased attention to the institutions of book production, regulation, and distribution, I think he overstates the degree to which the institution of the law can be detached from the questions taken up in these debates. As I will argue, not only does the federal court understand the free circulation of texts to be the ground and image of its authority, it seizes on statutory copyright as a means of strengthening its power against the competing claims of state courts.

3. Throughout this chapter I will be quoting from the transcript of the arguments of counsel and judges' opinions that was privately printed by Richard Peters: *Report of the Copy-Right Case of Wheaton v. Peters* (New York: James van Norden, 1834). This version of the case differs from the official account, which can be found in Peters, ed., *Reports of Cases Argued and Adjudged in the Supreme Court of the United States*, vol. 8 (Philadelphia: Desilver, Jun., and Thomas, 1834), 591–699, in a number of important ways. For the most part, the privately printed version is more expansive. Arguments that are abbreviated in Peters's *Reports* are written out in full; instead of being taken from the reporter's notes, J. R. Ingersoll's defense is taken from the copy that Ingersoll read at the hearing. Famously, Peters's official

account of the case omits Justice Baldwin's dissent which can be found in full in the privately printed copy. Unfortunately, this text omits Thomas Sergeant's comments, which can be found at Peters, *Reports*, vol. 8, 638–51, and Daniel Webster's remarks, which can be found at Peters, *Reports*, vol. 8, 651–54. Unless marked otherwise, all citations in the text are taken from the privately printed edition.

4. Rose, "The Author as Proprietor," 69–70. In revising and extending his argument in *Authors and Owners*, Rose tempers his sense of the inevitability of this development, shifting responsibility for the emergence of authorial proprietorship from generalized "forces" to the particular persuasiveness of a Lockean theory of property. And yet, in locating the origins of modern authorship in eighteenth-century British legal debate, Rose foreshortens the highly charged history of legal, political, and cultural contestation over authors' rights, creating a powerful sense of the unbroken continuity in Anglo-American culture of a concept that faced (and continues to face) significant resistance (125).

5. *The Letters of the Republic: Publication and the Public Sphere in Eighteenth-Century America* (Cambridge, Mass.: Harvard University Press, 1990).

6. One way to mark the erosion of the republican model of authorship within legal discourse is to note the way in which the rhetoric of personality emerges at the turn of the twentieth century as a justification of the author's right to his copy. Justice Holmes's well-known opinion in *Bleistein v. Donaldson Lithographing* (1903) serves as a good touchstone for this change. In ruling on the copyrightability of a series of chromolithographs Holmes notes: "The copy is the personal reaction of an individual upon nature. Personality always contains something unique. It expresses its singularity even in handwriting, and a very modest grade of art has in it something irreducible, which is one man's alone." See *Decisions of the United States Courts Involving Copyright and Literary Property, 1789–1900* (Washington, D.C.: U.S. Government Printing Office, 1980), vol. 13, 276. Holmes's definition of copyright as a personal right that depends on the individuation of handwriting, and his reliance on an expressive theory to ground the value of art signals a major departure from the language of the constitutional copyright provision and the Copyright Act of 1790, which justified the individual ownership of a printed text in terms of the public good, the disinterested and generalized "encouragement of learning" (Act of May 31, 1790, quoted in Solberg, *Copyright Enactments*, 32).

7. "American Literature, Public Policy, and the Copyright Laws before 1800," *Federal Copyright Records 1790–1800* (Washington D.C.: Library of Congress, 1980), xv–xxv.

8. For a detailed history of Wheaton's career as a court reporter and a social history of *Wheaton v. Peters*, see G. Edward White, *The Marshall Court and Cultural Change, 1815–1835*, vols. 3–4 of *The History of the Supreme Court of the United States* (New York: Macmillan, 1988), 384–426.

9. For a thorough treatment of *Wheaton v. Peters* in its institutional context, including a history of the publishing of Supreme Court reports and an excellent account of the internal politics of the Marshall court, see Craig Joyce, "The Rise of the Supreme Court Reporter: An Institutional Perspective on Marshall Court Ascendancy," *Michigan Law Review* 83 (1985): 1291–1391.

10. "The Author as Proprietor," 62, 65.

11. For a discussion of the way in which, prior to the adoption of the U.S. Constitution, state copyright statutes "mingled public benefit rationales with natural rights rhetoric" (97), see Jane Ginsburg, "A Tale of Two Copyrights: Literary Property in Revolutionary France and America," in *Publishing and Readership in Revolutionary France and America*, ed. Carol Armbruster (Westport, Conn.: Greenwood Press, 1993), 95–114.

12. The British press found the American fascination with Justice Yates's arguments unfathomable. As one reviewer noted, "it was strange to see the antiquated doctrine of Mr. Justice Yates in *Millar v. Taylor*, which was refuted at the time by the luminous intellect of a Mansfield, and has ever since been repudiated in Westminster Hall, revived in a court of justice on the other side of the Atlantic." Review of *Report of the Copy-Right Case of* Wheaton v. Peters, *Westminster Review* 24 (1836): 187–97, 192. Morton Horwitz's account of the post-Revolutionary demand for codification provides some ground for understanding the plaintiffs' reluctance to rely on Mansfield's authority. According to Horwitz, Mansfield's efforts at judicial reform raised American fears of the arbitrary exercise of judicial power. Mansfield's "luminous intellect" was rendered suspect by what Americans saw as his evasion of the letter of the law. Jefferson, for example, associated Mansfield's reasoning with an anti-democratic conspiracy, alleging that he sought "to render [the law] more uncertain under pretence of rendering it more reasonable." See Horwitz, *The Transformation of American Law, 1780–1860* (Cambridge, Mass.: Harvard University Press, 1977), 18.

13. See *English Reports*, vol. 98 (Edinburgh: William Green & Sons, 1901), 2401–3.

14. For a philosophical discussion of this confusion between the incorporeality of the right to property and the corporeality of the object, see C. B. Macpherson, *Property: Mainstream and Critical Positions* (Toronto: University of Toronto Press, 1978), 1–13.

15. Although presented as if at random, the watch, the table, and the guinea are all what Philip Fisher has called "model objects," objects that in philosophical, theological, and economic writing have traditionally been used to exemplify the relation of persons to things. "Pins, a Table, Works of Art," *Representations* 1 (1983): 43–57. Fisher identifies the watch as the dominant early-modern image of a self-contained world, the projection of human craftsmanship in the image of divine craftsmanship. He also discusses the table as its Platonic predecessor, the archetypical craft object that represents the incarnation of the idea in the mind of a single maker. The guinea is not so much an object as a medium of exchange, a representation of the mobility of objects in the world of commerce. That Paine aligns the book with this series of model objects gives some indication of the ambitiousness of his claims. Paine attempts to establish the book as an ideal commercial and aesthetic object, one that would remedy not only the alienation implicit in the fact of exchange but also that implicit in the act of aesthetic creation.

16. Peters, ed., *Reports*, vol. 8, 653.

17. "Morphology and the Book from an American Perspective," *Printing History* 17 (1987): 2–14, 4.

18. In the introduction to his chapter "Of Things Personal," Blackstone

notes that the common law traditionally "entertained a very low and contemptuous opinion of all personal estate . . . as only a transient commodity." See his *Commentaries on the Laws of England* (New York: W.E. Dean, 1846), vol. 2, 384.

19. John Locke, *Second Treatise of Government* (Indianapolis: Hackett Publishing Company, 1980), 18–30.

20. Locke, 19.

21. One might argue that this common-law fantasy has been largely fulfilled by contemporary copyright legislation. Since 1976, American copyright law has protected a work from the moment of its fixation in material form and preserved its status as private property for fifty years following the author's death; the 1998 Sonny Bono Act extended this term of protection for an additional twenty years. This radical increase in the duration of copyright protection, coupled with the substitution of the moment of composition for that of publication as the defining moment at which property is vested, testifies to the decline of the public sphere as the site of, and justification for, granting individual property in texts. And yet the legal difference between the trade in books and that of other mass-produced objects, becomes *more* legible as copyright is increasingly defined in common-law terms as compensation for an author's labor. As James Boyle has noted, copyright legislation grants to authors an unprecedented property right in the products of their labor, a residual right of ownership past the point of sale that would appear ludicrous should it be granted to pipefitters or autoworkers. See his *Shamans, Software, and Spleens*. That the copyright holder can restrict the behavior of the book purchaser (one may read a book but not photocopy it; one may refer to it, but not quote from it at length) represents the flip side of the reader's imagined intimacy with what he or she commonly mistakes as the sole producer of this commodity. Contemporary copyright law ratifies the author as an exception to ordinary labor and the book as an ideal commodity, one in which the depersonalization of mass-production is overcome in fantasy.

22. *English Reports*, vol. 98, 2361.

23. American copyright law worked at cross-purposes with the interests of industry so long as it failed to protect copyright holders against derivative works, destabilizing the object of property and undercutting its value by redistributing ownership to anyone who worked a slight variation on the text in question. As late as 1951 in *Alfred Bell v. Catalda Fine Arts*, Judge Frank articulated an extremely low standard for claiming property in a derivation, arguing that anything more than "a 'merely trivial' variation" provided grounds for the assertion of a new work. Ruling on a case of piracy in the visual arts, Frank suggested that poor copying or accidental disfigurement would produce a margin of difference ample enough for a new property claim: "A copyist's bad eyesight or defective musculature, or a shock caused by a clap of thunder, may yield sufficiently distinguishable variations. Having hit upon such a variation unintentionally, the 'author' may adopt it as his and copyright it" (*Decisions*, vol. 28, 42–51, 50). Frank's decision runs counter to a line of reasoning laid out by Judge Learned Hand in *Sheldon v. Metro-Goldwyn Pictures Corp.* (1936), where a broad similarity between texts was enough to establish infringement. Unlike Judge Frank, who thought authorship could be established through the introduction of minimal—even unintentional—differences, Judge

Hand argued that "no plagiarist can excuse the wrong by showing how much of his work he did not pirate" (*Decisions*, vol. 21, 255–66).

24. Interestingly, the majority left open the possibility of a federal common law, so long as the arbitrary and arcane nature of customary law could be ameliorated by publicity and ratified by collective assent. According to the majority opinion, "the common law could be made part of our federal system only by legislative adoption" (100).

25. Because the question of Wheaton's full compliance with the statute remained undecided, the Supreme Court remanded the case to a lower court for a jury trial to determine the facts. Wheaton failed to pursue the matter, however, both because of the expense of proceeding further with the case, and because the judges' unanimous ruling as to the noncopyrightability of their opinions had confined his property claim in the *Reports* to peripheral features such as headnotes, indexes, and digests of the arguments of counsel.

26. *Decisions*, vol. 17, 85–96.

27. "The Right to Privacy," *Harvard Law Review* (December 1890): 193–220, 207, 200. The fullest statement of the inalienability of the handwritten text, on which the right to privacy rests, is put forward by Justice McLean in *Bartlett v. Crittenden* (1849): "There is no law which can compel an author to publish. . . . His manuscripts, however valuable, cannot without his consent be seized by his creditors as property" (*Decisions*, vol. 13, 157). For a reading of the relation between copyright law and the right to privacy that differs markedly from my own, see Rose, *Authors and Owners*, 139–42.

28. Solberg, *Copyright Enactments*, 34–37.

29. ". . . if a book or books, [the author shall] give information by causing the copy of the record, which by said act he is required to publish in one or more of the newspapers, to be inserted at full length in the title-page or in the page immediately following the title of every such book or books" (Solberg, *Copyright Enactments*, 35).

30. John F. Whicher usefully situates *Wheaton v. Peters* in the context of the fight between state and federal powers set off by the "Great Steamboat Patent War," in "The Ghost of *Donaldson v. Beckett*: An Inquiry into the Constitutional Distribution of Powers over the Law of Literary Propety in the United States," *Bulletin of the Copyright Society of the USA*, Parts 1 and 2 (October 1861) and (February 1862).

31. For an account of American ambivalence toward the common law which, while deemed unnecessarily intricate and dangerously subject to manipulation, was also seen as a "bulwark of rights and liberties" (241), see Perry Miller, *The Life of the Mind in America: From the Revolution to the Civil War* (New York: Harcourt, Brace & World, 1965), 239–65.

32. *Crimes of Writing: Problems in the Containment of Representation* (New York: Oxford University Press, 1991), 16.

33. See the *American Jurist* 13 (1835), 484–86, which publishes selections from Peters's correspondence on this matter, including a letter impugning the judgment of the publisher of the rival reports and a letter soliciting a testimonial from Chief Justice Marshall as to the authenticity of Peters's *Reports*. In this correspondence,

Peters goes on the defensive, associating copying not with a dissemination that preserves liberty, but with degeneration. Newly attuned to the logic of the supplement, he complains that the mere fact of the existence of a rival report casts aspersions on the authority of his own production. The absolute publicity of Supreme Court opinions finally requires that Peters's *Reports* be authorized by the Chief Justice himself. That Justice Marshall's testimony to the "fidelity and accuracy" of Peters's *Reports* is necessarily detached from Peters's text, circulating in the back pages of the *American Jurist*, nicely illustrates the republican paradox by which the authority of print is secured by a multiplication of print authorities.

34. *Decisions*, vol. 14, 1267–73.

35. *Decisions*, vol. 14, 1784–95.

36. U.S. Constitution, Article 1, Section 8. For the argument that this clause reflects not a republican but a "utilitarian conception of literary activity" (72), see Grantland Rice, *The Transformation of Authorship*, 70–96. I would not want to draw too sharp a line between these rhetorics. As Rice notes, in American copyright discourse a defense of the free circulation of texts is often buttressed by instrumentalist public good rationales. Nevertheless, I would insist that the circumscription of authors' rights in American law is driven by an understanding of print-publicity as necessarily impersonal and as crucial to the imagination of popular sovereignty, not, as Rice would have it, by a conception of the public good as the aggregate of individual interests. As I see it, the utilitarian theory of print he describes is best embodied in the antebellum period by the publishing activities of the American Tract Society, which developed techniques of administration such as standardizing costs and gathering statistics far in advance of the publishing industry. For the development of what we think of as market logics outside the market for literary goods, see David Paul Nord, "Evangelical Origins," and "Systematic Benevolence: Religious Publishing and the Marketplace in Early Nineteenth-Century America," in *Communication and Change in American Religious History*, ed. Leonard Sweet (Grand Rapids, Mich.: William B. Eerdmans, 1993), 239–269.

37. See *Bleistein v. Donaldson Lithographing* (*Decisions*, vol. 13, 269–79). Holmes's decision in this case anticipated the 1909 recodification of copyright law, in which the 1790 statute's emphasis on useful works was expanded to cover "all the writings of an author" (17 U.S.C. § 4)

38. The historical significance of the patent-copyright analogy, which is frequently invoked in nineteenth-century copyright cases (often to opposite effects), is too involved for me take up here at length. Suffice it to say that, while the analogy to patent law buttressed the claims of the state (as Justice McLean pointed out in *Wheaton v. Peters*, no one ever claimed that the inventor had a natural or perpetual right to patent-protection [99]), figuring the text as a machine also worked in the interests of publishers by eliding the role of the press in textual production. Like patent law, American copyright justified an author's property with reference to the cultural function of his text. However, unlike patent law, which requires proof of originality and holds accidental copying to be infringing, nineteenth-century copyright law generally protected against mechanical duplication regardless of the originality of the text in question. In copyright cases,

independent re-origination is rarely held to be infringing. See, for example, *Sheldon v. Metro-Goldwyn Pictures Corp* (1936) where Judge Learned Hand playfully suggests that, "if by some magic a man who had never known it were to compose anew Keat's [sic] Ode on a Grecian Urn, he would be an 'author,' and, if he copyrighted it, others might not copy that poem, though they might of course copy Keats's" (*Decisions*, vol. 21, 263.)

The comparison of copyright to patent law generally plays off of this fundamental asymmetry, using the analogy of text and machine to smuggle in a notion of authorial "invention," even as it works to efface the author through an emphasis on the reproductive powers of the text itself. This emphasis on the text-as-machine also displaces the machine that produces the text. In the analogy with patent-law, the discourse of copyright rearticulates the common-law fantasy of the author-as-sole producer even as it seeks to invert this figure, establishing the producer as the sole author of the text. For an example of the surreptitious use of patent law to place publishers in the position of authors, see *Wheaton v. Peters* (99). For an excellent discussion of the differences between patent law and copyright, see *Alfred Bell v. Catalda Fine Arts* (1951), *Decisions*, vol. 28, 42–61.

39. *Decisions*, vol. 13, 645.

40. *Decisions*, vol. 14, 1726–27.

41. *Decisions*, vol. 14, 1723.

42. *A Treatise on the Law of Property in Intellectual Productions in Great Britain and the United States* (Boston: Little, Brown and Company, 1879), 181.

43. *Decisions*, vol. 15, 2484.

44. *Decisions*, vol. 15, 2485.

45. Walter Benjamin elucidates the disjunctive temporality of translation in his "The Task of the Translator," *Illuminations* (London: Fontana, 1982), 82.

46. In his critique of judicial reasoning in this case, Drone noted that, taken to its extreme, this decision would hold as noninfringing a version of *Uncle Tom's Cabin* that had been retranslated into English from the German translation (*A Treatise*, 455). While the Act of 1870 expanded copyright to include the right to translation, the narrowness with which the court defined the subject of copyright in this case outlived this specific holding. See for example *White-Smith Music Publishing Company v. Apollo Company* (1908) in which the court determined that copyright in a published song was not infringed by its material "translation" into music rolls for use in player pianos (*Decisions*, vol. 15, 2978).

47. *Decisions*, vol. 15, 2486.

48. "Democratic Social Space: Whitman, Melville, and the Promise of American Transparency," *Representations* 24 (1988): 60–101.

Chapter 2

1. *The Letters of Charles Dickens*, ed. Madeline House and Graham Storey (Oxford: Clarendon Press, 1974), vol. 3, 82.

2. "Resolutions of the New York Welcome Committee," quoted in William Glyde Wilkins, *Charles Dickens in America* (New York: Haskell House Publishers,

1970), 106. These resolutions characteristically link the reformist aims of Dickens's fiction with the American political project: "As Republicans we are bound to thank him who has, in his writings, so eloquently maintained the cause of the humble and oppressed" (105–6).

3. K. J. Fielding, *The Speeches of Charles Dickens* (New York: Oxford University Press, 1960), 25.

4. For Washington Irving's toast to international copyright and Cornelius Mathews's speech and toast in favor of the measure, see Wilkins, 139–48. Horace Greeley's *New York Tribune* also published strong editorials in favor of international copyright shortly before and directly following Dickens's New York speech. See Wilkins, 242–45.

5. As the editors of Dickens's *Letters* note, the Philadelphia publishing house of Carey & Lea paid Scott "an average of £75 for each of the *Waverly* novels" (vol. 3, 125n). Carey, Lea & Blanchard also sporadically sent payments to Dickens as a goodwill gesture and for the privilege of obtaining advance sheets of the last part of *Oliver Twist*. Upon returning from his American tour, however, Dickens refused badly needed payments for advance sheets of *American Notes* and subsequent novels. For Dickens's dealings with the Philadelphia publisher, see Robert L. Patten, *Charles Dickens and His Publishers* (New York: Oxford University Press, 1978), 95–98, 131. For his distribution of a printed circular to friends and acquaintances, asking them to "hold themselves aloof" from the system of reprinting by declining payments from newspaper republishers, see "To British Authors and Journals," July 7, 1842, *Letters*, vol. 3, 256–59. For his acceptance of payments for advance sheets after 1852, see Peter S. Bracher, "Harper & Brothers, Publishers of Dickens," *Bulletin of the New York Public Library* 79 (1976): 315–35. For a table documenting some of the payments made to foreign authors by American publishers in the antebellum period, see Wallace Putnam Bishop, "The Struggle for International Copyright in the United States" (Ph.D. dissertation, Boston University, 1959), 57–64.

6. See Terence Whalen, *Edgar Allan Poe and the Masses: The Political Economy of Literature in Antebellum America* (Princeton, N.J.: Princeton University Press, 1999), for a recent example of an author-centered approach to the period that dramatizes the collision of authorial ambitions with a monolithic and oppressive publishing system.

7. For a history of the right to petition and its use in the antebellum period, see David C. Frederick, "John Quincy Adams, Slavery, and the Disappearance of the Right of Petition," *Law and History Review* (Spring 1991): 113–55.

8. See Teresa Ann Murphy, *Ten Hours Labor: Religion, Reform, and Gender in Early New England* (Ithaca, N.Y.: Cornell University Press, 1992).

9. William Wiecek details the wide range of antebellum positions on slavery that found common ground in the "federal consensus." See his *The Sources of Antislavery Constitutionalism in America, 1760–1848* (Ithaca, N.Y.: Cornell University Press, 1977).

10. Solberg, *Copyright Enactments*, 31.

11. Solberg, *Copyright Enactments*, 34.

12. As Patterson explains, Section VII of the Statute of Anne "was aimed at the monopoly of the English booksellers and the Stationers' Company, and did

not legalize piracy of foreign works; it simply provided that the act should not be construed to prohibit 'the importation, vending, or selling' of books in a foreign language printed beyond the sea." *Copyright in Historical Perspective* (Nashville, Tenn.: Vanderbilt University Press, 1968), 199.

13. Even James J. Barnes's indispensable history of copyright agitation, *Authors, Publishers, and Politicians: The Quest for an Anglo-American Copyright Agreement, 1815–1854* (Columbus: Ohio State University Press, 1974) proceeds from a position that cannot help but naturalize the cause of authors' rights. As Barnes explains in his preface, his study details "why failure attended" (ix) the efforts of copyright agitators. Despite a healthy skepticism about the motives driving both sides of the debate, Barnes's account of the struggle is finally not about competing principles, but about the ways in which the cause of authors' rights ran up against publishers' interests. The tendency to view the struggle over international copyright from an authors'-rights perspective runs deep in the secondary criticism. See for example, Andrew J. Eaton, "The American Movement for International Copyright, 1837–60," *Library Quarterly* (April 1945): 95–122, who contrasts the "abstract ideals" of copyright advocates to the opposition's appeal to "economic advantage" (122), and Aubert J. Clark, *The Movement for International Copyright in Nineteenth-Century America* (Washington, D.C.: Catholic University of America Press, 1960), who summarizes the opposition's "specious arguments" (53). Lawrence H. Houtchens's opinion that opposition arguments were "far more persuasive" (22) than those of advocates is a notable exception. See his "Charles Dickens and International Copyright," *American Literature* 13 (March 1941): 18–28. For a more recent invocation of the hardships brought about by "the failure of nineteenth-century copyright law to extend protection to works by foreign authors," see Alice D. Schreyer, "Copyright and Books in Nineteenth-Century America," in *Getting the Books Out*, ed. Michael Hackenberg (Washington, D.C.: Center for the Book, 1987), 122.

14. As Barnes notes, Henry Clay put forward copyright bills in 1837, 1838, 1840, and 1842. A detailed report explaining the rationale behind the rejection of international copyright was produced by John Ruggles's Committee on Patents and the Patent Office in June 1838 (discussed below). A similarly unfavorable report was produced by the Judiciary Committee in May 1842, but it was neither discussed nor printed due to Clay's temporizing decision to postpone consideration of the bill. An Anglo-American Copyright treaty supported by Presidents Fillmore and Pierce was turned back by the Senate in 1854, marking the end of the most intense period of antebellum copyright agitation. See Barnes, 49–94, 177–262, and Houtchens.

15. For a detailed history of the vexed politics of early national public works, see Jonathan Lauritz Larson, *Internal Improvement* (Chapel Hill: University of North Carolina Press, 2001). For the centrality of debates over internal improvements to antebellum understanding of the limits of federal power, see Sellers.

16. "The International Copyright Question: Protest Against the Doctrine of the Democratic Review Thereon," *United States Magazine and Democratic Review* (June 1843): 609–14, 614.

17. *New World* (October 19, 1842), 288.

18. Foremost among these are Thorvald Solberg, the Register of Copyrights

under the new law, and publisher and copyright agitator George Haven Putnam. Their work remains an indispensable starting point for research despite its triumphalist cast. Neither compiler, however, adequately represents the texts and arguments of the opposition. See Solberg, "Bibliography of Literary Property," in R. R. Bowker, *Copyright: Its Law and Its Literature* (New York: Publishers' Weekly, 1886); *Copyright in Congress, 1789–1904* (Washington, D.C.: U.S. Government Printing Office, 1905), and *Copyright Enactments*. Ezra Greenspan identifies Putnam as the "chief publisher of pro-international copyright pamphlets" (89) and details his political work in *George Palmer Putnam: Representative American Publisher* (University Park: Pennsylvania State University Press, 2000), 342–47. See also Putnam, *The Question of Copyright* (New York: G.P. Putnam's Sons, 1896).

19. For lists of antebellum American authors who supported international copyright, see the petitions reprinted by Kenneth Cameron in "The Quest for International Copyright in the Thirtieth Congress," *ESQ: A Journal of the American Renaissance* 51 (1968): 108–36 and William Cullen Bryant, Francis L. Hawks, and Cornelius Mathews, *An Address to the People of the United States in Behalf of the American Copyright Club* (New York: American Copyright Club, 1843), 19–20. The Copyright Club's list of "Associate Members," however, must be treated with some skepticism in that it excludes only those authors who, when invited to join, explicitly declined membership. A pro-copyright petition, complete with facsimile signatures of over one hundred prominent nineteenth-century authors is appended to Bowker. For an analysis of Washington Irving's ambivalence about proprietary authorship despite his strong support for international copyright, see Rice, *The Transformation of Authorship*, 70–72.

20. Barnes, 66. Only a small number of these petitions were ordered to be printed by the House and Senate. The petitions indexed by Solberg in *Copyright in Congress* and discussed in this chapter should be considered a representative sample, not a complete listing.

21. As far as I am able to ascertain, no labor history of the print trades discusses worker agitation against the passage of an international copyright law. Evidence of labor organization can be found in the many petitions sent to Congress by printers, papermakers, and typographers' unions, discussed below. Joseph Campbell, to whom Cornelius Mathews contemptuously referred as a "paper-dealing tradesman" (*Arcturus* [March 1842]: 312), published a pamphlet in which he answered Mathews point for point. See his *Considerations and Arguments Proving the Inexpediency of an International Copyright Law* (New York: William E. Dean, 1844). References to public meetings of tradesmen in Boston, New York, and Philadelphia are scattered throughout the pro-copyright literature and the secondary histories. See William Cullen Bryant's pro-copyright editorial responding to "the paper-makers who belong to the Home League," *Power for Sanity: Selected Editorials of William Cullen Bryant*, ed. William Cullen Bryant II (New York: Fordham University Press, 1994), 171, and the report in the *Boston Mercantile Journal* of a "Convention of persons engaged in the manufacture of books" which assembled to discuss both duties on foreign books and the dangers of an international copyright law, reprinted in Wilkins, 246–47. See also Paul B. Davis, "Dickens and the American Press, 1842," *Dickens Studies* 4 (1968): 32–77, 69; Bishop, 114;

Eaton, 105, 116, 121; and Houtchens, 21. For an account of radicals' use of petitions to combat the extension of the term of domestic copyright in Britain, see Catherine Seville, *Literary Copyright Reform in Early Victorian England: The Framing of the 1842 Copyright Act* (New York: Cambridge University Press, 1999).

22. "The International Copyright Question," *United States Magazine and Democratic Review* 12 (February 1843): 113–22, 115.

23. See [Evert Duyckinck], "Literary Prospects of 1845," *American Review* (February 1845): 146–51. For the Young Americans' split with O'Sullivan over the copyright issue, see Perry Miller, *The Raven and the Whale: The War of Words and Wits in the Era of Poe and Melville* (1956); reprinted as *The Raven and the Whale: Poe, Melville, and the New York Literary Scene* Baltimore: Johns Hopkins University Press, 1997), 113, 122–23, and Chapter 5.

24. See Simms's two-part letter to Representative Isaac E. Holmes of South Carolina, *Southern Literary Messenger* (January 1844): 7–17 and (March 1844): 137–51, and [John Blair Dabney], "Reply to E.D. and Mr. Simms" *Southern Literary Messenger* (April 1844): 193–99 and (May 1844): 289–97.

25. For the *Public Ledger*'s opposition to international copyright, see Arno L. Bader, "Frederick Saunders and the Early History of the International Copyright Movement in America," *Library Quarterly* 8 (January 1938): 25–39, 36. For the working-class origins of the penny press, see Alexander Saxton, "Problems of Class and Race in the Origins of the Mass Circulation Press," *American Quarterly* 36 (Summer 1984): 211–34.

26. In addition to the efforts of Henry Clay in the late 1830s and early 1840s, active Whig support for the cause of international copyright came from Daniel Webster and his successor at the Department of State, Edward Everett, who were instrumental in brokering the 1853 treaty with Great Britain. Free-trade advocate and nullifier William C. Preston of South Carolina, to whom Francis Lieber addressed his pro-copyright treatise, *On International Copyright* (New York: Wiley & Putnam, 1840), might seem an exception to this rule, though his growing estrangement from the Democrats and strong alliance with the Whigs throughout the period of international copyright agitation suggests, rather, his strategic importance to a cross-sectional, bi-partisan coalition.

27. "Report, with Senate Bill No. 223," February 16, 1837, 24th Congress, 2d Session, *Senate Documents* No. 179, 1.

28. "Literary Property," *United States Magazine and Democratic Review* 2 (June 1838): 289–311, 307.

29. Philip H. Nicklin, *Remarks on Literary Property* (Philadelphia: P.H. Nicklin and T. Johnson, 1838), 32. The *Democratic Review* essay on "Literary Property," noted above, takes particular note of this passage.

30. "Memorial of a Number of Citizens of the United States, Praying an Alteration of the Law Regulating Copyrights," February 4, 1837, 24th Congress, 2d Session, *Senate Documents* No. 141, 1.

31. James Buchanan is the Democrat most visibly connected with opposition to international copyright in the Senate. Buchanan regarded the measure with suspicion from the moment Clay introduced the first international copyright bill, urging the Senate in "the interest of the reading people of the United States" to

"go beyond publishers and ascertain what would be the effect on the acquisition of knowledge in this vast country." *Register of Debates in Congress* (Washington, D.C.: Gales & Seaton, 1837), vol. 13, 670. He is also on record as having "expressed himself gratified to hear" that an adverse committee report had stalled the progress of Clay's 1842 bill. *Niles National Register*, May 11, 1842, cited in Houtchens, 21. There are strong indications that George Bancroft spoke publicly and persuasively against international copyright in 1842–43, crystallizing Democratic opposition and prompting O'Sullivan's explanation of its grounds in the *Democratic Review*. See Cornelius Mathews, *The Better Interests of the Country, in Connexion with International Copy-right* (New York: Wiley & Putnam, 1843), 8. Perry Miller confirms the speech, but does not cite his source. See *The Raven and the Whale*, 98–99, 113. Bancroft eventually signed a petition in favor of international copyright, but only on the principle of trade reciprocity, refusing the imputation that American authors were injured by the circulation of cheap foreign books. See the "Memorial of American Authors" appended to Bowker.

32. One gauge of the characteristic flexibility of the opposition is the fact that the two most influential anti-copyright treatises were written by Philip Nicklin, a fierce defender of free trade, and by protectionist economist and publisher Henry C. Carey.

33. See Sellers for the complexity of this double bind by which devolution of power from the center is exercised by federal decree (exemplified by Jackson's veto of the National Bank charter, and his removal of deposits). Jackson understands himself to be acting in the public interest with the only tools the Constitution gives him, and yet such action is equally comprehensible to Whigs as executive tyranny.

34. For a detailed comparison of payments to authors that argues that popular American writers did not suffer from competition with foreign reprints, see W. S. Tryon, "Nationalism and International Copyright: Tennyson and Longfellow in America." *American Literature* 24 (1952): 301–9.

35. *A Second Visit to the United States of North America* (New York: Harper & Brothers, 1849), vol. 2, 253. For a survey of antebellum attempts to regulate reading practices, see Lehuu, 126–55.

36. For evangelicals' innovative use of technologies of mass production and distribution for the circulation of tracts and bibles, see Nord, "Evangelical Origins." For the Sabbatarian controversy, in which evangelicals' effective use of the press prompted William Ellery Channing to denounce the ease with which voluntary organizations could bring public opinion "to bear tryannically against individuals or sects" (198), see Richard John, *Spreading the News: The American Postal System from Franklin to Morse* (Cambridge, Mass.: Harvard University Press, 1995), 169–205. For the abolitionists' "great postal campaign," which terrified anti-abolitionists in both South and North with "the vision of a well-organized, centrally directed propaganda machine," see Leonard L. Richards, *"Gentlemen of Property and Standing": Anti-Abolition Mobs in Jacksonian America* (New York: Oxford University Press, 1970), 71–81, and John, 257–80. For the importance of cheap print to the election of 1840 and allegations that former postmaster general Amos Kendall unfairly used his influence within the postal system to distribute party propaganda, see

Robert Gray Gunderson, *The Log Cabin Campaign* (Lexington: University of Kentucky Press, 1957), 86–7, 156–58.

37. "Memorials of John Jay and of William C. Bryant and Others, in Favor of an International Copyright Law," March 22, 1848, 30th Congress, 1st Session, *House of Representatives Miscellaneous Documents*. No. 76, 3.

38. November 5, 1836; quoted in Barnes, 60–61.

39. "Petition of Thomas Moore, and other Authors of Great Britain, Praying Congress to grant to them the Exclusive Benefit of their Writings Within the United States," February 2, 1837. 24th Congress, 2d Session, *Senate Documents* No. 134, 1.

40. For the intimate connection between the example of Scott and American support of international copyright as hereditary privilege, see obituaries of Scott, such as that in the *Museum of Foreign Literature, Science and Art* 21 (December 1832): [481], which proposes that Congress grant land to Scott's unmarried daughter and American copyright privileges to his son-in-law, John Gibson Lockhart. See also memorial speeches and pamphlets, such as John McVickar's *Tribute to the Memory of Sir Walter Scott* (New York: George P. Scott and Co., 1833), which calls for the passage of an international copyright law to "redeem a debt which in honor we long have owed" (42). I am indebted to Emily Todd for these references. The "Thomas Moore" petition cites McVickar's letter to the New York *American* as a way of ventriloquizing the connection between the lack of international copyright and Scott's demise. In his controversial after-dinner speech, Charles Dickens sentimentalizes what by 1842 is a longstanding feature of copyright advocacy.

41. Worried about endless litigation between English and American publishers as well as opposition from the public and the trade, Clay proposed that already reprinted works be excluded from protection, taking care to note that this category included "the great mass of the science and literature of the world." He also suggested that the law be "limited to the subjects of Great Britain and France," where reciprocal rights were all but assured, and, to ensure the availability of books, that copyright for foreign works be contingent on their publication "within reasonable time" (2).

42. Clay, 2.

43. "Memorial of a Number of Citizens of Boston, Praying the Passage of an International Copyright Law," April 24, 1838, 25th Congress, 2d Session, *Senate Documents* No. 398, 1.

44. It is interesting to note in this regard that the Provisional Congress of the Confederate States of America voted in its first session to enable its president to enter into reciprocal treaties for the extension of copyright privileges to foreign authors. See Resolution 15, *The Statutes at Large of the Provisional Government of the Confederate States of America*, ed. James M. Mathews (New York: William S. Hein & Company, 1988), 93.

45. "Memorial of a Number of Citizens of Boston," 2.

46. "Memorial of a Number of Citizens of New York, Praying the Passage of an International Copyright Law," April 24, 1838. 25th Congress, 2d Session, *Senate Documents* No. 399, 2.

47. "Memorial of a Number of Citizens of the United States," 1. This analogy is repeated in John Jay's important 1848 petition, which synthesizes the most

persuasive points made by petitioners on behalf of international copyright. See John Jay, "Memorials of John Jay and of William C. Bryant and Others, in Favor of an International Copyright Law," March 22, 1848, 30th Congress, 1st Session, *House of Representatives Miscellaneous Documents* No. 76.

48. Jay, 7–8. See also "Memorial of a Number of Citizens of New York," 1–2.

49. Jay, 7.

50. "Memorial of a Number of Citizens of New York," 1.

51. See for example John Ruggles's "Report, from the Committee on Patents and the Patent Office," June 25, 1838, 25th Congress, 2d Session, *Senate Documents* No. 494, in which he speculates on the reasons for American authors' eagerness to endorse the British authors' petition: "Indeed, the mind is induced to cast about for the means of reconciling the united and harmonious application of American and foreign authors for a law to relieve the former from injurious competition by the latter, in our literary market. It can be found only in the result it is calculated to produce, the taxing of the reading public of this country, for the joint benefit of both, as the reading public is taxed in England" (7).

52. "Memorial of Nahum Capen, of Boston, Massachusetts, on the Subject of International Copyright," 26th Congress, 1st Session, *House of Representatives Documents* No. 61, 6.

53. "Memorial of the Columbia Typographical Society of the City of Washington, Against the Enactment of an International Copy-Right Law," February 13, 1838, 25th Congress, 2d Session, *Senate Documents* No. 190, 1.

54. "Memorial of a Number of Persons Concerned in Printing and Publishing, Praying an Alteration in the Mode of Levying Duties on Certain Books, and Remonstrating against the Enactment of an International Copyright Law," June 15, 1843, 27th Congress, 2d Session, *Senate Documents* No. 323, 1–2.

55. Ruggles, 5.

56. "Remonstrance of the Inhabitants of Massachusetts, Against the Passage of an International Copyright Law," June 4, 1838, 25th Congress, 2d Session, *House of Representatives Documents* No. 416, 1.

57. For publishers', booksellers', bookbinders' and printers' support of international copyright, see Jay, 13–15.

58. Ruggles, 3.

59. "Memorial of the New York Typographical Society Against the Passage of an International Copyright Law," March 13, 1838, 25th Congress, 2d Session, *Senate Documents* No. 296, 2.

60. "Remonstrance of Inhabitants of Massachusetts," 3.

61. As Andrew Eaton notes, Frederick Marryat's *A Diary in America, Part Second* (1840), tied opposition to international copyright directly to southern resentment of Harriet Martineau's condemnation of slavery in her controversial travel narrative, *Society in America* (1837). According to Marryat, southern legislators were determined to do nothing that would assist Martineau in publicizing abolitionist doctrine, "forgetting that as a copyright would increase the price of a work, it would be the means of checking its circulation, rather than extending it" (quoted in Eaton, 112).

62. "Memorial of the New York Typographical Society," 2.

63. Ruggles, 4.

64. "Memorial of a Number of Persons Concerned in Printing and Publishing," 2. This attack on the dangers of a centralized publishing system was occasionally softened by an appreciation of social and cultural differences. For instance, John Ruggles conceded that "high prices are attended with less injurious effects in England" (4), where the density of the population enabled those who could not afford to buy books to be well served by libraries. By contrast, Ruggles argued, the sparseness and remoteness characteristic of American settlement required that books be kept cheap enough for laborers to purchase them.

65. For the continued importance of the resetting of type as a point of re-origination and mark of national difference, see the Chace Bill (1886), which garnered the support of the National Typographers Union by stipulating that foreign books seeking American copyright must be printed from type set in the United States, and the Platt-Simonds Copyright Act (1891), which was passed into law with a similar provision (Putnam, 52–53, 132).

66. Isaac Kramnick, "Republican Revisionism Revisited," *American Historical Review* 87 (1982): 629–64, and Carroll Smith-Rosenberg, "Domesticating 'Virtue': Coquettes and Revolutionaries in Young America," in *Literature and the Body: Essays on Populations and Persons*, ed. Elaine Scarry (Baltimore: Johns Hopkins University Press, 1988), 160–84.

67. "Memorial of a Number of Citizens of Philadelphia, Against the Passage of an International Copyright Law," January 15, 1838, 25th Congress, 2d Session, *Senate Documents* No. 102, 2. The text of this petition was submitted to Congress three times under different headings and with different lists of signatures attached. See also the "Memorial of Inhabitants of Philadelphia, Against an International Copyright Law," January 15, 1838, 25th Congress, 2d Session, *House of Representatives Documents* No. 117, and "Memorial of Richard Penn Smith and Others, Against the Passage of the Bill to Establish an International Copyright Law," April 10, 1838, 25th Congress, 2d Session, *Senate Documents* No. 369.

68. "Memorial of the New York Typographical Society," 3.

69. "Memorial of a Number of Persons Concerned in Printing and Publishing," 2.

70. For an analysis of the dynamic of center and periphery in the British book market, see Jerome Christensen, *Practicing Enlightenment: Hume and the Formation of a Literary Career* (Madison: University of Wisconsin Press, 1987), 193–96. Christensen argues that the London print monopolies constructed themselves in the image of state power, in part so that the extra-legal pressure they brought to bear on provincial publishers would carry quasi-legal force. Christensen's elaboration of the ways in which publishers' power was underwritten by the state provides a useful contrast to the American system in which anti-copyright publishers imagined the decentralization of the book market to underwrite state power.

71. *Irish Booksellers and English Writers 1740–1800* (Atlantic Highlands, N.J.: Humanities Press International, 1986), Chapters 3, 8, and 9.

72. *Letters on International Copyright* (Philadelphia: A. Hart, 1853), 29–32.

73. "Memorial of a Number of Citizens of Philadelphia," 3.

74. Ruggles, 5.

75. "Memorial of the New York Typographical Society," 3.

76. For a brief description and history of the stereotype process, see Philip Gaskell, *A New Introduction to Bibliography* (New York: Oxford University Press, 1972), 201–5.

77. Ordinary newspapers and trade circulars from this period bear witness to a lively trade in stereotype plates. For an analysis that links economies of scale in book production to the decreasing marginal cost of producing duplicate plates, see "Memorial of the New York Typographical Society," 3.

78. "Memorial of the New York Typographical Society," 3.

79. Ruggles, 7.

80. For a rich account of the negotiation of this treaty that details how its passage was compromised by the rise of organized lobbying, see Barnes, 177–262.

81. For elaboration of this position, see Ruggles and the two anti-copyright articles in *The Democratic Review*, "Literary Property," 290–92, and "The International Copyright Question," 118–20.

82. Thomas Jefferson,"Query XIX: Manufactures," *Notes on the State of Virginia* (New York: W.W. Norton, 1954), 164–65.

83. "Remonstrance of the Inhabitants of Massachusetts," 2–3.

84. "Memorial of a Number of Persons concerned in Printing and Publishing," 2, 1.

85. "Literary Property," 295. In this, the *Democratic Review*'s first pronounce ment on the issue, the reviewer adopts a qualified stance against international copyright, arguing that domestic legislation redefining copyright as a moral right granted in perpetuity must precede the passage of an international copyright law. But see also "The International Copyright Question" (1843) where O'Sullivan argues that the statutory nature of copyright in American and foreign law necessarily limits its reach "to the subjects of the legislating sovereignty" 121.

86. See the "Memorial of A Number of Citizens of Philadelphia," 2, and the "Remonstrance of Inhabitants of Massachusetts," 2–3.

87. Ruggles, 7.

88. "Memorial of a Number of Citizens of Philadelphia," 2.

89. "Memorial of Nahum Capen, of Boston Massachusetts," 8.

90. See for example, Pope's Epistles to Bathhurst and Burlington in *Poetry and Prose of Alexander Pope*, ed. Aubrey Williams (New York: Houghton Mifflin, 1969), 176–96, and Swift's "Epistle Dedicatory to His Royal Highness, Prince Posterity," *A Tale of A Tub* (New York: Oxford University Press, 1984), 75.

91. For "courtesy of the trade," see Eugene Exman, *The Brothers Harper* (New York: Harper & Row, 1965), 52–59, Barnes, 53–60, and John Tebbel, *A History of Book Publishing in the United States* (New York: R. R. Bowker, 1972) vol. 1, 208–9. For the Supreme Court ruling that "courtesy of the trade" was unenforceable at law, see *Sheldon v. Houghton* (1865), *Decisions*, vol. 13, 2373–79.

92. Quoted in Barnes, 55.

93. "Publishing Intimacy in *Leaves of Grass*," *ELH* 60 (1993): 471–501, 481–82.

94. For the sudden demise of the foreign reprints that were published as newspaper "extras," see Barnes, 18–29, who explains that they were vulnerable to

shifts in demand characteristic of a boom and bust economy, and to changes to the postal code that raised the cost of their circulation through the mails.

95. For a brief discussion of *Clayton v. Stone* (1829) the case that established that "a newspaper or price-current is not such a publication as falls under the protection of the copyright law" (*Decisions*, vol. 13, 640), see Chapter 1.

96. *Imagined Communities: Reflections on the Origin and Spread of Nationalism* (New York: Verso, 1983; revised edition, 1991), 36.

97. For a thorough discussion of the system of newspaper exchanges, see Richard Kielbowoicz, *News in the Mail: The Press, Post Office, and Public Information, 1700–1860s* (New York: Greenwood Press, 1989), 141–61.

Chapter 3

1. For Postmaster General and Jackson appointee Amos Kendall's "implicit rejection of the superiority of federal law" (271) when it came to postal employees' obligations to their communities, see John, *Spreading the News*, 257–80.

2. Letter to W. C. Macready, March 22, 1842, *Letters*, vol. 3, 156.

3. February 4, 1842, *Letters*, vol. 3, 50.

4. For an account of Dickens's precarious financial state—"mortgaged on all sides and possessing scarcely any copyrights of present value" (126)—and for an astute reading of the boldness of Dickens's and his publishers' gamble on the long-term benefits of the interruption of serialization, the year of respite, and the success of the travel narrative, see Patten, 119–38.

5. Dickens, quoting *Hamlet* III, i, 154, in a letter to John Forster, January 21, 1842, *Letters*, vol. 3, 15.

6. January 21, 1842, *Letters*, vol. 3, 15.

7. For a detailed account of Dickens's American reception, see Wilkins.

8. Wilkins, 32.

9. Wilkins, 23–24. William Cullen Bryant echoed this language in an editorial in the *New York Evening Post* the day of the New York dinner, claiming that Dickens's reception had articulated new, democratic criteria for excellence and honor: "a young man, without birth, wealth, title, or a sword, whose only claims to distinction are his intellect and heart, is received with a feeling that was formerly rendered only to emperors and kings." See Sidney Moss, *Charles Dickens' Quarrel with America* (Troy, N.Y.: Whitson Publishing Company, 1984), 2.

10. Moss, *Charles Dickens' Quarrel*, 3.

11. New Haven *Commercial Herald*, quoted in Wilkins, 95.

12. An editorial in the *New World* on February 12, 1842 put it bluntly: "Has Mr. Dickens yet to learn that to the very absence of such a law as he advocates, he is mainly indebted for his widespread popularity in this country? To that class of his readers—the dwellers in log cabins, in our back settlements—whose good opinion, he says is dearer to him than gold, his name would hardly have been known had an international copy-right law been in existence." Even the pro-copyright press drew the connection. Arguing that "the evil of which he complains should be remedied," the New York *Morning Courier* nevertheless regretted Dickens's

"ill-timed" comments, noting that his "reputation in the United States arises from the fact, that his writings have been placed within the reach of every reader by reason of their [sic] being no restriction upon the copyright" (quoted in Davis, 67).

13. In his New York speech, Dickens claimed a right to speak on copyright, "a question of universal literary interest," on the grounds that there had not been "the faintest unworthy reference to self in any word" he had addressed to his American audience (Fielding, 28). His published preface to a series of letters from British authors supporting international copyright similarly claims that "the sentiments that I have expressed on all public occasions . . . are not merely my individual sentiments, but are . . . the opinions of the great body of British authors" (Wilkins, 250; *Letters*, vol. 3, 213). Dickens's most ferocious attempt to deliver himself from the charge of self-interest came after his return to England when the *Edinburgh Review* alleged that he had gone to America "as a kind of missionary in the cause of International Copyright." Dickens vehemently replied in a letter to the *Times* that "It occurred to me to speak (as other English travellers connected with literature have done before me) . . . when I found myself in America" (Wilkins, 239–40). For analysis of the excessive and self-indicting nature of Dickens's protestations, see Moss, *Charles Dickens' Quarrel*, 60–66 and Alexander Welsh, *From Copyright to Copperfield: The Identity of Dickens* (Cambridge, Mass.: Harvard University Press, 1987), 38.

14. The American press was unaware that Dickens carried in his "portmanteau a petition for an international copyright law, signed by all the best American writers, with Washington Irving at their head" (Letter to John Forster, February 27, 1842, *Letters*, vol. 3, 92), although the *New World* suspected that "his *business* in visiting the United States at this season of the year—a season not usually chosen by travellers for pleasure" was "to procure, or to assist in procuring, the passage, by Congress, of an International Copy-right Law" (quoted in *Letters*, vol. 3, 83). For Dickens's presentation of this petition to Henry Clay, see Frederick Saunders, "A Reminiscence in Copyright History," *Publishers' Weekly* 33 (June 30, 1888), 988.

15. Letter to John Forster, February 24, 1842, *Letters*, vol. 3, 83.

16. For Dickens's prefatory letter, see *Letters*, vol. 3, 213; for the appended letters and memorial, see *Letters*, vol. 3, 621–624.

17. See for example the response of the *Boston Courier*, quoted in *Letters*, vol. 3, 215.

18. Letter to Daniel Maclise, March 22, 1842, *Letters*, vol. 3, 154.

19. Letter to Frederick Dickens, March 22, 1842, *Letters*, vol.3, 149. See also the newspaper report quoted in a footnote, which details one barber's use of Dickens's locks, *Letters*, vol. 3, 80.

20. See *Letters*, vol. 3, 74–75, and Wilkins, 152–60.

21. March 22, 1842, *Letters*, vol. 3, 145.

22. Letter to Henry Austin, May 1, 1842, *Letters*, vol. 3, 230.

23. The difficulty of thinking about authorial agency under conditions of unauthorized reprinting is not simply Dickens's problem; it is richly reflected in the criticism, which tends to overestimate the coordination of the American newspaper press as a way of assigning blame for the failure of Dickens's tour. Jerome Meckier's account of "The Newspaper Conspiracy of 1842" both reflects and

reflects on the problem when he describes Dickens as "the victim of an informal conspiracy" (41): how much design, how much responsibility can one attach to an act of unauthorized reprinting? The experience of the editors of the Worcester *Aegis* with the circulation of an intimate personal description of Dickens is pertinent here. Chagrined that their attempt to represent their "first impression" of Dickens had "travelled further" than they "could have anticipated," and had "found its way into papers where it will be likely to meet the eye of Mr. Dickens," the editors apologized for the effect their comments might have when read out of context (quoted in Davis, 64). While Dickens might indeed have suspected collusion, encountering this oddly detailed description of his physical characteristics in local papers in many of the places he visited, the offense is attributable to a decentralized and copy-hungry press, not an organized conspiracy. Dickens demonstrates his awareness of how authorial agency could be both exerted and effaced through this medium when suggests that Cornelius Felton send copies of the British authors' letters of support to four carefully chosen newspapers; see his "Letter to C.C. Felton," April 29, 1842, *Letters*, vol. 3, 214–15. Literary critics have been less resourceful than Dickens was in responding to the challenges to authorial and editorial agency posed by the system of reprinting. Despite their impressive mastery of the texts, the chain of events, and the social conditions that structured Dickens's tour, the need to blame and to exonerate individuals frequently locks Meckier and the chief defender of the American press, Sidney Moss, into recapitulating nineteenth-century charges of newspaper conspiracy and gentlemanly collusion rather than moving beyond them.

24. See his reference to the "Carmen of Hertford [sic], who presented themselves in a body in their blue frocks, among a crowd of well-dressed ladies and gentlemen, and bad me welcome through their spokesmen. They had all read my books, and all perfectly understood them" (letter to W. C. Macready, March 22, 1842, *Letters*, vol. 3, 158–59.

25. See Dickens's letters to John S. Bartlett and John Forster, February 24, 1842, *Letters*, vol. 3, 79, 85.

26. For Dickens's epistolary account of this episode, see his letter to John Forster, January 29, 1842, *Letters*, vol. 3, 33; for its incorporation into his travel narrative, see *American Notes for General Circulation*, Arnold Goldman and John Witley, eds. (New York: Penguin Books, 1985), 74. Dickens dissolves this ambiguity and erases his own vulnerability in *Martin Chuzzlewit*, ed. P. N. Furbank (New York: Penguin Books, 1995), where these figures become newsboys hawking sensationalist and exploitative penny dailies (317–18).

27. "Dickens's American Notes for General Circulation," by Q.Q.Q. [Samuel Warren], *Blackwood's Edinburgh Magazine* 52 (December 1842): 783–801; 787.

28. Although appearing in many twentieth-century editions, this chapter was first printed posthumously in Forster's biography. See John Forster, *The Life of Charles Dickens* (London: Chapman and Hall, 1872), vol. 1, 304–7.

29. See Dickens's letter to John Chapman, where he exclaims: "I have never in my life been so shocked and disgusted, or made so sick and sore at heart, as I have been by the treatment I have received here . . . in reference to the International Copyright," February 24, 1842, *Letters*, vol. 3, 76.

30. *From Copyright to Copperfield*, 43–73.

31. Forster, *Life of Charles Dickens*, vol. 1, 303.

32. *American Notes for General Circulation* (New York: Harper & Brothers, 1842).

33. *American Notes for General Circulation*, *New World* Extra Series, Numbers 32, 33 (New York, 1842), 47.

34. For a descriptive list of American reprints of *American Notes*, see Peter S. Bracher, "The Early American Editions of *American Notes*: Their Priority and Circulation," *Papers of the Bibliographical Society of America* 69 (1975): 365–76. Strikingly, British and American editions of a satirical response to Dickens's text preserve these differences in format. Compare the Harper edition of Henry Wood's pseudonymous *Change for the American Notes: In Letters from London to New York* (New York: Harper & Brothers, 1843), which was printed as an eighty-eight-page, double-columned octavo so that it could be bound along with their edition of *American Notes* as Volume 14 of the Harper's Library, to the edition published in London by Wiley & Putnam, in which generous margins and larger type spread the same text across 392 pages.

35. For an account of the difficulties inherent in navigating an economy that relied on a nonuniform paper currency, see David M. Henkin, *City Reading: Written Words and Public Spaces in Antebellum New York* (New York: Columbia University Press, 1998), 137–65.

36. In *American Notes*, Dickens refers to the now empty Bank of the United States as "the Tomb of many fortunes; the Great Catacomb of investment" (145), and uses "that ill-fated Cairo on the Mississippi"—Darius Holbrook's spurious bond scheme that lured British investors on promises of substantial returns from frontier development—as an example of "the bad effects such gross deceits must have when they exploded, in generating a want of confidence abroad, and discouraging foreign investment" (286, see also 215). For the now discredited biographical theory that Dickens's tour was motivated by speculation in the fraudulent Cairo City and Canal Company, see J. F. Snyder, "Charles Dickens in Illinois," *Journal of the Illinois State Historical Society* (1910): 7–22. "[T]his dismal Cairo" (215) is the model for Eden in *Martin Chuzzlewit*.

37. Andrew Jackson, "Veto Message" July 10, 1832, in *A Compilation of the Messages and Papers of the Presidents*, ed. James D. Richardson (New York: Bureau of National Literature, 1897), vol. 3, 1139–1154, 1154. Strikingly, Jackson's interpretation of the limitations of Congressional power in his veto message mentions "two subjects only" on which the Constitution grants Congress "the power to grant exclusive privileges or monopolies"—patents and copyrights (1147). While the issue of international copyright does not seem to have worried Jackson, his opposition to exclusive measures that benefited individuals at the expense of the public and his concern about foreign control over American banking were critical positions that were drawn on by those who opposed extending copyrights to foreign authors.

38. *Gold, Greenbacks, and the Constitution* (Berryville: The George Edward Durell Foundation, 1991), 14–17. For an account of Congressional debates over the issue of Treasury notes, see John Jay Knox, *United States Notes: A History of the*

Various Issues of Paper Money by the Government of the United States (New York: Charles Scribner's Sons, 1988), 40–62. I am indebted to Richard Doty of the National Museum of American History for helping me to identify *Brother Jonathan's* treasury note and for calling my attention to the importance of these financial instruments. An illustration of the note on which *Brother Jonathan's* parody is based may be found in Gene Hessler, *The Comprehensive Catalog of U.S. Paper Money* (Port Clinton, Ohio: BNR Press, 1992), 58.

39. Jackson, "Veto Message," 1144.

40. Jackson, "Veto Message," 1153.

41. Other American replies to Dickens's narrative also insist on his fundamental misunderstanding of the nature of American government. See in particular Thomas G. Cary, *Letter to a Lady in France on the Supposed Failure of a National Bank, the Supposed Delinquency of the National Government, the Debts of the Several States, and Repudiation; with Answers to Enquiries Concerning the Books of Capt. Marryat and Mr. Dickens* (Boston: Benjamin H. Greene, 1844), in which the author, in the guise of an American lady corresponding to an expatriate friend, offers a simplified account of the distribution of powers as a way of clearing the nation of responsibility for state-level debts. Cary defends the federal government's lack of jurisdiction in state affairs and compares the European suggestion that the U.S. government secure the debts of its repudiating states to asking "Queen Victoria in England to assume a few of the powers of the Pope, in order to settle the affairs of Ireland" (25).

42. For a reading of this section of *American Notes* as an example of the "streetwise sketch produced by the *flâneur*" (12), see William Sharpe, "A Pig upon the Town: Charles Dickens in New York," *Nineteenth-Century Prose* 23, no. 2 (Fall 1996): 12–24.

43. See letters to John Forster and Charles Sumner, March 13, 1842, *Letters*, vol. 3, 126–31.

44. See, for example, Dickens's evident pleasure in staying at a familiar hotel in Cincinnati (230), and his great relief whenever he can construct his narrative around a "Passage Out" and a "Passage Home" (144, 226, 261).

45. Dickens's description of Cairo, Illinois, is typical insofar as it insists on comparative and superlative degrees of bleakness without providing terms of comparison that would distinguish it from any other place: "At length, on the morning of the third day, we arrived at a spot so much more desolate than any we had yet beheld, that the forlornest places we had passed were, in comparison with it, full of interest" (215). But Dickens is spared from retrospectively re-imagining these places by continued lateral movement.

46. See "Representing Slavery in Nineteenth-Century Britain: The Anxiety of Non/Fictional Authorship in Charles Dickens' *American Notes* and William Brown's *Clotel*," in *Images of America: Through the European Looking Glass*, ed. William L. Chew III (Brussels: VUB University Press, 1997), 125–40. Noting the "literary inversion of Dickens's real-life priorities," Fabi argues that in Dickens's narrative, slavery becomes "the very visible, but nevertheless coded, literary signifier of that discontent with the United States which had initially coalesced around the (literarily invisible) issue of copyright" (132). I would alter her formula to emphasize the

instrumentality of slavery, not the substitution of one issue for the other. Slavery does not stand in for copyright so much as serve as an opportunity for Dickens to intervene in the culture of reprinting.

47. See Louise H. Johnson, "The Source of the Chapter on Slavery in Dickens's *American Notes,*" *American Literature* 14, no. 4 (January 1943): 427–30.

48. *American Slavery As It Is: Testimony of a Thousand Witnesses* (New York: Arno Press, 1968), [iv], [iii].

49. Dickens's attempt to establish a firm relationship between frontier violence and the institution of slavery continues to drift back to scenes of reading: "Do we not know that the worst deformity and ugliness of slavery are at once the cause and the effect of the reckless license taken by these freeborn outlaws? Do we not know that the man who has been born and bred among its wrongs; who has seen in his childhood husbands obliged at the word of command to flog their wives; women, indecently compelled to hold up their own garments that men might lay the heavier stripes upon their legs, driven and harried by brutal overseers in their time of travail, and becoming mothers on the field of toil, under the very lash itself; *who has read in youth and seen his virgin sisters read*, descriptions of runaway men and women, and their disfigured persons, which could not be published elsewhere, of so much stock upon a farm, or at a show of beasts:—do we not know that that man, whenever his wrath is kindled up, will be a brutal savage?" (283; emphasis mine). The violent American in this passage is above all a voyeur, an "overseer" both of the degradation of slave women and of his sisters' access to forbidden knowledge, a man made savage by seeing and reading.

50. This is a loose enough chain of cause and effect to implicate violence in England: "When knives are dawn by Englishmen in conflict let it be said and known: 'We owe this change to Republican Slavery'" (284).

51. *Southern Literary Messenger* 9 (January 1843): 63.

52. "Dickensonianna," *Southern Quarterly Review* 4 (October 1843): 306.

53. For the attempt to censor Dickens's text and its emergence as an abolitionist cause célèbre, see Sidney P. Moss, "South Carolina Contemplates Banning *American Notes*" in *American Episodes Involving Charles Dickens*, Sidney P. Moss and Carolyn J. Moss, eds., (Troy: The Whitston Publishing Company, 1999), 20–27.

54. *New World*, December 17, 1843, quoted in Moss, "South Carolina Contemplates," 22.

55. "The Newspaper Literature of America," *Foreign Quarterly Review* 30 (October 1843): 202.

56. See for example, Forster's discussion of the *Louisville Gazette*'s publication of charges that Daniel Webster had sexually harassed the wife of one of his clerks. Not only does the footnote begin to take over the page, Forster's selections from the *Gazette* suggest that the paper used the scandal to launch a critique of political patronage that is substantially no different than Forster's. Though Webster felt threatened enough to publish affidavits vigorously denying the "Anecdote of Daniel Webster," the ridiculous seduction line attributed to him in this story—"Madam, this is one of the prerogatives of my office"—and the *Gazette*'s extended critique of his misuse of official power suggest that the sexual scandal was a figure for and a means to address political abuses. See Forster, "Newspaper Literature," 216–19.

57. Americans' suspicions of Dickens's authorship were seemingly confirmed by his reference to this essay as "an able and perfectly truthful article" (289) in a footnote at the end of *American Notes*. For the newspaper scandal precipitated by this reference and the confidence with which Americans identified Dickens as "the author of that Review" (40), see Moss, *Charles Dickens' Quarrel*, 15–56. For the scholarly attribution of the article to Forster, see Moss, 325.

58. Forster, *Life of Charles Dickens*, vol. 1, 285.

59. See Moss, *American Episodes*, 28–52.

60. Welsh argues that *Martin Chuzzlewit* surpasses most books "in self-knowledge, once allowance has been made for its astonishing indirections" (15). According to Welsh, Dickens's multiple projections onto disparate characters "explains the special intensity and often hilarious incoherence of the novel" (45). For Dickens's projection onto Pecksniff, see 25–28; for his identification with the elder and younger Martin Chuzzlewits and with the murderer, Jonas Chuzzlewit, see 45–58.

61. *Commissioned Spirits: The Shaping of Social Motion in Dickens, Carlyle, Melville, and Hawthorne* (1979; reprint New York: Columbia University Press, 1989), 78.

62. That Nadgett is a figure for the serial novelist is particularly apparent in the scene where he conveys Jonas's secret to his employer, insisting on handing over his notes in installments and "[keeping] pace with the emotions of the reader" (666). Gerhard Joseph expands on Arac's analysis with an account of Dickens's "uneasiness about the stance of overview" (20); see his "Labyrinth and Library," *Dickens Studies Annual* 15 (New York: AMS Press, 1986): 1–22. Joseph's account of Dickens's ambivalence toward the elder Martin Chuzzlewit, the "arch manipulator of the plot's central motion" (16), applies as well to the morally more suspect Nadgett: the poison may yet be in the system.

63. Arac's analysis of Dickens's fascination with the unconscious co-presence of urban strangers anticipates Benedict Anderson's account in *Imagined Communities* (1983) of the importance of the spatiotemporal organization of the novel to the idea of nationhood. If, according to Anderson, the novel and the newspaper provide "the technical means for 'representing' the *kind* of imagined community that is the nation" (25), Dickens's reconception of urban space as an alternative to the haphazard simultaneity of American newspapers suggests signal differences in the kinds of communities that can be imagined through these media. In representing London in *Martin Chuzzlewit*, Dickens shifts away from the energetic but leveling disorder typical of the American newspaper, to the tense but undisclosed proximity of strangers set within a socioscape that promises to restore a deferred but implicit principle of order.

64. Gerhard Joseph similarly reads this scene as providing evidence of the complexity of Dickens's displacement of the copyright question into the pages of his novel. Joseph calls attention to the way in which Dickens condemns both Pecksniff's fraud and Martin's self-righteousness as he storms about exclaiming "I invented it. I did it all" (625). Joseph focuses on the way in which architecture in the novel becomes a language for addressing both the problem of unauthorized copying and the egotism of absolute claims to ownership. I would add only that it is the architecture of the novel—closely aligned, as Joseph notes, with the

disjointed and obscure urban space from which Mark and Martin first view Pecksniff—that allows for the ambivalent staging of this disclosure and for Mark's assurance to Martin and the reader that "it'll all come right in the end, sir; it'll all come right" (626). See Joseph, "Charles Dickens, International Copyright, and the Discretionary Silence of *Martin Chuzzlewit*," in *The Construction of Authorship: Textual Appropriation in Law and Literature*, ed. Martha Woodmansee and Peter Jaszi (Durham, N.C.: Duke University Press, 1994), 259–70.

65. Kate Field, *Pen Photographs of Charles Dickens's Readings: Taken from Life*, ed. Carolyn J. Moss (Troy, N.Y.: Whitston Publishing Company, 1998), 12. For a "Schedule of Dickens's Readings in America," see 96–99.

66. *Boston Daily Journal*, December 3, 1867, quoted in Moss, *Charles Dickens's Quarrel*, 271–72.

67. For a detailed account of the American press response to Dickens's 1868 tour, see Moss, *Charles Dickens's Quarrel*, 232–324.

68. For this arrangement, in which Ticknor & Fields promised to pay Dickens a royalty for each volume sold and to import and sell Chapman and Hall's "Illustrated Library Edition," see Moss, *Charles Dickens's Quarrel*, 213–15. Moss usefully documents the angry reaction of T. B. Peterson & Brothers to this arrangement. T. B. Peterson had been paying the Harper Brothers for access to advance sheets that the Harpers obtained by sending regular payments to Dickens. Notwithstanding Dickens's pride in the honorable nature of his agreement with Ticknor & Fields, one newspaper likened the arrangement to "selling that which was already sold" (217).

69. Advertisement, inside cover, *American Notes for General Circulation* (Boston: Ticknor & Fields, 1867).

Chapter 4

1. New York *Evening Mirror*, November 28, 1844, 3.

2. He may also be parrying her reference to *The Comedy of Errors*, in which Emelia is the mother of the twin gentleman, both named Antipholus, who are the masters of the two Dromios. Emelia re-appears in the last scene of the play to unscramble the plot's many confusions (Vi, 341–45).

3. Welby's poem was first published in book form in *Poems* (Boston: A. Tompkins, 1845), but likely circulated in the *Louisville Journal* and in a number of exchange papers before then. "The Little Step-Son" is most easily found in Rufus Wilmot Griswold's *The Female Poets of America* (Philadelphia: Carey and Hart, 1849), 331–32.

4. See for example, Felicia Hemans, "The Chamois Hunter's Love" and Elizabeth Barrett Browning's "Felicia Hemans" in *Victorian Women Poets: An Anthology*, ed. Angela Leighton and Margaret Reynolds (Cambridge: Blackwell, 1995), 18–19, 67–68.

5. See Griswold, 331–32.

6. Poe first published "Lenore," a revision of his early poem, "A Paean," in James Russell Lowell's short-lived Boston magazine, *The Pioneer* (February 1843):

60–61. Thomas Ollive Mabbott speculates that Poe published the relineated version shortly after he moved to New York in April, 1844, possibly in Mordecai Noah's *Sunday Times*. But scholars have found no original for the Jackson *Advocate* copy; neither have they been able to locate the relevant issue of the *Advocate* itself. See Mabbott's *The Collected Works of Edgar Allan Poe*, vol. 1 (Cambridge, Mass.: Belknap Press, 1969), 332–33.

7. See Mabbott, *Collected Works*, vol. 1, 356, and Eliza Richards, " 'The Poetess' and Poe's Performance of the Feminine," *Arizona Quarterly* 55, no. 2 (Summer 1999): 1–29.

8. "The Raven," l. 10, Edgar Allan Poe, *Poetry and Tales*, ed. Patrick F. Quinn (New York: Literary Classics of the United States, 1984), 81. References to this reader's edition will be noted by page number in the text, except where revisions or alterations introduced in the history of a text's reprinting require reference to Mabbott's scholarly edition.

9. "What Is an Author?" 101–20, 109.

10. For Poe's claim that his composition of "The Raven" began with the choice of "the long *o* as the most sonorous vowel, in connection with *r* as the most producible consonant," see "The Philosophy of Composition," *Essays and Reviews*, ed. G. R. Thompson (New York: Literary Classics of the United States, 1984), 18. Burton Pollin speculates that Poe's "Lenore" is directly indebted to Frances Sargent Osgood's "Leonor" in "Poe and Frances Osgood, as Linked through 'Lenore,' " *Mississipi Quarterly* 46, no. 2 (1993): 185–97. Mabbott, too, mentions a number of popular poems to which Poe might have been indebted, including Margaret Davidson's "Lenore" and Felicia Hemans's "Forest Sanctuary" (*Collected Works*, vol. 1, 330–31). My point, however, is that these texts are now visible to us only as precursors of *Poe's* poem. For a bold attempt to engineer a critical context that would enable us to read like Welby and Willis, that is, with a rich sense of the imbrication of Poe's poetic practice with that of the women poets of his day, see Eliza Richards, " 'The Poetess,' " and "Lyric Telegraphy: Women Poets, Spiritualist Poetics, and the 'Phantom Voice' of Poe," *Yale Journal of Criticism* 12, no. 2 (1999): 269–94. Quinn selects the long-line version of "Lenore" for publication in *Poetry and Tales*, 68–69; the Pindaric version can be found in Mabbott, *Collected Works*, vol. 1, 334–36.

11. For essays that read "The Philosophy of Composition" as a restaging of Poe's concerns in "The Raven," see Debra Fried, "Repetition, Refrain, and Epitaph," *ELH* 53, no. 3 (Fall 1986): 615–39, Leland S. Person, Jr. "Poe's Composition of Philosophy: Reading and Writing 'The Raven,' " *Arizona Quarterly* 46, no. 3 (Fall 1990): 1–15, and Barbara Johnson, "Strange Fits: Poe and Wordsworth on the Nature of Poetic Language," in *The American Face of Edgar Allan Poe*, ed. Shawn Rosenheim and Stephen Rachman (Baltimore: Johns Hopkins University Press, 1995), 89–99.

12. Letter from N. P. Willis to George Pope Morris, October 17, 1858, quoted in Dwight Thomas and David K. Jackson, eds., *The Poe Log: A Documentary Life of Edgar Allan Poe, 1809–1849* (Boston: G.K. Hall, 1987), 473.

13. See "Marginalia," December 1844, reprinted in Thompson, ed., *Essays and Reviews*, 1354.

14. "The Aristidean," *Broadway Journal* (May 3, 1845), reprinted in *Collected Writings of Edgar Allan Poe*, ed. Burton Pollin, vol. 3, part 1 (New York: Gordian Press, 1986), 108.

15. Whitman scholars will recognize "Richard Parker's Widow," which was identified as the work of "Walter Whitman" with the addition of the initials "W.W." in the index of the first volume of the journal.

16. Though the review was published in April 1845, it was not attributed to Poe until the initials E.A.P were affixed to its title in the index to vol. 1 of the *Aristidean*, published no sooner than December 1845 when the final issue of the volume was printed. A notice in the New York *Evening Mirror*, April 29, 1845, assumed that, given the anonymity of the review, the journal's editor, Thomas Dunn English, would be held responsible for it.

17. *Poe's Literary Battles: The Critic in the Context of His Literary Milieu* (Carbondale: Southern Illinois University Press, 1963), 177. Biographers and critics are divided in their treatment of Poe's authorship of the review: Arthur Hobson Quinn restricts his analysis of the Longfellow War to the articles that appeared in the *Broadway Journal* (*Edgar Allan Poe: A Critical Biography* [1941; reprint, Baltimore: Johns Hopkins University Press, 1998], 454–45), but later attributes the *Aristidean* review to Poe (474). Kenneth Silverman deems the review a "close collaboration," based in part on the use of such words as "purloin and purloining." *Edgar A. Poe: Mournful and Never-Ending Remembrance* (New York: HarperCollins, 1991), 253. The editors of *The Poe Log*, however, are unwilling to attribute the review to Poe, describing it as "written by the editor Thomas Dunn English, apparently after some consultation with Poe" (529).

18. Thompson places this review at the end of the "Little Longfellow War" sequence in Thompson, ed., *Essays and Reviews*, 759–77. Leonard Cassuto relies on the *Aristidean* review to represent the entire series in his *Edgar Allan Poe: Literary Theory and Criticism* (New York: Dover Publications, 1999), 84–99.

19. For Poe's disavowal of editorship of the *Aristidean*, see the *Broadway Journal*, March 29, 1845, reprinted in Pollin, ed. *Collected Writings*, vol. 3, part 1, 69. For a general account of Poe's and English's collaboration see Sidney P. Moss, *Poe's Major Crisis: His Libel Suit and New York's Literary World* (Durham, N.C.: Duke University Press, 1970), 26–28.

20. The narrative of their falling out, which reads like a bizarre enactment of the interlaced plots of "William Wilson" and "The Purloined Letter," gets staged in public in the summer of 1846, but their relationship begins to unravel as early as December 1845 with the demise of the *Broadway Journal* and English's involvement in the scandal of Mrs. Ellett's missing letters. Strikingly, the public declaration that seems most to irk English is Poe's allegation that their relationship is wholly mediated by print: "I do not personally know Mr. English" (Moss, *Poe's Major Crisis*, 35). For summaries, documentation, and analysis of this episode see Moss and Joseph Moriarty, *A Literary Tomahawking: The Libel Action of Edgar Allan Poe vs. Thomas Dunn English* (self-published, 1963).

21. William Doyle Hull, "A Canon of the Critical Works of Edgar Allan Poe" (Ph.D. dissertation, University of Virginia, 1941), iii–iv.

22. The two largest sections of Thompson's edition, "Reviews of British and

Continental Authors" and "Reviews of American Authors and American Literature," are arranged alphabetically by author's name, suggesting the triumph of
the values of an author-centered literary nationalism. But it is not at all clear, for
instance, that Poe's review of the American reprint of the anonymously published
Peter Snook, A Tale of the City; Follow Your Nose; and other Strange Tales, By the
Author of "Chartley," the "Invisible Gentleman," &c. &c., a collection of magazine
essays that Poe inferred were written by a number of authors, fits comfortably
under either its national or its authorial designation.

23. *Edgar Allan Poe and the Masses: The Political Economy of Literature in Antebellum America* (Princeton, N.J.: Princeton University Press, 1999), 113. William
Doyle Hull marked the "Paulding-Drayton" review as "definitely not Poe's" (3),
and J. V. Ridgely made the case against its inclusion in the canon in "The Authorship of the 'Paulding-Drayton Review,'" *Poe Studies Association Newsletter* 20, no. 2
(Fall 1992). Whalen reprises and extends these arguments in his chapter "Average
Racism," 111–46.

24. It should not go without saying that I am entirely indebted to Mabbott,
and to Poe scholars such as Burton Pollin, Dwight Thomas, David K. Jackson, and
Kent Ljungquist, who have compiled an excellent working record of the many print
vehicles in which authorized and unauthorized versions of Poe's texts appeared.
My argument rather, is with historicist critics who take this work as given, ignoring the disorderly and multiple publication histories of Poe's texts in favor of the
chronology of composition established by Mabbott. Kevin Hayes has recently
argued for the importance of antebellum print genres to understanding Poe's work
in *Poe and the Printed Word* (New York: Oxford University Press, 2000).

25. Echoing a longstanding critical tradition, Terence Whalen associates
Poe's poetry with the romantic prehistory of his discovery that the logic of capitalism required him to market his writing to a mass audience. See *Edgar Allan Poe
and the Masses*, 9.

26. Thomas Ollive Mabbott's facsimile edition of *Al Aaraaf*, (New York: Facsimile Text Society, 1933), 71, makes clear the potential double reference of the note.

27. Mabbott notes that Poe's reference is to the song, "Mary," in Chapter 12
of Scott's *The Pirate* (1822). See *Collected Works*, vol. 2, 124.

28. "The Authority Effect: Poe and the Politics of Reputation in the Pre-
Industry of American Publishing," *Arizona Quarterly* 49, no. 3 (Autumn 1993):
1–19, 6.

29. "The Stout Gentleman" is a dense figure for Anglo-American literary
commerce. Irving first introduced this elusive character in a story-telling sequence
in *Bracebridge Hall* (1822), where his tale serves as an example of "that mysterious
and romantic narrative so greedily sought after at the present day" (*Bracebridge
Hall, Tales of a Traveller*, and *The Alhambra* [New York: Literary Classics of the
United States, 1991], 60). In *Tales of a Traveller* (1824) Irving informs readers that
"the author of Waverley" has indicated "that he was himself the Stout Gentleman
alluded to" (389). In including "the stout gentleman" in his group of literati, Poe
invokes Irving's and Scott's public declarations of mutual admiration, pronouncements that were conducted with coy disavowal of personal intimacy across a figure for the elusiveness of the author's public persona: the stout gentleman is a

man "of more than ordinary dimensions" (389) who is glimpsed only at the point of his disappearance from the scene. For Scott's identification with this figure, see "Prefatory Letter to *Peveril of the Peak*," *The Prefaces to the Waverley Novels*, ed. Mark A. Weinstein (Lincoln: University of Nebraska Press, 1978), 58–69, 62.

30. For the publication history of this tale, see Mabbott, *Collected Works*, vol. 2, 51–82. For the formative influence of *Blackwood's Edinburgh Magazine* on Poe, see Michael Allen, *Poe and the British Magazine Tradition* (New York: Oxford University Press, 1969). Herbert G. Eldridge discusses the American popularity of reprinted editions of Moore's early poetry in "The American Republication of Thomas Moore's *Epistles, Odes, and Other Poems*: An Early Version of the Reprinting 'Game,'" *Papers of the Bibliographic Society of America* 62, no. 2 (1968): 199–205.

31. My reading of Poe's narrative posture in these tales differs from that of Kenneth Dauber, who usefully distinguishes Poe's favored modes of burlesque and hoax from satire and parody: "Poe does not ridicule his audience's faith so much as he plays upon it, takes advantage of it. He does not, as in satire or parody, expose its assumptions, but exaggerates them, taking the assumptions themselves as his medium." *The Idea of Authorship in America: Democratic Poetics from Franklin to Melville* (Madison: University of Wisconsin Press, 1990), 135. Whereas Dauber maintains that Poe's turn to the burlesque is proof of his will to preempt and dominate his reader, I argue that Poe's immersion in the genres he mocks is a rhetorical strategy that responds to the American popularity of reprinted British fiction. To work a change on Dauber's damning phrase, I would maintain that the "conceptualization of others as those who are to be stolen from" (135) is not exclusive to Poe but a cultural norm; moreover, it is a form of relation to culture that by definition cannot be mastered.

32. Michael Allen's study of the influence of *Blackwood's Magazine* on Poe's writing stresses Poe's adoption of the hoaxing and scandal-generating tactics of the early volumes, arguing that Poe's *Blackwood's* persona enabled him to enact a sense of superiority to his audience. Allen fails to note, however, how readily available to middle-class Americans *Blackwood's* was at mid-century, both in cheap reprint editions, and in the form of individual articles circulating in eclectic magazines. For example, the first 12 issues of *Littell's Living Age* (May 25–August 3,1844) contain at least 12 excerpts from *Blackwood's*, ranging from a sober essay on "The British Fleet" (No. 2) to trifles such as "Hair Cutting" (No. 9), and romantic historical tales such as "The Heart of the Bruce" (No. 12).

33. "Exordium to Critical Notices," Thompson, ed., *Essays and Reviews*, 1027–28. For an earlier statement of this philosophy, which links European excellence in "Polite Literature" to the existence of a substantial leisure class and to institutions such as "magnificently endowed Academies," see Poe's review "Joseph Rodman Drake—Fitz-Greene Halleck," *Southern Literary Messenger* (April 1836), in Thompson, ed., *Essays and Reviews*, 505.

34. *Broadway Journal* (October 4, 1845), reprinted in Pollin, ed., *Collected Writings*, vol. 3, part 1, 273. Poe's complicated critique of literary nationalism, which deftly sidesteps the question of international copyright by coming out in favor of an independent national criticism, can also be found in Thompson, ed., *Essays and Reviews*, 1076–78.

35. "Poe's Alpha Poem: The Title of 'Al Aaraaf,'" *Poe Studies* 22, no. 2 (December 1989): 35–39.

36. See *The Poe Log*, 282.

37. Poe publishes this version of the poem anonymously in *Burton's Gentleman's Magazine* (October 1839): 75. For the history of its publication in multiple versions, see Mabbott, ed., *Collected Works*, vol. 1, 233–36. For the contrary argument that both Poe and antebellum culture clearly distinguished between the manuscript and print circulation of poems, see Hayes, *Poe and the Printed Word*, 17–29.

38. Although Mabbott acknowledges that it is impossible to be certain whether the personally addressed "To Marie Louise" or the depersonalized "To _____ _____ _____" was published first, Quinn chooses to reprint the more general of the two versions, maintaining the widest possible field of reference for the poem's apostrophic terminus: "With thy dear name as text, though bidden by thee, / I cannot write– I cannot speak or think, / . . . Gazing, entranced, adown the gorgeous vista, / . . . To where the prospect terminates—*thee only*." See Mabbott, ed., *Collected Works*, vol. 1, 405–9, and Quinn, ed., *Poetry and Tales*, 88.

39. *Burton's Gentleman's Magazine* (August 1839), 99. Though Poe attaches his name to the publication of "To Ianthe in Heaven" in the July issue of *Burton's*, and will publish "To _____" anonymously in the October edition, this version of "To the River _____" falls somewhere in between authorial endorsement and omission of the signature, marked only by the initial "P."

40. As Mabbott notes, Byron's "Stanzas to the Po" clearly provided Poe with the rhetorical structure on which "To the River _____" is based. Poe's poem can be read as a response to Byron's question to the river, dramatizing Poe's narcissistic recognition that his own "image deeply lies" within Bryon's object of address, and his strategic realization that, like the river in Byron's poem, Poe's poetry might serve to mediate the relation between Byron and his female readers. Byron asks of the Po:

> What if thy deep and ample stream should be
>   A mirror of my heart, where she may read
> The thousand thoughts I now betray to thee,
>   Wild as thy wave, and headlong as thy speed!

Poe's reply raises the ante by comparing the river to an admirer—in this version, the poet himself—who returns the lady's gaze. While Byron's poem offers up the river/ poem as a "mirror" of the poet's heart, Poe's reflects back the image of the woman reader. For Poe's shift to a third-person identification of the owner of "the heart" in ll. 11 and 13, see Mabbott, ed., *Collected Works*, vol. 1, 135.

41. A number of Poe's "extravaganzas" parody their narrators' residual attachment to genealogy despite their inability to provide a legitimate account of origins. See for example, "Lionizing," where the narrator asserts: "my name, I believe, is Robert Jones, and I was born somewhere in the city of Fum-Fudge" (212); and "The Man That Was Used Up," which begins: "I cannot just now remember when or where I first made the acquaintance of that truly fine-looking fellow, Brevet Brigadier General John A. B. C. Smith" (307).

42. Compare Poe's similar invocation of "Romance" in "The Visionary": "It was at Venice, beneath the covered archway there called the 'Ponte di Sospiri,' that met me for the third or fourth time the person of whom I speak. It is, however, with a confused recollection that I recall to mind the circumstances of that meeting. Yet I remember—ah! How should I forget?—the deep midnight, the Bridge of Sighs, the beauty of woman and the Demon of Romance who stalked up and down the narrow canal" (Mabbott, ed., *Collected Works*, vol. 2, 151). The slippage between Poe's title character, the visionary, and his personification of genre was perhaps a little too evident here. In revising the tale in 1845, Poe made it less likely that the reader will mistake his personification for "the person of whom I speak," referring to "the Genius of Romance *that* stalked up and down the narrow canal" (151; emphasis mine).

43. *The Letters of Edgar Allan Poe*, ed. John Ward Ostrom (New York: Gordian Press, 1966), vol. 1, 57–58.

44. Terence Whalen reads this letter as an early instance of what would become a well-developed theory of effect in "The Philosophy of Composition." In making this connection, however, he overstates Poe's investment in his control over publication. In quoting the letter, Whalen elides Poe's reference to the suspension of authority across reprinting. See *Edgar Allan Poe and the Masses*, 7–9.

45. As Dayan writes, "Poe takes the mouth of a lady and turns it into the mind of a man." *Fables of Mind: An Inquiry into Poe's Fiction* (New York: Oxford University Press, 1987), 136. See also Whalen, 8.

46. The *Lady's Book*, in which "The Visionary" first appeared, was at the time known as the *Monthly Magazine of Belles-Lettres and the Arts*. *Graham's Lady's and Gentleman's Magazine*, which Poe edited in 1841–42, began life as *The Casket and Philadelphia Monthly Magazine, Embracing Every Department of Literature: Embellished with Engravings, the Quarterly Fashions, and Music* (1839–40) and circulated under the titles *Graham's Magazine of Literature and Art* (1843), *Graham's American Monthly Magazine of Literature, Art and Fashion* (1843–55), and *Graham's Illustrated Magazine of Literature, Romance, Art, and Fashion* (1856–58), all the while trying to hold off the competition provided by monthlies such as *Sartain's Union Magazine of Literature and Art* (1849–52)

47. "Arthur Gordon Pym and the Novel Narrative of Edgar Allan Poe," *Nineteenth-Century Literature* (1992): 349–61. For the "planned absurdity" of the passages on stowage in *Pym*, see Burton Pollin, "Notes and Comments," *Collected Writings*, vol. 1, 251–52.

48. "Poe's Secret Autobiography," in *The American Renaissance Reconsidered*, ed. Walter Benn Michaels and Donald Pease (Baltimore: Johns Hopkins University Press, 1985), 58–89, 82.

49. See Baudelaire's "New Notes on Edgar Poe" (1857), in which he argues that "in order to encourage credulity, to delight the stupidity of his contemporaries [Poe] has stressed human sovereignty most emphatically and has very ingeniously fabricated hoaxes flattering to the pride of *modern man*" (124). Reprinted in Lois Hyslop and Francis E. Hyslop, Jr., *Baudelaire on Poe* (State College, Penn.: Bald Eagle Press, 1952), 119–44.

50. "Poe's Other Double: The Reader in the Fiction," *Criticism* 24, no. 4 (1982): 341–61, 342.

51. See *Reading at the Social Limit: Affect, Mass Culture, and Edgar Allan Poe* (Stanford, Calif.: Stanford University Press, 1995), especially 174–223.

52. My reading here goes against the grain of a longstanding tradition in Poe studies of understanding romantic irony as Poe's tool for sifting a select group of discerning readers out of a mass-cultural audience. Major texts in this tradition include G. R. Thompson, *Poe's Fiction: Romantic Irony in the Gothic Tales* (Madison: University of Wisconsin Press, 1973) and Dennis Eddings, ed., *The Naiad Voice: Essays on Poe's Satiric Hoaxing* (Port Washington, N.Y.: Associated Faculty Press, 1983). Recent critics draw on this tradition in their focus on the hoax and the crypt as synechdoches for Poe's writing. As interpretive models, both hoax and crypt call attention to hidden and deferred meanings; both also recuperate generic or tonal indeterminacy through the delayed but exaggerated return of the author. For the elaboration of the hoax as a master-trope for Poe's writing, see Louis Renza, "Poe's Secret Autobiography," and Terence Whalen, *Edgar Allan Poe and the Masses*. For Renza's reconsideration of Poe's strategies of withholding as socially significant, not privative, see "Poe and the Issue of American Privacy," in *A Historical Guide to Edgar Allan Poe* (New York: Oxford University Press, 2001), 167–88. For the model of the crypt, see Joseph Riddel, *Purloined Letters*, and Shawn Rosenheim, *The Cryptographic Imagination: Secret Writing from Edgar Allan Poe to the Internet* (Baltimore: Johns Hopkins University Press, 1997). Rosenheim provocatively associates Poe's experiments in secret writing with characteristically twentieth-century modes of interpretation.

53. *United States Magazine and Democratic Review* (May 1845): 455–60. Duyckinck wrote this piece shortly after he became literary editor of the *Democratic Review*, giving it the status of a statement on editorial policy. See Perry Miller, *The Raven and the Whale*, 130.

54. Putting principles into practice, Poe uses the occasion of Duyckinck's article to re-circulate an old critique of an American reprint of *Peter Snook*, an anonymously published grab bag of British magazine fiction. Poe initially justifies this review of a reprint of "English light literature" on the grounds that it offers a model of "the brief and piquant article, slightly exaggerated in all its proportions" for the emulation of American magazinists (Thompson, ed., *Essays and Reviews*, 189). Poe added an extended disquisition on magazine writing to the review when he republished it in the *Broadway Journal*. See Pollin, ed., *Collected Writings*, vol. 3, part 1, 136–43.

55. Duyckinck complains that American magazines have failed to provide "a keen, just, appreciative character of our worthies," abandoning the task to British authors: "Here is a field where the genuine writers of the country should come to one another's help and not leave the best characters of our authors and statesmen, as is the fact at present, to be written abroad. If we wish to learn anything of our great men, beyond of course the fact that they are *great*, we must go to Miss Martineau and the foreign reviews" (459).

56. Justifying the book organization of his diverse tales in terms of a Lockean faculty psychology seems to have been a long-standing idea of Poe's. See his 1836 letter to Harrison Hall, sometime publisher of the Philadelphia miscellany, *The Port-Folio*, in which he refers to his evolving manuscript under the title "On the Imaginative Faculties." *Letters*, vol. 1, 103.

57. For an early example of Poe's reluctance to be identified with a particular style, see his "Preface" to *Tales of the Grotesque and Arabesque* (1840), reprinted in Quinn, ed., *Poetry and Tales*, 129–30. Here Poe strives to define a mode of "unity" that would not be taken by readers as a proxy for his consciousness, thereby limiting the range of future writing. Poe distances himself from the stylistic consistency suggested by his title through the unsettling use of the subjunctive: "The epithets 'Grotesque' and 'Arabesque' will be found to indicate with sufficient precision the prevalent tenor of the tales here published. But from the fact that, during a period of some two or three years, I have written five-and-twenty short stories whose general character may be so briefly defined, it cannot be fairly inferred—at all events it is not truly inferred—that I have, for this species of writing, any inordinate, or indeed any peculiar taste or prepossession. I may have written with an eye to this republication in volume form, and may, therefore, have desired to preserve, as far as a certain point, a certain unity of design. This is indeed, the fact; and it may even happen that, in this manner, I shall never compose anything again" (129).

58. Thompson, ed., *Essays and Reviews*, 670.

59. The class privilege which undergirds this refusal is strongly marked in the narrative structure of "Hyperion" and erupts into discourse in an early scene, where Longfellow's hero proposes the capacious temporality of literary scholarship as a corrective to the urgencies of literary journalism: "perhaps the greatest lesson which the lives of literary men teach us, is told in a single word: Wait!—Every man must patiently bide his time. He must wait. More particularly in lands, like my native land, where the pulse of life beats with such feverish and impatient throbs, is the lesson needful. Our national character wants the dignity of repose. . . . The voices of the Present say, 'Come!' But the voices of the Past say, 'Wait!'." *Hyperion* (Boston: Ticknor & Fields, 1844), 80. The insouciance with which Longfellow refashions aristocratic privilege as moral injunction must indeed have been infuriating for Poe.

60. See "Poe, Longfellow, and the Institution of Poetry," *Poe Studies* 33, nos. 1, 2 (2000): 23–28.

61. "From Poe to Valéry," in *The Recognition of Edgar Allan Poe*, ed. Eric W. Carlson (Ann Arbor: University of Michigan Press, 1970), 205–19, 207.

62. See *American Renaissance: Art and Expression in the Age of Emerson and Whitman* (New York: Oxford University Press, 1941), xii.

63. Elmer characterizes Poe as the "undead" of the American canon, linking his problematic literary legacy to the exclusion of mass-culture and its affects from the high-cultural tradition. See Chapter 1 of his *Reading at the Social Limit*.

64. Writers with capital commonly countered the displacement of the author by taking on the role of publisher, editor, or distributor. For instance, William Cullen Bryant financed the entire production and distribution of his first volume of poems, offering the books to retailers on consignment. In their early careers, both Washington Irving and James Fenimore Cooper paid for the production of their books and sold entire editions to middlemen for distribution. Prescott, Longfellow, and Lowell commonly invested in the stereotype plates to their books, leasing them to printers should there be a demand for a second edition. For an account of

authorial involvement in the process of book production see Charvat, *Literary Publishing in America*, 38–60.

65. "Reminiscences of Poe by John H .B. Latrobe," in *Edgar Allan Poe: A Memorial Volume*, ed. Sara Sigourney Rice (Baltimore: Turnbull Brothers, 1877), 58.

66. Quoted in Jay B. Hubbell, "Charles Chauncey Burr: Friend of Poe," *PMLA* 69 (September 1954): 833–40, 838.

67. Rice, "Reminiscences," 59.

68. As Hubbell explains, Latrobe's testimonial was first printed by Charles Chauncey Burr in the pro-slavery, secessionist New York monthly, *The Old Guard*, as part of the post-Civil War struggle to reclaim Poe for the South. See "Poe and His Biographer, Griswold," *The Old Guard* (June 1866) 353–58. Latrobe greatly elaborated his account of the meeting when he spoke at the dedication of the Poe monument in Baltimore, November 17, 1875. See Rice, "Reminiscences," 57–62.

69. The *Saturday Visiter* warned authors that relinquishing their property rights was a condition of entering the contest: "We wish those who may write for either of the premiums to understand that all manuscripts submitted will become the property of the Publishers." See *The Poe Log*,130.

70. Hubbell, 838.

71. See the *Lady's Book* 8 (January 1834).

72. In discussing "The Visionary," I will quote the 1834 version of the tale, the variants for which can most easily be found in Mabbott, ed., *Collected Works*, vol. 2, 148–66.

73. *Letters*, vol. 1, 20.

74. *The Poe Log*, 62–63.

75. *Southern Literary Messenger* (February, 1836): 209. Mabbott also reprints the spoof, *Collected Works*, vol. 2, 259–90. For an astute analysis of Poe's "Autography" as a meditation on the way in which "personality was seen to emerge from a generic publicity" (40), see Elmer, *Reading at the Social Limit*, 37–43.

76. *Southern Literary Messenger*, 212.

77. *The Poe Log*, 346.

78. Poe published three slightly different versions of the *Prospectus of* the Penn Magazine in June and August 1840, and January 1841. Facsimile reprints of these texts can be found in Jacob N. Blanck, *Bibliography of American Literature*, vol. 7 (New Haven, Conn.: Yale University Press, 1983), 116–19. Poe published his *Prospectus of* The Stylus in March of 1843, reprinted in Thompson, ed., *Essays and Reviews*, 1033–35.

79. For the source and translation of Poe's epigraph, see Mabbott, *Collected Works*, vol. 1, 329, and Burton Pollin, *Discoveries in Poe* (Notre Dame, Ind.: University of Notre Dame Press, 1970), 206–95.

80. To compare this daguerreotype to the original, see Michael J. Deas, *The Portraits and Daguerrotypes of Edgar Allan Poe* (Charlottesville: University Press of Virginia, 1989), 59, 80. Rice's altered daguerreotype was also used by James A. Harrison as the frontispiece to vol. 4 of his *Complete Works of Edgar Allan Poe* (New York: George D. Sproul, 1902). I thank William Pannapacker for this reference.

Chapter 5

1. Sidney Moss's *Poe's Literary Battles* is the definitive account of Poe's oppo-sition to the literary cliques, while Claude Richard's "Poe and Young America," *Studies in Bibliography* 21 (1968): 25–58, provides the most thorough account of Poe's concessions.

2. Poe had received biographical treatment once before as part of the "Poets and Poetry of Philadelphia" series published in the Philadelphia *Saturday Museum* in 1843. This biography was written by H. B. Hirst in collaboration with Poe, and included selections from his published poems and laudatory opinions on Poe's writ-ings excerpted from newspapers, magazines, and private correspondence. How-ever, it does not seem to have received much notice outside of the Philadelphia newspapers; as the title of the series suggests, it was intended primarily for local consumption. See *The Poe Log*, 398–402. Poe sent Lowell a copy of this early biog-raphy to assist him in preparing his essay for *Graham's*.

3. Magazines did not routinely copyright their contents until late in the cen-tury, so even editors and proprietors regularly surrendered control over future pub-lication of a text upon issue of the magazine. Poe's editing of the *Broadway Journal*, however, was directly related to his desire to establish a different form of owner-ship over his writing, both in terms of his ability to profit from its success (rather than accepting a flat fee for his contribution, regardless of sales), and in terms of his ability to control the medium in which his writing appeared. His frustrating experience as an editor of *Graham's* seems to have hardened his resolve on both counts: while watching the circulation figures for this magazine climb, Poe had to remain content with his editor's salary. He later complained, "If, instead of a paltry salary, Graham had given me a tenth of his Magazine, I should feel myself a rich man to-day." See *Letters*, vol. 1, 192. In addition, he had to suffer the indignity of watching Graham become wealthy and spend increasingly lavish amounts for illus-trations and fashion plates. Unfortunately, the part-share arrangement Poe signed with Briggs, and his eventual full-ownership of the *Broadway Journal*, failed to gener-ate the profits he expected. For a detailed account of this agreement and the finan-cial reasons for the *Journal's* collapse, see Heyward Ehrlich, "Briggs's Dilemma and Poe's Strategy," reprinted in Pollin, ed., *Collected Writings*, vol. 3, part 2, xii–xxxi.

4. A list of the texts that Poe reprinted in vol. 1 of the *Broadway Journal* can be found in Quinn, 456n.; a list of those reprinted in vol. 2 can be found in George E. Woodberry *The Life of Edgar Allan Poe*, vol. 2 (New York: Houghton Mifflin Co., 1909), 149n. The importance of these reprintings has not been lost on contemporary textual editors. While Mabbott's *Collected Works* cross-references variant versions of each tale, Patrick Quinn's *Poetry and Tales* has in nearly every case taken the *Broadway Journal* revision to be authoritative.

5. See Richard, "Poe and Young America."

6. "Exordium," in Thompson, ed., *Essays and Reviews*, 1027.

7. See Thompson, ed., *Essays and Reviews*, 823–33

8. New York *Mirror*, August 1823, [1].

9. Review of Lambert Wilmer, *Quacks of Helicon*, in Thompson, ed., *Essays and Reviews*, 1007.

10. There is strong evidence to suggest that this is the way in which Poe desired his alliance with the literary nationalists to be perceived. In an important *Broadway Journal* editorial expressing "the most earnest sympathy in all the hopes, and the firmest faith in the capabilities of 'Young America,'" Poe stops short of explicitly endorsing their project, while at the same time claiming a stake in their success. Just as affiming "sympathy in *hopes*" and "faith in *capabilities*" dodges the question of support of present action, so Poe's most explicit declaration of solidarity is characterized by a signal evasion. Poe writes of Young America, "We look upon its interests as our own" suggesting that his investment is not ideological, but strategic or economic. See Pollin, ed., *Collected Writings*, vol. 3, part 1, 171. For Poe's later renunciation of Young America, see his unpublished manuscript, "*The Living Writers of America*: A Manuscript by Edgar Allan Poe," ed. Burton Pollin, *Studies in the American Renaissance* (1991): 151–211.

11. A facsimile of this title page can be found in *The Poe Log*, 541.

12. Although early in his career Lowell had been an enthusiastic supporter of the Young Americans, the publication of *The Pioneer* marked a parting of their ways. Lowell broke ranks in the first issue by calling for a "natural," not a "national" literature. Worse still, the second issue included an anonymous puff written by Poe praising all *The Pioneer*'s critical notices *except* that of Mathews's *Puffer Hopkins*, which Poe termed "one of the most trashy novels that ever emanated from an American press" (*The Pioneer*, January 1843, "Introduction," and February 1843, back cover). Poe's comment instigated a quarrel between Lowell and Mathews, formalizing the split that had become apparent in their rhetoric. Lowell's falling out with the Young Americans occurred just as Poe had taken on the young poet, engaging him in a friendly correspondence, soliciting contributions for *The Stylus*, and publishing a flattering but admonitory review of his second book of poetry. Lowell's essay succeeds in bridging the gap between Poe's aesthetics and the discourse of literary nationalism largely because Lowell sets out to perform this kind of mediation in the first place, using the essay to reconcile the competing claims of two of his most formative influences.

13. "Our Contributors, No. XVII: Edgar Allan Poe," *Graham's Magazine* (February 1845); reprinted in *The Shock of Recognition*, ed. Edmund Wilson (New York: Doubleday, Doran & Co., 1943), 5–20.

14. Quoted in Miller, *The Raven and the Whale*, 111.

15. *The Pioneer*, January 1843, 1–2.

16. The figure of the stillborn child is important for Lowell, and for his relation with Poe. See for instance Poe's praise of "The Legend of Brittany," a poem that centers on this figure (Thompson, ed., *Essays and Reviews* 809–14), and Lowell's 1849 essay "Nationality in Literature" (*North American Review*; reprinted in *Literary Criticism of James Russell Lowell*, ed. Herbert F. Smith [Lincoln: University of Nebraska Press, 1969], 116–31). In this essay Longfellow displaces Poe as the exemplar of Lowell's critical ideals, while the image of the stillborn child is displaced by the image of an enduring pregnancy. Self-consciously revising his position in his biography of Poe, Lowell refers in this essay to "the period of gestation which a country must go through, ere it bring forth a great poet" and urges "Let us not be in any hurry to resort to a Caesarian operation" (13).

17. "Bryant's American Poets," *Arcturus* 1, no. 1 (December 1840): 24–29.

18. "Prospectus of the Stylus," *Philadelphia Saturday Museum*, March 4, 1843, in Thompson, ed., *Essays and Reviews*, 1035.

19. "Prospectus of the Penn Magazine," in Blanck, *Bibliography*, vol. 7, 116.

20. Review of *Twice Told Tales*, in Thompson, ed., *Essays and Reviews*, 569–77.

21. "The Philosophy of Composition," in Thompson, ed., *Essays and Reviews*, 14.

22. "She Was a Phantom of Delight," ll. 21–22, in *William Wordsworth*, ed. Stephen Gill (New York: Oxford University Press, 1984), 292–93.

23. A kind of anti-biography of a professional literary man at the end of his career, "Thingum Bob" seems at least partially intended to deflate what Poe referred to in a letter to Lowell as his "well-intended flatteries" (*Letters*, vol. 1, 264–65). Poe cites the line as he delivers on the ponderous pun of his title, transforming his literary lion's triumph into a comment on the generic nature of literary fame. The eponymous hero gloats: "Yes; I have made history. My fame is universal. . . . You cannot take up a common newspaper in which you shall not see some allusion to the immortal THINGUM BOB. It is Mr. Thingum Bob said so, and Mr. Thingum Bob wrote this, and Mr. Thingum Bob did that. But I am meek and expire with an humble heart. After all, what is it?—this indescribable something which men will persist in terming "genius?" I agree with Buffon—with Hogarth—it is but *diligence* after all" (Quinn, ed., *Poetry and Tales*, 786).

24. *Evening Mirror*, January 20, 1845, quoted in *The Poe Log*, 491.

25. *Morning News*, January 25, 1845, quoted in *The Poe Log*, 492–94.

26. Although many readers undoubtedly knew Poe to be the author of *Arthur Gordon Pym*, the poems that appeared in Griswold's *Poets and Poetry of America* (1842) the tales collected in the *Tales of the Grotesque and Arabesque* (1840) or those circulated in the *Southern Literary Messenger*, *Burton's*, or *Graham's*, there exist numerous testimonies to readers' ignorance of significant portions of Poe's work. Poe's reputation as an author was scattershot, disarticulated by both genre and region. For example, early in 1845 Charles Briggs mentioned in a letter to Lowell that he was unfamiliar with "The Gold Bug," a tale which had been a popular sensation in Philadelphia (*The Poe Log*, 494). Likewise, soon after the publication of Griswold's anthology, *Poet's Magazine* scornfully asked of Poe, "Who ever dreamed that the cynical critic, the hunter up of small things, journeyman editor of periodicals, and Apollo's man of all work . . . wrote *Poetry?*" (*The Poe Log*, 368). Poe attributed this ignorance to the erratic nature of magazine readership. In a letter to Charles Anthon, he complained that "unless the journalist collects his various articles, he is liable to be grossly misconceived and misjudged by men . . . who see, perhaps, only a paper here and there, by accident—often only one of his mere extravaganzas, written to supply a particular demand" (*Letters*, vol. 1, 270–71).

27. For the textual history of "The Fall of the House of Usher," see *The Poe Log*, 267–73, 278, 305, 307; for "The Purloined Letter," see 470, 489–91, 540, 543.

28. According to a contemporary, Thomas Wyatt paid Poe to appear as the nominal author of an abridged edition of Wyatt's *Manual of Conchology* (1838). Poe's "authorship" enabled Wyatt to circumvent his publisher, who held the copyright and feared a cheap edition would undercut sales of the more expensive

edition. Wyatt apparently trusted that Poe was someone "whom it would be idle to sue for damages" (*The Poe Log*, 259).

29. Review of "The Quacks of Helicon," Thompson, ed., *Essays and Reviews*, 1009.

30. *Evening Mirror*, January 14, 1845, *The Poe Log*, 487.

31. For a detailed history of the Young America movement, see Miller, *The Raven and the Whale*, and Edward L. Widmer, *Young America: The Flowering of Democracy in New York City* (New York: Oxford University Press, 1999).

32. [John O'Sullivan], "Introduction," *United States Magazine and Democratic Review* (October 1837): 1–15, 15.

33. *Ibid.*, 14.

34. [John O'Sullivan], "Review of Twice-Told Tales," *United States Magazine and Democratic Review* (February 1842) 198.

35. "The International Copyright Question," 118.

36. See "Editor's Table," *Knickerbocker* (April 1842): 384–85 for an example of Lewis Gaylord Clark's attempt to rearticulate the need for copyright within the bounds of Whig restraint.

37. "Necessity for a National Literature," *Knickerbocker* (May 1845): 416–17.

38. "The Literary Prospects of 1845," *American Review* (February 1845): 148.

39. *Graham's Magazine*, September 1842, 122.

40. Terence Whalen gives a markedly different account of the antebellum literary marketplace's "tendency toward overproduction" (11) in *Edgar Allan Poe and the Masses*, 11–17. What he takes to be a settled economic condition, I identify as a Whig reaction to an emerging market; where he argues that Poe takes refuge from "overproduction" by imagining "a mind whose comprehension—and productivity—could expand without limit" (15), I emphasize the literary nationalists' attempt to enlist Poe's judgment in the regulation of this market.

41. See *Wiley and Putnam's Literary Newsletter* (April 1845), 306. For a publishing history of these series, see Ezra Greenspan, "Evert Duyckinck and the History of Wiley and Putnam's Library of American Books, 1845–1847," *American Literature* 64, no. 4 (1992): 677–93.

42. Charles Briggs was explicit in acknowledging the role Lowell's essay played in his taking on Poe as a contributor, editor, and eventually part-owner of the *Broadway Journal*. As Briggs explained to Lowell, "For my own part, I did not use to think well of Poe, but my love for you, and implicit confidence in your judgment, led me to abandon all my prejudices against him, when I read your account of him" (*The Poe Log*, 519).

43. "Marginalia," December 1844, in Thompson, ed., *Essays and Reviews*, 1346.

44. See "'Es Lässt Sich Nicht Screiben': Plagiarism and 'The Man of the Crowd,'" in Rosenheim and Rachman, *The American Face of Edgar Allan Poe*, 49–87. See also David Leverenz, "Poe and Gentry Virginia" in Rosenheim and Rachman, 210–36, for an account of Poe's textual elaboration of what Leverenz identifies as a typically southern pseudo-aristocracy.

45. *Evening Mirror*, 27 February 1845, quoted in Moss, *Poe's Literary Battles*, 167.

46. *Morning News*, 1 March 1845, *The Poe Log*, 509.

47. *Evening Mirror*, 1 March 1845.

48. Miller, 99. For an account of Boston and New York conservatives' championing of Longfellow in response to the Young Americans, see Miller, *The Raven and the Whale*, 22, 99, 130, 282.

49. "Longfellow's *Waif*," *Evening Mirror*, January 13–14, 1845, in Thompson, ed., *Essays and Reviews*, 698.

50. That Longfellow intended to play upon the ambiguous property-status of "fugitive" or uncollected magazine verse is clear from his epigraph which is taken from Book IV of Spenser's *Faerie Queene*: "A waif the which by fortune came / Upon your seas, he claimed as property / And yet nor his, nor his in equity, but / Yours the waif by high prerogative" (IV.12.33–36). This is the voice of Cymodeche imploring Neptune to release Florimell from her captivity at the hands of Proteus who "claimed" her while she was drifting on the sea. Casting the book itself in the role of Florimell, Longfellow tacitly disavows property in the volume, suggesting that his editorial appropriation of these poems is no more legitimate than Proteus's seizure. And yet Poe is right to question a such a gesture of renunciation. By invoking the romance-context to justify his collection, Longfellow obscures the origin of these poems, refiguring authorship as accidental (and fortunate) dispossession. What is more, in addressing the reader in the role of Neptune, Longfellow seeks to restore ownership not to the poems' authors, but to the sovereign reader. Longfellow's epigraph bears out Poe's offhand comments on the volume's manipulative tone and structure. Longfellow's overt disavowal of property rights conceals a powerful bid to act as the instrument of their rearticulation.

51. Thompson, ed., *Essays and Reviews*, 705.

52. Critics are divided on the issue of the identity of Outis, many speculating that Outis was Poe himself, attempting to generate scandal in the form of an antagonistic exchange. The true identity of Outis, however, is less important than the fact that it is in dialogue with a personification of anonymity and impersonality that Poe conducts his most extensive treatment of the problem of plagiarism. Arguments over whether the entire episode was staged by Poe, or whether his response was a defensive overreaction to a legitimate outside challenge, drive accounts of the Longfellow War back to the extremes of authorial control and authorial surrender that Poe was troubling in this series of responses. For the most recent sparring in the debate over the identity of Outis, see Burton Pollin, "Poe as Author of the 'Outis' Letter and 'The Bird of the Dream,'" *Poe Studies* 20, no. 1 (1987): 10–15; Kent Ljungquist and Buford Jones, "The Identity of 'Outis': A Further Chapter in the Poe-Longfellow War," *American Literature* 60, no. 3 (1988): 402–15; and the exchange between Pollin and Dwight Thomas in *Poe Studies Newsletter*, 17, no. 2 (1989).

53. Like the Young Americans, Poe directs his attack at a split target, representing Outis's anonymity both as evidence of a gentlemanly conspiracy, and as a form of mob violence. Poe claims that Outis has resorted to anonymity "with the view of decrying by sheer strength of lungs—of trampling down—of rioting down—of mobbing down any man with a soul that bids him come out from the general corruption of our public press" (741). And yet hovering behind this characterization of anonymous publication as mob aggression is an image of Outis as an aristocrat who, like Longfellow, cleverly manipulates the technology of print.

Outis is an "anonymous gentleman" who "manufactures" similarities between poems through the use of typography, "appealing from the ears to the eyes of the most uncultivated classes of the rabble" (729). Print circulation may be a dangerous form of popular power, but Poe suspects that this power is within the control of the elite.

54. "Plagiarism," *United States Magazine and Democratic Review* (April 1845):413.

55. See *The Poe Log*, 573. The source of this report, Rufus Wilmot Griswold, is famously unreliable when it comes to the life of Poe, and so it seems safe to speculate that Poe's decision to read a juvenile poem may have been motivated by something more than sheer desperation. For an account of the Lyceum disaster that reads Poe's recitation of "Al Aaraaf as a good faith gesture towards the interests of the Boston audience, see Ottavio M. Casale, "The Battle of Boston: A Revaluation of Poe's Lyceum Appearance," *American Literature* 45 (1973): 423–428.

56. "Editorial Miscellany," *Broadway Journal*, November 1, 1845, reprinted in Pollin, ed., *Collected Writings*, vol. 3, 299. Poe's proprietary claim to self-exposure should be understood against the backdrop of another form of exposure over which he had little control: *The Raven and Other Poems*, which included "Al Aaraaf" along with ten other "Poems Written in Youth," had been in press since early October and was due to be issued by the second week of November. For the publication history of this volume, see Mabbott's introduction to Edgar Allan Poe, *The Raven and Other Poems* (New York: Columbia University Press, 1942), iv–xxi. Poe's private revelation of the fraud he had carried off could be considered a preemptive strike, an attempt to assert control over evidence that would soon appear in public.

57. Cornelia Wells Walter, *Evening Transcript*, October 18, 1845, quoted in *The Poe Log*, 579.

58. Comments on the impropriety of Poe's inclusion of juvenilia in this volume are widespread: see for example reviews in the New York *Anglo-American* and the Philadelphia *North American*, cited in *The Poe Log*, 593–95; see also Margaret Fuller's *Daily Tribune* review, and Lewis Gaylord Clark's *Knickerbocker* review, both reprinted in *Edgar Allan Poe: The Critical Heritage*, ed. I. M. Walker (New York: Routledge and Kegan Paul, 1986).

59. William Gilmore Simms, *The Southern Patriot*, November 10, 1845, quoted in *The Poe Log*, 588.

60. See, for example, T. S. Eliot's association of Poe with poetic adolescence in "From Poe to Valéry," and Henry James's assertion that "an enthusiasm for Poe is the mark of a decidedly primitive stage of reflection" (Carlson, ed., *The Recognition*, 66)

61. See for example the November issue of the temperance journal *The New England Washingtonian*, cited in *The Poe Log*, 690, and John Sullivan Dwight's review of *The Raven and Other Poems* in the *Harbinger*, reprinted in Walker, *Edgar Allan Poe*, 236–39.

62. Pollin, ed., *Collected* Writings, vol. 3, 299.

63. See for example, Kenneth Silverman, *Edgar A. Poe*, 266–70.

64. *The Poe Log*, 642.

65. Sheridan, *The Rivals*, vol. 3, noted in Pollin, ed., *Collected Writings*, vol. 4, 229.

Chapter 6

1. For the publication history of "The Raven," see Mabbott, ed., *Collected Works*, vol. 1, 359–64. For a sense of the breadth of the poem's unauthorized circulation in the form of popular parodies, see Mabbott, 352.

2. That the degree of *The Scarlet Letter*'s success was unexpected is indicated by the fact that Hawthorne's publishers reset the type twice before committing the volume to stereotype. According to C. E. Frazer Clark, Jr., Ticknor and Fields had run through two editions of 2500 copies each before stereotyping the book on September 9, 1850. See his *Nathaniel Hawthorne: A Descriptive Bibliography* (Pittsburgh: University of Pittsburgh Press, 1978), 16.1–16.3.

3. Fields to Hawthorne, August 20, 1850, quoted in William Charvat, "Introduction," *The House of the Seven Gables* (Columbus: Ohio University Press, 1965), xv.

4. For an account of Fields's innovative publication and distribution strategies, see Brodhead's *The School of Hawthorne* (New York: Oxford University Press, 1986), 48–66. Brodhead argues convincingly that Fields's most significant achievement was the identification and marketing of specific writers as a cultural elite, a group that included Longfellow, Emerson, Hawthorne, Holmes, Lowell, and Whittier. The groundbreaking essay on Fields's merchandising tactics is William Charvat, "James T. Fields and the Beginnings of Book Promotion, 1840–1855" (1964), reprinted in *The Profession of Authorship* 168–189.

5. See "Judging Books by Their Covers: House Styles, Ticknor and Fields, and Literary Promotion," in *Reading Books: Essays on the Material Text and Literature in America*, ed. Michelle Moylan and Lane Stiles (Amherst: University of Massachusetts Press, 1996), 75–100.

6. Brodhead, 56.

7. Brodhead, 58. See also Jane Tompkins, *Sensational Designs: The Cultural Work of American Fiction, 1790–1860* (New York: Oxford University Press, 1985), 3–39.

8. In *Practicing New Historicism*, Catherine Gallagher and Stephen Greenblatt turn to figures of suspended animation to connect the "conditional mood" (196) of the nineteenth-century novel with modes of skepticism in scientific, economic, and medical discourses. I will focus more closely on the temporal axis of the novel's unfolding, reading instances and figures of suspended animation as allegories of authorship as well as allegories of reading.

9. Nathaniel Hawthorne, *Tales and Sketches* (New York: Literary Classics of the United States, 1982), 1150.

10. "The Firing of Nathaniel Hawthorne," *Essex Institute Historical Collections* 114 (April 1978): 64, 66. Many of Hawthorne's defenders alluded to his national reputation as a means of lifting him above the concerns of local politicians—in Hawthorne's words, the "slang-whangers—the vote distributors—the Jack Cades" (61) who reaped the benefits of patronage after a change of administration. *The Albany Atlas*, for example, referred to Hawthorne as "the gentle Elia of our American literature" (65) while the *Philadelphia Evening Bulletin* argued that, as a literary man and *not* a political appointee, Hawthorne should be "saved from the pinch of poverty" by "the bestowal of the government patronage" (66). Perhaps in recoil from what was ultimately a losing strategy, Hawthorne suggests in the "Preface"

that his actual reputation was intensely local. Referring only to the dissemination of his tales in book form, Hawthorne writes: "The circulation of the two volumes was chiefly confined to New England; nor was it until long after this period, if it even yet be the case, that the Author could regard himself as addressing the American Public, or indeed, any Public at all. He was merely writing to his known or unknown friends" (1151). If in the wake of the Custom House firing it had served Hawthorne's local, political purposes to be known as a national literary figure, the occasion of Fields's republication of *Twice-Told Tales* offered Hawthorne a spectacular form of erasure: the national production of the Hawthorne persona as a local and apolitical figure.

11. "Nathaniel Hawthorne and His Mother," *Feminism and American Literary History* (New Brunswick, N.J.: Rutgers University Press, 1992), 36–56.

12. See letters 59–72 in *The Letters, 1813–1843*, vol. 15 of *The Centenary Edition of the Works of Nathaniel Hawthorne*, ed. Thomas Woodson, L. Neal Smith, and Norman Holmes Pearson (Columbus: Ohio State University Press, 1984), 228–47.

13. Quoted in Horatio Bridge, *Personal Recollections of Nathaniel Hawthorne* (New York: Harper and Brothers, 1893), 94. Hawthorne's letters to Bridge concerning his editorial rewriting and promotion of Bridge's *Journal of an African Cruiser* (1845) suggest an author who is confident of his abilities, proud of his publishing connections, and known to be possessed of a good reputation.

14. The phrase is Nina Baym's, whose *The Shape of Hawthorne's Career* (Ithaca, N.Y.: Cornell University Press, 1976) remains the most influential account of the career as a whole.

15. Hawthorne's ironic disregard for minor writing in the "Preface" to *Twice-Told Tales* contrasts sharply with his early enthusiasm for writing children's books, by definition a minor genre. In a letter to Longfellow concerning a possible collaboration, Hawthorne writes expansively about "entirely [revolutionizing] the whole system of juvenile writing," acknowledging that minor writing is not incompatible with literary ambition: "Seriously, I think that a very pleasant and peculiar kind of reputation may be acquired in this way—we will twine for ourselves a wreath of tender shoots and dewy buds, instead of such withered and dusty leaves as other people crown themselves with; and what is of more importance to me, though of none to a Cambridge Professor, we may perchance put money in our purses" *Letters, 1813–1843*, 266–67.

16. *The Province of Piety: Moral History in Hawthorne's Early Tales* (Cambridge, Mass.: Harvard University Press, 1984), 485.

17. For an account of the terms of reception of Hawthorne's early fiction, see Tompkins.

18. See C. E. Frazer Clark, Jr.'s invaluable *Nathaniel Hawthorne: A Descriptive Bibliography*, A 2.28, A 2.48, A 19.1.a, C2. While not a comprehensive list of the reprinting of Hawthorne's tales—a bibliographic feat which is as yet impossible due to the inadequately indexed state of nineteenth-century periodicals—Clark's volume represents the best information available.

19. See C. E. Clark, A 2.1, A 2.4, A 2.39–40, A 2.51, A 19.10, C 8, C 11, C 19. It is striking that Griswold's selections are all what we would consider minor

fiction: "A Rill from the Town Pump," "David Swan," "The Celestial Railroad," and a selection from "Buds and Bird Voices" (C. E. Clark, C19).

20. See C. E. Clark, A 2.4.

21. All of these remarks are taken from reviews found in John L. Idol, Jr. and Buford Jones, eds., *Nathaniel Hawthorne: The Contemporary Reviews* (New York: Cambridge University Press, 1994), 20, 21, 27, 30.

22. *American Romanticism*, 97.

23. Review of *Twice Told Tales* and *Mosses from an Old Manse*, *Godey's Lady's Book* (November 1847), reprinted in Thompson, ed., *Essays and Reviews*, 578.

24. Review of Twice-Told Tales, *Graham's Magazine* (May 1842) in Thompson, ed., *Essays and Reviews*, 574. Poe comments that he "had good reason for so supposing"; his evidence is most probably the laudatory reviews of *Twice Told Tales* published by Longfellow in the *North American Review* immediately in the wake of the 1837 and 1842 editions.

25. Hawthorne self-deprecatingly refers to the volume as "'twice-told tediousness'" in a letter to Longfellow (*Letters 1843–1853*, vol. 16 of *The Centenary Edition of the Works of Nathaniel Hawthorne*, ed. Thomas Woodson, L. Neal Smith, and Norman Holmes Pearson [Columbus: Ohio State University Press], 249), alluding to Shakespeare's *King John* III iv 108: "Life is as tedious as a twice-told tale." Nevertheless, his title seems designed to reclaim the already-printed tales and sketches by transposing them into an imaginary oral context, a provocation taken up by Park Benjamin and Elizabeth Palmer Peabody in their reviews of the volume. See Idol and Jones, 27–34.

26. Kristie Hamilton argues for the importance of sketch as a form to a wide range of American writers in *America's Sketchbook: The Cultural Life of a Nineteenth-Century Literary Genre* (Athens: Ohio University Press, 1998). John Bryant's genealogy of repose as a narrative stance would also be crucial to a more thorough reconsideration of Hawthorne's sketches. See his *Melville and Repose: The Rhetoric of Humor in the American Renaissance* (New York: Oxford University Press, 1993).

27. See Sandra Tomc, "An Idle Industry: Nathaniel Parker Willis and the Workings of Literary Leisure," *American Quarterly* 49, no. 4 (December 1997): 780–805, for a provocative analysis of the importance of literary idleness to the articulation of entrepreneurial professionalism.

28. Note the parenthetical, accidental correspondence between the conditions of composition and Hawthorne's narrative persona. Hawthorne nominally refuses to identify the two but also courts such an identification: "With the foregoing characteristics, proper to the productions of a person in retirement (which happened to be the Author's category, at the time) the book is devoid of others that we should quite as naturally look for" (1152).

29. James T. Fields, *Yesterdays with Authors* (Boston: Houghton, Mifflin and Company, 1885), 51.

30. *Letters, 1843–1853*, 460–61.

31. Nathaniel Hawthorne, *The House of the Seven Gables* (New York: Penguin Books, 1986), 12.

32. See Walter Michaels, *The Gold Standard*, Brook Thomas, *Cross-Examinations of Law and Literature: Cooper, Hawthorne, Stowe, and Melville* (New York:

Cambridge University Press, 1987), and Milette Shamir, "Hawthorne's Romance and the Right to Privacy," *American Quarterly* 49; no. 4 (1997): 746–79.

33. Michaels, 109. For other accounts of the novel as shaped by fantasies of escape from the market see Gilmore and Thomas.

34. For a reading of the novel in these terms, see Thomas, *Cross-Examinations*.

35. I write in the spirit of Michael Bell's introduction to the novel, where he asserts that Hawthorne "well knew that in *The House of the Seven Gables* he was in important respects moving away from the romantic into something like novelistic realism." Bell's introduction to the Oxford World Classics edition of the novel is reprinted in *Culture, Genre, and Literary Vocation: Selected Essays on American Literature* (Chicago: University of Chicago Press, 2001), 54–64.

36. *Letters, 1843–1853*, 369.

37. *Letters, 1843–1853*, 371.

38. See for example, Gilmore, who notes that Hepzibah "resembles her creator both in her history of isolation and her need to earn a living," although he also maintains that she "is not an artist-figure" (100).

39. Hawthorne's emphasis on mockery throughout this chapter and his careful description of Hepzibah's toilet despite depriving his narrator of direct oversight suggests that he may well have Alexander Pope's mock-epic "The Rape of the Lock" in mind as a model for bringing his formal ambitions into line with the all-too-obvious declension of modern life.

40. *Letters, 1813–1843*, 456. For the editors' doubts about the authenticity of this letter, see Thomas Woodson, "Introduction," *Letters, 1813–1843*, 64. Even if this episode was constructed by Connolly in hindsight, it still speaks to the way *The House of the Seven Gables* recalls the narrative structure of Hawthorne's early children's books.

41. For an account of the publication history of these volumes, which were issued and reissued in a number of different formats in the 1840s and early '50s, see Roy Harvey Pearce, "Historical Introduction," *True Stories from History and Biography*, vol. 6 of *The Centenary Edition of the Works of Nathaniel Hawthorne* (Columbus: Ohio State University Press, 1972), 287–311.

42. Although Hawthorne associated writing for children with writing for profit, and wrote a number of tales and sketches clearly designed for the juvenile market, the stories themselves and the books and magazines in which they were published do not maintain a strong distinction between the two audiences. For example, "The Gentle Boy," first published in *The Token* (1832), was reprinted in *The Juvenile Key* (March, April 1832), while "Little Annie's Ramble," first published in a gift-book for children, *Youth's Keepsake* (1835), carried the signature "By the Author of 'The Gentle Boy.'" While until recently, scholars have treated "Little Annie's Ramble" as "lovingly sentimental hackwork" (Pearce, 288), the English publisher, Milner and Sowerby took it to be representative of Hawthorne's early fiction, republishing selections from *Twice Told Tales* under the title *Little Annie's Ramble, and Other Tales* (1853). See C. E. Clark, A 2.12. For a detailed treatment of "Little Annie's Ramble," see Elizabeth Freeman, "Honeymoon with a Stranger: Pedophiliac Picaresques from Poe to Nabokov," *American Literature* 70, no. 4 (December 1998): 863–97. For an account of the centrality of writing for children

to Hawthorne's career, see Karen Sánchez-Eppler, "Hawthorne and the Writing of Childhood," *The Cambridge Companion to Nathaniel Hawthorne* (New York: Cambridge University Press, forthcoming 2002).

43. *Letters, 1813–1843*, 252. But see also his letter to George Hilliard, in which Hawthorne qualifies his use of the term: "If I am to support myself by literature, it must be by what is called drudgery, but which is incomparably less irksome, as a business, than imaginative writing—by translation, concocting of school-books, newspaper scribbling &c," *Letters, 1843–1853*, 23.

44. *Letters, 1813–1843*, 266.

45. *Letters, 1813–1843*, 288. See similar assertions at 252 and 267. For Hawthorne's attempts throughout the 1840s to collaborate in the publication of texts for the use of schools, see Pearce.

46. *Letters, 1813–1843*, 502.

47. See Brown, *Domestic Individualism*, 81.

48. "Class, Culture, and the Trouble with White Skin in Hawthorne's *The House of the Seven Gables*," *Yale Journal of Criticism* 12, no. 2 (1999): 249–68. See also Robert K. Martin, "Haunted by Jim Crow: Gothic Fictions by Hawthorne and Faulkner," in *American Gothic: New Interventions in a National Narrative*, ed. Robert K. Martin and Eric Savoy (Iowa City: University of Iowa Press, 1998), 129–42.

49. See *Peter Parley's Universal History on the Basis of Geography* (New York: William Robinson, 1837). I am indebted to Scott Karambis for this observation.

50. Compare Hawthorne's insistence on the "rich depth" (95) of her voice when he depicts the domestic preparations for Clifford's arrival to his later depiction of the "croak" of her voice "as ineradicable as sin" (134). This later scene, which stresses Hepzibah's "innumerable sins of emphasis" (134) when reading, enacts what it describes, maintaining with a strange tenacity that Hepzibah should be held responsible for an instance of aesthetic failure. For Hawthorne's invocation of Hepzibah as the occasion for a later rupture in narrative time, see the drawn-out scene in which she goes to fetch Clifford at Judge Pyncheon's behest. The alternation of force and reluctance in this episode reprises the temporal stutter of the opening scenes (240–48).

51. *The Scarlet Letter* (New York: Penguin Classics, 1986), 65–66.

52. See "Hawthorne and the Writing of Childhood."

53. As Freeman details, Hawthorne loads this tale with intimations of perversity and sexual danger without, in the end, threatening Little Annie. Although her stroll with a stranger comes close to turning into a narrative of abduction, both Annie and a tidy moral are safely delivered home by the end of the sketch.

54. See also Hawthorne's introduction to *Biographical Stories for Children* (1842), in which he expresses a similar willingness to trade breadth of public reception for importance across the lifespan of individual children.

55. Richard Gray, " 'Hawthorne: A Problem': *The House of the Seven Gables*," in *Nathaniel Hawthorne: New Critical Essays*, ed. A. Robert Lee (New York: Vision Press, 1982), 88–109, 92.

56. *The Production of Personal Life: Class, Gender, and the Psychological in Hawthorne's Fiction* (Stanford, Calif.: Stanford University Press, 1991), 144–61. See

also Susan Van Zanten Gallagher, "A Domestic Reading of *The House of the Seven Gables*," *Studies in the Novel* 21, no. 1 (1992): 1–13. Strongly aligning Hawthorne's perspective with Phoebe's, Marianne Noble argues that Hawthorne "endorses a sentimental epistemology" (275) in "Sentimental Epistemologies in *Uncle Tom's Cabin* and *The House of the Seven Gables*," in *Separate Spheres No More: Gender Convergence in American Literature, 1830–1930*, ed. Monika M. Elbert (Tuscaloosa: University of Alabama Press, 2000), 261–81.

57. For discussions of the problem of unity of the novel, see Gray and William Charvat, "Introduction." Strikingly, although Hawthorne worried in a letter to Horatio Bridge that he had "refined on the principal character too much" (*Letters, 1843–1853,* 406), scholars have been unable to decide to which character he refers.

58. For Catherine Sedgwick's opinion that "Little Phoebe" was "the one redeeming force" within the novel, see Pfister, 157. For the reprinting of "The Breakfast-Table" in *The (Old) Farmer's Almanack* (1852), see C. E. Clark, C23.

59. See Julian Hawthorne, *Hawthorne and His Circle* (New York: Harper Brothers, 1903), 15.

60. See for example the narrator's swerve into emotional, third-person appeals on behalf of "a character" where Beauty "should exist as the chief attribute" (108); "persons who have wandered, or been expelled out of the common track of things" (140); and "that great chaos of people whom an inexplicable Providence is continually putting at cross-purposes with the world" (149).

61. I am indebted here to Neill Matheson, who elaborates on the novel's association of sexuality with questions of taste in his unpublished conference paper, "Clifford's Dim Unsatisfactory Elegance," Modern Language Association, 2001.

62. For a consideration of Hawthorne's desire for transparency within the broader tradition of sketch-writing, see Teresa Toulouse, "Seeing Through 'Paul Pry': Hawthorne's Early Sketches and the Problem of Audience," *Critical Essays on Hawthorne's Short Stories*, ed. Albert von Frank (Boston: G. K. Hall & Co., 1991), 203–19.

63. Hawthorne describes Clifford's intermittent consciousness as an oscillation between waking and dreamlike states in which the idea of a gradual transition is so unthinkable it can only be understood as unbearable repetition: "Had Clifford, every time that he emerged out of dreams so lifelike, undergone the torture of the transformation from a boy into an old and broken man, the daily recurrence of the shock would have been too much to bear" (170). The threat of a "daily recurrence of the shock" links Clifford's limited perception to Hepzibah's enslavement to the shop-bell's call to market and to the "torture of the transformation" of literary regimes.

64. For the mutually constituting logics of racial and class transgression in this episode, see Anthony. For Hawthorne's feminization of subjection to commerce, see Brown; for women as a medium of exchange in the novel, see Teresa Goddu, "The Circulation of Women in *The House of the Seven Gables*," *Studies in the Novel* 23, no. 1 (Spring 1991): 119–27.

65. My argument here echoes that of Peter Bellis in his "Mauling Governor Pyncheon," *Studies in the Novel* 26, no. 3 (1994): 199–217.

66. Gilmore, 112.

67. *The Transformation of Authorship*, 176.

Coda

1. See Eugene Exman, *The Brothers Harper*, for a description of Norton's periodical and tour. The first independent trade magazine, the *American Publisher's Circle and Literary Gazette*, was founded in 1855 by the New York Book Publishers' Association; it served both as a nexus for the trade and as a vehicle for lobbying for international copyright. See Greenspan, *George Palmer Putnam*, 358–74.

2. *A Fictive People*, 55–68.

3. See *The Western Book Trade: Cincinnati as a Nineteenth-Century Publishing and Book-Trade Center* (Columbus: Ohio University Press, 1961).

4. "A Word at the Start," vol. 1 (June 1850): [1]–2.

5. For the nationalist underpinning and aims of the magazine, see Charles Briggs's anonymous editorial, "Introductory," *Putnam's Monthly: A Magazine of Literature, Science, and Art* 1 (January 1853): [1]–3. For Putnam's arrangement with the London publisher Sampson Low, see Greenspan, *George Palmer Putnam*, 290–92. Greenspan's research suggests that Putnam carries forward in muted form the literary property debates of the 1840s. Seeking an appropriate audience for his new periodical, Putnam purchased the subscription list of the recently disbanded *American Whig Review*.

6. Circulation figures for *Putnam's* can be found in Greenspan, *George Palmer Putnam*, 295. For *Harper's*, see Edward E. Chielens, ed., *American Literary Magazines: The Eighteenth and Nineteenth Centuries* (Westport, Conn.: Greenwood Press, 1986), 168.

7. See the chart reproduced in Exman, *The Brothers Harper*, 358.

8. *Decisions*, vol. 15, 2484.

9. *Decisions*, vol. 15, 2486.

10. See "Imperfect Title," 142–52. Noting Grier's sudden shift to the use of a female pronoun in this passage, Homestead argues that the final sentences of the decision may be addressed directly to Stowe, implicating Stowe in the system she despises by suggesting that she trades in Uncle Tom as assuredly as her slave-trader Haley.

11. "Uncle Tomitudes," *Putnam's Monthly* 1 (January 1853): 97–102, 99. Joan Hedrick estimates that, while 300,000 copies of the novel were sold in the United States in the first year of publication, a million and a half copies were sold in Great Britain alone. See *Harriet Beecher Stowe: A Life* (New York: Oxford University Press, 1994), 223, 233.

12. Quoted in Hedrick, 234.

13. See "International Copyright," *United States Review* (April 1853): 352–55 (the *United States Magazine and Democratic Review* changed its name to the *United States Review* in January 1853. In the text I will refer to the magazine by the name by which it was popularly known in the 1840s and '50s, "The Democratic"). For evidence of British publishers' embrace of cheap printing, see Chapman and Hall's 1850 "Cheap Edition" of Dickens's *American Notes* which they sold for 5 shillings, one quarter of the price of the 1842 edition. This 175–page double-columned book is comparable both in format and in cost to American reprints.

14. Clear signs that the Democrats do not simply or easily embrace the Whig

position include their championing of rural citizens, "stigmatized as ignorant and vulgar" (108), who read only newspapers, and their refusal to identify with British authors. They make a point of noting that their support of international copyright does not derive "from any sympathy with the sordid clamors of the British press" (114)

15. "National Literature, and the International Copy-Right Treaty," *United States Review* (August 1853): 97–117, 98. This detailed critique targets laws of primogeniture and entail, the English constitution, the Parliamentary system of representation, and the much-vaunted freedom of the press which, "like every other species of British freedom . . . is a mere shadow without substance; a cheat and a hypocrite whenever it comes to practical application to the great mass of the people" (109).

Bibliography

"Advertisement." *Sartain's Union Magazine of Literature and Art* (November 1849): 320.

Allen, Michael. *Poe and the British Magazine Tradition*. New York: Oxford University Press, 1969.

Altick, Richard D. *The English Common Reader: A Social History of the Mass Reading Public*. 1959. Reprint Columbus: Ohio University Press, 1998.

Amory, Hugh. "Proprietary Illustration: The Case of Cooke's *Tom Jones*." In *An Index of Civilisation*, ed. Ross Harvey, Wallace Kirsop, and B. J. McMullin, 137–47. Victoria: Centre for Bibliographical and Textual Studies, 1993.

Amory, Hugh, and David D. Hall, eds. *The Colonial Book in the Atlantic World*. Vol. 1 of *A History of the Book in America*. New York: Cambridge University Press, 2000.

Anderson, Benedict. *Imagined Communities: Reflections on the Origin and Spread of Nationalism*. 1983. Rev. ed. New York: Verso, 1991.

Anthony, David. "Class, Culture, and the Trouble with White Skin in Hawthorne's *The House of the Seven Gables*." *Yale Journal of Criticism* 12, no. 2 (1999): 249–68.

Arac, Jonathan. *Commissioned Spirits: The Shaping of Social Motion in Dickens, Carlyle, Melville, and Hawthorne*. 1979. Reprint New York: Columbia University Press, 1989.

Auerbach, Jonathan. "Poe's Other Double: The Reader in the Fiction." *Criticism* 24, no. 4 (1982): 341–61.

Bader, Arno L. "Frederick Saunders and the Early History of the International Copyright Movement in America." *Library Quarterly* 8 (January 1938): 25–39.

Baker, Thomas N. *Sentiment and Celebrity*. New York: Oxford University Press, 1999.

Barnes, James J. *Authors, Publishers, and Politicians: The Quest for an Anglo-American Copyright Agreement 1815–1854*. Columbus: Ohio State University Press, 1974.

Barthes, Roland. "From Work to Text." In *Textual Strategies: Perspectives in Post-Structuralist Criticism*, ed. Josué V. Harari, 73–81. Ithaca, N.Y.: Cornell University Press, 1979.

Baudelaire, Charles. *Baudelaire on Poe*. Ed. Lois Hyslop and Francis Hyslop. State College, Pa.: Bald Eagle Press, 1952.

Baym, Nina. *Feminism and American Literary History*. New Brunswick, N.J.: Rutgers University Press, 1992.

———. *The Shape of Hawthorne's Career*. Ithaca, N.Y.: Cornell University Press, 1976.

Bell, Michael Davitt. "Conditions of Literary Vocation." In *The Cambridge History of American Literature*, vol. 2, 9–123. New York: Cambridge University Press, 1995.

———. *Culture, Genre, and Literary Vocation: Selected Essays on American Literature*. Chicago: University of Chicago Press, 2001.

Bellis, Peter. "Mauling Governor Pyncheon." *Studies in the Novel* 26, no. 3 (1994): 199–217.

Benjamin, Walter. *Illuminations*. London: Fontana, 1982.

Bentham, Jeremy. *Works of Jeremy Bentham*. Vol. 1. Edinburgh: William Tait, 1843.

Bishop, Wallace Putnam. "The Struggle for International Copyright in the United States." Ph.D. dissertation, Boston University, 1959.

Blackstone, William. *Commentaries on the Laws of England*. Vol. 2. New York: W. E. Dean, 1846.

Blanck, Jacob N., ed. *Bibliography of American Literature*. Vol. 7. New Haven, Conn.: Yale University Press, 1983.

Bowker, R. R. *Copyright: Its Law and Its Literature*. New York: Publishers' Weekly, 1886.

Boyle, James. *Shamans, Software and Spleens: Law and the Construction of the Information Society*. Cambridge, Mass.: Harvard University Press, 1996.

Bracher, Peter S. "The Early American Editions of *American Notes*: Their Priority and Circulation." *Papers of the Bibliographical Society of America* 69 (1975): 365–76.

———. "Harper & Brothers, Publishers of Dickens." *Bulletin of the New York Public Library* 79 (1976): 315–35.

Bridge, Horatio. *Personal Recollections of Nathaniel Hawthorne*. New York: Harper and Brothers, 1893.

Briggs, Charles. "Introductory." *Putnam's Monthly: A Magazine of Literature, Science, and Art* 1, no. 1 (January 1853): 1–3.

Brodhead, Richard. *The School of Hawthorne*. New York: Oxford University Press, 1986.

Bromell, Nicholas. *By the Sweat of the Brow: Literature and Labor in Antebellum America*. Chicago: University of Chicago Press, 1993.

Brown, Gillian. *Domestic Individualism: Imagining Self in Nineteenth-Century America*. Berkeley: University of California Press, 1990.

Bryant, John. *Melville and Repose: The Rhetoric of Humor in the American Renaissance*. New York: Oxford University Press, 1993.

Bryant, William Cullen. *Power for Sanity: Selected Editorials of William Cullen Bryant, 1829–1861*. Ed. William Cullen II Bryant. New York: Fordham University Press, 1994.

Bryant, William Cullen, Francis L. Hawks, and Cornelius Mathews. *An Address to the People of the United States in Behalf of the American Copyright Club*. New York: American Copyright Club, 1843.

Bugbee, Bruce W. *Genesis of American Patent and Copyright Law*. Washington D.C.: Public Affairs Press, 1967.

Cameron, Kenneth. "The Quest for International Copyright in the Thirtieth Congress." *ESQ: A Journal of the American Renaissance* 51 (1968): 108–36.

Campbell, Joseph. *Considerations and Arguments Proving the Inexpediency of an International Copyright Law*. New York: William E. Dean, 1844.

Capen, Nahum. "Memorial of Nahum Capen, of Boston, Massachusetts, on the Subject of International Copyright." *House of Representatives Documents* 26-61 (1st Sess. 1838).

Carey, Henry C. *Letters on International Copyright*. Philadelphia: A. Hart, 1853.

Carlson, Eric W., ed. *The Recognition of Edgar Allan Poe*. Ann Arbor: University of Michigan Press, 1970.

Cary, Thomas G. *Letter to a Lady in France on the Supposed Failure of a National Bank, the Supposed Delinquency of the National Government, the Debts of the Several States, and Repudiation; with Answers to Enquiries Concerning the Books of Capt. Marryat and Mr. Dickens*. Boston: Benjamin H. Greene, 1844.

Casale, Ottavio M. "The Battle of Boston: A Reevaluaton of Poe's Lyceum Appearance." *American Literature* 45 (1973): 423–28.

Cassuto, Leonard. *Edgar Allan Poe: Literary Theory and Criticism*. New York: Dover Publications, 1999.

Chartier, Roger. *Forms and Meanings*. Philadelphia: University of Pennsylvania Press, 1995.

———. *The Order of Books*. Trans. Lydia G. Cochrane. Stanford, Calif.: Stanford University Press, 1994.

Charvat, William. "Introduction." In *The House of the Seven Gables*, ed. Fredson Bowers, xv–xxviii. Columbus: Ohio University Press, 1965.

———. *Literary Publishing in America, 1790–1850*. Philadelphia: University of Pennsylvania Press, 1959.

———. *The Profession of Authorship in America, 1800–1870*. Columbus: Ohio State University Press, 1968.

Chielens, Edward, ed. *American Literary Magazines: The Eighteenth and Nineteenth Centuries*. Westport, Conn.: Greenwood Press, 1986

Christensen, Jerome. *Practicing Enlightenment: Hume and the Formation of a Literary Career*. Madison: University of Wisconsin Press, 1987.

Clark, Aubert J. *The Movement for International Copyright in Nineteenth-Century America*. Washington, D.C.: Catholic University of America Press, 1960.

Clark, C. E. Frazer. *Nathaniel Hawthorne: A Descriptive Bibliography*. Pittsburgh: University of Pittsburgh Press, 1978.

Clark, Lewis Gaylord. "Editor's Table." *The Knickerbocker* (April 1842): 384–85.

Clay, Henry. *Report, with Senate Bill No. 223, Senate Documents* 24-179 (2d Sess. 1837).

Colacurcio, Michael. *The Province of Piety: Moral History in Hawthorne's Early Tales*. Cambridge, Mass.: Harvard University Press, 1984.

Cole, Richard Cargill. *Irish Booksellers and English Writers 1740–1800*. Atlantic Highlands, N.J.: Humanities Press International, 1986.

"Correspondence." *Littell's Living Age* 1 (May 11, 1844).

"Correspondence." *Littell's Living Age* 2 (May 25, 1844).

Dabney, John Blair. "Reply to E.D. and Mr. Simms." *Southern Literary Messenger* (April–May 1844): 193–99, 289–97.

Darnton, Robert. *The Business of Enlightenment: A Publishing History of the* Encyclopédie *1775–1800*. Cambridge, Mass.: Harvard University Press, 1979.

———. "What Is the History of Books?" In *Reading in America: Literature & Social History*, ed. Cathy Davidson, 27–52. Baltimore: Johns Hopkins University Press, 1989.

Dauber, Kenneth. *The Idea of Authorship in America: Democratic Poetics from Franklin to Melville*. Madison: University of Wisconsin Press, 1990.

Davidson, Cathy, ed. *Reading in America: Literature & Social History*. Baltimore: Johns Hopkins University Press, 1989.

Davis, Paul. "Dickens and the American Press, 1842." *Dickens Annual* 4 (1968): 32–77.

Dayan, Joan. *Fables of Mind: An Inquiry Into Poe's Fiction*. New York: Oxford University Press, 1987.

De Prospo, R. C. "Poe's Alpha Poem: The Title of Al Aaraaf." *Poe Studies* 22, no. 2 (December 1989): 35–39.

Deas, Michael J. *The Portraits and Daguerreotypes of Edgar Allan Poe*. Charlottesville: Univeristy Press of Virginia, 1989.

Decisions of the United States Courts Involving Copyright and Literary Property, 1789–1900. Vols. 13–15. Washington, D.C.: Government Printing Office, 1980.

Decisions of the United States Courts Involving Copyright, 1909–1914. Vol. 17. Washington, D.C.: Government Printing Office, 1928.

Decisions of the United States Courts Involving Copyright, 1935–1937. Vol. 21. Washington D.C.: Government Printing Office, 1938.

Decisions of the United States Courts Involving Copyright, 1951–1952. Vol. 28. Washington D.C.: Government Printing Office, 1954.

Derrida, Jacques. *Of Grammatology*. Trans. Gayatri Chakravorty Spivak. Baltimore: Johns Hopkins University Press, 1974.

Dickens, Charles. *American Notes for General Circulation*. *New World* Extra Series, Nos. 32, 33. New York, 1842.

———. *American Notes for General Circulation*. New York: Harper & Brothers, 1842.

———. *American Notes for General Circulation*. London: Chapman and Hall, 1850.

———. *American Notes for General Circulation*. Boston: Ticknor & Fields, 1867.

———. *American Notes for General Circulation*. Ed. Arnold Goldman and John Whitley. New York: Penguin Books, 1985.

———. *The Letters of Charles Dickens*. Ed. Madeline House and Graham Storey. Vol. 3. Oxford: Clarendon Press, 1974.

———. *Martin Chuzzlewit*. Ed. P. N. Furbank. New York: Penguin Books, 1995.

"Dickensonianna." *Southern Quarterly Review* 4 (October 1843): 292–309.

Douglas, Ann. *The Feminization of American Culture*. New York: Knopf, 1977.

Drone, Eaton S. *A Treatise on the Law of Property in Intellectual Productions in Great Britain and the United States*. Boston: Little, Brown and Company, 1879.

Duyckinck, Evert. "Bryant's American Poets." *Arcturus* 1 (December 1840): 24–29.

———. "Literary Prospects of 1845." *American Review* (February 1845): 146–51.

———. "On Writing for the Magazines." *United States Magazine and Democratic Review* (May 1845): 455–60.

———. "Plagiarism." *United States Magazine and Democratic Review* (April 1845): 413–15.

Duyckinck, Evert, and George L. Duyckinck. *Cyclopedia of American Literature*. Philadelphia: W. M. Rutter & Co., 1875.

Eaton, Andrew J. "The American Movement for International Copyright." *Library Quarterly* 15 (April 1945): 95–122.

Eddings, Dennis, ed. *The Naiad Voice: Essays on Poe's Satiric Hoaxing*. Port Washington, N.Y.: Associated Faculty Press, 1983.

Eldridge, Herbert G. "The American Republication of Thomas Moore's *Epistles, Odes, and Other Poems*: An Early Version of the 'Reprint Game.'" *Papers of the Bibliographic Society of America* 62, no. 2 (1968): 199–205.

Eliot, T.S. "From Poe to Valéry." In *The Recognition of Edgar Allan Poe*, ed. Eric W. Carlson, 205–19. Ann Arbor: University of Michigan Press, 1970.

Elmer, Jonathan. *Reading at the Social Limit: Affect, Mass Culture, and Edgar Allan Poe*. Stanford, Calif.: Stanford University Press, 1995.

English Reports. Vol. 98. Edinburgh: William Green & Sons, 1901.

Exman, Eugene. *The Brothers Harper*. New York: Harper & Row, 1965.

Fabi, M. Giulia. "Representing Slavery in Nineteenth-Century Britain: The Anxiety of Non/Fictional Authorship in Charles Dickens' *American Notes* and William Brown's *Clotel*." In *Images of America: Through the European Looking Glass*, ed. William L. Chew III, 125–40. Brussels: VUB University Press, 1997.

Fabian, Ann. *The Unvarnished Truth: Personal Narratives in Nineteenth-Century America*. Berkeley: University of California Press, 2000.

Febvre, Lucien, and Henri-Jean Martin. *The Coming of the Book: The Impact of Printing 1450–1800*. Trans. Geoffrey Nowell-Smith and David Wooton. London: New Left Books, 1976.

Field, Kate. *Pen Photographs of Charles Dickens's Readings: Taken from Life*. Ed. Carolyn J. Moss. Troy, N.Y.: Whitson Publishing Company, 1998.

Fielding, K. J. *The Speeches of Charles Dickens*. New York: Oxford University Press, 1960.

Fields, James T. *Yesterdays with Authors*. Boston: Houghton Mifflin and Company, 1885.

Fisher, Philip. "Democratic Social Space: Whitman, Melville, and the Promise of American Transparency." *Representations* 24 (1988): 61–101.

———. "Pins, A Table, Works of Art." *Representations* 1 (1983): 43–57.

Forster, John. *The Life of Charles Dickens*. 3 Vols. London: Chapman and Hall, 1872–74.

———. "The Newspaper Literature of America." *Foreign Quarterly Review* 30 (October 1843): 197–222.

Foucault, Michel. "What Is an Author?" In *The Foucault Reader*, ed. Paul Rabinow, 101–20. New York: Pantheon Books, 1984.

Franklin, John. *Narrative of a Journey to the Shores of the Polar Sea*. London: J. Murray, 1823.

Frederick, David C. "John Quincy Adams, Slavery, and the Disappearance of the Right of Petition." *Law and History Review* (Spring 1991): 113–55.

Freeman, Elizabeth. "Honeymoon with a Stranger: Pedophiliac Picaresques from Poe to Nabokov." *American Literature* 70, no. 4 (1998): 863–97.

Fried, Debra. "Repetition, Refrain, and Epitaph." *ELH* 53, no. 3 (Fall 1986): 615–39.

Gallagher, Catherine, and Stephen Greenblatt. *Practicing New Historicism*. Chicago: University of Chicago Press, 2000.

Gallagher, Susan Van Zanten. "A Domestic Reading of *The House of the Seven Gables.*" *Studies in the Novel* 21, no. 1 (1992): 1–13.

Gaskell, Philip. *A New Introduction to Bibliography*. New York: Oxford University Press, 1972.

The Gift: A Christmas and New Year's Present for 1840. Philadelphia, 1840.

Gilmore, Michael T. *American Romanticism and the Marketplace*. Chicago: University of Chicago Press, 1985.

——. "Politics and the Author's Career: Two Cases." In *Reciprocal Influences: Literary Production, Distribution, and Consumption in America*, ed. Stephen Fink and Susan S. Williams, 199–212. Columbus: Ohio State University Press, 1999.

Gilreath, James. "American Literature, Public Policy, and the Copyright Laws Before 1800." In *Federal Copyright Records 1790–1800*, xv–xxv. Washington D.C.: Library of Congress, 1980.

Ginsburg, Jane. "A Tale of Two Copyrights: Literary Property in Revolutionary France and America." In *Publishing and Readership in Revolutionary France and America*, ed. Carol Armbruster, 95–114. Westport, Conn.: Greenwood Press, 1993.

Gitelman, Lisa. "Arthur Gordon Pym and the Novel Narrative of Edgar Allan Poe." *Nineteenth-Century Literature* (1992): 349–61.

Goddu, Teresa. "The Circulation of Women in *The House of the Seven Gables.*" *Studies in the Novel* 23, no. 1 (Spring 1991): 119–27.

Goodrich, Samuel. *Recollections of a Lifetime, or Men and Things I Have Seen: In a Series of Familiar Letters to a Friend, Historical, Biographical, Anecdotal, and Descriptive*. 2 vols. New York: Miller, Orton, and Mulligan, 1856.

Gray, Richard. "'Hawthorne: A Problem': *The House of the Seven Gables.*" In *Nathaniel Hawthorne: New Critical Essays*, ed. A. Robert Lee, 88–109. New York: Vision Press, 1982.

Greenspan, Ezra. "Evert Duyckinck and the History of Wiley and Putnam's Library of American Books, 1845–1847." *American Literature* 64, no. 4 (1992): 677–93.

——. *George Palmer Putnam: Representative American Publisher*. University Park: Pennsylvania State University, 2000.

Griswold, Rufus Wilmot, ed. *The Female Poets of America*. Philadelphia: Carey and Hart, 1849.

Gross, Robert A, and Mary Kelley, eds. *A History of the Book in America*. Vol. 2. New York: Cambridge University Press, 2003.

Groves, Jeff. "Judging Books by Their Covers: House Styles, Ticknor and Fields, and Literary Promotion." In *Reading Books: Essays on the Material Text and Literature in America*, ed. Michelle Moylan and Lane Stiles, 75–100. Amherst: University of Massachusetts Press, 1996.

Gunderson, Robert Gray. *The Log Cabin Campaign*. Lexington: University of Kentucky Press, 1957.

Hall, David D. *Worlds of Wonder, Days of Judgment: Popular Religious Belief in Early New England*. New York: Alfred A. Knopf, 1989.

Hamilton, Kristie. *America's Sketchbook: The Cultural Life of a Nineteenth-Century Literary Genre*. Athens: Ohio University Press, 1998.

Hawthorne, Julian. *Hawthorne and His Circle*. New York: Harper Brothers, 1903.

Hawthorne, Nathaniel. *The House of the Seven Gables*. New York: Penguin Books, 1986.

——. *The Letters, 1813–1843*. Vol. 15 of *The Centenary Edition of the Works of Nathaniel Hawthorne*, ed. Thomas Woodson, L. Neal Smith, and Norman Holmes Pearson. Columbus: Ohio State University Press, 1984.

——. *The Letters, 1843–1853*. Vol. 16 of *The Centenary Edition of the Works of Nathaniel Hawthorne*, ed. Thomas Woodson, L. Neal Smith, and Norman Holmes Pearson. Columbus: Ohio State University Press, 1984.

——. *The Scarlet Letter*. New York: Penguin Classics, 1986.

——. *Tales and Sketches*. New York: Literary Classics of the United States, 1982.

——. *True Stories from History and Biography*. Vol. 6 of *The Centenary Edition of the Works of Nathaniel Hawthorne*. Columbus: Ohio State University Press, 1972.

Hawthorne, Nathaniel, and Elizabeth Hawthorne. *Peter Parley's Universal History on the Basis of Geography*. New York: William Robinson, 1837.

Hayes, Kevin. *Poe and the Printed Word*. New York: Oxford University Press, 2000.

Hedrick, Joan. *Harriet Beecher Stowe: A Life*. New York: Oxford University Press, 1994.

Henkin, David. *City Reading: Written Words and Public Spaces in Antebellum New York*. New York: Columbia University Press, 1998.

Hesse, Carla. *Publishing and Cultural Politics in Revolutionary Paris, 1789–1800*. Berkeley: University of California Press, 1991.

Hessler, Gene. *The Comprehensive Catalog of U.S. Paper Money*. Port Clinton, Ohio: BNR Press, 1992.

Homestead, Melissa. "Imperfect Title: Nineteenth-Century American Woman Authors and Literary Property." Ph.D. dissertation, University of Pennsylvania, 1998.

Hoover, Merle Montgomery. *Park Benjamin, Poet & Editor*. New York: Columbia University Press, 1948.

Horwitz, Morton. *The Transformation of American Law, 1780–1860*. Cambridge, Mass.: Harvard University Press, 1977.

Houghton, Walter E. "Periodical Literature and the Articulate Classes." In *The Victorian Periodical Press: Samplings and Soundings*, ed. Joanne Shattock and Michael Wolff, 3–27. Toronto: University of Toronto Press, 1982.

Houtchens, Lawrence H. "Charles Dickens and International Copyright." *American Literature* 13 (March 1941): 18–28.

Hubbell, Jay B. "Charles Chauncey Burr: Friend of Poe." *PMLA* 69 (1954): 833–40.

Hull, William Doyle. "A Canon of the Critical Works of Edgar Allan Poe." Ph.D. dissertation, University of Virginia, 1941.

Idol, John L., and Buford Jones, eds. *Nathaniel Hawthorne: The Contemporary Reviews*. New York: Cambridge University Press, 1994.

"International Copyright." *United States Review* (April 1853): 352–55.

"The International Copyright Question." *United States Magazine and Democratic Review* 12 (February 1843): 113–22.

"The International Copyright Question: Protest Against the Doctrine of the Democratic Review Thereon." *United States Magazine and Democratic Review* (June 1843): 609–14.

Irving, Washington. *Bracebridge Hall, Tales of a Traveller, and The Alhambra*. New York: Literary Classics of the United States, 1991.

Irwin, John. *American Hieroglyphics: The Symbol of the Egyptioan Hieroglyphics in The American Renaissance*. New Haven, Conn.: Yale University Press, 1980.

Jackson, Andrew. "Veto Message." In *A Compilation of the Messages and Papers of the Presidents*, ed. James D. Richardson. New York: Bureau of National Literature, 1897.

Jackson, Virginia. "Poe, Longfellow, and the Institution of Poetry." *Poe Studies* 33, no. 1–2 (2000): 23–28.

Jaszi, Peter. "Toward a Theory of Copyright: The Metamorphosis of Authorship." *Duke Law Journal* (1991): 455–502.

Jay, John. "Memorials of John Jay and of William Cullen Bryant and Others, in Favor of an International Copyright Law," *House of Representatives Miscellaneous Documents* 30-76 (1st Sess. 1848).

Jefferson, Thomas. *Notes on the State of Virginia*. New York: W. W. Norton, 1954.

John, Richard. *Spreading the News: The American Postal System from Franklin to Morse*. Cambridge, Mass.: Harvard University Press, 1995.

Johns, Adrian. *The Nature of the Book: Print and Knowledge in the Making*. Chicago: University of Chicago Press, 1998.

Johnson, Barbara. "Strange Fits: Poe and Wordsworth on the Nature of Poetic Language." In *The American Face of Edgar Allan Poe*, ed. Shawn Rosenheim and Stephen Rachman, 89–99. Baltimore: Johns Hopkins University Press, 1995.

Johnson, Louise H. "The Source of the Chapter on Slavery in Dickens's *American Notes*." *American Literature* 14, no. 4 (January 1943): 427–30.

Joseph, Gerhard. "Charles Dickens, International Copyright, and the Discretionary Silence of Martin Chuzzlewit." In *The Construction of Authorship: Textual Appropriation in Law and Literature*, ed. Martha Woodmansee and Peter Jaszi, 259–70. Durham, N.C.: Duke University Press, 1994.

——. "Labyrinth and Library." *Dickens Studies Annual* 15 (1986): 1–22.

Joyce, Craig. "The Rise of the Supreme Court Reporter: An Institutional Perspective on Marshall Court Ascendancy." *Michigan Law Review* 83 (1985): 1291–391.

Kelley, Mary. *Private Woman, Public Stage: Literary Domesticity in Nineteenth-Century America*. New York: Oxford University Press, 1984.

Kielbowicz, Richard B. *News in the Mail: The Press, Post Office, and Public Information, 1700–1860s*. New York: Greenwood Press, 1989.

Knox, John Jay. *United States Notes: A History of the Various Issues of Paper Money by the Government of the United States*. New York: Charles Scribner's Sons, 1988.

Kramnick, Isaac. "Republican Revisionism Revisited." *American Historical Review* 87 (1982): 629–64.

Larson, Jonathan Lauritz. *Internal Improvement*. Chapel Hill: University of North Carolina Press, 2001.

Latrobe, John H. B. "Poe and His Biographer, Griswold." *The Old Guard* (June 1866): 353–58.

Lehuu, Isabelle. *Carnival on the Page: Popular Print Media in Antebellum America*. Chapel Hill: University of North Carolina Press, 2000.

Leighton, Angela, and Margaret Reynolds, eds. *Victorian Women Poets: An Anthology*. Cambridge: Blackwell, 1995.

Leverenz, David. "Poe and Gentry Virginia." In *The American Face of Edgar Allan Poe*, ed. Shawn Rosenheim and Stephen Rachman, 210–36. Baltimore: Johns Hopkins University Press, 1995.

Levine, Lawrence. *Highbrow/Lowbrow: The Emergence of Cultural Hierarchy in America*. Cambridge, Mass.: Harvard University Press, 1988.

Lieber, Francis. *On International Copyright*. New York: Wiley & Putnam, 1840.

"Literary Property." *United States Magazine and Democratic Review* 2 (June 1838): 289–311.

Ljungquist, Kent, and Buford Jones. "The Identity of 'Outis': A Further Chapter in the Poe-Longfellow War." *American Literature* 60, no. 3 (1988): 402–415.

Locke, John. *Second Treatise of Government*. Indianapolis: Hackett Publishing Company, 1980.

Longfellow, Henry Wadsworth. *Hyperion*. Boston: Ticknor & Fields, 1844.

Lott, Eric. *Love and Theft: Blackface Minstrelsy and the American Working Class*. New York: Oxford University Press, 1993.

Lowell, James Russell. "Nationality in Literature." *North American Review* (July 1849). Reprinted in *Literary Criticism of James Russell Lowell*, ed. Herbert F. Smith, 116–31. Lincoln, Neb.: University of Nebraska Press, 1969.

———. "Our Contributors, No. XVII: Edgar Allan Poe." In *The Shock of Recognition*, ed. Edmund Wilson, 5–20. New York: Doubleday, Doran & Co., 1943.

Lyell, Charles. *A Second Visit to the United States of North America*. New York: Harper & Brothers, 1849.

Macpherson, C. B. *Property: Mainstream and Critical Positions*. Toronto: University of Toronto Press, 1978.

Madison, James, Alexander Hamilton, and John Jay. *The Federalist Papers*, ed. Isaac Kramnick. New York: Penguin Books, 1987.

Martin, Robert K. "Haunted by Jim Crow: Gothic Fictions by Hawthorne and Faulkner." In *American Gothic: New Interventions in a National Narrative*, ed. Robert K Martin and Eric Savoy, 129–42. Iowa City: University of Iowa Press, 1998.

Matheson, Neill. "Clifford's Dim Unsatisfactory Elegance." Modern Language Association, 2001.

Mathews, Cornelius. "An Appeal to American Authors and the American Press in Behalf of International Copyright." *Graham's Magazine* (September 1842): 121–24.

———. *The Better Interests of the Country, in Connexion with International Copyright*. New York: Wiley & Putnam, 1843.

Matthiessen, F. O. *American Renaissance: Art and Expression in the Age of Emerson and Whitman*. New York: Oxford University Press, 1941.

The May Flower, for MDCCCXLVI. Boston, 1846.

The Mayflower, for MDCCCXLVII. Boston, 1848.

McHenry, Elizabeth. *Forgotten Readers: African-American Literary Societies, 1830–1940.* Durham, N.C.: Duke University Press, 2002.

McKenzie, D. F. *Bibliography and the Sociology of Texts.* London: British Library, 1986.

McVickar, John. *Tribute to the Memory of Sir Walter Scott.* New York: George P. Scott and Co., 1833.

Meckier, Jerome. *Innocent Abroad: Charles Dickens's American Engagements.* Lexington: University Press of Kentucky, 1990.

"Memorial of the Columbia Typographical Society of the City of Washington, Against the Enactment of an International Copy-Right Law," *Senate Documents* 25-190 (2d Sess. 1838).

"Memorial of Inhabitants of Philadelphia, Against an International Copyright Law," *House of Representatives Documents* 25-117 (2d Sess. 1838).

"Memorial of the New York Typographical Society Against the Passage of an International Copyright Law," *Senate Documents* 25-296 (2d Sess. 1838).

"Memorial of a Number of Citizens of Boston, Praying the Passage of an International Copyright Law," *Senate Documents* 25-398 (2d Sess. 1838).

"Memorial of a Number of Citizens of New York, Praying the Passage of an International Copyright Law," *Senate Documents* 25-399 (2d Sess. 1838).

"Memorial of a Number of Citizens of Philadelphia, Against the Passage of an International Copyright Law," *Senate Documents* 25-102 (2d Sess. 1838).

"Memorial of a Number of Citizens of the United States, Praying an Alteration of the Law Regulating Copyrights," *Senate Documents* 24-141 (2d Sess. 1837).

"Memorial of a Number of Persons Concerned in Printing and Publishing, Praying an Alteration in the Mode of Levying Duties on Certain Books, and Remonstrating Against the Enactment of an International Copyright Law," *Senate Documents* 27-323 (2d Sess. 1843).

"Memorial of Richard Penn Smith and Others, Against the Passage of the Bill to Establish an International Copyright Law," *Senate Documents* 25-369 (2d Sess. 1838).

Michaels, Walter Benn. *The Gold Standard and the Logic of Naturalism.* Berkeley: University of California Press, 1987.

Miller, Perry. *The Life of the Mind in America: From the Revolution to the Civil War.* New York: Harcourt, Brace & World, 1965.

———. *The Raven and the Whale: The War of Words and Wits in the Era of Poe and Melville.* 1956. Reprint. *The Raven and the Whale: Poe, Melville, and the New York Literary Scene.* Baltimore: Johns Hopkins University Press, 1997.

Moriarty, Joseph. *A Literary Tomahawking: The Libel Action of Edgar Allan Poe vs. Thomas Dunn English.* Self-published, 1963.

Moss, Sidney P. *Charles Dickens' Quarrel with America.* Troy, N.Y.: Whitson Publishing Company, 1984.

———. *Poe's Literary Battles: The Critic in the Context of His Literary Milieu.* Carbondale: Southern Illinois University Press, 1963.

———. *Poe's Major Crisis: His Libel Suit and New York's Literary World.* Durham, N.C.: Duke University Press, 1970.

———. "South Carolina Contemplates Banning *American Notes.*" In *American Episodes Involving Charles Dickens*, edited by Sidney Moss and Carolyn J. Moss, 20–27. Troy, N.Y.: Whitson Publishing Company, 1999.

Mowitt, John. *Text: The Genealogy of an Antidisciplinary Object.* Durham, N.C.: Duke University Press, 1992.

Mulcaire, Terry. "Publishing Intimacy in *Leaves of Grass.*" *ELH* 60 (1993): 471–501.

Murphy, Teresa Ann. *Ten Hours Labor: Religion, Reform, and Gender in Early New England.* Ithaca, N.Y.: Cornell University Press, 1992.

"National Literature, and the International Copy-Right Treaty." *United States Review* (August 1853): 97–117.

"Necessity for a National Literature." *The Knickerbocker* (May 1845): 416–17.

Newbury, Michael. *Figuring Authorship in Antebellum America.* Stanford, Calif.: Stanford University Press, 1997.

Nicklin, Philip H. *Remarks on Literary Property.* Philadelphia: P. H. Nicklin and T. Johnson, 1838.

Nissenbaum, Stephen. *The Battle for Christmas.* New York: Vintage Books, 1997.

———. "The Firing of Nathaniel Hawthorne." *Essex Institute Historical Collections* 114 (April 1978): 57–86.

Noble, Marianne. "Sentimental Epistemologies in *Uncle Tom's Cabin* and *The House of the Seven Gables.*" In *Separate Spheres No More: Gender Convergence in American Literature, 1830–1930,* ed. Monika M. Elbert, 261–81. Tuscaloosa: University of Alabama Press, 2000.

Nord, David Paul. "The Evangelical Origins of Mass Media in America, 1815–1835." *Journalism Monographs* 88 (May 1984): 1–30.

———. "Systematic Benevolence: Religious Publishing and the Marketplace in Early Nineteenth-Century America." In *Communication and Change in American Religious History,* ed. Leonard Sweet, 239–69. Grand Rapids, Mich.: William B. Eerdmans, 1993.

"Notices of Littell's Living Age." *Littell's Living Age* 1 (April 11–August 3 1844): 3–6.

"Obituary of Scott." *Museum of Foreign Liteature, Science, and Art* 21 (December 1832): [481].

The Opal: A Pure Gift for the Holy Days. New York, 1844.

O'Sullivan, John. "Introduction." *United States Magazine and Democratic Review* (October 1837): 1–15.

———. "Review of Twice-Told Tales." *United States Magazine and Democratic Review.* (February 1842): 197–98.

Patten, Robert. *Charles Dickens and His Publishers.* New York: Oxford University Press, 1978.

Patterson, Lyman Ray. *Copyright in Historical Perspective.* Nashville, Tenn.: Vanderbilt University Press, 1968.

Pearce, Roy Harvey. "Historical Introduction." In *True Stories from History and Biography,* 287–311. Columbus: Ohio State University Press, 1972.

Person, Leland S. "Poe's Composition of Philosophy: Reading and Writing 'The Raven.'" *Arizona Quarterly* 46, no. 3 (Fall 1990): 1–15.

Peters, Richard. "Letters." *American Jurist* 13 (1835): 484–86.

———. *Report of the Copy-Right Case of Wheaton v. Peters*. New York: James van Norden, 1834.

———, ed. *Reports of Cases Argued and Adjudged in the Supreme Court of the United States*. Vol. 8. Philadelphia: Desilver, Jun. and Thomas, 1834.

"Petition of Thomas Moore, and Other Authors of Great Britain, Praying Congress to Grant to Them the Exclusive Benefit of Their Writings Within the United States," *Senate Documents* 24-134 (2d Sess. 1837).

Pfister, Joel. *The Production of Personal Life: Class, Gender, and the Psychological in Hawthorne's Fiction*. Stanford, Calif.: Stanford University Press, 1991.

Poe, Edgar Allan. *Al Aaraaf*. Edited by Thomas Ollive Mabbott. New York: Facsimile Text Society, 1933.

———. *The Collected Works of Edgar Allan Poe*. Ed. Thomas Ollive Mabbott. Cambridge, Mass.: Belknap Press, 1969–78.

———. *Collected Writings of Edgar Allan Poe*. Ed. Burton Pollin. New York: Gordian Press, 1981–86.

———. *Complete Works of Edgar Allan Poe*. Ed. James A. Harrison. New York: George D. Sproul, 1902.

———. *Essays and Reviews*. Ed. G. R. Thompson. New York: Literary Classics of the United States, 1984.

———. "Lenore." *Pioneer* (February 1843): 60–61.

———. *The Letters of Edgar Allan Poe*. Ed. John Ward Ostrom. New York: Gordian Press, 1966.

———. *Poetry and Tales*. Ed. Patrick Quinn. New York: Literary Classics of the United States, 1984.

———. *The Raven and Other Poems*. Ed. Thomas Ollive Mabbott. New York: Columbia University Press, 1942.

Pollin, Burton. *Discoveries in Poe*. Notre Dame, Ind.: University of Notre Dame Press, 1970.

———. "The Living Writers of America: A Manuscript by Edgar Allan Poe." *Studies in the American Renaissance* (1991): 151–211.

———. "Poe and Frances Osgood, as Linked Through 'Lenore.'" *Mississippi Quarterly* 46, no. 2 (1993): 185–97.

———. "Poe as Author of the 'Outis' Letter and 'The Bird of the Dream.'" *Poe Studies* 20, no. 1 (1987): 10–15.

Poole, William Fred, Editor. *Poole's Index to Periodical Literature*. New York: Charles B. Norton, 1853.

Pope, Alexander. *Poetry and Prose of Alexander Pope*. Ed. Aubrey Williams. New York: Houghton Mifflin, 1969.

Putnam, George Haven. *The Question of Copyright*. New York: G. P. Putnam's Sons, 1896.

Quinn, Arthur Hobson. *Edgar Allan Poe: A Critical Bibliography*. 1941. Reprint. Baltimore: Johns Hopkins University Press, 1998.

Rachman, Stephen. "'Es Lasst Sich Nicht Schreiben': Plagiarism and 'The Man of the Crowd.'" In *The American Face of Edgar Allan Poe*, ed. Shawn Rosenheim and Stephen Rachman, 49–87. Baltimore: Johns Hopkins University Press, 1995.

Radway, Janice A. *Reading the Romance: Women, Patriarchy, and Popular Literature*. 1984. Reprint. Chapel Hill: University of North Carolina Press, 1991.

Register of Debates in Congress. Vol. 13. Washington D.C.: Gales & Seaton, 1837.

"Remonstrance of the Inhabitants of Massachusetts, Against the Passage of an International Copyright Law," *House of Representatives Documents* 25-416 (2d Sess. 1838).

Renza, Louis. "Poe and the Issue of American Privacy." In *A Historical Guide to Edgar Allan Poe*, ed. J. Gerald Kennedy, 167–88. New York: Oxford University Press, 2001.

———. "Poe's Secret Autobiography." In *The American Renaissance Reconsidered*, ed. Walter Benn Michaels and Donald Pease, 58–89. Baltimore: Johns Hopkins University Press, 1985.

"Review of Charles Dickens, *American Notes for General Circulation*." *Southern Literary Messenger* 9 (January 1843): 58–62.

"Review, *Report of the Copy-Right Case of Wheaton v. Peters*." *Westminster Review* 24 (1836): 187–97.

Rice, Grantland. *The Transformation of Authorship in America*. Chicago: University of Chicago Press, 1997.

Rice, Sara Sigourney, ed. *Edgar Allan Poe: A Memorial Volume*. Baltimore: Turnbull Brothers, 1877.

Richard, Claude. "Poe and Young America." *Studies in Bibliography* 21 (1968): 25–58.

Richards, Eliza. "Lyric Telegraphy: Women Poets, Spiritualist Poetics, and the 'Phantom Voice' of Poe." *Yale Journal of Criticism* 12, no. 2 (1999): 269–94.

———. "'The Poetess' and Poe's Performance of the Feminine." *Arizona Quarterly* 55, no. 2 (Summer 1999): 1–29.

Richards, Leonard L. *"Gentlemen of Property and Standing": Anti-Abolition Mobs in Jacksonian America*. New York: Oxford University Press, 1970.

Riddel, Joseph. *Purloined Letters: Originality and Repetition in American Literature*. Baton Rouge: Louisiana State University Press, 1995.

Ridgely, J.V. "The Authorship of the 'Paulding-Drayton Review.'" *Poe Studies Association Newsletter* 20, no. 2 (Fall 1992): 1–6.

Romero, Laura. *Home Fronts: Domesticity and Its Critics in the Antebellum United States*. Durham, N.C.: Duke University Press, 1997.

Rose, Mark. "The Author as Proprietor: *Donaldson v. Becket* and the Genealogy of Modern Authorship." *Representations* 23 (1988): 51–85.

———. *Authors and Owners: The Invention of Copyright*. Cambridge, Mass.: Harvard University Press, 1993.

Rosenheim, Shawn. *The Cryptographic Imagination: Secret Writing from Edgar Allan Poe to the Internet*. Baltimore: Johns Hopkins University Press, 1997.

Rowe, John Carlos. *Through the Custom House: Nineteenth-Century American Fiction and Modern Theory*. Baltimore: Johns Hopkins University Press, 1982.

Ruggles, John. "Report, from the Committee on Patents and the Patent Office," *Senate Documents* 25-494 (2d Sess. 1838).

Sánchez-Eppler, Karen. "Hawthorne and the Writing of Childhood." In *The Cambridge Companion to Nathaniel Hawthorne*. New York: Cambridge University Press, forthcoming 2002.

Saunders, David. *Authorship and Copyright*. New York: Routledge, 1992.

Saunders, Frederick. "A Reminiscence in Copyright History." *Publishers' Weekly* 33 (June 30, 1888): 998.

Saxton, Alexander. "Problems of Class and Race in the Origins of the Mass Circulation Press." *American Quarterly* 36 (Summer 1984): 211–34.

Scherman, Timothy. "The Authority Effect: Poe and the Politics of Reputation in the Pre-Industry of American Publishing." *Arizona Quarterly* 49, no. 3 (Autumn 1993): 1–19.

Schreyer, Alice D. "Copyright and Books in Nineteenth-Century America." In *Getting the Books Out*, ed. Michael Hackenberg, 121–36. Washington, D.C.: Center for the Book, 1987.

Scott, Sir Walter. *The Prefaces to the Waverley Novels*. Ed. Mark A. Weinstein. Lincoln: University of Nebraska Press, 1978.

Secord, James A. *Victorian Sensation*. Chicago: University of Chicago Press, 2000.

Sellers, Charles. *The Market Revolution: Jacksonian America, 1815–1846*. New York: Oxford University Press, 1991.

Seville, Catherine. *Literary Copyright Reform in Early Victorian England: The Framing of the 1842 Copyright Act*. New York: Cambridge University Press, 1999.

Shamir, Milette. "Hawthorne's Romance and the Right to Privacy." *American Quarterly* 49, no. 4 (1997): 746–79.

Sharpe, William. "A Pig Upon the Town: Charles Dickens in New York." *Nineteenth-Century Prose* 23, no. 2 (Fall 1996): 12–24.

Silverman, Kenneth. *Edgar A. Poe: Mournful and Never-Ending Remembrance*. New York: Harper Collins, 1991.

Simms, William Gilmore. "Letter." *Southern Literary Messenger* (January–March 1844): 7–17; 137–51.

Smith-Rosenberg, Carroll. "Domesticating 'Virtue': Coquettes and Revolutionaries in Young America." In *Literature and the Body: Essays on Populations and Persons*, ed. Elaine Scarry, 160–84. Baltimore: Johns Hopkins University Press, 1988.

Snyder, J. F. "Charles Dickens in Illinois." *Journal of the Illinois State Historical Society* (1910): 7–22.

Solberg, Thorvald, ed. *Copyright Enactments of the United States, 1783–1906*. Washington, D.C.: Government Printing Office, 1906.

——. *Copyright in Congress 1789–1904*. Washington D.C.: Government Printing Office, 1905.

The Statutes at Large of the Provisional Government of the Confederate States of America. Ed. James M. Mathews. New York: William S. Hein & Company, 1988.

Stewart, Susan. *Crimes of Writing: Problems in the Containment of Representation*. New York: Oxford University Press, 1991.

Stoddard, Roger. "Morphology and the Book from an American Perspective." *Printing History* 17 (1987): 2–14.

Stokes, Melvin, and Stephen Conway, eds. *The Market Revolution in America: Social, Political, and Religious Expressions, 1800–1880*. Charlottesville: University Press of Virginia, 1996.

Sutton, Walter. *The Western Book Trade: Cincinnati as a Nineteenth-Century Publishing and Book-Trade Center*. Columbus: Ohio University Press, 1961.

Swift, Jonathan. *A Tale of a Tub*. New York: Oxford University Press, 1984.

Taylor, George Rogers. *The Transportation Revolution, 1815–1860*. New York: M.E. Sharpe, 1951.

Tebbel, John. *A History of Book Publishing in the United States*. Vol. 1. New York: R. R. Bowker, 1972.

Teichgraeber, Richard F. *Sublime Thoughts/Penny Wisdom: Situating Emerson and Thoreau in the American Market*. Baltimore: Johns Hopkins University Press, 1995.

Thomas, Brooks. *Cross-Examinations of Law and Literature: Cooper, Hawthorne, Stowe, and Melville*. New York: Cambridge University Press, 1987.

Thomas, Dwight, and David K. Jackson, eds. *The Poe Log: A Documentary Life of Edgar Allan Poe, 1809–1849*. Boston: G. K. Hall & Co., 1987.

Thompson, G. R. *Poe's Fiction: Romantic Irony in the Gothic Tales*. Madison: University of Wisconsin Press, 1973.

Timberlake, Richard. *Gold, Greenbacks, and the Constitution*. Berryville: George Edward Durell Foundation, 1991.

The Token: A Christmas and New Year's Present. Boston, 1831.

The Token: A Christmas and New Year's Present. Boston, 1832.

The Token and Atlantic Souvenir: A Christmas and New Year's Present. Boston, 1836.

Tomc, Sandra. "An Idle Industry: Nathaniel Parker Willis and the Workings of Literary Leisure." *American Quarterly* 49, no. 4 (December 1997): 780–805.

Tompkins, Jane. *Sensational Designs: The Cultural Work of American Fiction, 1790–1860*. New York: Oxford University Press, 1985.

Toulouse, Teresa. "Seeing Through 'Paul Pry': Hawthorne's Early Sketches." In *Critical Essays on Hawthorne's Short Stories*, ed. Albert Von Frank, 203–19. Boston: G. K. Hall & Co., 1991.

Tryon, W. S. "Nationalism and International Copyright: Tennyson and Longfellow in America." *American Literature* 24 (1952): 301–9.

"Uncle Tomitudes." *Putnam's Monthly: A Magazine of Literature, Science, and Art* 1, no. 1 (January 1853): 97–102.

Veeser, H. Aram, ed. *The New Historicism*. New York: Routledge, 1989.

Walker, I. M., ed. *Edgar Allan Poe: The Critical Heritage*. New York: Routledge and K. Paul, 1986.

Wall, Edward C. *Cumulative Author Index for Poole's Index to Periodical Literature, 1802–1906*. Ann Arbor, Mich.: Pierian Press, 1971.

Warner, Michael. *The Letters of the Republic: Publication and the Public Sphere in Eighteenth-Century America*. Cambridge, Mass.: Harvard University Press, 1990.

Warren, Samuel. "Dickens's American Notes for General Circulation." *Blackwood's Edinburgh Magazine* 52 (December 1842): 783–801.

Warren, Samuel, and Louis Brandeis. "The Right to Privacy." *Harvard Law Review* (December 1890): 193–220.

Weinstein, Cindy. *The Literature of Labor and the Labors of Literature*. New York: Cambridge University Press, 1997.

Welby, Amelia. *Poems*. Boston: A. Tompkins, 1845.

Weld, Theodore. *American Slavery As It Is: Testimony of a Thousand Witnesses*. New York: Arno Press, 1968.

The Wellesley Index to Victorian Periodicals. 5 vols. Toronto: University of Toronto Press, 1966.

Welsh, Alexander. *From Copyright to Copperfield: The Identity of Dickens.* Cambridge, Mass.: Harvard University Press, 1987.

Whalen, Terence. *Edgar Allan Poe and the Masses: The Political Economy of Literature in Antebellum America.* Princeton, N.J.: Princeton University Press, 1999.

Whicher, John F. "The Ghost of *Donaldson v. Beckett*: An Inquiry Into the Constitutional Distribution of Powers Over the Law of Literary Property in the United States." *Bulletin of the Copyright Society of the United States of America* (October; February 1961–62).

White, G. Edward. *The Marshall Court and Cultural Change, 1815–1835.* Vols. 3–4 of *The History of the Supreme Court of the United States.* New York: Macmillan Publishing Company, 1988.

Widmer, Edward. *Young America: The Flowering of Democracy in New York City.* New York: Oxford University Press, 1999.

Wiecek, William M. *The Sources of Antislavery Constitutionalism in America, 1760–1848.* Ithaca, N.Y.: Cornell University Press, 1977.

Wilkins, William Glyde. *Charles Dickens in America.* 1911. Reprint. New York: Haskell House Publishers, 1970.

Williams, Susan S. *Confounding Images: Photography and Portraiture in Antebellum American Fiction.* Philadelphia: University of Pennsylvania Press, 1997.

Winship, Michael. *American Literary Publishing in the Mid-Nineteenth Century: The Business of Ticknor and Fields..* New York: Cambridge University Press, 1995.

——. "The Transatlantic Book Trade and Anglo-American Literary Culture in the Nineteenth Century." In *Reciprocal Influences: Literary Production, Distribution, and Consumption in America,* ed. Steven Fink and Susan S. Williams, 98–122. Columbus: Ohio State University Press, 1999.

Wood, Henry. *Change for the American Notes: In Letters from London to New York.* New York: Harper & Brothers, 1843.

——. *Change for the American Notes: In Letters from London to New York.* London: Wiley & Putnam, 1843.

Woodberry, George E. *The Life of Edgar Allan Poe.* 2 vols. New York: Houghton Mifflin Co., 1909.

Woodmansee, Martha. "The Genius and the Copyright: Economic and Legal Conditions of the Emergence of the 'Author.'" *Eighteenth-Century Studies* 17, no. 4 (1984): 425–48.

Woodmansee, Martha, and Mark Osteen. *The New Economic Criticism: Studies at the Intersection of Literature and Economics.* New York: Routledge, 1999.

"A Word at the Start." *Harper's Monthly Magazine* 1, no. 1 (June 1850): [1]–2.

Wordsworth, William. *William Wordsworth.* Ed. Stephen Gill. New York: Oxford University Press, 1984.

Zboray, Ronald. *A Fictive People: Antebellum Economic Development and the American Reading Public.* New York: Oxford University Press, 1993.

Index

Acknowledgments

I am grateful for the generous support this project has received from a variety of sources. Funding from the Bibliographical Society of America, a Kate B. and Hall J. Peterson fellowship at the American Antiquarian Society, and an NEH-Newberry Library fellowship made the archival work that undergirds this study possible, as did release from teaching at both Harvard University and Rutgers University. Formal and informal discussions with staff and fellows at the American Antiquarian Society, the Newberry Library, and the Center for the Critical Analysis of Contemporary Culture at Rutgers University offered an indispensable medium for the development of my thinking.

A version of Chapter 1 appeared in *American Literary History* 9, no. 1 (Spring 1997): 21–59; I thank Gordon Hutner for his encouragement and Oxford University Press for permission to reprint this essay here. The last section of Chapter 4 also concluded a talk I gave at the English Institute in 1995; it was published as "The Duplicity of the Pen," in *Language Machines: Technologies of Literary and Cultural Production*, ed. Jeffrey Masten, Peter Stallybrass, and Nancy Vickers (New York: Routledge, 1997), 39–71. I thank Peter Stallybrass and Jeffrey Masten for their editorial guidance, and Routledge, Inc. for permission to reprint this material. An earlier version of Chapter 5 first appeared in *The American Face of Edgar Allan Poe*, ed. Shawn Rosenheim and Stephen Rachman (Baltimore: Johns Hopkins University Press, 1995), 271–304, reprinted by permission of the Johns Hopkins University Press. The first two sections of Chapter 6 were written for an Ohio State University conference in honor of William Charvat and were published as "The Problem of Hawthorne's Popularity" in *Reciprocal Influences: Essays on Literary Production, Distribution, and Consumption in America*, ed. Steven Fink and Susan S. Williams (Columbus: Ohio State University Press, 1999), 36–54. I thank Susan Williams for the invitation and for overseeing the process of publication.

John Irwin provoked my interest in Edgar Allan Poe and did much to shape my thinking about literary property; I thank him for his unwavering confidence in my work. Among my teachers at Johns Hopkins I owe special thanks to Sharon Cameron, Jerome Christensen, and Neil Hertz. I am grateful to a number of friends who nurtured and inspired me in those years, among them Loren Council, Charles Dove, Neill Matheson, Meg Russett, Robert Schreur, and Kim Wheatley. Charles Rutheiser deserves special thanks for seeing me through this project's early incarnations with patience and good humor. I was fortunate to begin my career at Harvard, which offered a rich environment for scholarship and teaching. For encouragement and provocation, I thank in particular Lawrence Buell, Philip Fisher, Marjorie Garber, David Hall, and Barbara Johnson. For their intellectual liveliness, saving wit, and sustaining companionship, I thank Philip Harper, Jeffrey Masten, Wendy Motooka, Jonah Siegel, and Lynn Wardley.

Giving talks at a variety of institutions afforded me the opportunity to hone my arguments and learn from my audiences. I thank Chris Looby and the American Studies Workshop at the University of Chicago; Bob Gross, Rich Lowry, and the William and Mary American Studies Colloquium; Peter Stallybrass and the University of Pennsylvania Seminar in the History of Material Texts; Sharon Baris, Ellen Spolsky and Bar-Ilan University; Teresa Murphy and the American Studies Program at City College of the City University of New York; Laurie Shannon and the Duke University English Department; Margaret Groesbeck and the Amherst College Friends of the Library; and Leah Marcus and the Vanderbilt University English Department.

Early exposure to the collections of the American Antiquarian Society and to the extraordinary people who make them available to scholars opened my eyes to the importance of the history of the book for the study of American literature. For their uncommon generosity and bottomless reservoirs of knowledge, I remain indebted to Gigi Barnhill, Nancy Burkett, Joanne Chaison, Alan Degutis, Ellen Dunlap, John Hench, Tom Knoles, Marie Lamoreux, Caroline Sloat, and the late Joyce Tracy. The staff at the Newberry Library did much to broaden my archival horizons; I thank in particular Paul Gehl, Jim Grossman, Hjordis Halverson, and Fred Hoxie. Margaret Groesbeck and Michael Kasper made the Amherst College Library feel like home. Graduate students in classes on "The Literary Marketplace in America" at both Harvard and Rutgers worked with me to develop many of these arguments; I am grateful to both those whose work I cite in the notes and those whose influence on my thinking is less easy to trace. For assistance with research, I thank Amy King, Bill Pannapacker, and Jeffrey Scraba.

Rutgers University has offered an ideal climate for intellectual risk and development. As department chairs, Barry Qualls, Larry Scanlon, and Cheryl Wall have been unfailingly supportive. Americanist colleagues Virginia Jackson, Myra Jehlen, and Michael Warner each took on extra work so as to release me to my writing; I thank them for their foresight and their generosity. For the pleasures of conversation and intellectual debate, I thank in particular Derek Attridge, Marianne DeKoven, Elin Diamond, Brent Edwards, Billy Galperin, Marcia Ian, Jonathan Kramnick, Michael McKeon, Bruce Robbins, and Carolyn Williams.

Numerous friends and colleagues read and commented on chapters-in-progress. For insights, inspiration, and suggestions for revision, I thank James Boyle, Jay Clayton, Stephen Engelmann, Ann Fabian, Jim Green, Bob Gross, Teresa Goddu, Jay Grossman, Elaine Hadley, David Hall, Virginia Jackson, Amy Kaplan, Neill Matheson, Michael Moon, Stephen Nissenbaum, Bob Patten, Barry Qualls, Stephen Rachman, Eliza Richards, Mark Rose, Karen Sánchez-Eppler, Emily Todd, Lynn Wardley, Michael Warner, Elizabeth Wingrove, Michael Winship, and Elizabeth Young. I was extraordinarily lucky in my readers at the University of Pennsylvania Press. I am grateful to Ezra Greenspan for his astute commentary on the first set of chapters, and to Jan Radway for her exacting and inspiring reading of the entire manuscript. Peter Stallybrass has supported this project from its earliest stages. I thank him for his galvanizing enthusiasm and for immeasurably enriching the conversation between literary theory and the history of the book. Jerry Singerman made the decision to publish with Penn an easy one. I thank him for sound advice and spirited encouragement.

Finishing a book that was so long in the making has proved unusually difficult. For sustaining friendship I thank Ann Fabian, Lisa Gitelman, Jay Grossman, Janet Halley, Martin Harries, Suvir Kaul, Ania Loomba, Mary Kasper, Michael Kasper, Jeffrey Masten, Michael Moon, Mary Russo, Eve Sedgwick, Hal Sedgwick, Jonah Siegel, Dan Warner, and Nancy Yusef. For the considerable gift of saying the right thing at the right time, I thank Elin Diamond, Jonathan Goldberg, Yopie Prins, Carolyn Williams, and Elizabeth Young. For helping to keep body and soul together, I thank Mia Engelmann, Pat Hertz, Donna Kelley, Andrea Matura, Marjan Mohenson, Donna Orange, and Jane Silane. My siblings, Robert, Christina, and James McGill, and my extended family, David Cranson, Gabrielle McGill, Leslie Parker, Bill Spanos, and Marianne Spanos, have been an ongoing source of support; I thank them for their generosity and their patience with the demands of academia. Completing the manuscript would have been impossible without the active intervention of an extraordinary group of friends. For their watchful care and brilliant engagements with the work-in-progress, I thank Stephen Engelmann, Virginia Jackson, Sophia Mihic, Lynn Wardley, and Elizabeth Wingrove.

My parents, Robert and Daphne McGill, made this book possible both through their loving support and through their example: my father always read aloud the copyright page of children's books, while my mother always insisted that we look things up. Andrew Parker made this book possible in ways that defy enumeration. His wit and intelligence thread their way through its better passages; his love has made the world outside its pages a splendid place indeed. I dedicate this book to them with gratitude and pleasure.